D1231693

THE OXFORD HISTORY OF THE BRITISH EMPIRE

COMPANION SERIES

THE OXFORD HISTORY OF THE BRITISH EMPIRE

Volume I. *The Origins of Empire*
EDITED BY Nicholas Canny

Volume II. *The Eighteenth Century*
EDITED BY P. J. Marshall

Volume III. *The Nineteenth Century*
EDITED BY Andrew Porter

Volume IV. *The Twentieth Century*
EDITED BY Judith M. Brown and Wm. Roger Louis

Volume V. *Historiography*
EDITED BY Robin W. Winks

THE OXFORD HISTORY OF THE BRITISH EMPIRE
COMPANION SERIES

India and the British Empire
Douglas M. Peers and Nandini Gooptu

Britain's Experience of Empire in the Twentieth Century
Andrew Thompson

Scotland and the British Empire
John M. MacKenzie and T. M. Devine

Black Experience and the Empire
Philip D. Morgan and Sean Hawkins

Gender and Empire
Philippa Levine

Ireland and the British Empire
Kevin Kenny

Missions and Empire
Norman Etherington

Environment and Empire
William Beinart and Lotte Hughes

Australia's Empire
Deryck Schreuder and Stuart Ward

Settlers and Expatriates: Britons over the Seas
Robert Bickers

Migration and Empire
Marjory Harper and Stephen Constantine

THE OXFORD HISTORY OF THE BRITISH EMPIRE

COMPANION SERIES

Wm. Roger Louis, CBE, D.Litt., FBA

*Kerr Professor of English History and Culture, University of Texas, Austin
and Honorary Fellow of St Antony's College, Oxford*

EDITOR-IN-CHIEF

British North America in the Seventeenth and Eighteenth Centuries

EDITED BY

Stephen Foster

OXFORD

UNIVERSITY PRESS

OXFORD
UNIVERSITY PRESS

Great Clarendon Street, Oxford, OX2 6DP,
United Kingdom

Oxford University Press is a department of the University of Oxford.
It furthers the University's objective of excellence in research, scholarship,
and education by publishing worldwide. Oxford is a registered trade mark of
Oxford University Press in the UK and in certain other countries

Published in the United States of America by Oxford University Press
198 Madison Avenue, New York, NY 10016, United States of America

British Library Cataloguing in Publication Data
Data available

Library of Congress Cataloging in Publication Data
Data available

ISBN 978-0-19-920612-4

Jacket illustration: Sea Captains Carousing in
Surinam, c.1752-58 (oil on bed ticking), Greenwood,
John (1727-92) © Saint Louis Art Museum, Missouri,
USA/Museum Purchase/The Bridgeman Art Library.

FOREWORD

The purpose of the five volumes of the Oxford History of the British Empire was to provide a comprehensive survey of the Empire from its beginning to end, to explore the meaning of British imperialism for the ruled as well as the rulers, and to study the significance of the British Empire as a theme in world history. The volumes in the Companion Series carry forward this purpose. They pursue themes that could not be covered adequately in the main series while incorporating recent research and providing fresh interpretations of significant topics.

Wm. Roger Louis

ACKNOWLEDGEMENTS

"Great creatures lie long in the womb" was, appropriately enough, intended to describe an early episode in the creation of the British Empire in America. Although we hope this volume has interesting and useful things to say on this same subject, it makes no claims to greatness. It has, however, partaken in full of John Donne's extended gestation. A great many debts have accordingly been accumulated along the course of its progress, and it is right and proper that at least the most prominent of them be recognized here.

We wish to thank in particular Wm. Roger Louis, the general editor of both the original five-volume *Oxford History of the British Empire* and of the subsequent Companion series, for (amongst other things) his regular doses of encouragement and his unstinted optimism at moments when frustration, if not outright despair, might have been the more apposite emotion. Similarly, we have much to be grateful for in having had Stephanie Ireland of Oxford University Press to do the hands-on work of shuttling the evolving volume along its incidented route to publication. Our appreciation extends as well to Cathryn Steele and Emma Barber of Oxford University Press, and to Peter Marshall for a critical reading of our work that was as generous as it was searching. Thanks are also due to Natalie Kalich for her help in putting the book together in electronic form, and to Nick Bromley, our copy editor, as well as to our proof reader Francis Eaves.

Stephen Foster, the editor of this volume, is, yet again, deeply obligated to the Newberry Library and to Verna Foster for their forbearance, manifested in different ways but much tried in both instances. And, finally, he wishes to use this occasion to remember the late Robin W. Winks, who examined him in the field of British Imperial history half a century ago, when it was a very different thing from at present, and who then, some thirty years later, as editor of the fifth volume of the *Oxford History,* encouraged the revival of his interest in the subject, tolerating with equal good humor both his eccentricities and his digressions.

CONTENTS

LIST OF MAPS

CONTRIBUTORS

TROY BICKHAM (D.Phil., Oxford) is an Associate Professor in the Department of History and Ray A. Rothrock '77 Fellow in the College of Liberal Arts at Texas A&M University, and holds a joint appointment with its branch campus in Qatar. His publications include *Savages within the Empire: Representations of American Indians in Eighteenth-Century Britain* (2005), *Making Headlines: The American Revolution as Seen Through the British Press* (2008), and *The Weight of Vengeance: The United States, the British Empire and the War of 1812* (2012).

ROBERT E. DESROCHERS, Jr. (Ph.D., Johns Hopkins) is an Assistant Professor in the Department of History at Emory University. His publications include "Slave for Sale Advertisements and Slavery in Massachusetts, 1704–1781," *William and Mary Quarterly* (2002), and he is currently working on a book-length study of slavery, print, and identity in eighteenth-century Massachusetts.

STEPHEN FOSTER (Ph.D., Yale) is Distinguished Research Professor (Emeritus) in the Department of History at Northern Illinois University. His publications include *The Long Argument: English Puritanism and the Shaping of New England Culture, 1570–1700* (1991) and the chapter on British North America in the seventeenth and eighteenth centuries in *The Oxford History of the British Empire, V, Historiography* (1999).

JEREMY GREGORY (D.Phil., Oxford) is Professor of the History of Christianity at the University of Manchester where he is also Head of the School of Arts, Languages and Cultures. His publications include *The Speculum of Archbishop Thomas Secker, 1758–68* (1995), *Restoration, Reformation, and Reform, 1660–1828: Archbishops of Canterbury and their Diocese* (2000), and (as editor) *John Wesley. Tercentenary Essays* (2005). His current long-term projects include a study of the Church of England in New England, and he is the editor of *Establishment and Empire: The Development of the Church of England, 1662–1829* for the forthcoming Oxford History of Anglicanism.

EVAN HAEFELI (Ph.D., Princeton) is an Associate Professor in the Department of History at Columbia University. His most recent book is *New Netherland and the Dutch Origins of American Religious Liberty* (2012).

DANIEL J. HULSEBOSCH (J.D., Columbia Law School, Ph.D., Harvard) is the Charles Seligson Professor of Law at the New York University School of Law. His publications include *Constituting Empire: New York and the Transformation of Constitutionalism in the Atlantic World, 1664–1830* (2005) and "A Civilized Nation: The Early American Constitution, the Law of Nations, and the Pursuit of International Recognition," *New York University Law Review* (2010).

KEN MACMILLAN (Ph.D., McMaster) is Professor of History at the University of Calgary. He is the editor of *John Dee: The Limits of the British Empire* (2004) and author of *Sovereignty and Possession in the English New World: The Legal Foundations of Empire, 1576–1640* (2006) and *The Atlantic Imperial Constitution: Center and Periphery in the English Atlantic World* (2011).

NANCY L. RHODEN (Ph.D., Princeton) is an Associate Professor of History at the University of Western Ontario. She is the author of *Revolutionary Anglicanism: The Colonial Church of England Clergy during the American Revolution* (1999), and has edited and co-edited several anthologies.

JAY SEXTON (D.Phil., Oxford) is University Lecturer and Tutorial Fellow in American History at Corpus Christi College, Oxford. His publications include *Debtor Diplomacy: Finance and American Foreign Relations in the Civil War Era, 1837–1873* (2005) and *The Monroe Doctrine: Empire and Nation in Nineteenth-Century America* (2011).

SARAH YEH (Ph.D., Brown) teaches Atlantic History at Concord Academy (Concord, MA). Her work on the British Caribbean includes her doctoral dissertation, "'In an Enemy's Country': British Culture, Identity, and Allegiance in Ireland and the Caribbean, 1688–1763" (2006).

LIST OF ABBREVIATIONS

AHR	*American Historical Review*
BL	British Library
JBS	*Journal of British Studies*
OHBE	*The Oxford History of the British Empire*, ed. Wm. Roger Louis (Oxford, 1998–99)
WMQ	*William and Mary Quarterly*

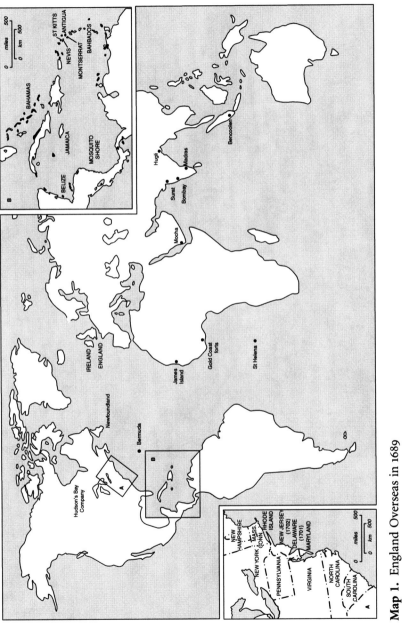

Map 1. England Overseas in 1689

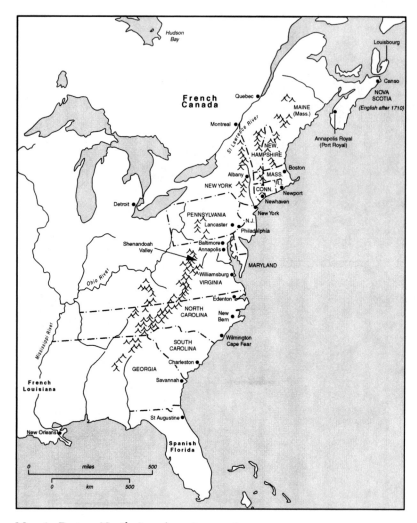

Hudson
Bay

Louisbourg

Canso

**French
Canada**

Quebec

NOVA
SCOTIA

(English after 1710)

MAINE
(Mass.)

Montreal

St. Lawrence River

Annapolis Royal
(Port Royal)

NEW
HAMPSHIRE

Albany

Boston

MASS.

R.I.

CONN.

Newhaven

Newport

NEW YORK

Detroit

PENNSYLVANIA

Lancaster

N.J.

New York

Philadelphia

Ohio River

Shenandoah
Valley

Baltimore

Annapolis

Williamsburg

MARYLAND

VIRGINIA

Edenton

Mississippi River

NORTH
CAROLINA

New
Bern

Wilmington
Cape Fear

SOUTH
CAROLINA

Charleston

GEORGIA

Savannah

**French
Louisiana**

St Augustine

New Orleans

**Spanish
Florida**

0   miles   500

0   km   500

Map 2. Eastern North America, 1690–1748

Map 3. Indian Peoples and European Colonies in Mid-Eighteenth-Century North America

1

Introduction

The What and Why of this Volume*

Stephen Foster

In the fifth and final volume of *The Oxford History of the British Empire*, the editor of this Companion took note of a resurgent interest in placing early American history in a transatlantic and Imperial context but suggested that it had mostly run its course.[1] A subsequent, follow up essay at soothsaying was gloomier still on the same subject. Mercifully, it was never published. As it happens, the imperiled lines of inquiry did not entirely disappear and *empire* as a generic concept currently enjoys a certain modishness. What did subsequently come in for radical questioning was the one thing that had been taken for granted in the course of the earlier prognostications: the very subject of early American history itself—of what the term comprehends or can be made to comprehend and whether a few years from now anyone will continue to make it, whatever *it* is, an object of study. This unexpected turn of events, one way or another, mostly indirectly but never inadvertently, provides the background to the individual chapters in this volume and to the collective shape of the whole.

Until this recent unsettling, the history of "early America" conventionally began with the coming of Europeans to the New World for the purposes of settlement. Some attention was of necessity always given to "pre-Columbian" America, to things European and especially English (not British) at the time of colonization, and to the other European empires in the Americas.

---

* The author wishes to thank Troy Bickham, T.H. Breen, and Evan Haefeli for reading earlier versions of this chapter, as well as the Seminar in Imperial History at the University of Texas, Austin for providing (*felix culpa*) a venue for a false but by no means unfruitful start upon it.

[1] Stephen Foster, "British North America in the Seventeenth and Eighteenth Centuries," in Robin W. Winks (ed.), *OHBE*, V, *Historiography* (Oxford, 1999), pp. 90–2.

These obligations duly fulfilled, the subject in question became British North America in the seventeenth and eighteenth centuries, meaning, once appropriate notice was taken of the West Indies and Nova Scotia, the thirteen colonies that formed the United States in 1776. The organizing conceit of early American historiography was in fact just how the colonial period lead in to what came next. Was there a relatively straightforward development over two centuries in which the gradual creation of an American nationality led in time to an appropriate political independence? Or did the colonies' status as units in a world-wide empire so dominate their character that the newly independent United States itself became the retroactive creator of the nationality it nominally merely celebrated?[2]

As the pile of proclamations of new orders of the ages grows and grows, this classic poser increasingly seems to belong to another world, recoverable only in sepia-tinted photographs of one or another era of now lost innocence. In recent decades, the conventional geography of early America and even to a degree its familiar chronology have been rearranged, extended, perhaps distended. The Caribbean has taken on a new salience as more fundamentally American than Plymouth Rock while, on the North American mainland itself, the Spanish "Borderlands" (the American South West) now loom large, a sprawling entity labeled "the South East" (roughly the Gulf Coastal Plain and some adjoining territory at both ends) is making its presence felt, and the Pacific North West has an occasional look in. Absence of coverage of Alaska, acquired by the United States only in 1867, is periodically lamented, and it would appear that Hawaii may also soon find its way into the colonial period by way of the study of "indigeneity."[3] In turn, cast off from its traditional temporal and conceptual moorings, the historiography of the Revolution and Early National Periods is in danger of being reduced to the antecedentless beginnings of America in the nineteenth

---

[2] Foster, "British North America," in Winks (ed.), *OHBE*, V, pp. 74–80, 88–90.

[3] A good example of the territorial reach of the new geography is Alan Taylor, *American Colonies* (New York, 2001), which includes the Great Plains, all of French America, and the British West Indies. (For Alaska and Hawaii see pp. 444–77.) For indigeneity see Douglas Kiel, "The Politics of Indigeneity: North American and Pacific Histories," *Journal of Social History*, XLIV (2010–2011), pp. 239–45, as well as the instance of the D'Arcy McNickle Center for American Indian History at the Newberry Library adding "and Indigenous Studies" to its original title in order to comprehend "the history of the aboriginal peoples under the jurisdiction of the US in the Philippine Islands and Hawaii," <http://www.newberry.org/american-indian-studies-ayer-collection-philippine-and-hawaiian-history>.

century.[4] It has even been suggested that we are witnessing the rejection of "linear-driven" historiography entirely "as against the fragment, the episode, or the fugitive subaltern subject."[5]

A proliferation of "forums" and "round tables" in learned journals, along with works of multiple authorship of the "new directions in..." variety, provide further evidence that the practitioners of early American history are treading a terrain of uncertain dimensions and shifting borders. These overlapping, somewhat inbred, colloquies take as their primary target history divided up by country, which, it is held, uncritically organizes accounts of the past around a largely factitious entity, the nation state. Some critiques would go beyond the well-known inadequacies of national history to indict it as, in effect, legitimating and "naturalizing" racial and economic oppression.[6] Such sentiments are not entirely new. In the first half of the previous century Charles M. Andrews, H.E. Bolton, and Carlton J.H. Hayes, among other academic luminaries, issued the same sort of warnings as at present about the unhappy consequences of an overly purposive, hermetically sealed vision of America's past. None of their alternative contexts, however, made much headway except in the case of Andrews, who was arguably so successful at separating out the history of British America from that of the independent United States that his subject all but disappeared for a time from university curricula.[7] The unhappy fate of these earlier attempts should serve as a needful caution against any premature rejoicing at the downfall of blinkered old practices. We have been here before.

In the latest and perhaps most searching attempt at a radically reformed conception of early America, the larger whole of which it is to be made a part is the Atlantic "basin," meaning both the ocean itself and the coasts of the four continents bordering it. Atlanticism, however, enjoys an unusually broad constituency precisely because it is more a vehicle of the

---

[4] Older colonial American survey texts frequently went up to 1789 or at least 1783. By contrast, Taylor, *American Colonies* and T. H. Breen and Timothy Hall, *Colonial America in an Atlantic World: A Story of Creative Interaction* (New York, 2004) end in 1776. Cf. also n. 7 below.

[5] Tony Ballantyne and Antoinette Burton, "Postscript: Bodies, Genders, Empires: Reimagining World Histories," in Ballantyne and Burton (eds), *Bodies in Contact: Rethinking Colonial Encounters in World History* (London, 2005), pp. 419–20.

[6] Cf. Robin Blackburn, "Haiti, Slavery, and the Age of the Democratic Revolution," *WMQ*, 3rd ser., LXIII (2006), pp. 643–74, and Jack P. Greene, "Colonial History and National History: Reflections on a Continuing Problem," *WMQ*, 3rd ser., LXIV (2007), pp. 235–50.

[7] Foster, "British North America," in Winks (ed.), *OHBE*, V, pp. 79–80.

prevailing substantive indeterminacy and methodological uncertainty than a resolution of it. As one veteran contributor to the succession of forums and round tables has put it, "Atlantic history is a notoriously fluid construct."[8] *Volatile* would do as well or better for a concept that seems to be forever spilling over into a genuinely global history, on the one hand, or breaking down, on the other, into assorted fragments (the Black Atlantic, the Red Atlantic, the Green Atlantic, as well as Atlantics organized by nation, such as the British Atlantic or the French Atlantic).[9]

Quite apart from this instability, the varieties of Atlanticism on display have suspiciously national shadings and priorities.[10] British Atlanticists, for example, while not without their jurisdictional disputes, can at least routinely canvas several new ways of seeing their past—Greater Britain, the Atlantic Archipelago, Britain in Europe, Britain in the World—and sometimes opt for an eclecticism that would likely bring near universal derision down on the head of any American Atlanticist ingenuous enough to attempt a similar form of compromise.[11] Equally, Brazilians of Atlanticist bent,

---

[8] Eliga H. Gould, "Atlantic History and the Literary Turn," *WMQ*, 3rd ser., LXV (2008), p. 175.

[9] A useful discussion of the tendency of Atlanticism to globalize may be found in the forum "Beyond the Atlantic": Alison Games, "Beyond the Atlantic: English Globetrotters and Transoceanic Connections," *WMQ*, 3rd ser., LXIII (2006), pp. 675–92, Philip J. Stern, "British Asia and British Atlantic: Comparison and Connections," ibid., pp. 693–712, Paul W. Mapp, "Atlantic History from Imperial, Continental, and Pacific Perspectives," ibid., pp. 713–24, Peter Coclanis, "Atlantic World or Atlantic/World?," ibid., pp. 725–42. The term "Black Atlantic" is usually attributed to Robert Farris Thompson, *Flash of the Spirit: African and Afro-American Art and Philosophy* (New York, 1983), pp. xiv, xv. The talismanic text, however, is Paul Gilroy, *The Black Atlantic: Modernity and Double Consciousness* (Cambridge, MA, 1993). "Red Atlantic" describes "the movement of western hemisphere indigenes and indigenous wealth, ideas, and technology around the Atlantic basin from 1000 ce to 1800" (http://www.indigenouspeoplesissues.com/index.php?). However, cf. Paul Cohen, "Was there an Amerindian Atlantic? Reflections on the Limits of a Historiographical Concept," *History of European Ideas*, XXIV (2008), pp. 388–410. The "Green Atlantic" can be found in Kevin Wheland, "The Green Atlantic: Radical Reciprocities between Ireland and America in the Long Eighteenth Century," in Kathleen Wilson (ed.), *A New Imperial History: Culture, Identity, and Modernity in Britain and the Empire, 1660–1840* (Cambridge, 2004), pp. 216–38. The earliest use of a national Atlantic in the title of a book of which I am aware is Ian K. Steele, *The English Atlantic, 1675–1740: An Exploration of Communication and Community* (New York, 1986). On the French Atlantic, see the special issue "New Perspectives on the Atlantic," (ed.), Allan Potofsky, *History of European Ideas*, XXIV (2008).

[10] This paradoxical situation is brought out in exemplary fashion in Jack P. Greene and Philip D. Morgan (eds), *Atlantic History: A Critical Appraisal* (New York, 2009).

[11] Trevor Burnard, "The British Atlantic," in Green and Morgan (eds), *Atlantic History*, pp. 111–36, esp. pp. 113–15. See also Tony Claydon, " 'British' History in the Post-Revolutionary

welcoming the attention to be given to their country's connections to the Indian Ocean in the new dispensation, must be puzzled by the attempts of many Americanists of an avowedly similar persuasion to rule out the very same area as in any serious way connected to their version of an Atlantic world.[12] And despite the commercial primacy of the Netherlands among the European powers, marked by trading centers extending from Curaçao to Nagasaki, an historian of the Dutch Atlantic feels obliged to apologize for his subject on the grounds that, most of the time, it does not involve territorial acquisition in the manner of British North America, even though the metropolitan British themselves in the eighteenth century thought of their own empire in the first instance in terms of its global reach and the commercial and maritime power it represented, rather than the number of hectares flying the union jack.[13]

World," in Glen Burgess (ed.), *The New British History: Founding a Modern State, 1603–1715* (London, 1999), pp. 115–37, Tim Harris, "Critical Perspectives: The Autonomy of English History?" ibid., pp. 266–86, and Tony Claydon, *Europe and the Making of England, 1660–1760* (Cambridge, 2007), pp. 9–12.

[12] For Brazil and the Indian Ocean see Sueann Caulfield, "In Conversation with … João José Reis," *Perspectives on History*, XLVI (2008), pp. 18–20. The interdiction of Asia is most pronounced in Bernard Bailyn, *Atlantic History: Concept and Contours* (Cambridge, MA, 2005), pp. 91–2, is criticized in the four pieces cited in n. 9 above (especially Coclanis, "Atlantic World or Atlantic/World?" pp. 729–30), and is defended in Nicholas Canny, "Atlantic History and Global History," in Greene and Morgan (eds), *Atlantic History*, pp. 321–32.

[13] Benjamin Schmidt, "The Dutch Atlantic: From Provincialism to Globalism," in Greene and Morgan (eds), *Atlantic History*, pp. 163–87. For the case for the centrality of the Anglo-Dutch rivalry to European economic development generally see David Ormrod, *The Rise of Commercial Empires: England and the Netherlands in the Age of Mercantilism, 1650–1750* (Cambridge, 2003). For other discussions of the Dutch in the New World, cf. John J. McCusker and Russell R. Menard, "The Sugar Industry in the Seventeenth Century: A New Perspective on the Barbadian 'Sugar Revolution,'" in Stuart B. Schwartz (ed.), *Tropical Babylon: Sugar and the Making of the Atlantic World, 1450–1680* (Chapel Hill, NC, 2004), pp. 289–330; April Lee Hatfield, *Atlantic Virginia: Intercolonial Relations in the Seventeenth Century* (Philadelphia, 2004); Jan de Vries, "The Dutch Atlantic Economies," in Peter A. Coclanis (ed.), *The Atlantic Economy during the Seventeenth and Eighteenth Centuries: Organization, Practice, and Personnel* (Columbia, SC, 2005), pp. 1–29; Claudia Schnurmann, "Atlantic Trade and American Identities: The Correlation of Supranational Commerce, Political Opposition, and Colonial Regionalism," ibid., pp. 186–204; Christian J. Koot, *Empire at the Periphery: British Colonies, Anglo-Dutch Trade, and the Development of the British Atlantic, 1621–1713* (New York, 2011); and Nathan Perl-Rosenthal and Evan Haefeli (eds), "Anglo-Dutch Revolutions," special issue of *Early American Studies*, X (Spring 2012). On the relationship between commerce and empire as understood by the British, cf. T.H. Breen, "An Empire of Goods: The Anglicization of Colonial America, 1690–1776," *JBS*, XXV (1986), pp. 467–99; Philip Lawson, "Sources, Schools and Separation: The Many Faces of Parliament's

Interestingly, the American academy withholds *de jure* recognition of this historiographic polyvalence. For its purposes, you are an Atlantic power only to the extent that you dispossess indigenous people, make widespread use of plantation slavery, and tease out racial and cultural boundaries in well-documented fashion.[14] The starkness of these axioms is the product not, as some would have it, of the hypnotic spell of the Circe theory but of something far less negotiable—moral commitment. A deep seated fear of being in collusion with the ill deeds on which the nation was founded has attached itself to the writing of early American history in the United States. Whether the sins be of omission or commission, in a universe built out of language and run by one or another form of myth, purportedly deficient historiographical practice can be presented as a quasi-eucharistic reenactment of the original racial enslavement, territorial sequestration, and cultural suppression of the colonial period.[15] So, economic historians of

Role in Anglo-American History to 1783," in Lawson (ed.), *Parliament and the Atlantic Empire* (Edinburgh, 1995), pp. 18–27; P. J. Marshall, "Introduction," in P. J. Marshall (ed.), *OHBE*, II, *The Eighteenth Century* (Oxford, 1998), pp. 4–9; Bob Harris, "War, Empire, and the 'National Interest' in Mid-Eighteenth Century Britain," in Julie Flavell and Stephen Conway (eds), *Britain and America Go to War: The Impact of War and Warfare in Anglo-America, 1754–1815* (Gainesville, FL, 2004), pp. 13–40; Eliga H. Gould, "Fears of War, Fantasies of Peace: British Politics and the Coming of the American Revolution," in Gould and Peter S. Onuf (eds), *Empire and Nation: The American Revolution in the Atlantic World* (Baltimore, 2005), pp. 19–34; N. A. M. Rodger, *The Command of the Ocean: A Naval History of Britain, 1649–1815*, pbk. edn (New York, 2006), p. 180; Troy Bickham, "Eating the Empire: Intersections of Food, Cookery and Imperialism in Eighteenth-Century Britain," *Past & Present*, 198 (February, 2008), pp. 71–109.

[14] Systematic and sustained programmatic statements can be found in Alan I. Karras, "The Atlantic World as a Unit of Study," in Karras and J.R. McNeil (eds), *Atlantic American Societies: From Columbus through Abolition, 1492–1888* (London, 1992), pp. 1–15, and in Bailyn, *Atlantic History*, where (p. 56) the clash of "hearth cultures" is given a literal centrality. Cf. James Sidbury and Jorge Cañizares-Esguerra, "Mapping Ethnogenesis in the Early Modern Atlantic," *WMQ*, 3rd ser., LXVIII (2011), pp. 181–208, as well as the commentary following, pp. 209–46, esp. Patrick Griffin, "A Plea for a New Atlantic History," pp. 236–9.

[15] For lexical genocide, cf. Laura M. Stevens, *The Poor Indians: British Missionaries, Native Americans, and Colonial Sensibility* (Philadelphia, 2004), esp. pp. 22, 179, 192–4, 197, 200–2; Jean M. O'Brien, *Firsting and Lasting: Writing Indians out of Existence in New England* (Minneapolis, 2010), esp. pp. xi–xxvi; James H. Merrell, "Second Thoughts on Colonial Historians and American Indians," *WMQ*, 3rd ser., LXIX (2012), pp. 451–512, as well as the sources cited there and in the commentary following, pp. 513–40. A critical evaluation of the power attributed to language and myth can be found in Richard Price, "One Big Thing: Britain, Its Empire, and their Imperial Culture," *JBS*, XLIV (2006), pp. 602–27. Cf. also Alan Knight, "The Myth of the Mexican Revolution," *Past & Present*, 209 (November, 2010), pp. 223–73, where the overall argument is still pertinent to the relevant trends in early American historiography.

the slave trade and slavery, who have laboriously established in terrible detail its size, profitability, and demographic cost, are held to further its appalling practices by treating its victims in the aggregate, thereby reaffirming the "commodification" that the Middle Passage imposed.[16] By the same logic, any work of historiography that is monocultural, in the sense of organized around what Europeans did, however global the scope and broad the canvas, implicitly legitimates European domination of others. *Nolens volens*, an historian of empire is an imperialist.[17]

No wonder then that the "discussion" of the different forms of organizing the American past is such a cacophony. This collection, abjuring the addictive charms of disputatiousness, is deliberately a flank attack on the impasse rather than a head on assault. At the least, it will raise the question of the relevance of the British Empire in the history of North America in the seventeenth and eighteenth centuries in such a forceful way as to preclude the matter subsequently slipping back into the oblivion of the Great Unasked. Each of the following chapters grapples with two related issues: whether it made a difference to people living in North America that they were subjects of an empire and, further, if so, whether it mattered that the empire in question was British. Some chapters give their verdict in passing, some directly but, in either case, the reader should be able in the end to come away with some overall sense of the "colonialness" of the colonies and of the ways Great Britain, even after the independence of the United States, was a force in its history.

Readers who have not been immersed in the world of manifestos, forums, "meditations," and exchanges over contested terminology may wonder why this undertaking is necessary in the first place. Surely the Empire is so large an elephant in the North American room that it will be stumbled upon eventually and incorporated in one way or another into whatever larger story is in progress. That this situation does not invariably obtain in practice, at least not at present, can be attributed to two quite distinct causes. One is the familiar overenthusiasm of those who have come across something new and significant; the other, very different from the first, is the gravitational pulls

---

[16] See Stephanie Smallwood, *Saltwater Slavery: A Middle Passage from Africa to American Diaspora* (Cambridge, MA, 2007) and the reviews of this work, especially Sharla Fett, <http://www.h-net.org/reviews/showrev.php?id=13735>, along with the works cited there.

[17] For a concise statement of this argument see Amy Turner Bushnell, "Indigenous America and the Limits of the Atlantic World, 1493–1825," in Greene and Morgan (eds), *Atlantic History*, pp. 191–221, esp. pp. 191–5.

within the historiography of America that are so formidable as to, sooner or later, defeat every effort to place the subject in a broader context.

As an example of the first phenomenon, take the ways in which, in defiance of Eurocentrism, the entire Atlantic basin is organized around "circuits" and "circulations," movements of populations, commodities, and cultures between the continents that are so cyclonic in scope and shape and so heterogeneous and agglomerative in content as to rank with light years and geological eras as concepts that are in a literal sense unimaginable. In reaction to this high level of abstraction, Atlanticist monographic studies often resort to "microhistories," closely analyzed discrete events or single lives in which the outsized generalizations of the programmatic statements can be made flesh.[18] Mediating between the Grand Forces and the almost desperate particularizations are the "networks," a term that mostly refers to medium sized, patterned forms of connections by which people on both sides of the Atlantic do business, lobby or finesse politicians, pass information, undertake scientific investigations, and so on. Emphasis in such studies falls on how these networks function—not how they *malfunction*. Yet scholarship on transatlantic political connections warns of just how partial, intermittent, and incomplete the ligaments of the Atlantic world were.[19] Studies of what was necessary to have an effective imperial network in the nineteenth and early twentieth centuries indirectly make the same point, highlighting what was *not* available earlier.[20] Economic historians would similarly caution that commercial networks encouraged inefficiencies ("rent seeking")

[18] The case for the urgent necessity of the microcosm in Atlanticist scholarship is well made in Lara Putnam, "To Study the Fragments/Whole: Microhistory and the Atlantic World," *Journal of Social History*, XXXIX (2005–6), pp. 615–30.

[19] Such studies include Michael G. Kammen, *A Rope of Sand: The Colonial Agents, British Politics, and the American Revolution* (Ithaca, NY, 1968), Bernard Bailyn, *The Origins of American Politics* (New York, 1968), and Alison Gilbert Olson, *Making the Empire Work: London and American Interest Groups, 1690–1790* (Cambridge, MA, 1992).

[20] See Simon J. Potter, "Webs, Networks, and Systems: Globalization and Mass Media in the Nineteenth- and Twentieth-Century British Empire," *JBS*, XLVI (2007), pp. 456–621, and Christopher Hilliard, "The Provincial Press and the Imperial Traffic in Fiction, 1870s–1930s," *JBS*, XLVIII (2009), pp. 653–73. Broader ranging discussions can be found in James Belich, *Replenishing the Earth: The Settler Revolution and the Rise of the Anglo-World, 1783–1939* (New York, 2009), and Gary B. Magee and Andrew S. Thompson, *Empire and Globalisation: Networks of People, Goods and Capital in the British World, c. 1850–1914* (Cambridge, 2010), as well as the "Round-Table" devoted to the latter work in *British Scholar*, III (2010), pp. 139–60.

and point to the unfortunate consequences of dependence on family connections for business transactions.[21] The most reliable networks for providing the kinds of information otherwise unavailable to most merchants were those of pariah groups, especially the Quakers and the Jews, because they had to be effective for the collective survival of their members and (not coincidentally) incorporated formal disciplinary institutions for dealing with and publicizing transgressions. For any overseas trader not so "privileged" arguably the best way to get a purchase on the economy in the course of engaging in an inherently risky business was to take advantage of the increasing volume of broadly available *public* knowledge.[22] Lacunae, distortions, and inadequacies—the kinds of things with which the history of empires is positively stuffed—can be quite as significant historically as the precarious linkages Atlanticism celebrates, but they play little part in studies committed to describing a presumptively viable "Atlantic world."[23] There, happily, despite means of communication and transportation that came to seem primitive in the extreme even by the standards of the mid-nineteenth century, circulations are free, circuits are unbroken, systems are very systematic, and empires accordingly are reduced to mere cartographic fantasies.

The second problem, the phoenix-like tendency to explain America entirely in terms of internal developments, can most easily be illustrated in the premier growth area of American Atlanticism, the innovative scholarship dealing with the reciprocal cultural "interaction" between Native

---

[21] Nuala Zahedieh, *The Capital and the Colonies: London and the Atlantic Economy, 1660–1700* (Cambridge, 2010), pp. 55–7, 106–36; S.D. Smith, *Slavery, Family, and Gentry Capitalism in the British Atlantic: The World of the Lascelles, 1648–1834* (Cambridge, 2006), p. 357. Cf. Gloria L. Main, "'They Were All Atlanticists Then'," *WMQ*, 3rd ser., LXIII (2006), pp. 385–92, as well as Julian Hoppit, *Risk and Failure in English Business, 1700–1800* (Cambridge, 1987), pp. 59–62, 68–70, 100–3, 177–8.

[22] Cf. Nuala Zahedieh, "Making Mercantilism Work: London Merchants and Atlantic Trade in the Seventeenth Century," *Transactions of the Royal Historical Society*, 6th ser., IX (Cambridge, 1999), pp. 143–58; Zahedieh, *The Capital and the Colonies*, pp. 101–13; S.D. Smith, "The Account Book of Richard Poor, Quaker Merchant of Barbados," *WMQ*, 3rd ser., LXVI (2009), pp. 605–28; Perry Gauci, *The Politics of Trade: The Overseas Merchant in State and Society, 1660–1720* (Oxford, 2001), pp. 156–66; John J. McCusker, "The Demise of Distance: The Business Press and the Origins of the Information Revolution in the Early Modern Atlantic World," *AHR*, CX (2005), pp. 295–321; Sheryllyne Haggerty, *The British-Atlantic Trading Community, 1760–1810: Men, Women, and the Distribution of Goods* (Leiden, 2006), pp. 109–41.

[23] See the chapter in this volume on Atlantic integration by Nancy Rhoden.

Americans and various types of Europeans and Euro-Americans.[24] Empires, whether British, French, or Spanish, cannot be entirely neglected in this literature. Their world wars had their American theatres, their attempts to prevent conflict produced treaties and employed interpreters, their efforts to spread their respective forms of Christianity were important to cultural exchanges. Only limited significance, however, is usually given to the specifically *imperial* aspects of these activities because of the prior imperative to restore agency, indeed, even personality to Native Americans, who become perforce the main actors in the narrative. When this literature does turn its attention to the British, the individuals whose perspective is adopted are the cultural brokers in the Indian Agency and a handful of proconsular types presumptively kept from doing their best by a stereotypically distant, myopic Whitehall. From the contraction of British power in the trans-Appalachian West after 1765 to the final abandonment of the attempt to retain some kind of protectorate over the Indian groups on American soil at the end of the War of 1812, in every case insufficient weight is given to recurrent fears of Imperial overstretch, the exigencies of world-wide warfare, or the entanglements and embarrassments of European diplomacy, while the political liabilities of supporting Indian allies and the limitations in the resources, cultural no less than material, of even those in British public life who would be their advocates all go virtually unremarked upon.[25] The brave initial

[24] The classic study along these lines is Richard White, *The Middle Ground: Indians, Empires, and Republics in the Great Lakes Region, 1650–1815* (New York, 1991), which has added a term to the historian's lexicon. A good conspectus of earlier approaches to the subject is Andrew R. L. Cayton and Fredrika J. Teute (eds), *Contact Points: American Frontiers from the Mohawk Valley to the Mississippi, 1750–1830* (Chapel Hill, NC, 1998), while a broad sampling of more recent preoccupations can be found in Daniel P. Barr (ed.), *The Boundaries between Us: Natives and Newcomers along the Frontiers of the Old Northwest Territories, 1750–1850* (Kent, OH, 2006).

[25] On Great Britain's domestic and geopolitical predicaments, cf. Patrick K. O'Brien, "Inseparable Connections: Trade, Economy, Fiscal State and the Expansion of Empire," in Marshall (ed.), *OHBE*, II, pp. 53–77; N. A. M. Rodger, "Sea-Power and Empire, 1688–1793," ibid., pp. 168–83; Michael Duffy, "World-Wide War and British Expansion, 1793–1815," ibid., pp. 184–207; John Shy, "The American Colonies in War and Revolution, 1748–1783," ibid., pp. 300–24; Rajat Kanta Ray, "Indian Society and the Establishment of British Supremacy," ibid., pp. 518–20; Brendan Simms, *Three Victories and a Defeat: The Rise and Fall of the First British Empire, 1714–1788* (London, 2007), pp. 503–10, 654–61; Michael Duffy, *Soldiers, Sugar and Seapower: The British Expedition to the West Indies and the War against Revolutionary France* (Oxford, 1987), pp. 41–58, 107–8, 126–9, 137–9; Christopher D. Hall, *British Strategy in the Napoleonic War, 1803–15* (Manchester, 1992), pp. 77–8, 91–2, 187–8, 196–8; Bradford Perkins, *Castlereagh and Adams: England and the United States, 1812–1823* (Berkeley, 1964), pp. 68–9, 71–2, 74–101, 102–11. For the ambivalent British attitude towards their Indian allies see Troy Bickham, *Savages within the Empire: Representations of American*

commitment to reduce American history to a segment of a much larger story embracing four continents has succumbed in its turn to the mandatory autochthony to which American historiography regularly reverts.

No one in this volume pretends that Imperial history lacks its own share of blind spots and weak points.[26] Rather, the chapters that follow are intended as co-belligerents with Atlantic history in the same long, incidented campaign to place American history in a wider setting. Before this argument can even begin, however, one more apologia must be rolled out in deference to the tense, really rather overladen state of current scholarship: the British West Indies have a chapter of their own and receive some attention in other chapters, but the working assumption throughout this volume is that they can never be entirely assimilated into a common history with the mainland colonies.

All informed students of this period accept the proposition that any history of British North America is incomplete without an account of the mainland's relationship with the Caribbean. Proponents of subsuming the respective histories of the two areas under a single coherent narrative and explanatory structure would go further. They insist that the affinities between the North American and the West Indian colonies have been obscured by a narrow-minded, nationalist, and "overdetermined" reading of the American Revolution and by embarrassed attempts to make slavery an exception in American life when it should be seen as the central boss of European colonization everywhere in the New World. All of the British colonies in the New World are to be ranged along a "continuum" based on the percentage of slaves in their population and, as a corollary to this proposed taxonomy, British North America from the Chesapeake southwards is held to have had more in common with the Sugar Islands than with the contiguous mainland colonies to its north. Once these twin propositions are examined in any detail, however, they become fuzzy at best and, to the extent that they are taken seriously, have the potential to create serious confusion of multiple sorts.

Indians in Eighteenth-Century Britain (Oxford, 2005) and the same author's chapter in this volume, as well as Stevens, *The Poor Indian*, Kate Flint, *The Transatlantic Indian, 1776–1930* (Princeton, 2009), pp. 26–52, and Tim Fulford, *Romantic Indians: Native Americans, British Literature, and Transatlantic Culture* (Oxford, 2006).

[26] See the survey of Imperial lapses in Carole Shammas, "Introduction," in Elizabeth Mancke and Carole Shammas (eds), *The Creation of the British Atlantic World* (Baltimore, 2005), pp. 1–16.

The very concept of the Caribbean as a colonial American "region" is hard to sustain. The two main foci of the British Sugar Islands, Jamaica and Barbados, are almost twelve hundred miles apart, four times the distance from New York to Fort Niagara or Philadelphia to Fort Pitt, and winds and currents made communication between them notoriously difficult. Further, *Caribbean* takes in a much more variegated group of colonies than the more traditional mainland groupings, even when compared to the miscellaneous amalgam that goes under the label "Middle Colonies." Yet, for all this variety, the area has no real equivalent in centrality or staying power among its indigenous peoples to the Iroquois or the Creek Indians. Again, unlike the mainland, the Caribbean was composed of the colonies of various European powers jumbled together in close proximity. As a consequence, in time of war the threat to any British island, with the partial exception of Barbados, was not merely of exposed frontiers and sharply increased risks for ships at sea but of full scale invasion by organized military forces, as well as the possibility of severe privation because of the interruption of food supplies.[27] In all these fundamental respects the West Indies were distinctive—that is, more like each other, despite their extraordinary variety, than like their mainland counterparts, regardless of the predomin-ance of slaves in the labor force of both areas.

Aggregative generalizations are another serious sticking point. It is pos-sible to make some general statements about British North America as a whole, though any proposition would be in need of immediate qualification to account for regional variations. Factoring the West Indies into the same equations hopelessly skews the results in their direction. Between 1655 and 1808, over a million slaves were shipped to Jamaica alone, roughly the same figure as for *all* immigrants, slave and free, to British North America. Nonetheless, at the time of the American Revolution the total slave popula-tion of Jamaica was only 200,000, three-quarters of whom were first generation Africans. European migration, perhaps half a million individuals in all, was, if anything, less successful in demographic terms, leaving the island with its characteristic situation of a tiny population of whites vastly

---

[27] Steele, *English Atlantic*, p. 36; Richard B. Sheridan, "The Formation of Caribbean Planta-tion Society, 1689–1748," in Marshall (ed.), *OHBE*, II, pp. 397–8; Andrew Jackson O'Shaugh-nessy, *An Empire Divided: The American Revolution and the British Caribbean* (Philadelphia, 2000), pp. 73–5.

outnumbered by a labor force of African slaves, who were replacements for earlier African slaves and who would themselves for the most part be replaced in their turn.[28] These figures are sufficiently dramatic (if that is the right term) to justify a prominent place in any broad account of British America, whatever its primary focus. Nonetheless, the horrific calculus also points back to the major reason (in addition to vulnerability to naval attack) why the West Indian colonies went their separate way at the Revolution: the fear that conflict with Britain would be an occasion for servile insurrection.

These two built-in deterrents to separation, absent in the mainland colonies, can be augmented by a third abiding feature of West Indian life: the far greater degree to which the Caribbean plantocracy was integrated into (and often parasitic upon) its metropolitan counterpart. You are presumably in no great hurry to declare your independence from the place which educates your children, provides you with your technical expertise in medicine and the law, and is also where you wish to spend your later days, provided you have piled up sufficient funds to do so.[29] Well before 1776 these distinctive circumstances all combined to make the Caribbean different in kind from the mainland and not merely in degree.

The concept of a continuum (alternatively a spectrum) was probably created to address this obvious deficiency in the argument for an amalgamated history of British America. Ranged at the far end of the proposed scale, the Sugar Islands can be presented as what the mainland, or at least the slave labor economies of the colonial South, was in some way tending towards even if they could never quite get there. Again, however, the claim does not wear well, even at its strongest point, the resemblance between Low Country South Carolina and Barbados. The two areas in juxtaposition represent the crucial point where the jump is made, allegedly seamlessly,

[28] Trevor Burnard and Kenneth Morgan, "The Dynamics of the Slave Market and Slave Purchasing Patterns in Jamaica, 1655–1788," *WMQ*, 3rd ser., LVIII (2001), pp. 205–28. See also: Philip D. Morgan, "The Black Experience in the British Empire, 1680–1810," in Marshall (ed.), *OHBE*, II, 467–70; Trevor Burnard, "European Migration to Jamaica, 1655–1780," *WMQ*, 3rd ser., LIII (1996), pp. 769–96; Trevor Burnard, *Mastery, Tyranny, and Desire: Thomas Thistlewood and his Slaves in the Anglo-Jamaican World* (Chapel Hill, NC, 2004), pp. 16–17.

[29] J.R. Ward, "The British West Indies in the Age of Abolition, 1748–1815," in Marshall (ed.), *OHBE*, II, pp. 433–4; O'Shaughnessy, *An Empire Divided*, pp. 19–33. See also the discussion in the chapter by Sarah Yeh in this volume.

from North America to the West Indies. Barbadians, it is frequently pointed out, were the single largest group among the European founding generation of South Carolina, and the subsequent development of the mainland colony in many ways duplicated that of the island from which they came.[30] The African/British ratios fluctuated at around three or four to one in both Barbados and the Carolina Low Country, while the phenomenon of absenteeism was not as pronounced in Barbados as in the other Sugar Islands and had a rough equivalent in the South Carolina planter elite managing their scattered plantations through agents while they remained based in Charleston.[31] There was even a West Indian style expatriate community of South Carolinians living in London on the eve of the Revolution, though it would be extravagant to characterize them as an "interest."[32]

Instructive as the pairing of South Carolina and Barbados is, it cannot be stretched to bear the argumentative burden put upon it. At the most, it creates a bridge to nowhere. Barbados is easily the most distinctive of the major British island possessions, the one most unlike the others. Similarly, Low Country South Carolina is not just like the Chesapeake but more so: its flora and fauna (and the pathogens that went with them) are really the only genuinely tropical elements in the ecosystems of the original thirteen colonies, other than the immediately adjacent Georgia low country, and the per capita value of its exports was also unprecedented— that is, on a West Indian scale—when compared to anywhere to its north.[33] The strong family resemblance between the two colonies, therefore, does little by itself to bring, say, Maryland or Antigua into the proposed extended kinship network.

And then there is the Insuperable. South Carolina revolted, Barbados did not. From the resistance to the Stamp Act onwards, the South Carolina

---

[30] Robert M. Weir, *Colonial South Carolina: A History* (Millwood, NY, 1983), pp. 50–1, 60–1; Peter A. Coclanis, *The Shadow of a Dream: Economic Life and Death in the South Carolina Low Country* (New York, 1989), pp. 21–2, 61; S. Max Edelson, *Plantation Enterprise in Colonial South Carolina* (Cambridge, MA, 2006), pp. 41–4. Cf., however, a critique of Barbadian influence in Louis H. Roper, *Conceiving Carolina: Proprietors, Planters, and Plots, 1662–1729* (New York, 2004).

[31] Ward, "The British West Indies in the Age of Abolition," in Marshall (ed.), *OHBE*, II, p. 433 (Table 19.2); Edelson, *Plantation Enterprise in Colonial South Carolina*, pp. 127–9, 153–4.

[32] Julie Flavell, *When London was Capital of America* (New Haven, 2010), pp. 16–26.

[33] O'Shaughnessy, *An Empire Divided*, p. 6; Coclanis, *The Shadow of a Dream*, pp. 35–43, 77, 91.

Commons House of Assembly regularly displayed a truculence that would not have been out of place in Virginia or Massachusetts. There were certainly signs of hesitancy in the last year or so before the Revolution, as there were elsewhere in America. Nonetheless, in July of 1776 through its representatives at Philadelphia, the planter elite of South Carolina voted for independence, albeit a day late.[34] The individuals who did so may have been, as has been argued, members of that very elastic category, the reluctant revolutionaries.[35] The designation, at least as apposite to the political elites of Pennsylvania or New York, among other places, still begs the question. If the South Carolina elite had really assessed their situation in terms basically similar to that of the great planters of Barbados or any other sugar island, it is unlikely that they would have allowed themselves to be forced into participating in the Revolution. The alternative of turning Tory was always there, and many people did take it—but never in sufficient numbers to suggest that South Carolina was simply a Caribbean island that had been beached on the Atlantic coastal plain.

One should not make a fetish of temporal and geographical classifications, which are always in need of variances and renegotiations if they are to retain their explanatory value. The historians of the Caribbean have responded creatively to this inherent slipperiness in ways that may recommend themselves to historians of the mainland facing similar puzzles. For the most part, they currently favor a pan-Caribbean approach that emphasizes the commonalities among the various ex-colonial islands without much reference to their respective imperial pasts.[36] One can object that sometimes whether one island was once French and another British or Spanish does in fact matter and still admire the underlying flexibility that informs their manner of proceeding. A "Greater Caribbean" has been proposed, for example, organized around vulnerability to hurricanes and therefore including South Carolina and Georgia, but the geographical area so designated does not necessarily preclude the mainland region from

---

[34] Weir, *Colonial South Carolina*, pp. 291–332.

[35] Robert Olwell, *Masters, Slaves, and Subjects: The Culture of Power in the South Carolina Low Country, 1740–1790* (Ithaca, NY, 1998), pp. 226–43. Cf. Weir, *Colonial South Carolina*, pp. 332–4.

[36] B.W. Higman, "The British West Indies," in Winks (ed.), *OHBE*, V, pp. 134–45. All recent histories of the Caribbean emphasize its commonalities, but there are differences in the choice of organizing themes. Cf. Gad Heuman, *The Caribbean* (London, 2006), Frank Moya Pons, *History of the Caribbean: Plantations, Trade and War in the Atlantic World* (Princeton, 2007), and B.W. Higman, *A Concise History of the Caribbean* (New York, 2011).

simultaneous or subsequent consideration as part of either the South East or the American colonial South. If the subject were to be disease vectors, the Greater Caribbean could arguably be extended to the Chesapeake and on occasion Philadelphia, while in the case of trade patterns and the routes by which communication proceeded along them the area could be stretched even further north to take in Boston.[37] Such taxonomic promiscuity may seem dangerously "undertheorized." Nonetheless, in the face of the self-fueling, ever more subtle "conversations" about methodology that pre-occupy much of early American historiography at present it is difficult to imagine any course other than a Caribbean-style pragmatism that can return attention to the subjects of the inquiry in their own right.

Somehow, at some point, the overlapping, fragmented entities that come under the heading *British North America* in a variety of different historio-graphies will be patched back together into a coherent whole or, more likely, a number of different coherent wholes, in spite of all the a priori objections. Within a very few years of the present author pronouncing that a workable alignment of Imperial and ethnohistorical scholarship was improbable, studies of the Seven Years' War and the Albany Plan of Union, paying no heed to probabilities, went ahead and successfully combined the two.[38] To tempt fate with a final prophecy, more along the same lines is likely as the students of the American Indians in the first centuries of Contact, who have already produced some of the most remarkable scholarship of recent decades, shed their apologetic and polemical stance. The same perhaps can be said with equal or greater emphasis for historians of slavery and the slave trade. In the interim, partial answers to incomplete questions will have to do if any progress is to be made along the lines the various alternative forms of categorization are meant to achieve. This Companion

---

[37] Cf. Matthew Mulcahy, *Hurricanes and Society in the British Greater Caribbean, 1624–1783* (Baltimore, 2006); J.R. McNeil, *Mosquito Empires: Ecology and War in the Greater Caribbean, 1620–1914* (New York, 2010), pp. 15–62; Steele, *The English Atlantic*, pp. 24–8, 37, 256–8.

[38] Fred Anderson, *The Crucible of War: The Seven Years' War and the Fate of Empire in British North America, 1754–1766* (New York, 2000); Timothy J. Shannon, *Indians and Colonists at the Crossroads of Empire: the Albany Congress of 1754* (Ithaca, NY, 2000). Mention should also be made of the pioneering work along the same lines of Daniel K. Richter, especially *The Ordeal of the Longhouse: The Peoples of the Iroquois League in the Era of European Colonization* (Chapel Hill, NC, 1992) and, among more recent titles, of Jon Parmenter, *The Edge of the Woods: Iroquoia, 1534–1701* (East Lansing, MI, 2010), and Gail D. MacLeitch, *Imperial Entanglements: Iroquois Change and Persistence on the Frontiers of Empire* (Philadelphia, 2011).

is intended as an addition to this mosaic. As such, without any gestures towards prescription, proscription, or imprecation, it is committed to the reader.

Select Bibliography

DAVID ARMITAGE, et al., "AHR Forum: The New British History in Atlantic Perspective," *American Historical Review*, CIV (1999), pp. 426–500.

DAVID ARMITAGE and MICHAEL J. BRADDICK (eds), *The British Atlantic World, 1500–1800* (Basingstoke, Hants. and New York, 2002).

BERNARD BAILYN, *Atlantic History: Concept and Contours* (Cambridge, MA, 2005).

BERNARD BAILYN and PATRICIA L. DENAULT (eds), *Soundings in Atlantic History: Latent Structures and Intellectual Currents, 1500–1830* (Cambridge, MA, 2009).

ALISON GAMES, et al., "Forum: Beyond the Atlantic," *William and Mary Quarterly*, Third Series, LXIII (2006), pp. 675–742.

JACK P. GREENE, et al., "Colonial History and National History: Reflections on a Continuing Problem," *William and Mary Quarterly*, Third Series, LXIV (2007), pp. 235–86.

JACK P. GREENE and PHILIP D. MORGAN (eds), *Atlantic History: A Critical Appraisal* (New York, 2009).

ALAN I. KARRAS and J.R. McNEIL (eds), *Atlantic American Societies: From Columbus through Abolition, 1492–1888* (London, 1992).

RICHARD PRICE, "One Big Thing: Britain, Its Empire, and their Imperial Culture," *Journal of British Studies*, LIV (2006), pp. 602–27.

ERIC SLAUTER, et al., "The 'Trade Gap' in Atlantic Studies: A Forum on Literary and Historical Scholarship," *William and Mary Quarterly*, Third Series, LXIV (2008), pp. 135–86.

KATHLEEN WILSON (ed.), *A New Imperial History: Culture, Identity, and Modernity in Britain and the Empire, 1660–1840* (Cambridge, 2004).

2

British North America in the Empire

An Overview

Stephen Foster and Evan Haefeli

The overseas empires of the nations of early modern Europe were such various and composite arrangements that it is possible to characterize them according to any one of a wide variety of rubrics. In the recent scholarly literature they seem to come across most often as so many states of mind. Much of the narrative of empire has devolved into an account of one or another of the ways in which Europeans got into serious conflicts whenever they came up against other peoples (mainly indigenes and enslaved Africans) with different assumptions about how the world worked and for what purposes. Certainly, culture was an important part of matters imperial, and historical understanding has profited by moving beyond purely European modes of thought. This much said, to begin at so abstract a level with ontologies and cosmologies is to enter the story, in good epic fashion, *in medias res*. Be it Jamestown or Speightstown, Boston or Fort Stanwix, the Europeans who came together with other peoples in various cross-cultural "contact points" did so on the basis of more limited but more explicit claims. Empires in the first instance were assertions of authority and exercises of power made on a regular basis by institutionalized means according to a well-developed rationale.[1] Simultaneously, they were also intended to be extractive machines transferring wealth and creating value for the benefit of those who sponsored them.

---

[1] See the chapter by Kenneth MacMillan in this volume, and the same author's *Sovereignty and Possession in the English New World: The Legal Foundations of Empire, 1576–1640* (Cambridge, 2006), as well as David Armitage, *The Ideological Origins of the British Empire* (Cambridge, 2000).

As both the premier power in Europe and the first proper holder of dominion in the New World, Spain was the archetypal example of how dynastic power and influence, as well as national economic performance, seemed a function of imperial expansion. Thus Richard Hakluyt in his *Discourse of Western Planting* of 1584 announced that England by getting a slice of "that waste firmament of America" not yet Spanish would at one go set the poor at work as shipwrights and sailors, make England "lordes of all those sees," and "spoile Phillipps Indian navye" in order to "abate the pride of Spaine and of the supporter of the greate Antechriste of Rome, and to pull him downe in equallitie to his neighbour princes, and consequently to cutt of[f] the common mischefes that come to all Europe by the peculiar aboundaunce of his Indian treasure."[2] Allowing for the ominous implications of "waste firmament," there are no indigenous peoples per se to be dispossessed nor Africans to be enslaved in this familiar statement of the logic of empire. Once theory was put into practice both would come easily enough—but only as corollaries to the fundamental theorem that colonial wealth equaled European power.

Self-evident on first assertion, the connection between the two constituent elements, war and economic growth, could rarely be maintained for long in subsequent discussions. By the time Louis XIV had become the prince to be pulled down to equality with his neighbors, writers on economic topics treated the Imperial Wars as little more than an appendage to their respective rhapsodies on the excellent use of colonies. Colonies were there to produce commodities not otherwise available for which there was a substantial market in Europe or, less frequently, Africa and Asia. These same commodities should arrive in England in English ships manned by English crews, thereby subsidizing English maritime industries, and then were to be processed in some way that set the English poor at work. Finally, along with domestic manufactures, the colonial products were to be re-exported to the Continent or elsewhere at a high profit to produce the much coveted favorable balance of payments. The theory and practice of colonization had become (for some) a relatively simple matter. John Cary, in his 1695 *Essay on the State in Relation to its Trade, its Poor, and its Taxes, for Carrying on the Present War against France,* had in fact little relevant to say on the Nine Years' War. Instead, he weighed the various forms of English overseas

---

[2] *A Discourse Concerning Western Planting, Written in the Year 1584* (ed.), Charles Deane, *Documentary History of the State of Maine* (Cambridge, MA, 1877), II, p. 155.

trade in a standard issue balance and found some wanting. The West Indian and African trades were "the most profitable of any we drive." The slave trade in particular "doth occasionally give so vast an Imployment to our People both by Sea and Land" and also provided "the Hands whereby our Plantations are improved, and 'tis by their Labours such great Quantities of Sugar, Tobacco, Cotton, Ginger, and Indigo, are raised."[3] At the opposite extreme, the New England colonies were held "to bring least Advantage to this Kingdom." Instead of producing what was unobtainable elsewhere for export to the Mother Country they traded mainly with the other colonies in "Fish, Deal-Boards, Pipe-staves, Horses, and such like," as well as home-grown provisions, "and from thence fetch their respective Growths, which they after send to Foreign Markets, and thereby injure the Trade of *England.*" New England should, therefore, be prevented from trading with any place but England or dealing in anything that could be made or grown at home. Compensation would be given in "*Negroes* on easie Terms."[4]

Subsequently much reprinted in whole or part, Cary's *Essay* is the work of an author who barely understood multilateral trade, had no grasp of the size or nature of wartime financing, and thought the high interest the government had to pay for its loans was the product of stock jobbing rather than because they looked at the time like very risky propositions.[5] Charles Davenant, Cary's much better informed, infinitely more sophisticated contemporary, and one of the founding figures of "political arithmetic" cannot be faulted on any of these grounds.[6] Yet even he apparently felt that colonies bereft of slave labor growing staple crops were in need of some fancy footwork to justify their continued existence. "The Northward Parts," meaning all of the colonies of the mainland except Virginia (treated as a special case), were to be valued because they fed the West Indies which produced the treasured tropical products, so that "the Southward and

---

[3] John Cary, *An Essay on the State of England in Relation to its Trade, its Poor. and its Taxes, for Carrying on the Present War against France* (Bristol, 1695), pp. 65, 75.

[4] Cary, *An Essay*, pp. 70–1 (quotation), 94–6.

[5] Cary, *An Essay*, pp. 31–2, 170–8.

[6] Cf. Terence Hutchinson, *Before Adam Smith: The Emergence of Political Economy, 1662–1776* (Oxford, 1988), pp. 42–55; David Ormrod, *The Rise of Commercial Empires: England and the Netherlands in the Age of Mercantilism, 1650–1750* (Cambridge, 2003), esp. pp. 55–9; Nuala Zahedieh, *The Capital and the Colonies: London and the Atlantic Economy, 1660–1700* (Cambridge, 2010), esp. pp. 1–16, 42–4. For a different view of Davenant, as essentially *the* Tory ideologue on the economy, see Steve Pincus, "Rethinking Mercantilism: Political Economy, the British Empire, and the Atlantic World in the Seventeenth and Eighteenth Centuries," *WMQ,* 3rd ser., LXIX (2012), pp. 24–8.

Northward Colonies, having such a mutual Dependance upon each other, all Circumstances considered, are almost equally Important."[7] In contrast to Cary and many others, Davenant did not regard domestic consumption as a necessary evil. No less presciently, he discovered that the mainland colonies would make good markets for English goods. For all that, he still had his own particular quarrel with the people of New England because their substantial ship building industry might, if not checked, make them a naval power in their own right, "which if suffer'd, we cannot expect to hold 'em long in our Subjection."[8]

If the anomaly of New England only deepened over time, in every other respect by the third decade of the eighteenth century, if not earlier, most of the North American mainland was doing what it was supposed to do. One may argue about the degree to which the force majeure of Acts of Parliament restricting the channels of colonial trade brought about this obliging turn of affairs and how much of it was a simple matter of the increasing strengths of the British economy, which rendered illegal trade unnecessary or at least not worth the risk except where potential profits were extremely high.[9] In any event, the widespread adoption of slave labor, improvements in methods of growing and shipping, and the cultivation of Continental markets for American tobacco pushed the Chesapeake colonies of Virginia and Maryland into their golden age and gave Great Britain that most desirable of commodities: a staple that was predominantly re-exported. In South Carolina, slave-grown rice cultivation, in its infancy when Cary and Davenport wrote, provided a second major re-export crop. The Middle Colonies of New York, New Jersey, and Pennsylvania, while not quite so dutiful, could still justify their existence as the major suppliers of wheat and other bread products to the West Indies, the source for the most valuable of British

---

[7] Charles Davenant, *Discourses on the Publick Revenues, and on the Trade of England* (London, 1698), II, pp. 225–37 (quotation at p. 230). The definition of the term *Northward Parts* can be found at p. 225.

[8] Davenant, *Discourses*, pp. 205–9 (quotations at pp. 205, 208).

[9] Different points of view on this question may be found in: Nuala Zahedieh, "Overseas Expansion and Trade in the Seventeenth Century," in Nicholas Canny (ed.), *OHBE*, I, *The Origins of Empire* (Oxford, 1998), pp. 398–422; Patrick K. O'Brien, "Inseparable Connections: Trade, Economy, Fiscal State, and the Expansion of Empire, 1688–1815," in P. J. Marshall (ed.), *OHBE*, II, *The Eighteenth Century* (Oxford, 1998), pp. 53–77; Ormrod, *The Rise of Commercial Empires*, esp. pp. 23–7, 98–9; Zahedieh, *The Capital and the Colonies*, esp. pp. 36–41; and, most recently, Christian J. Koot, *Empire at the Periphery: British Colonies, Anglo-Dutch Trade, and the Development of the British Atlantic, 1621–1713* (New York, 2011).

imports. Even Massachusetts, the prime malefactor in a scapegrace region, had at least the saving grace of sending almost two thirds of its exports of dried fish to the same destination. Increases in prosperity and population in the colonies, in their turn, meant that, by the eve of the Revolution, North American markets accounted for about a quarter of British total exports and the West Indies for about an eighth.[10]

There is an obvious enough skeleton at this particular feast. Studies of Native American slavery, of the coming of slavery to Barbados before sugar became the dominant crop, and of the increase in the size of the slave labor force in so improbable a place as mid-eighteenth-century Boston all point to the ubiquity of the not-so-peculiar institution.[11] The British in the American colonies resorted to slaves as a source of labor everywhere it was remotely practical, as rapidly as circumstances would permit and in a great variety of ingenious forms, including plantations without staples in North Carolina and staple agriculture without large plantations on the Maryland Eastern Shore.[12] Even in the early Chesapeake, the plantation region conventionally singled out for an alleged reluctance to switch from indentured servants to slave labor, the transition actually began as far back as 1640, was well and decisively underway by 1670, and had already reached the point where slaves outnumbered servants on the large plantations by 1690.[13] For its predominant labor force the region's subsequent "golden age" of improved productivity and cost effective economies meant only longer hours, harder work, more intensive surveillance, and possibly less food.[14]

---

[10] Jacob M. Price, "The Imperial Economy, 1700–1776," in Marshall (ed.), *OHBE*, II, pp. 78–104, esp. Table 4.6 (p. 103). Cf. Ormrod, *The Rise of Commercial Empires*, pp. 71–2.

[11] Cf. Alan Gallay, *The Indian Slave Trade: The Rise of the English Empire in the American South, 1670–1717* (New Haven, 2002); Russell R. Menard, *Sweet Negotiations: Sugar, Slavery, and Plantation Agriculture in Early Barbados* (Charlottesville, VA, 2006); Robert E. Desrochers, Jr., "Slave-For-Sale Advertisements and Slavery in Massachusetts, 1704–1781," *WMQ*, 3rd ser., LIX (2002), pp. 623–65, and the same author's chapter in this volume.

[12] Harry Roy Merrens, *Colonial North Carolina in the Eighteenth Century: A Study in Historical Geography* (Chapel Hill, NC, 1964), pp. 85–92; Lorena S. Walsh, *Motives of Honor, Pleasure, and Profit: Plantation Management in the Colonial Chesapeake* (Chapel Hill, NC, 2010), pp. 554–86.

[13] Walsh, *Motives of Honor, Pleasure, and Profit*, pp. 200–3; John C. Coombs, "The Phases of Conversion: A New Chronology for the Rise of Slavery in Early Virginia," *WMQ*, 3rd ser., LXVIII (2011), pp. 332–60.

[14] Walsh, *Motives of Honor, Pleasure, and Profit*, pp. 475–6, 521, 622–5, 636–7.

Enslaved individuals constituted only about a fifth of the population of the British colonies on the mainland at the time of the American Revolution. Nonetheless, of the top five North American exports by value, three—tobacco, rice, and indigo—were largely slave grown products and accounted for roughly two-thirds of the whole, while much of the second most valuable commodity—bread and flour—was destined for the slave population of the West Indies, as was the larger share of dried fish, the smallest of the five. Admittedly, not everything produced in British North America followed Davenant's happy harmony of Northward and Southward parts. Pennsylvania, for example, sent somewhat more bread and flour to the Wine Islands and southern Europe than it did to the Sugar Islands, and the New England ship builders supplying the region's formidable merchant marine also made good money selling their ships in England.[15] But it still remains difficult, if not impossible, to imagine a prosperous colonial economy *anywhere* in British North America without slave grown products or the profits made from the sale of colonial produce carried in colonial ships to the West Indies for consumption mainly by slaves.

If Davenant's political economy is neglectful of the casualties accumulated in the prosecution of its schemes, it is also appears radically incomplete in a second, less obvious way once attention shifts to the other half of Hakluyt's equation. From the Glorious Revolution of 1689 to the Peace of Paris of 1763, Great Britain was engaged in warfare on a large scale for about half of the years under consideration, and every one of these wars had an American theatre. In this alternate version of political arithmetic, war was not an interruption in the normal state of things but a central part of that "normal." From such a perspective, the colonies appeared rather differently from when they were marshaled in order of the value of their exports. Jamaica, for example, was a jewel in the crown well before its sugar production became significant because of its ability to suck up silver from the Spanish Empire, which was then used to help pay for the masts and naval stores from the Baltic trade that kept the Royal Navy afloat. That same silver

---

[15] The variety and distribution of colonial export activity on the eve of the Revolution can be taken in conveniently through the maps in Lester J. Cappon, et al. (eds), *Atlas of Early American History: The Revolutionary Era, 1760–1790* (Princeton, 1976), pp. 26–7, which are constructed from the sources discussed on p. 103. See also Thomas Doerflinger, *A Vigorous Spirit of Enterprise: Merchants and Economic Development in Revolutionary Philadelphia* (Chapel Hill, NC, 1986), pp. 108–13; Jacob M. Price, "A Note on the Value of Colonial Exports of Shipping," *Journal of Economic History*, XXXVI (1976), pp. 704–24.

also made possible the profits from the East Indian trade that generated in their turn yet more silver to underwrite the logistics of Marlborough's victories in the War of the Spanish Succession.[16] By the same logic, the Duke of Newcastle in 1750 could speak of the "northern colonies, which are inestimable to us," meaning by *northern* the erstwhile Imperial pariahs of New England and (probably) New York. They were the front-line colonies in military operations in America that prevented the French bringing their full force to bear in Europe, so that "if we lose our American possessions, or the influence and weight of them, in time of peace, France will, with great ease, make war with us whenever they please hereafter."[17]

In the wonderful alchemy of war, the last were first and the first were last. The presumed economic liabilities of the New England colonies were precisely what made them valuable. A flexible, decentralized, and increasingly well-organized trade network tied Boston and the port towns to near and distant hinterlands and provided the hard tack, small beer, salt pork, dried onions, and so on for the merchant, whaling, and fishing fleets. It could also, when needed, provision amphibious expeditionary forces, as in the abortive assault on Quebec in 1711 and the successful siege of Louisbourg in 1745.[18] Equally, the trades and facilities that built and kept the New England merchant and fishing fleets in repair (and that so alarmed Davenant) also refitted British Royal Navy ships that, prior to the founding of

[16] Nuala Zahedieh, "The Merchants of Port Royal, Jamaica, and the Spanish Contraband Trade," *WMQ*, 3rd ser., XLIII (1986), pp. 570–93; D.W. Jones, *War and Economy in the Age of William III and Marlborough* (Oxford, 1988), pp. 274–307.

[17] William Coxe, *Memoirs of the Administration of the Right Honourable Henry Pelham, Collected from the Family Papers, and Other Authentic Documents* (London, 1829), II, pp. 345, 345–6. For the context, see T.R. Clayton, "The Duke of Newcastle, the Earl of Halifax, and the American Origins of the Seven Years' War," *Historical Journal*, XXIV (1981), p. 576; Brendan Simms, *Three Victories and a Defeat: The Rise and Fall of the First British Empire, 1714–1788* (London, 2007), pp. 367–8.

[18] Cf. James E. McWilliams, *Building the Bay Colony: Local Economy and Culture in Early Massachusetts* (Charlottesville, VA, 2007), esp. pp. 149–50; Ian K. Steele, *The English Atlantic, 1675–1740: An Exploration of Communication and Community* (New York, 1986), pp. 63–6. For examples of the extent of the integration of the New England economy, see Bruce H. Mann, *Neighbors and Strangers: Law and Community in Early Connecticut* (Chapel Hill, NC, 1987), pp. 11–12; W.T. Baxter, *The House of Hancock: Business in Boston, 1724–1775* (Cambridge, MA, 1945), pp. 104–5, 112. For the expeditions see Thomas Hutchinson, *The History of the Colony and Province of Massachusetts-Bay* (ed.), Lawrence Shaw Mayo (Cambridge, MA, 1936), II, pp. 142–7, 309–16; G. A. Rawlyk, *Yankees at Louisbourg*, Univ. of Maine Studies, 2nd ser., LXXXV (Orono, ME, 1967), pp. 113–14.

Halifax, had no other place to go in North America for the same services.[19] Better still, from the latter stages of King Philip's War onwards semi-professionalized mixed groups of dependent allied Indians and footloose Europeans under the command of local *condottieri* (to use Richard Johnson's analogy) were available on demand for carrying on "wilderness warfare" in the ugliest possible way, while the pool of surplus young men marking time before they could inherit or buy land had an all too obvious use in the recruitment of larger expeditionary forces.[20] At the opposite end of British America, in the Caribbean, the situation was also inverted. Valuable as the Caribbean islands were for their sugar, molasses, and rum, they were also difficult to defend. In addition, the imbalance between slave and free populations that provided so much per capita purchasing power for the latter also necessitated the stationing of regular troops in the area at considerable expense to Great Britain because of the unwillingness of the legislatures of the islands to pick up much of the cost.[21] There should be no surprise, then, at the decision in 1763 to keep Canada, of no great worth in itself but a major menace to colonial security, rather than the sugar islands of Guadelupe and Martinique, a choice that would have compounded the overstretch of British military resources.[22]

In the Lower South, just as in the Caribbean, the political arithmetician's delight was the strategist's nightmare. South Carolina added to its existing liabilities—a long coastline, a slave majority in the Low Country, and the proximity of the Spanish in Florida—by provocative behavior toward the neighboring Indian populations. Both the Yamasee War of 1715–16 and the Cherokee War of 1760–1 demonstrated the near total incapacity of the colony to use its considerable resources to mount any kind of effective military operation. Georgia, created to be a buffer for South Carolina, ended up in the same predicament as the colony it was supposed to shield

---

[19] John Brewer, *The Sinews of Power: War, Money and the English State, 1688–1788* (New York, 1989), p. 35; Michael Duffy, "The Foundations of British Naval Power," in Michael Duffy (ed.), *The Military Revolution and the State, 1500–1800*, Exeter Studies in History, I (Exeter, 1980), p. 61.

[20] Fred Anderson, *A People's Army: Massachusetts Soldiers and Society in the Seven Years' War* (Chapel Hill, NC, 1984), pp. 26–39; Harold E. Selesky, *War and Society in Colonial Connecticut* (New Haven, 1990), pp. 67–95, 166–94; Richard R. Johnson, "The Search for a Usable Indian: An Aspect of the Defense of Colonial New England," *Journal of American History*, LXIV (1977), p. 641.

[21] See above, chap. I ("Introduction"), nn. 27, 28; John Shy, *Toward Lexington: The Role of the British Army in the Coming of the American Revolution* (Princeton, 1965), pp. 34–5.

[22] Simms, *Three Victories and a Defeat*, pp. 475–7.

and had to be rescued by the annexation of Florida in 1763.[23] Only North Carolina, generally dismissed as "Lubberland" for the alleged stupidity and indolence of its inhabitants, *was* defensible from naval attack thanks to the Outer Banks, and it also served an important military function in the provision of tar, pitch, and turpentine for the Royal Navy.[24]

The Upper South and the Middle Colonies were less predictable. Maryland exported a valuable staple in the form of tobacco and simultaneously provided foodstuffs for the West Indies and Philadelphia, but to all intents and purposes it sat out the Imperial Wars because of the perpetual quarrel between the assembly and the proprietors of the colony, the Calverts. Virginia looked to be doing much the same thing between 1689 and 1713 but the size of the colony and the wealth generated by its tobacco economy endowed it with sufficient means to mount credible military efforts in the last two Imperial Wars. Virginia famously participated with enthusiasm in the failed siege of Cartagena in 1741, sending not only troops but the only royal governor to participate in the expedition, while the colony's undisguised lust for land in the Ohio Country gave a Virginia militia unit the dubious honor of firing the first shot in the American theatre of the Seven Years' War. After the successful expedition to take Fort Duquesne in 1758, the colony's own interests were less immediately involved in the progress of the war and its cooperation flagged for a time, only to revive in full for the final campaigns in North America in 1761 and 1762.[25]

Pennsylvania was something of a cross between Virginia and Maryland. The British military would spend substantial sums in Philadelphia, by 1760 the largest city in America.[26] Well-placed Pennsylvanians also were prominent among those casting sheep's eyes at the Ohio Country. On the other side of the balance, conflicts between the colonial assembly and the propri-

---

[23] Daniel K. Richter, "Native Peoples of North America and the Eighteenth-Century British Empire," in Marshall (ed.), *OHBE*, II, pp. 351–2; Ian K. Steele, *Warpaths: Invasions of North America* (New York, 1994), pp. 165–6; Fred Anderson, *The Crucible of War: The Seven Years' War and the Fate of Empire in British North America, 1754–1766* (New York, 2000), pp. 467–71; John L. Bullion, "Securing the Peace: Lord Bute, the Plan for the Army, and the Origins of the American Revolution," in Karl W. Schweizer (ed.), *Lord Bute: Essays in Re-interpretation* (Leicester, 1988), p. 31.

[24] Merrens, *Colonial North Carolina in the Eighteenth Century*, pp. 85–92.

[25] Cf. James Titus, *The Old Dominion at War: Society, Politics, and Warfare in Late Colonial Virginia* (Columbia, SC, 1991), pp. 120–48; Steele, *Warpaths*, pp. 198–9; Anderson, *The Crucible of War*, pp. 229–30, 320–3, 519.

[26] John J. McCusker and Russell R. Menard, *The Economy of British America, 1607–1789*, 2nd edn (Chapel Hill, NC, 1991), pp. 194–7.

etors, the Penn family, threatened the same kind of paralysis as in Maryland, and Quaker dominance of the legislature made explicit participation in any kind of military effort difficult. The passing of Quaker control, however, and the fear that the whole of the Ohio Country would go by default to Virginia, led Pennsylvania to become a useful part of the British war effort in the Seven Years' War—until it got what it wanted. The proprietor–assembly conflict promptly resurfaced once Fort Duquesne was captured, and for the rest of the war the ensuing stalemate resulted in considerable suffering for Europeans and Indians alike in the exposed western areas of the colony.[27]

New Englanders complained that the neighboring colony of New York "always kept itself in a State of Neutrality, contributing nothing to the common Safety," and its reputation for non-stop fractious, obdurate political imbroglios seemed to preclude significant government activity of any sort.[28] As the loci of the conflict with the French moved south and west towards the Great Lakes and Lake Champlain, however, New York took an increasing part in the last two Imperial conflicts and managed to tie with Connecticut for second place for the size of its share of Parliamentary reimbursements to the colonies for their military expenditures. Taken together with the front-runner, Massachusetts, the three colonies received three quarters of the total sums disbursed between 1749 and 1763, amply justifying Newcastle's insistence on their strategic centrality to Empire in America.[29]

Whether the subject is the location of Jamestown or the design of the ships that carried the first migrants there, to a greater or lesser degree the influence of warfare can be detected in every aspect of the British Empire from its inception.[30] The wars of the long eighteenth century, in particular, were too large in scope, went on for too long, and involved spending what

[27] Anderson, *The Crucible of War*, pp. 160–1, 322–4, 519. Cf. Matthew C. Ward, *Breaking the Backcountry: The Seven Years' War in Virginia and Pennsylvania* (Pittsburgh, 2004), and Jane T. Merritt, *At the Crossroads: Indians and Empires on the Mid-Atlantic Frontier, 1700–1763* (Chapel Hill, NC, 2003), pp. 274–99.

[28] Jeremiah Dummer, *A Defence of the New-England Charters* (London, 1721), p. 26; Alan Tully, *Forming American Politics: Ideals, Interests, and Institutions in Colonial New York and Pennsylvania* (Baltimore, 1994), pp. 213–56.

[29] Anderson, *The Crucible of War*, pp. 320–1, 388–9; Julian Gwyn, "British Government Spending and the North American Colonies, 1740–1775," *Journal of Imperial and Commonwealth History*, VIII (1980), p. 79.

[30] John C. Appleby, "War, Politics, and Colonization, 1558–1625," in Canny (ed.), *OHBE*, I, pp. 71–2; N. A. M. Rodger, "Guns and Sails in the First Phase of English Colonization, 1500–1650," in ibid., pp. 96–7.

was by colonial standards inconceivably large sums of money for the situation to be otherwise. Some facets of colonial life were less touched by military conflict than others, but the specifically Imperial ones—the economy, colonial governance, and the trilateral relationship of the metropole, the colonists, and the American Indians, as well as British American self-conception—all were shaped by the stimulus of war in fundamental and significant ways.

Perhaps the most telling example of this proposition is the process by which a colony's lower house, in imitation of the House of Commons, leveraged its control of revenue to encroach, fracas by fracas, on the power of the royally-appointed executive.[31] War figures in this particular narrative as the instance of legislative aggrandizement par excellence. An assembly that would vote funds for military expenditures only on the condition of specifying what went to whom and that also demanded the sole right to supervise these expenditures trenched on the royal prerogative with a vengeance, but it was still likely to win its point and gain a lasting precedent at the expense of royal government.[32] By the end of the Seven Years' War, the presumed loss of metropolitan control through these means had become something of a commonplace. Soame Jenyns, minor poet and member of the Board of Trade, merely repeated the received wisdom when he defended parliamentary taxation of the colonists as the only way left to recover a generation's worth of forfeited royal authority:

Can any Time be more proper to oblige them [the colonies] to settle handsome Incomes on their Governors, than when we find them [the governors] unable to procure a Subsistence on any other terms than those of breaking all their Instructions, and betraying the Rights of their Sovereign?[33]

The generation of Charles M. Andrews and his student, Leonard W. Labaree, made much of these extortionate transactions conducted under the heading

---

[31] P. J. Marshall, "The First British Empire," in Winks (ed.), *OHBE*, V, pp. 43–53; C. A. Bayly, "The Second British Empire," in ibid., pp. 54–72.

[32] See the chapter by Daniel Hulsebosch in this volume.

[33] Soame Jenyns, *The Objections to the Taxation of our American Colonies, by the Legislature of Great Britain, Briefly Consider'd*, 2nd edn (London, 1765), pp. 13–14. Cf. Jack P. Greene, "Martin Bladen's Blueprint for a Colonial Union," *WMQ*, 3rd ser., XVII (1960), p. 529; John Campbell, Earl of Loudon to the Duke of Cumberland, December 26, 1756, in Stanley Pargellis (ed.), *Military Affairs in North America, 1748–1765, Selected Documents from the Cumberland Papers in Windsor Castle* (New York, 1936), p. 273.

"the power of the purse," a stock phrase of the time dubbed by John Dickinson (referring to one of its variations) as "a common, but strong expression."[34] Later scholarship has added some important context by pointing out that the phenomenon was an aspect of the aggressive self-promotion of colonial elites, so that the matters of home rule and who shall rule at home were already closely linked well before the Revolution. And we have been further reminded that the House of Commons was also consolidating its power at the same time as the colonial assemblies. When these two parallel lines of development finally crossed (as they can in history, if not in geometry), there was a predictable train wreck.[35]

The constitutional high road to Lexington outlined here is a part of the whole, but only a part. Taking a longer view—the one thing a Jenyns or Dickinson could *not* do—uncovers countercurrents pulling Imperial governance in an opposite direction. Prior to 1689, the dominant fact of colonial governance had been the metropolitan power's *lack* of effective power. Until almost the end of the seventeenth century, Virginia remained the only mainland royal colony and (with Barbados and Jamaica) one of only three British colonies in the New World in which the executive was responsible directly to the crown rather than to a proprietor or an electorate. In a sense, Sir William Berkeley, Virginia's longtime governor, was a large fraction of the British Empire all by himself. By virtue of his membership of a prominent court family, he had far more immediate access to the top level of English government than any other official in the New World, either at the time or subsequently, and was restrained only by a complaisant legislature largely in awe of him.[36] Elsewhere things Imperial enjoyed an existence that was at best intermittent. In a sense, the Rump Parliament had laid down the basic parameters by which the Empire might be defined when

[34] Stephen Foster, "British North America in the Seventeenth and Eighteenth Centuries," in Winks (ed.), *OHBE*, V, pp. 74–8; [John Dickinson], *Letters from a Farmer in Pennsylvania, to the Inhabitants of the British Colonies*, 2nd edn (Philadelphia, 1768), p. 43.

[35] Jack P. Greene, *The Quest for Power: The Lower Houses of Assembly in the Southern Royal Colonies, 1689–1776* (Chapel Hill, NC, 1963); Ian K. Steele, "The Anointed, the Appointed, and the Elected: Governance of the British Empire, 1689–1784," in Marshall (ed.), *OHBE*, II, pp. 105–27. For the broader context see also Jack P. Greene, *Peripheries and Center: Constitutional Development in the Extended Polities of the British Empire and the United States, 1607–1788* (Athens, GA, 1986).

[36] Warren M. Billings, *Sir William Berkeley and the Forging of Colonial Virginia* (Baton Rouge, LA, 2004); G.E. Aylmer, *The Crown's Servants: Government and Civil Service under Charles II, 1660–1685* (Oxford, 2002), p. 158.

it passed the Navigation Acts of 1650 and 1651, restricting the channels within which colonial commerce could pass and confining the nationality of its carrying trade to English ships manned mostly by English crews. The Restoration parliaments of Charles II re-enacted their own version of this legislation and tightened up its provisions while, from time to time, various executive bodies, most notably the Lords of Trade and Plantations, were created or re-created to oversee the trade of the Empire and the welfare of the colonies generally.[37] All the same, G.E. Aylmer is more than justified in characterizing the colonial policy of the period as analogous to the Cheshire Cat, with its unhappy tendency to fade away entirely except for the grin.[38] The standing institutions of Imperial governance barely existed.

Towards the end of the reign of Charles II, seriatim upheavals in the southern colonies coupled with a destructive Indian war in New England finally created something resembling a sense of urgency in Whitehall. The ensuing attempts at centralization in the early 1680s can, if necessary, be dignified as a *policy*, although they are actually separate, stuttering initiatives arguably informed by a common spirit. The most important result of this flurry of activity was the revocation of the charters of the New England colonies and their incorporation into a single unit, the Dominion of New England, to be ruled by a royal governor without the necessity of an elected legislature. The standing machinery of government of Charles II had reached a point where, if sufficiently galled, it could effect serious change at home and in the colonies—but only for a limited duration and by mustering some heroic efforts. It might, under the right circumstances, conquer; it could not, for want of continuing institutional mechanisms, occupy, administer, or superintend.[39]

James II, who succeeded to the English throne in 1685, is credited with an ambitious plan for an essentially autocratic overseas empire.[40] Whatever his aspirations, under the best of circumstances his resources were still seriously inadequate in comparison with his successors. He did benefit from a surge

---

[37] Michael J. Braddick, "The English Government, War, Trade, and Settlement, 1625–1688," in Canny (ed.), *OHBE*, I, pp. 286–308; Robert M. Bliss, *Revolution and Empire: English Politics and the American Colonies in the Seventeenth Century* (Manchester, 1990), pp. 57–60; Carla Gardina Pestana, *The English Atlantic in an Age of Revolution, 1640–1661* (Cambridge, MA, 2004), pp. 170–5.

[38] Aylmer, *The Crown's Servants*, p. 255.

[39] Aylmer, *The Crown's Servants*, pp. 271–8; Richard S. Dunn, "The Glorious Revolution and America," in Canny (ed.), *OHBE*, I, pp. 447–51.

[40] Steve Pincus, *1688: The First Modern Revolution* (New Haven, 2009), pp. 372–81.

in English trade unprecedented in strength and duration and from improvements at the Treasury in tapping this new wealth, as well as decades of improvement in the Royal Navy, a civil service of a more respectable size than previously, and a permanent, professionalized military establishment. The combined efforts of soldiers, sailors, and clerks still enabled him to do no more than carry through in a more sustained and energetic fashion the spasmodic initiatives begun in the later years of the reign of his brother.[41] Given more years of James as king, there might have been more amalgamated dominions of the New England variety. His government of the colonies, that is, would still have been the same "all or nothing" game.

After 1689, it was at last possible to think of colonial governance in different terms. Such staples of early imperialism as the Board of Trade and the panoply of vice-admiralty courts and customs officials that came in with the Enforcement Act of 1696 are just so many additional instances of the efflorescence of institutions and institutionalization generally in the same period, which also comprehended the Bank of England, the National Debt, and a standing army funded by the annual Mutiny Act. They are all products of the exigencies and opportunities of the quarter century of warfare on the grand scale that commenced with the accession of William and Mary, when England, and then Britain, was able to "to set out such Fleets and Armies as were never heard of among our Ancestors."[42] Whitehall could now attempt what earlier could not have been so much as fantasized, that is, introduce institutionalized forms of royal control into colonial governance and then wait for a variety of *modi vivendi* between them and the various entrenched elements of local autonomy to take hold in what became an empire of protracted negotiations, appeals, and petitions. One should not overweight the role of Whig principles in bringing about this change of tack. Sir Edmund Andros, Francis Nicholson, and William Blathwayt, stalwarts of James's day, all found postings of importance in the new order, and there were movements in Parliament for the "reunion" of

---

[41] Brewer, *The Sinews of Power*, pp. 94–5; N. A. M. Rodger, *The Command of the Ocean: A Naval History of Britain, 1649–1815*, pbk. edn (New York, 2006), pp. 181–200, esp. pp. 187–9; John Childs, *The Army, James II, and the Glorious Revolution* (Manchester, 1980); Dunn, "The Glorious Revolution and America," in Canny (ed.), *OHBE*, I, pp. 451–4.

[42] Davenant, *Discourses on the Publick Revenues*, p. 222.

the colonies with the Mother Country in 1701–2, 1706, and 1715.[43] Much of the motivation behind this willingness to settle for half measures was the pragmatic realization that wars on the magnitude of what took place between 1689 and 1713 were best fought without a repetition of the serial insurgency in the New World colonies that had marked the previous two decades.

In the end, the mixed governance of the Empire tossed together in these years turned out to be the cheapest solution available that could both bring real dividends in terms of taxable transatlantic commerce and also contribute to the prosecution of world wars. Along the way, however, a permanently unfinished Imperial constitution made for some colorful, much reported and much remembered colonial politics. Upon his replacement as royal governor in 1722, Virginia's Alexander Spotswood followed up on his long-running, frustrating fight with the grandees of the assembly by becoming a local magnate and over-mighty subject in his own right, complete with castle on the Rappahannock in the county that bears his name. His less fortunate contemporary, Samuel Shute, governor of Massachusetts, left the colony abruptly in 1723, possibly in fear for his life, and unsuccessfully demanded a permanent military force stationed in Boston as the condition for his return.[44] The tenures of George Clinton in New York (1743–53) or Sir Thomas Robinson in Barbados (1742–47) could be mined for similar material easily enough.[45] Chronicling individual imbroglios obscures the broader process by which, after 1689, a state capable of negotiation gradually became a given in the way things were done. Recovering the great English political tradition of complaint and reform, the colonies developed various semi-formal grievance mechanisms that, whatever the verdict rendered in any particular case, became an integral part of their constitution as that term was then understood. Even the colony of Rhode

[43] Dunn, "The Glorious Revolution and America," in Canny (ed.), OHBE, I, pp. 457–65; Aylmer, The Crown's Servants, pp. 172–9; Richard R. Johnson, Adjustment to Empire: The New England Colonies, 1675–1715 (New Brunswick, NJ, 1981), pp. 249–51.

[44] Emory G. Evans, A "Topping People": The Rise and Decline of Virginia's Old Political Elite, 1680–1790 (Charlottesville, VA, 2009), pp. 45–71; William Pencak, War, Politics, and Revolution in Provincial Massachusetts (Boston, 1981), pp. 65–76; Stephen Foster, "Another Legend of the Province House: the Belcher-Shirley Duel and the Misconstruction of the Imperial Relationship," The New England Quarterly, LXXVII (2004), pp. 204–5.

[45] Stanley N. Katz, Newcastle's New York: Anglo-American Politics, 1732–1753 (Cambridge, MA, 1968), pp. 164–244; James Henretta, "Salutary Neglect": Colonial Administration under the Duke of Newcastle (Princeton, 1972), pp. 227–31.

Island, self-governing from its foundation and insistent that its precious charter rendered any proposed parliamentary regulation of its affairs un- warranted, in time accepted the legitimacy of appeals from its courts to the Privy Council. Liberty *and* authority were both secreted in the interstices of procedure, once there were procedures to proceed along and with them, of course, assorted backrooms in which to make deals to abet, modify, or, from time to time, frustrate the formal processes of governance.[46]

As an account of the fate of Empire in the New World, the claims for a progressive Imperial integration are at least as persuasive as the older narratives of relentless legislative encroachments on royal power and can be furthered with a considerable variety of evidence. One can, for example, point to the colonial idealization of William III and the early Hanoverians as heroic Protestant warrior monarchs, or take note of Americans vigorously aping the manners, clothing fashions, and architectural styles of British gentility, or express surprise at the number of colonists of a military bent willing to enlist in the British Army during the Seven Years' War or seeking officers' commissions almost up until the Revolutionary War broke out.[47] Momentarily, it is possible to forget that the whole thing ended badly and that it really did not take very long to do so. The longtime minister of Cambridge, Massachusetts, Nathaniel Appleton, born a subject of William and Mary, died a citizen of the United States. Just one lifetime, long but certainly not preternatural, could witness both the awkward beginnings of royal government in its new, post-1689 form and its violent denouement in war and revolution.[48] The end of empire will be discussed at the end of this chapter; here, however, it would be appropriate to take notice of two ubiquitous contemporary misconceptions that from an early date lay as

---

[46] Cf. the chapter in this volume by Daniel Hulsebosch; Mary Sarah Bilder, *The Transatlantic Constitution: Colonial Legal Culture and the Empire* (Cambridge, MA, 2004); and Alison Gilbert Olson, *Making the Empire Work: London and American Interest Groups, 1690–1790* (Cambridge, MA, 1992).

[47] Cf. Brendan McConville, *The King's Three Faces: The Rise and Fall of Royal America, 1688–1776* (Chapel Hill, NC, 2006); Richard L. Bushman, *The Refinement of America: Persons, Houses, Cities* (New York, 1992); Cary Carson, et al. (eds), *Of Consuming Interests: The Style of Life in the Eighteenth Century* (Charlottesville, VA, 1994); Shy, *Toward Lexington*, pp. 140–8, 354; as well as the secondary literature discussed in Foster, "British North America in the Seventeenth and Eighteenth Centuries," in Winks (ed.), *OHBE*, V, pp. 87–8.

[48] Clifford Shipton, et al. (eds), *Sibley's Harvard Graduates*, V, *Biographical Sketches of Those Who Attended Harvard College in the Classes 1701–1712* (Cambridge, MA, 1937), pp. 599–609.

dead weights on the thinking of both the professional Imperial administrators and the objects of their attentions in the colonies.

Once there was a Board of Trade and a customs service, there were
correspondence and internal memos. Then there were further memos referring to the earlier memos, and after that more of the same.[49] A significant
segment of this mountain of self-referential material consisted of apologies
from one official or another, most frequently the royal governors, offering
exculpatory explanations for instructions that had to be left unexecuted or
at least seriously modified. Preoccupied as they were with shifting responsibility to refractory colonists and systemic weaknesses, memorialists were
not inclined to draw attention either to the extent to which the Empire in its
full regalia was the latecomer to the American colonies or to the sheer
variety of different histories that unfolded as royal government was introduced in different colonies at different times.[50] Instead, officialdom's foundation myth posited some putative original and uniform Imperial authority
in America that had been seriously impaired in all the colonies and was
fading rapidly in some.[51]

Take as examples Virginia and Massachusetts a few decades on from the
unhappy regimes of Spotswood and Shute. Sir William Gooch, the governor
after the governor who succeeded Spotswood, prided himself on his ability
to avoid conflict. In consequence, in most accounts of his regime he comes
across as giving away the store to keep the burgesses and the council sweet.
But Gooch also accomplished what Spotswood had singularly failed at: he
got the assembly to enact a tobacco inspection scheme in 1730 that improved
the quality of one of Great Britain's most valuable re-export crops and he
then convinced Whitehall to accept it in the teeth of the organized hostility
of the London mercantile interests.[52] In Massachusetts, Jonathan Belcher,
the governor after the governor who replaced Shute, earned a reputation as
a man so confrontational that he nearly started the Revolution thirty years
early but who still obtained little or nothing from the recurrent uproars he
provoked.[53] One particularly blatant failure is taken to be his abandonment

---

[49] Brewer, *Sinews or Power*, pp. 241–9.

[50] Brewer, *Sinews of Power*, pp. 6, 22, 132.

[51] Jack P. Greene, "Transatlantic Colonization and the Redefinition of Empire in the Early
Modern Era," in Christine Daniels and Michael V. Kennedy (eds), *Negotiated Empires: Centers
and Peripheries in the Americas, 1500–1820* (New York, 2002), pp. 267–82.

[52] Evans, *A "Topping People"*, pp. 78–89.

[53] Foster, "Another Legend of the Province House," *New England Quarterly*, LXXVII, pp. 180–1.

in 1735 of his demand, as instructed, for a permanent fixed salary. Belcher did, however, make substantial constitutional gains for the prerogative in three other areas: the exclusive right to name the Speaker of the House of Representatives; the sole right to call an adjournment of the legislature; and the executive's unconditional control of money warrants. Even the settlement of 1735 was a partial victory for Belcher in that the Massachusetts General Court agreed to vote for appropriations at the beginning of any given legislative year so that the governor was not in perpetual fear of punishment if he did not act as required in the course of the session.[54] The lugubrious take on the regimes of the two men was possible only because of a mindset that equated any part of the ordinary business of political trade-offs with the surrender of rights that for all practical purposes the crown had never possessed.[55]

When royal governors contested the presumptively lost prerogative, the colonists replied with a variety of counter-arguments: disputatious readings of the terms of various colonial charters; appeals to English legal precedents or prescriptive right; invocations of the inherent rights of Englishmen. One common kind of claim, a little different from any of these, is of particular interest because it informs many of the others, is contractual without being in the least Lockean, and rests upon the same degree of fuzziness about the origins of Imperial governance as the guiding assumptions of the Board of Trade. The most extensive statement of this rather visceral assertion of entitlement, earned and inherited, is Jeremiah Dummer's *Defence of the New-England Charters*.

Widely regarded as the most brilliant Harvard scholar of his generation, Dummer served as the agent of one or more New England colonies during the second and third decades of the eighteenth century, in which capacity he honed his apologetic skills defending the New England colonial charters against repeated attempts at revocation.[56] The culmination of these efforts, the *Defence*, was published in both London and Boston in 1721, the same year the Board of Trade produced a benchmark oversized memorandum on

---

[54] Richard L. Bushman, *King and People in Provincial Massachusetts*, pbk. edn (Chapel Hill, NC, 1992), pp. 111–21.

[55] A good example of this kind of lament is the Board of Trade report of 1721, discussed in Craig Yirush, *Settlers, Liberty, and Empire: The Roots of Early American Political Theory, 1675–1775* (New York, 2011), pp. 183–7.

[56] Clifford Shipton, et al. (eds), *Sibley's Harvard Graduates*, IV, *Biographical Sketches of Those Who Attended Harvard College in the Classes 1690–1700* (Cambridge, MA, 1933), pp. 454–68.

the failings of Imperial governance.[57] Dummer had heard it all before, and his *Defence* preempts objections in a twisting, circumlocutory argument that keeps doubling back on itself. The claim at its core, however, is simplicity itself: the colonial charters amount to "Præmiums for Services to be perform'd, and therefor are to be consider'd as Grants upon a *valuable Consideration*." This "consideration" (that which turns a conditional promise into a binding contract) was the founding of colonies at great personal cost and hardship "to increase the Nation's Commerce and enlarge her Dominions." The New England colonies have satisfied their side of the agreement "even beyond what was ever hop'd or expected," and, therefore, to remove the charters now "after the Service has bin so successfully perform'd, is abhorrent from all Reason, Equity, and Justice."[58]

Just what the New England charters endow the colonists with in return for their expenses and exertions is spelled out in a little detail. It is not land, for Dummer insists that all of America that was habitable originally belonged of right to the native inhabitants and was obtained from them the only legitimate way, by purchase.[59] Instead, what the charters offer the colonies is the right of self-government in exchange for the heroic efforts they will have to make to create settlements. Once the bargain is sealed by the first generation of colonists, this contractual right, as a kind of beneficent original sin, is passed down to future generations inviolable. If the founding planters, Dummer speculates, could have "foreseen that their Privileges were such *transitory Things*, as to last no longer than their Work should be done, and their Settlements compleated, they had never engag'd in so hazardous and difficult an Enterprize . . . and those Countries which have since added so much to the Wealth and Greatness of the Crown might have bin a barren Wilderness to this Day; or what is worse and more probable, might have bin fill'd with *French* Colonies, whereby France would have reign'd sole Mistress of *North America*."[60]

Dummer's tract is the most systematic version of an argument with a long pedigree and wide reach. In a less developed form, it can be found as early as 1647, when Governor Berkeley induced the Virginia assembly to protest an

---

[57] Charles L. Sanford, "The Days of Jeremiah Dummer, Colonial Agent" (Ph.D. diss., Harvard University, 1952), pp. 349–64; Yurish, *Settlers, Liberty, and Empire*, pp. 98–110.

[58] Jeremiah Dummer, *Defence of the New-England Charters*, pp. 7, 13.

[59] Dummer, *Defence of the New-England Charters*, pp. 13–14.

[60] Dummer, *Defence of the New-England Charters*, pp. 14, 15–16.

Act of Parliament prohibiting trade with the Dutch on the grounds that would-be colonists and potential investors were lured to adventure purse and person in the colony by the promise of autonomy, what the assembly termed "the Conditionall reward & [recompense] propounded for our Undertakings in those rugged paths of Plantation."[61] The continuing appeal of this same logic is evidenced by the reprint of "that excellent defense" (as Samuel Adams called Dummer's tract) in Boston in 1745 and then again in both Boston and London in 1765. There are also distinct echoes of the same angry resentment at those who would take away what was dearly earned in so manifest a way in Isaac Barré's famous speech against the Stamp Act on February 6, 1765, in which he terms the Americans "Sons of Liberty." In the parliamentary debates over repeal of the Act a year later, the *Defence* was used as evidence by both sides and its author referred to as "Mr. Dummer, than whom, it was said, no Man better understood the Nature and Extent of the Colonial Constitutions."[62]

One would not want to use either the longevity of the *Defence* or the Board of Trade's serial lamentations to resurrect some version of a permanent conflict in which the colonies steadily march down the road to independence, almost from their creation. The contestations of the years immediately before the Revolution are far deeper, the theoretical assertions and counter-assertions far less capable of compromise, the presiding spirit far more one of unqualified absolutes in explicit conflict, than in earlier confrontations. But when push finally began to come to shove after 1763, the rival narratives of lost prerogatives and broken aboriginal contracts would add their mite to the mutual intransigence that inflamed the growing conflict.

One aspect of the colonial side of these intertwined antinomies throws some light on the ways in which the colonists viewed the indigenous

---

[61] Billings, *Sir William Berkeley*, pp. 101–2. Barbados found something similar to pronounce in 1651 in *A Declaration Set Forth by the Lord Lieutenant Generall the Gentlemen of the Councell and Assembly Occasioned from the View of a Printed Paper* (Hagh [The Hague], 1651), and the East India Company took a parallel line in the last quarter of the seventeenth century, adapted to their own distinctive status. Philip J. Stern, *The Company-State: Corporate Sovereignty and the Early Modern Foundations of the British Empire in India* (New York, 2011).

[62] Harry Alonzo Cushing (ed.), *The Writings of Samuel Adams* (New York, 1904–8), II, p. 444; Jared Ingersoll to Thomas Fitch, February 11, 1765, New Haven Colony Historical Society, *Papers*, IX (New Haven, 1918), pp. 310–12; Charles Garth to Messrs. Tilighman, Murdock, and Ringgold, March 5, 1766, *Maryland Historical Magazine*, VI (1911), p. 296. Publication data for the *Defence* is taken from estc.bl.uk, s.v. "Dummer."

population of America. Over time, the force of the argument for autonomy was liable to become increasingly attenuated. There was a distinct limit to how angry one could get about the breach of a promise made to one's great grandparents, and those on the other side of the dispute could argue that, after several generations of settlement, circumstances had so altered as to render the original promise irrelevant. At the very moment when Dummer was composing the *Defence*, apologists for the omnicompetence of statute were already advancing claims that the public good necessitated some one body be in a position to alter or abolish outdated arrangements grown inconvenient but not legally forfeit. The argument would gain progressively wider support in Britain in the course of the eighteenth century and be trotted out at as a commonplace during the Revolutionary crisis.[63]

A powerful rejoinder was ready to hand for any attack on colonial rights made along these lines. In his speech in opposition to the Stamp Act, Isaac Barré, who had served at Louisbourg and Quebec, made much of how the colonists in going to America "exposed themselves to almost all the hardships to which human Nature is liable, and among others to the Cruelties of a Savage foe, the most subtle and I take upon me to say the most formidable of any People upon the face of Gods Earth." Forty-four years earlier, Jeremiah Dummer had expatiated in the same vein, reeling off in his *Defence* a long, lurid list of hardships that ends "to sum up [i.e., crown] their Misfortunes, they found themselves inevitably engag'd in a War with the Natives."[64] In both instances, the savages and their savagery were invoked with some relish as a way of extending indefinitely the presumptive bargain of the founding period. In recurrent war, the original sacrifice was re-enacted, the foundational conditions re-fulfilled, and the attendant entitlements implicitly re-authorized in full.

In the interests of polemical utility, Dummer knowingly papered over a significant change within his own lifetime. As Dummer himself acknowledged elsewhere, the Imperial Wars had given the recurrent conflicts a

---

[63] Julian Hoppit, "Compulsion, Compensation and Property Rights in Britain, 1688–1833," *Past & Present*, 210 (February, 2011), pp. 93–128; "William [*sic*] Pym," *London General Evening Post*, August 20, 1765, reprinted in *Newport Mercury*, October 28, 1765 and from there in Edmund S. Morgan (ed.), *Prologue to Revolution: Sources and Documents on the Stamp Act Crisis, 1764–1766* (Chapel Hill, NC, 1959), pp. 97–9.

[64] New Haven Colony Hist. Soc., *Papers*, IX, p. 310; Dummer, *Defence of the New-England Charters*, p. 8.

whole new dimension.[65] Recent historiography tends to side with Dummer's *Defence* and take King Philip's War (1675–76) as the *locus classicus* of Indian-colonist warfare. Dummer himself knew better. Terrible as it was, King Philip's War was far more like the Pequot War or Opechancanough's two "uprisings" in the Chesapeake than the series of world wars that began in 1689 between Britain and France, aided by their respective allies of the moment. Only fourteen months in all elapsed between the Wampanoag's initial attack on Swansea in June 1675 and the death of their leader Philip on August 12, 1676; by October of the same year all the fighting outside Maine had ceased. No treaty marked the end of the war because victory, whatever the cost, was complete. If, however, the Wampanoag had had access to more gunpowder when their stocks ran low and to food supplies when their harvests were destroyed, King Philip's War might have looked more like what was to come.[66] Thus Dummer's tell-tale remark in the *Defence* that, once the Indians were "animated and assisted by the *French* of *Canada,*" Massachusetts had enjoyed "but few Intervals of Peace, and those very short ones from that Time [1689] to this Day," an observation that could be extended to much of British North America.[67]

As their names suggest, the Imperial Wars were characterized by length— nine years and seven years—and they were ended by treaties that were little more than truces of uncertain duration. In the colonies it was not always possible to say even this much. The Yamasee War, (Lt. Governor William) Dummer's War, and Pontiac's War, amongst others, were all cases in point of conflicts that continued or were reignited in the colonies without regard to the peace proclaimed by a European treaty. Over time, the horribly monotonous rhythm of extended, mostly inconclusive warfare and the insecurity, reflexive brutality, privation, and epidemic and endemic disease that went with it eliminated most of what chance there was for coexistence between the British colonists and the Native Americans.

An ethnohistorian might interject at this point that placing so much stress on the importance of Empire rehearses the old sin of depriving the Native American of *their* history, which has a very different set of dates and cast of characters than those ordained by some European war originating in

---

[65] [Jeremy Dummer], *A Letter to a Noble Lord concerning the Late Expedition to Canada* (London, 1712), pp. 8–9.

[66] Steele, *Warpaths*, pp. 104–7.

[67] Dummer, *Defence of the New-England Charters*, p. 24.

the death of a Spanish or Austrian monarch. The Imperial Wars were more often than not superimposed on local conflicts with their own purposes and termini. Dummer's War (or Father Rasle's War or Gray Lock's War), for example, can be seen as a continuation of the Anglo-French duel in North America and as another round in the struggle between Catholic and Protestant empires, but in fact, while the Abenaki made war with Massachusetts and New Hampshire and received aid from New France, they carried on the conflict for reasons very much their own and remained at peace with neighboring New York.[68] In reply, it is still possible to insist that attention to the needs of European-driven international warfare can re-introduce a degree of temporality into accounts of European-Indian warfare (*pace* Jeremy Dummer's *inevitably*) as well as place individual conflicts within the larger conflagrations that came to engulf the globe after 1689. The leading example would be the role in the Imperial Wars of the much-studied Iroquois. They were the group the British were most anxious to recruit in their conflicts with France and, eventually, with the independent United States. They were also the Indians with whom the British public in the eighteenth century had the greatest acquaintance.[69]

The Iroquois were not an especially formidable power in terms of numbers. At a strength of perhaps 4,200 men, the New England expedition that took Louisbourg in 1745 was significantly larger than the total number of Iroquois warriors who could be raised in any one place at any one time. The Iroquois advantage, rather, was both cultural and logistical. While they were never entirely free of faction, cultural arrangements such as the condolence ceremony on the death of a leader and the recitation of the Deganawidah Epic had virtually eliminated intra-Iroquois aggression. This unique *pax Iroquoiana* facilitated the development of lines of communication and trade routes of exceptional efficiency.[70] Eventually, the Iroquois became past masters at the wartime skills of scouting, gathering intelligence, and skirmishing, as well as adepts in the conduct of diplomacy. In the most remarkable instance, different parties of Iroquois treating respectively with the French and the English in 1701 were well aware of each other's

---

[68] Richter, "Native Peoples of North America and the Eighteenth-Century British Empire," in Marshall (ed.), *OHBE*, II, pp. 350–63; Colin G. Calloway, *The Western Abenakis of Vermont, 1600–1800: War, Migration, and the Survival of an Indian People* (Norman, OK, 1990), pp. 113–31.

[69] See the chapter by Troy Bickham in this volume.

[70] Jon Parmenter, *The Edge of the Woods: Iroquoia, 1534–1701* (East Lansing, MI, 2010), pp. xliii–xlix.

negotiations, an advantage that allowed the Iroquois to set the terms of peace with both parties.[71]

The question for this discussion is how to characterize such a situation within the overall scope of British North America and then how to account for its eventual passing. Here the obvious analogy—it has already been made—is with the contemporary situation on the Indian Subcontinent. One school would see the East India Company in the eighteenth century as simply another, unusually aggressive, territorial power on the Subcontinent trying to maximize its share in the squabbling and intrigues following the effective collapse of Mughal power.[72] There was no Mughal Empire to disintegrate in North America, and the Iroquois, unlike the Company, were indigenous to the continent where they exercised sway. But they can still plausibly be seen as a quasi-imperial power, jockeying for territory, trade, and influence along with the English and French from the 1680s onward. Through informed, eyes-open diplomacy combined with effective military power, they cemented their hegemony over the non-League Iroquoian people and from there created (via their leveraging of European alliances) spheres of influence among the Algonquian peoples in the surrounding regions, from the Great Lakes to Pennsylvania. The extent of Iroquois power on the North American continent turned their alliance with the English into a one-way tributary arrangement in which they gained freedom of movement throughout contested areas (especially the Southern backcountry), the ability to get the best deal on the fur trade by way of open competition between the various European traders, and some degree of effective "rent seeking" as the new power brokers between both of the European powers and many of the North Eastern Indians.

Once the Iroquois made the choice to become a major player in the eighteenth-century version of the Great Game, they could no more extricate themselves from European geopolitics than they could abandon the global markets they had entered into a century and more earlier. The practice of empire has a logic of its own, as well as some very distinctive liabilities. An

---

[71] Parmenter, *The Edge of the Woods*, Chaps. 5–6, esp. pp. 248–73. For subsequent events, up until the 1790s, cf. Timothy J. Shannon, *Iroquois Diplomacy on the Early American Frontier* (New York, 2008).

[72] Cf. P. J. Marshall, "The British in Asia: Trade to Dominion," in Marshall (ed.), *OHBE*, II, pp. 487–507, esp. pp. 495–501; P. J. Marshall, *The Making and Unmaking of Empires: Britain, India, and America, c. 1750–1783* (Oxford, 2005), chap. 4, esp. pp. 119–21.

obvious one was acting imperiously: when the Iroquois got around to appeasing colonial land hunger by deeding territory occupied by the Delaware, a one-time "pillar" of the Long House (the metaphor for the Iroquois Confederation) and sometime ally had clearly become a subject people.[73] Empires and quasi-empires are also notoriously vulnerable to loss of influence over the powers within their general orbit if there is any very public dent in their mystique. On this count, the Iroquois suffered a significant reversal by their cession of a portion of their own lands in the Treaty of Fort Stanwix in 1768.[74] Most serious of all, in a process that grows by feeding upon itself, empires can fall prey to a degree of militarization, and here too the Iroquois proved a text-book instance.

Warfare, along with hunting, the premier masculine vocation among the Iroquois, had originally been constrained by a number of cultural institutions, as well as by the ability of the Iroquois League as a body to remain neutral in the Imperial Wars.[75] Independent groups of Iroquois warriors in search of material rewards and status were recruited, however, with increasing frequency as the Anglo-French wars intensified. By the late 1760s, British backed "Pine Tree" warrior chiefs were a power in their own right. They had little interest in heeding female counsel, originally a famous and distinguishing Iroquois practice, and in time they largely shrugged off the control of the hereditary clan chiefs as well. But they did retain their close ties to their sponsors, the British.[76] By the outbreak of the Revolutionary war, many of the Iroquois were so dependent on the British that the League had neither the inclination nor the means, material or diplomatic, to keep up either their neutrality or their unity.[77] They had exchanged the role of imperial equal for British client state and as such were merely one consideration among many in the calculations of an overstretched global power.

It was not their fate alone: the western confederacy led by Blue Jacket and Little Turtle and, a little later, that under the leadership of Tecumseh

[73] Merritt, At the Crossroads, pp. 29–33, 170–1, 192–6; Gail D. MacLeitch, Imperial Entanglements: Iroquois Change and Persistence on the Frontiers of Empire (Philadelphia, 2011), pp. 32, 122–3.

[74] MacLeitch, Imperial Entanglements, p. 188; Shannon, Iroquois Diplomacy, pp. 174–5.

[75] Jon Parmenter, "After the Mourning Wars: The Iroquois as Allies in Colonial North American Campaigns, 1676–1760," WMQ, 3rd ser., LXIV (2007), pp. 39–82.

[76] MacLeitch, Imperial Entanglements, pp. 228–9.

[77] However, the Iroquois did avoid a civil war. See Karim M. Tiro, The People of the Standing Stone: The Oneida Nation from the Revolution through the Era of Removal (Amherst, MA, 2011).

suffered the same humiliation of seeing their interests sacrificed by British ministries forced to decide on what military resources to commit to North America as opposed to the West Indies, Europe, South Africa, and South Asia.[78] The Indians of the American South fared no better: the Creeks, the very rough equivalent of the Iroquois in the Southern British mainland colonies, also augmented their strength through confederations, created a furor with a celebrity delegation to England, and did their best to play off Spain, France, Britain, and (at a later date) the United States against each other. They too ended up divided, dispossessed, and dependent.[79]

Such a state of affairs may seem a world away from the very beginning of the eighteenth century, when the Iroquois could make law to French and British alike and the Creek were a dreaded force in the South East, but it represents the climax of developments begun then. The wars that defined European history between 1688 and 1815 gradually caught up people all over the globe in their toils and fixed the boundaries within which they could act. Victory, to the extent that it was achievable, came to depend less on skill or valor than on the brutal ability to raise and supply forces of unprecedented size, suffer significant, perhaps appalling casualties, and then find the means to repeat the same process as often as needed. Everybody involved was obliged to learn the same brutal lesson. "Without money it was impossible to assemble an army or prosecute war" may sound like a Ciceronian commonplace tossed off on the floor of the Constitutional Convention at Philadelphia in 1787, but it is the observation of the Maratha leader Daulat Rao Sindia, who succeeded to the throne of Gwalior in 1794 and after a long and incidented series of campaigns found himself ultimately overpowered by the British in 1803.[80] The very same point was understood equally well by Henry Dundas in Whitehall, who held that "all modern Wars are a contention of purse, and unless some very peculiar circumstance occurs to divert

---

[78] Richter, "Native Peoples of North America and the Eighteenth-Century British Empire," in Marshall (ed.), *OHBE*, II, pp. 363–70; Daniel P. Barr, *Unconquered: The Iroquois League at War in Colonial America* (Westport, CT, 2006), pp. 139–63. See also Michael Duffy, "World-Wide War and British Expansion, 1793–1815," in Marshall (ed.), *OHBE*, II, pp. 184–207.

[79] Richter, "Native Peoples of North America and the Eighteenth-Century British Empire," in Marshall (ed.), *OHBE*, II, pp. 351–69 passim.

[80] Rajat Kanta Ray, "Indian Society and the Establishment of British Supremacy," in Marshall (ed.), *OHBE*, II, p. 516. Cf. Max M. Edling, "'So Immense a Power in the Affairs of War': Alexander Hamilton and the Restoration of Public Credit," *WMQ*, 3rd ser., LXIV (2007), pp. 287–326.

the lead into another channel the Minister of Finance must be the Minister of War." No doubt this logic was just as comprehensible to Joseph Brant of the Mohawks, Alexander McGillivray of the Creek Confederacy, or, especially, Blue Jacket of the Shawnee and Little Turtle of the Miamis, who defeated two American armies in succession in 1790 and 1791 only to fall victim to a third at Fallen Timbers in 1794.[81]

Eighteenth-century people in both Europe and America had little choice other than to acknowledge finance and warfare as among the barest of the bare facts of life. Current historiography is not similarly burdened, and its preferred focus is instead the social and cultural dynamics within colonial society. This shift in interest, which tends to see colonial culture as created locally, has evolved in tandem with its opposite, a growing preoccupation with the progressive Anglicization of British North America. The rival trends are not in themselves some unyielding crux that must be resolved in favor of one alternative or another. Allowing for a wide variety of other possible influences, however, British North America was also significantly affected by its Imperial context. In trying to come to grips with just how this was the case, the much invoked *Anglicization* turns out to be at once a useful concept and a very elusive quiddity.

Forty years after the term first entered the early American studies lexicon, there is still no firm consensus on exactly what *Anglicization* comprehends. Its original champion, John Murrin, used the concept to challenge the conventional view that a proto-American culture gradually developed in the colonies over the course of the eighteenth century and had prepared the ground for a distinct nation well before 1776.[82] Murrin held instead that the direction of change was quite the opposite. "British North America in fundamental ways became more European, more English, in the eighteenth century. The growth of cities, the spread of printing and newspapers, the rise of the professions, and the emulation of British political culture all encouraged this trend." Colonial patriotism was Imperial and British, and the colonists "saw themselves as part of an expanding *British*

---

[81] Dundas to William Pitt the Younger, July 4, 1794, in A. Aspinwall and E. Anthony Smith (eds), *English Historical Documents*, XI (London, 1959), p. 124; John Sugden, *Blue Jacket: Warrior of the Shawnees* (Lincoln, NE, 2000), esp. pp. 188–207; Max M. Edling, *A Revolution in Favor of Government: Origins of the U.S. Constitution and the Making of the American State* (Oxford, 2003), pp. 47–58, 129–46.

[82] John Murrin, "Anglicizing an American Colony: The Transformation of Provincial Massachusetts" (Ph.D. thesis, Yale University, 1966).

nation and empire. Loyalty to colony meant loyalty to Britain. The two were expected to reinforce one another."[83] Later versions of the Anglicization argument presented the process as more fraught: eighteenth-century "Americans" were held to have been ambivalent about their provincial status and to have suffered from some kind of "cultural schizophrenia."[84] More recently still, the model of Anglo-American cultural convergence has been further modified by bringing in an "archipelagic" dimension. Though European Americans remained mostly English by birth or descent, the argument is that after the Union of 1707, "Americans did not become culturally English so much as British," and even then, "American colonists did not identify with everything British" but rather as "provincial Britons, citizens of the British provinces, with a particular provincial point of view." Scots in the colonies criticized the "previously unchallenged authority of the metropolis" by envisioning a "future American empire" that was more than England writ large, while an absentee Dean of Derry and future bishop of the Church of Ireland, the philosopher George Berkeley, proclaimed "Westward the Course of Empire," during his stay in Rhode Island.[85]

Colonial Americans were only too happy to accept the role of the representative Britons of the future. In 1771, two College of New Jersey graduates took up Berkeley's theme in *A Poem on the Rising Glory of America* delivered at the college's commencement. Philip Freneau, born in New York of Huguenot ancestry, and Hugh Henry Brackenridge, born in Scotland, embodied the multi-ethnic origins of eighteenth-century European Americans as well as their continuing investment in very British cultural frameworks. Freneau and Brackenridge held that the "northern realms" of America had been "discover'd by Britannia for her sons." They foresaw the rise of "Science" in America as new, North American versions of treasured British cultural heroes: a "Homer and a Milton" where once "num'rous tawny tribes" had "swarm'd." (Freneau and Brackenridge shared

---

[83] John Murrin "A Roof Without Walls: The Dilemma of American National Identity," in Richard Beeman, et al. (eds), *Beyond Confederation: Origins of the Constitution and American National Identity* (Chapel Hill, NC, 1987), pp. 336–40 (quotations on pp. 336, 338).

[84] T. H. Breen, *The Marketplace of Revolution: How Consumer Politics Shaped American Independence* (Oxford, 2004), pp. 166–72 (quotation on p. 167).

[85] Ned Landsman, *From Colonials to Provincials: American Thought and Culture, 1680–1760* (New York, 1997), esp. pp. 1–7, 176–80 (quotations on pp. 3, 6, 177, 178).

Dummer's vision of Americans having earned a special place within the Empire through their triumphs over the indigenous "savage sons.")[86] After 1776, New England writers like Joel Barlow, John Trumbull, and Timothy Dwight incorporated the same trope as the centerpiece of a new United States nationalism. Until the Declaration of Independence, however, Americans of European origin (like Australians and British Canadians at a later date) imagined themselves not as a new form of humanity but rather as the better sort of Briton, truer to the metropole's essential virtues than the inhabitants of Britain itself.[87]

The colonists were pragmatic in the ways they mixed and matched their British heritage. There was, for example, virtually no sympathy for the Jacobite cause in North America, yet transported Jacobite prisoners of the '15 were easily incorporated into American society, and the fiercely Protestant Massachusetts militiamen marched to the rhythm of the notorious Jacobite tune *The White Cockade* when confronting British regulars at Concord bridge.[88] A drunken brawl in a Cumberland County, Virginia tavern in June 1766 provides a more intimate example of the ways British reference points could get crossed in America. John Chiswell, one of the colony's slave-owning planter elite, overwhelmed by the debts he had fallen into, confronted the British merchant and creditor Robert Routledge. Calling Routledge a "villain who came to Virginia to cheat and defraud men of their property," a "Scotch rebel," and a "Presbyterian fellow," Chiswell ran his sword through the poor man—who actually hailed from the county of Cumberland on the *English* side of the border with Scotland. In fact, Chiswell himself was the son of a Scottish immigrant.[89] Clearly, for a

---

[86] Philip Freneau, *A Poem on the Rising Glory of America, Being an Exercise Delivered at the Public Commencement at Nassau-Hall, September 25, 1771* (Philadelphia, 1772), pp. 4, 9, 24.

[87] Cf. Gordon S. Wood, *The Americanization of Benjamin Franklin* (New York, 2004), Kariann Akemi Yokota, *Unbecoming British: How Revolutionary America Became a Postcolonial Nation* (Oxford, 2011), and Julie Flavell, *When London was Capital of America* (New Haven, 2010). For the continued use of the Americanization model, see Jon Butler, *Becoming America: The Revolution before 1776* (Cambridge, MA, 2000), and Susan Lindsey Lively, "Going Home: Americans in Britain, 1740–1776" (Ph.D. thesis, Harvard University, 1997).

[88] Geoffrey Plank, *Rebellion and Savagery: The Jacobite Rising of 1745 and the British Empire* (Philadelphia, 2006); Margaret Sankey, *Jacobite Prisoners of the 1715 Rebellion: Preventing and Punishing Insurrection in Early Hanoverian Britain* (Aldershot, 2005), pp. 59–76; David Hackett Fischer, *Paul Revere's Ride* (Oxford, 1994), p. 211.

[89] Woody Holton, *Forced Founders: Indians, Debtors, Slaves and the Making of the American Revolution in Virginia* (Chapel Hill, NC, 1999), pp. 39–44.

Virginia planter, regardless of his heritage, Scots were both a parasitical element in the Chesapeake economy (where they played a large role in the tobacco trade) and a symbol of disloyalty in the colonial version of the Imperial cultural fantasy. Chiswell's imaginary amalgam of treasonous Scotsmen was neither a copy of a British original nor an accurate representation of the ancestry of mid-eighteenth-century Virginians. Rather, it creatively combined the tensions in mid-eighteenth-century transatlantic economic relations with the previous two hundred years of conflict in the British Isles.

The distinctive nature of colonial British identity was shaped as well by the other European groups in America. Substantial pockets of Dutch culture in the Hudson Valley and northern New Jersey carried the legacy of the former colony of New Netherland. Substantial eighteenth-century immigration brought elements of Scotch-Irish and German influence to the architecture, foodways, language, and religion of Pennsylvania and the Southern backcountry. Something of a French tincture to life in parts of New England, New York, and the Carolinas could be credited to the Huguenot diaspora. A slightly different geographical configuration, from Rhode Island to New York, Philadelphia, Charleston, and Savannah, identified another, older diaspora in the form of a small but growing Jewish community.[90] Portions of the Delaware Valley could boast of a Swedish and Finnish heritage derived from the short-lived colony of New Sweden.[91] Even where the same groups were present in Britain itself, the chemistry differed sharply from that to be found in the colonies. The North American colonies were an integral part of a British Imperial world, but any such admission has to be qualified by an acknowledgment that, indigenous and African influences aside, their relationship to Europe was distinctive. Therein lay much of the attraction of Anglicization. Thanks to the wide range of options on

[90] A sample of recent work on European ethnic diversity in British North America includes Patrick Griffin, *The People with No Name: Ireland's Ulster Scots, America's Scots Irish, and the Creation of a British Atlantic World, 1689–1764* (Princeton, 2001); Philip Otterness, *Becoming German: The 1709 Palatine Migration to New York* (Ithaca, NY, 2004); William Pencak, *Jews and Gentiles in Early America, 1654–1800* (Ann Arbor, MI, 2005); Bertrand van Ruymbeke, *From New Babylon to Eden: The Huguenots and their Migration to Colonial South Carolina* (Columbia, SC, 2006); Mark Häberlein, *The Practice of Pluralism: Congregational Life and Religious Diversity in Lancaster, Pennsylvania, 1730–1820* (University Park, PA, 2009); Roger Panetta (ed.), *Dutch New York: The Roots of Hudson Valley Culture* (New York, 2009).

[91] Evan Haefeli, "The Revolt of the Long Swede: Transatlantic Hopes and Fears on the Delaware, 1669," *Pennsylvania Magazine of History and Biography*, LXXX (2006), pp. 137–80.

offer, colonists could easily find what they sought within the culture of the Empire, from the aristocratic pretensions of some Southern grandees to the Levelling inclinations that New Englanders were repeatedly accused of. Decades of selective Anglicization did not make the peoples of the colonies more homogeneous; it just provided greater, if still limited, legitimacy for their differences.

Given the numbers of Native Americans that they dispossessed, and of Africans that they enslaved, some kind of commitment to racialist doctrines was almost a necessary precondition for the peace of mind of most Anglo-Americans. But, as Benjamin Franklin's famous derogatory descriptions of German immigrants attest, non-British Europeans could be victims of attitudes that were very similar, if not quite so pernicious. Nor was there much evidence in colonial America of inter-regional fellow feeling. Only the Revolutionary crisis drove together a group of self-identified Britons who had up until then loved their king much more than their American neighbors. The "most conspicuous fault line" among the regions set New England off from everyone else. Other Americans harbored a deep resentment of the ostentatious sense of moral superiority they attributed to the inhabitants of the "Eastern states." Lewis Morris, Jr. of New York and New Jersey left a lasting sense of this antagonism in his will of 1762 when he stipulated that his son, the future American patriot Gouverneur Morris, was to receive the "best Education that is to be had in Europe or America but my Express Will and Directions are that he be never sent for that purpose to the Colony of Connecticut least he should imbibe in his youth that low Craft and cunning so Incident to the People of that Country...." To be either English American or British American was to be part of a wider world of resentments, conflicts, bitter historical memories, and unfulfilled aspirations. Often enough "Americans discovered that they really did not like each other very much."[92]

These serious ethnic divisions paralleled an increase in the distance between social classes. When the Declaration of Independence proclaimed the equality of the human race, it was assuming as a given a situation that was in many ways at odds with what had been the dominant trend in the colonies. Earlier, in the seventeenth century, colonial society had indeed been both significantly more rural and significantly more egalitarian than its

---

[92] Murrin, "Roof Without Walls," pp. 343–4.

English equivalent. In the eighteenth century, however, as the colonies became more like England in various ways, they also developed a visible, Anglicized hierarchy of wealth and power. And in either century, European Americans aspired mainly not to equality but to respectability, a state that took inequality and social distinctions for granted. Hence, the colonists' quest for refinement in their homes and furniture, the flaunted reading of contemporary British literature, such as Addison and Steele's *Spectator*, which reinforced a sense of the provinces' moral superiority to the decadent metropolis, and the wearing of London fashions, which, along with the rapidly expanding habit of drinking tea (with the concomitant display of an elaborate tea service), advertised an individual's means and refinement. The most ambitious of the colonists strove to attain the trappings of the lesser aristocracy through the possession of a landed estate.[93] No mainland colony, however, ever offered the degree of opportunity for ascent into the aristocracy to be found in the West Indies and especially eighteenth-century Jamaica. There the planter elite, amongst the richest men in the world, dispensed with Anglicization and just moved back to England or Scotland to buy huge estates, while a lesser fish such as the infamous Thomas Thistlewood, no planter at all but merely the proprietor of a livestock pen, could own as many slaves as a member of the Virginia gentry.[94]

Expansion in transatlantic trade provided the means, whether cash or credit, for colonists to hang British portraits on their walls, place British books on their shelves to accompany their Bibles, and delight their palates by making use of an expanding range of British-made culinary equipment. The greater availability and affordability of imported goods, in turn, could simultaneously improve the lives of most of the colonial population of European descent while offering the colonial elites already in place powerful tools for taking on new airs of sophistication to dramatize the growing gap between themselves and their presumptive inferiors. Those not quite so well off, but still endowed with some modicum of substance, talent, and aspiration, took their own stab at gentility through that great cultural solvent,

[93] See nn. 47, 83, and 84 above, as well as Kevin Sweeney, "Mansion People: Kinship, Class, and Architecture in Western Massachusetts in the Mid Eighteenth Century," *Winterthur Portfolio*, XIX (1984), pp. 231–55.

[94] Barry Higman, *Plantation Jamaica: Capital and Control in a Colonial Economy* (Kingston, Jamaica, 2005), pp. 1–18; Trevor Burnard, *Mastery, Tyranny, and Desire: Thomas Thistlewood and his Slaves in the Anglo-Jamaican World* (Chapel Hill, NC, 2004), pp. 38–67.

the Enlightenment. As postulant *philosophes*, they cultivated the image of cultivating knowledge in order to transcend the status customarily attached to their workaday occupations. Benjamin Franklin is only the most famous of the ambitious individuals who founded voluntary societies for just this purpose.[95]

Colonial savants included both the Jonathan Edwardses, who used the new learning to reaffirm the workings of providence in human affairs, and the Cadwallader Coldens, who insisted that a rule-bound impersonal mechanism governed every aspect of the cosmos. All used similar empirical methods, read the same accounts of the latest advances in natural philosophy, and corresponded with the Royal Society. Some also composed histories of their colonies, vigorously disabusing the British of the habit of thinking of the colonies as "wild, boundless, inhospitable, uncultivated desarts" and claiming a place for their respective localities (and themselves) within an expanded map of the British world.[96]

Growing inequality in eighteenth-century North America generally did not create the unbridgeable fissures that divided society in Britain because the expansion in both domestic and international markets for colonial goods provided opportunities for smallholders no less than estate owners and it created urban centers of varying sizes where the possibilities for advancement were greater and more diverse than in the countryside. After all, a runaway Boston apprentice with a skill to sell like Benjamin Franklin could become a gentleman in Philadelphia and then a celebrity, while his son could rise to the rank of royal governor. Though opportunities varied for individuals by status, region, and period, they existed to some degree everywhere and were widely expected to continue to do so. Well into the eighteenth century, the steady acquisition of indigenous lands enabled a large percentage of free colonists of limited means, both native born and

[95] John Fea, *The Way of Improvement Leads Home: Philip Vickers Fithian and the Rural Enlightenment in Early America* (Philadelphia, 2008); Konstantin Dierks, "Letter Writing, Masculinity, and American Men of Science, 1750–1800," *Explorations in Early American Culture*, special supplemental issue of *Pennsylvania History: A Journal of Mid-Atlantic Studies*, LXV (1998), pp. 167–98; David Jaffee, "Village Enlightenment in New England, 1760–1820," *WMQ*, 3rd ser., XLVII (1990), pp. 327–46.

[96] Cf. Michael P. Winship, *Seers of God: Puritan Providentialism in the Restoration and Early Enlightenment* (Baltimore, 1996); John Michael Dixon, "Cadwallader Colden and the Rise of Public Dissension: Politics and Science in Pre-Revolutionary New York" (Ph.D. diss., University of California, Los Angeles, 2007); L.F.S. Upton, *The Loyal Whig: William Smith of New York and Quebec* (Toronto, 1969), pp. 38, 39.

immigrants, to eventually acquire a farm of their own. Already, in the 1740s, wealthy colonial speculators had begun forming land companies to cash in on the expected drive across the Appalachian Mountains, and after the destruction of the French Empire from the West there seemed to be little to prevent this form of economic expansion and social mobility from continuing indefinitely.[97]

The land companies were mostly unsuccessful but their very existence testified to the growth in number, strength, and diversity of colonial households. Within these households, through the medium of gender, the most mundane of everyday activities developed an intimate symbiosis with the dynamics of an expanding Imperial economy. By the early eighteenth century, a balanced sex ratio for those of European descent had been achieved for virtually all of the North American colonies, facilitating the rapid expansion of the population—and all that followed from it.[98] Women acquired and deployed the growing number of things that the "empire of goods" made available to enhance the possibilities in life and enliven the routine of their households. In a real sense, the British Empire and the women of the colonies (predominantly, but not exclusively, European) reinforced each other's influence. Colonial women needed the goods that the vast increase in transatlantic trade brought with it to establish an economic role for themselves and proclaim their status and that of their families. The makers, shippers, and purveyors of things British and Imperial needed the repeated, regular exercise of individual choices by the women of the colonies as the active agents of consumption at the end of the long chain of transactions that constituted the import side of the eighteenth-century colonial economy. This role, commanding in its own way, would be recognized in a left-handed manner during the Revolutionary crisis when consumption of imported "luxuries"

[97] See McCusker and Menard, *The Economy of British America*, pp. 211–358. Recent studies include Cathy Matson, *Merchants and Empire: Trading in Colonial New York* (Baltimore, 1998); Simon Middleton, *From Privileges to Rights: Work and Politics in Colonial New York City* (Philadelphia, 2006); Anthony S. Parent, Jr., *Foul Means: The Formation of a Slave Society in Virginia, 1660–1740* (Chapel Hill, NC, 2003); Daniel Vickers, *Farmers and Fishermen: Two Centuries of Work in Essex County, Massachusetts, 1630–1850* (Chapel Hill, NC, 1994); Barry Levy, *Town Born: The Political Economy of New England from its Founding to the Revolution* (Philadelphia, 2009).

[98] Cf. Gloria Main, *Peoples of a Spacious Land: Families and Cultures in Colonial New England* (Cambridge, MA, 2001); Carole Shammas, *A History of Household Government in America* (Charlottesville, VA, 2002), chapters 2–4.

and especially the consummate cultural symbol of the British Empire, tea, was disparaged as debilitating and feminine, even as women's propensity for consuming British goods was seen as a potentially weak link in the colonial struggle against non-importation.[99]

The standard representations of colonial domestic life are an added oddity in this situation: whether in paintings, lace, or literature, they blithely ignore the commercial networks in which households were deeply embedded to concentrate instead on bucolic, pastoral motifs.[100] The same could be said of their British counterparts to some degree, but the bucolic imagery of peaceful, tamed, cultivated landscapes had an extra, ironic level of meaning in the colonies: it represented mastery over originally indigenous land acquired in the Indian wars that were so important to the colonists' sense of attachment to the country in which they lived. In contrast with Britain, where land ownership was progressively more concentrated and many of the largest landholders depended on activities other than agriculture for their primary source of income, in America acquisition of land was the only ready source the colonists had for increasing their profits, unless they could farm more intensively by acquiring significant amounts of (presumably forced) labor relatively cheaply. Maritime trade rather than conquest may have knit together the British Empire, but the trade rested on the constant acquisition and exploitation of land in North America. In order to have trade to tax, the Empire facilitated the supply of indentured European immigrants and enslaved Africans to the colonies to work the land at low cost, and it secured the colonists' possession of both land and labor by fending off the rival claims of the French and Spanish allies of their indigenous enemies. As a result, colonial land ownership remained relatively widespread and aspirations to yeoman or gentry status had a broader purchase in the population at large than in the metropole. American Anglicizing, therefore, centered on the re-creation of a society and culture that was becoming a thing of distant memory at home (to the extent that

[99] Breen, *Marketplace of Revolution*, pp. 279–89, 306–7. Cf. Carole Shammas, *The Pre-Industrial Consumer in England and America* (Oxford, 1990); Kathleen Wilson, "Empire, Gender, and Modernity in the Eighteenth Century," in Philippa Levine (ed.), *Gender and Empire*, *OHBE* Companion Series (Oxford, 2004), pp. 18–19.

[100] Zara Anishanslin, "Portrait of a Woman in a Silk Dress: The Hidden Histories of Aesthetic Commodities in the Eighteenth-Century British Atlantic World" (Ph.D. diss., University of Delaware, 2009).

it had ever existed at all)—and this paradox was what it was, paradox-ical, because America was part of an Empire.[101]

The diversity and flexibility of what it meant to be British in America (along with many of the inherent contradictions) are equally evident in the religious awakenings of the mid-eighteenth century. The itinerant evangel-icals who shook the colonial landscape from 1740 onwards had their roots in the British Isles and retained strong connections with their counterparts there. The resultant increase in theological conflict and ecclesiastical schisms rendered American religion contentious and divided in ways that were already of long standing in Britain.[102] The simultaneous renewal of warfare with the Catholic empires of France and Spain, on the other hand, provided a basis for unity among most Anglo-American Protestants. Protestantism broadly construed was a cornerstone of British American patriotism, and anti-Catholicism or anti-popery was its necessary analogue. War coupled with revival cut two ways, strengthening the notion of a common cause uniting colonies and metropole but also reinforcing British Americans in their belief that they represented the core values of an otherwise imperiled Britishness.[103]

The Imperial Wars graphically underscored how the more the colonists came to identify with the Empire, the more they imagined themselves to be equal partners and crucial players in the Imperial game. Imperial warfare cut off the regular flow of goods from Britain, raised prices, inflated currencies, and generally made it more difficult to display one's status and Britishness through ostentatious consumption, but the wars also provided a range of opportunities to demonstrate American adherence to the British cause, from filling supply contracts to preaching fiery sermons to enlisting to fight. From 1689 through the mid-1750s, the colonists did most of the fighting (and funding of the fighting) in their theaters of the Imperial Wars.

---

[101] Jack P. Greene, "Empire and Identity from the Glorious Revolution to the American Revolution," in Marshall (ed.), *OHBE*, II, pp. 208–30. Cf. Armitage, *The Ideological Origins of the British Empire*, pp. 172–4.

[102] Thomas S. Kidd, *The Great Awakening: The Roots of Evangelical Christianity in Colonial America* (New Haven, 2007) argues for a distinctive Americanness. Landsman, *Colonials to Provincials*, pp. 92–122 and Boyd Stanley Schlenther, "Religious Faith and Commercial Empire," in Marshall (ed.), *OHBE*, II, pp. 128–50 provide a British context.

[103] Owen Stanwood, "Catholics, Protestants, and the Clash of Civilizations in Early Amer-ica," in Chris Benecke and Christopher S. Grenda (eds), *The First Prejudice: Religious Tolerance and Intolerance in Early America* (Philadelphia, 2011), pp. 218–40.

In return, they profited from increased economic opportunities in trade and privateering, acquisition of large amounts of land hitherto in American Indian possession, access to the status only official military service could provide, and the chance to dominate peoples and places that did not have the good fortune to be British. The strength of this dynamic continued unabated after the Revolution among the loyalist Americans, who participated with the same commitment as their predecessors in the continuing expansion of the British Empire.[104]

Perhaps the most salient instance of the tensions generated by an inherently Janus-faced Imperial culture was the colonists' conscious imitation of Parliament. The American sense of pride in the sophistication and maturity of their own legislatures was physically incarnated in the new buildings housing the colonial assemblies built up and down the seacoast in the decades immediately before the Revolutionary crisis.[105] Yet as far back as 1720, Jeremy Dummer took time off from writing the *Defence* to warn the Massachusetts House of Representatives against the practice of publishing its journals annually for fear they would make the colonial legislature seem too like the British Parliament:

People here are very apt to read these things with jealous eyes; and when they find in the same journals, that all business is transacted in the Council and Assembly, and the conferences managed between the two houses with the same decency and solemnity as in the parliament of Great Britain, they fancy us to be a little kind of sovereign state, and conclude for certain that we shall be so in time to come, and that the crown will not be able to reduce us at so great a distance from the throne.[106]

---

[104] Richard R. Johnson, "Growth and Mastery: British North America, 1690–1748," in Marshall (ed.), *OHBE*, II, pp. 276–99; David Syrett, "The Raising of American Troops for Service in the West Indies during the War of Austrian Succession, 1740–1," *Historical Research*, LXXIII (2000), pp. 20–32; Carl E. Swanson, "American Privateering and Imperial Warfare, 1739–1748," *WMQ*, 3rd ser., XLII (1985), pp. 357–82; John Shy, "The American Colonies in War and Revolution," in Marshall (ed.), *OHBE*, II, pp. 300–8; John Ferling, "The New England Soldier: A Study in Changing Perceptions," *American Quarterly*, XXXIII (1981), pp. 26–45; Maya Jasanoff, *Liberty's Exiles: American Loyalists in the Revolutionary World* (New York, 2011).

[105] Carl Lounsbury, "The Public Buildings of British America," in Daniel Maudlin and Bernard Herman (eds), *Building the British Atlantic World 1600–1850* (Chapel Hill, NC, forthcoming).

[106] Dummer to [Massachusetts General Court], April 8, 1720, Massachusetts Historical Society, *Collections*, 3rd ser., I (Boston, 1825), pp. 144–5.

By 1765, metropolitan skepticism about the unwonted prodigiousness of colonial politics applied wholesale to just about every American colony. No follower of Chatham or Rockingham but "Anti-Sejanus" (James Scott), champion of the Stamp Act, predicted the inevitably of colonial independence. "The Americans imbibe notions of independence and liberty with their very milk, and will some time or other shake off all subjection." Strong measures alone could put off the evil day and "keep them in dependence for some years longer."[107] Scott could not see the visible and growing Anglicization of the Americans for what it was, a demonstration of the enthusiastic, *equal* participation by the colonies in the enterprise of British imperialism, any more than the colonists could fathom why their own desires for expansion and mastery were in any way incompatible with the fundamental purpose of the British Empire. Resistance and Independence when they finally came were a deliberate, conscious choice, but it is difficult to see either emerging inevitably out of the culture of the colonies without the intrusion of a British political force, Parliament, perceived as alien and claiming to legislate for "America," thereby creating a nation out of a cartographer's abstraction. In John Murrin's phrase, "America was Britain's idea."[108]

Two later chapters will take on the closing *peripeteia* of British North America at a more appropriate length. What may be useful here in the concluding portion of this chapter is a brief further survey of some of the ways in which the successes of the British Empire, the things that allowed it to work and mitigated the impact of its more fractious features, were also in their own ways instrumental in its ultimate undoing. One can start with *British* and proceed from there to *Empire.*

As the American colonies were becoming more genuinely Imperial they were also changing from English to British. There had been some Irish Catholic immigration to the West Indies early on in the seventeenth century but, otherwise, migrants from England had dwarfed in numbers those from the rest of the British Isles and the Continent. Not so the eighteenth century, which in the case of European immigrants was quite solidly Scottish.[109] This

---

[107] *London Chronicle,* February 13, 1766, reprinted in Edmund S. Morgan and Helen Morgan (eds), *The Stamp Act Crisis: Prologue to Revolution,* 2nd edn (New York, 1962), p. 134.

[108] Murrin, "Roof without Walls," p. 339. See also the chapter by Sarah Yeh in this volume.

[109] James Horn, "British Diaspora: Emigration from Britain, 1680–1815," in Marshall (ed.), *OHBE,* II, pp. 28–52.

change was neither gradual nor evenly distributed, however and, in most places for most of the century, colonists of English origin remained a majority of the European inhabitants and a large majority of the inhabitants of British origin or descent.[110] Ethnically, culturally, and politically, the North American colonists remained too English to accept a "British" (i.e., peripheral) role within the Empire. Most of them regarded people who came to the colonies from what were seen as the margins of the metropole with suspicion.

The Ulster Scots, the earliest of the new migrants and the single largest group from the British Isles in the eighteenth century, were concentrated in central Pennsylvania and the Southern backcountry, largely out of sight and unconsidered except when less than salutary neglect caused such affairs as the Paxton Boys' massacre of Conestoga Indians or the Regulation movements in the Carolinas. Scots from Scotland were not so easily written off. Although the great migration from Scotland occurred only in the last decade or two, at most, before the Revolution, the host societies categorized these later Scots according to notions established earlier from their experience of the much smaller number of Scotsmen on the make who had migrated to the colonies to fill relatively high profile positions as professionals (doctors, lawyers, educators, clergy) in a society short of educated talent, or as merchants backed by considerable reserves of capital in an economy that dearly needed it, or, most significantly for the purposes of this discussion, as servants of the Empire, civil and military.[111] There was always a tang of foreignness about Imperial administration because some of its representatives, Scottish or, to a lesser extent, Irish, were seen as members of a class of people suspect in origin and politics and presumptively lingering just long enough to make their pile and return home to build some Scottish or Irish castle with their dubiously acquired fortunes.[112]

As the Revolution approached, this edgy suspicion, already too near the surface to be termed merely "latent," became pervasive and hyperbolic: to give in to Imperial demands would be to become "hewers of wood and drawers of water" to "the lowest cow-herds in Scotland" and "every Scotch

---

[110] Thomas L. Purvis, "The European Ancestry of the United States Population, 1790," WMQ, 3d ser., XLI (1984), Table II, p. 98.

[111] T.M. Devine, Scotland's Empire, 1600–1815 (London, 2003), pp. 49–101, 108, 140–63.

[112] Alan L. Karras, Sojourners in the Sun: Scottish Migrants in Jamaica and the Chesapeake, 1740–1800 (Ithaca, NY, 1992), pp. 118–69, esp. pp. 120, 158–9.

shoeblack."[113] Similarly, in the most popular cartoon of the Stamp Act crisis, on both sides of the Atlantic, *The Repeal*, the funeral procession of "Miss Ame-Stamp" features two jurists bearing mourning banners engraved with the white rose and thistle (emblems of the exiled Stuarts and of Scotland, respectively) walking before the coffin while the much hated Earl of Bute follows behind as the chief mourner. The destination is a tomb flanked by two skulls labeled, respectively, 1715 and 1745 for the Jacobite rebellions of those years.[114]

Outrageous as this stereotype was, it had an objective correlative, or, more properly, the distant cousin of one in Scottish and Irish loyalism in Revolutionary America.[115] Consider, for example, the line of Auchmuty over three generations. Robert Auchmuty, Sr. (1687–1750) of County Longford was an Irish Ascendancy younger son, pure and simple, obliged to secure his own fortune by one of those familiar alternatives, the clergy, law, medicine, or the military. He chose law, perhaps because the ban on Catholic practitioners in Ireland created opportunities for Protestants. Even so, his situation was precarious without the permanent subsidy of fees and salary from office holding, and a fair proportion of the Irish plums invariably went to English placemen. *Faute de mieux*, Auchmuty migrated to Boston in 1716, where his trained talents brought a higher rate of return and in two years, by a process of infiltration, he found a job with the government in the Court of Vice-Admiralty. By the time of his death thirty-two years later he had gone native sufficiently to become a founding member of the Land Bank, but he also helped to reinvigorate a transatlantic law suit that sought to make Anglicanism the state-supported religion of the New England colonies and, while serving as the Massachusetts agent to Whitehall, he created a tumult by calling for stricter enforcement of the laws regulating trade.[116] Of his two sons, Robert, Jr. (1725–1788) found, like his

---

[113] William Lee to Robert Carter Nicholas, March 6, 1775, in Worthington Chauncy Ford (ed.), *Letters of William Lee* (Brooklyn, NY, 1891), I, pp. 142, 142n.

[114] F.G. Stephens and E. Hawkins, *Catalogue of Prints and Drawings in the British Museum: Division I, Political and Personal Satires*, IV (London, 1883), pp. 368–73. A large-scale reproduction of the cartoon itself can be found in Joan D. Dolmetsch, *Rebellion and Reconciliation: Satirical Prints on the Revolution at Williamsburg* (Williamsburg, VA, 1976), p. 38, and for a copy online see http://www.history.org/history/teaching/tchcrpc1.cfm.

[115] Devine, *Scotland's Empire, 1600–1815*, pp. 179–87.

[116] *American National Biography*, s.v., "Auchmuty, Robert, Sr." Cf. Bilder, *The Transatlantic Constitution*, p. 88; Clifford Shipton, et al. (eds), *Sibley's Harvard Graduates, Biographical Sketches of Those Who Attended Harvard College in the Classes 1726–1730*, VIII (Boston, 1951),

father, a position with the vice-admiralty courts. He was also one of the counsel for the crown in the Writs of Assistance case in 1761, one of the counsel for the defense of the soldiers on trial for the Boston Massacre in 1770, a member of the commission appointed to investigate the burning of the revenue cutter, *Gaspee,* in 1772 and, from an early date, a prominent loyalist.[117] The other son, Samuel (1722–77), after a failed career with the vice-admiralty court, took Anglican orders and moved to New York where he became a media star ministering to successively more gorgeous churches. He regularly identified "Dissent" (as he called the other denominations in New York) with republicanism and lobbied for the extension of episcopal establishment to the whole of the colony and for the taxation of "Dissenters" for its support. Both Robert and Samuel were obliged to flee their respective colonies. Samuel returned to New York upon the British occupation and died there a few months later; Robert died in exile in England.[118]

Samuel Auchmuty had three sons, all of whom joined the British army during the Revolution. One died in prison, one settled in Rhode Island, and the third, another Samuel (1758–1822), was a founding father of the second British Empire. He remained in the army after the Revolution and shipped to India, where he came under the wing of Cornwallis and served in the Second Mysore War and the Rohilla War. Subsequent exploits took him to Egypt, South America, and back to India, where he commanded at the capture of Java in 1810. His final posting, as General Sir Samuel Auchmuty, completed the circle: he was sent to Dublin in 1821 as commander-in-chief of the British army in Ireland.[119]

Apart from the near timeless quality of this kind of family saga—the ancestry of Field Marshall Montgomery comes to mind—the most remarkable thing about it is the capacity of three generations of colonial Americans, spanning one hundred and thirty-five years in all, to retain their original proconsular character undiluted. One thing the Auchmutys were *not* were the kinds of loyalists made familiar by Mary Beth Norton: colonists

pp. 499–506; John A. Schutz, *William Shirley: King's Governor of Massachusetts* (Chapel Hill, 1961), p. 72.

[117] *American National Biography,* s.v., "Auchmuty, Robert, Jr."; Clifford Shipton, et al. (eds), *Sibley's Harvard Graduates, Biographical Sketches of Those Who Attended Harvard College in the Classes 1746–1750,* XII (Boston, 1962), pp. 12–16.

[118] Clifford Shipton, et al. (eds), *Sibley's Harvard Graduates,* XI, *Biographical Sketches of Those Who Attended Harvard College in the Classes 1741–1745* (Boston, 1960), pp. 115–27.

[119] *Oxford Dictionary of National Biography,* s.v. "Auchmuty, Sir Samuel."

very like their patriot fellows, catapulted into an exile's fate to their own bewilderment by what should have been relatively small differences compared to all that was held in common.[120] Instead, the Auchmutys strongly suggest that the Imperial establishment fostered some kind of self-perpetuating culture that set its members apart in some degree from the bulk of the inhabitants of the colonies among whom they lived.

To be sure, counter-examples can be found. Francis Hopkinson, signer of the Declaration of Independence, was also the son of a judge of the Court of Vice-Admiralty. John Witherspoon, another signer, was one of the educated Scottish immigrants who found opportunities in America unavailable back home. But any such objection does not really nullify the sheer density of the evidence provided by instances such as the Auchmutys (or the Indian agents, John Stuart and Sir William Johnson, or Johnson's uncle, the famously entrepreneurial naval officer Sir Peter Warren), especially when taken in conjunction with the verdict of the revolutionaries themselves, blinkered and bigoted as it may have been. Embedded in the colonies or merely in transit, the representatives of the Empire in the colonies were a serious structural weakness: their ambiguous position in American society could be a provocation at any time and became an accelerant of no little force after 1763.

We are still left with the question of the origin of the Revolutionary crisis and, especially, of its unexpected suddenness and intensity in the immediate aftermath of an Imperial triumph. The one indisputably new element on the scene after 1763 is the sudden prominence of Parliament. The largest single section of the Declaration of Independence is taken up with just this matter. But it is worth inquiring as to just how original this formidable weapon of Empire actually was once it was deployed. The various acts that taxed the colonies were effectively innovations. The *purposes* for which the money was to be applied, on the other hand, were at least as old as the Board of Trade, as were the various "reforms" of colonial governance that accompanied the revenue measures and eventually displaced them in priority: financial independence for the officers of royal government in the colonies; expansion and strengthening of Admiralty Court jurisdiction; exemption of royal officials from the interference of local courts; the stationing of a garrison in Boston.[121]

---

[120] Mary Beth Norton, *The British-Americans: The Loyalist Exiles in England, 1774–1789* (Boston, 1972).

[121] P. J. Marshall, "The Thirteen Colonies in the Seven Years' War: The View from London," in Julie Flavell and Stephen Conway (eds), *Britain and America Go to War: The Impact of War and Warfare in Anglo-America, 1754–1815* (Gainesville, FL, 2004), pp. 69–94.

The lack of any very substantial evolution in bureaucratic attitudes is an important problem, but the logically prior question should be why some of these recurring vintage remedies for the government of the colonies had not been put in force earlier. Long before 1763, there were enough stand-offs between crown and colonies sufficient to trigger *something* by way of a reform effort, and the threat to refer the controversy with the colonies to Parliament for an unappealable settlement in the crown's favor was of long standing. But from the early years of Walpole to the Pitt-Newcastle ministry during the Seven Years' War, the same deep-rooted hesitancy about any substantial overhaul of colonial governance by Parliament ultimately prevailed in the repetitive series of alarms and excursions. Not everyone shared Newcastle's open contempt for the House of Commons, but no one in any of the ministries of which he was a member wanted to take it on as a regular partner in governing the colonies. In part, their skepticism stemmed from a jealous regard for their own power in wielding the royal prerogative in the king's name, in part from the fear that any extended parliamentary discussion of colonial affairs would turn into an attack on the reigning ministry for its purported failures in its stewardship of the Empire, and in part from a justified concern that an uncontrolled Commons was the last body on earth that should be let loose on a regular basis in so sensitive an area.[122]

When successive Whitehall regimes became actively involved in the politicking between royal governors and the elected part of the colonial legislatures, usually in times of war or when executive–legislative conflicts in a colony threatened to get out of hand, they resorted to rewards, trades, and on occasion bluster; but no impasse, however deeply rooted, was ever allowed to become irresolvable. In the 1720s, for example, on two distinct occasions Whitehall and the lower house of the Massachusetts General Court were locked in mortal combat in which unqualified claims of rights guaranteed by the colonial Charter were ranged against prerogative powers so deeply inherent in the king's majesty as to be immune from all question. In the course of the first dispute, occasioned by a memorial from Governor Shute after his flight from Massachusetts, the Board of Trade, with an

---

[122] Reed Browning, *The Duke of Newcastle* (New Haven, 1975), pp. 134–8; Paul Langford, "Old Whigs, Old Tories, and the American Revolution," *Journal of Imperial and Commonwealth History*, VIII (1980), pp. 114–18; Marshall, "The Thirteen Colonies in the Seven Years' War," in Flavell and Conway (eds), *Britain and America Go to War*, pp. 85–8.

almost shrill enthusiasm, endorsed his report indicting the colony's General Court. The Attorney General and Solicitor General followed afterwards with an equally emphatic confirmation.[123] Forfeiture of the Charter seemed assured. Then, *mirabile dictu*, a new Attorney General (none other than Sir Philip Yorke, the future Lord Chancellor Hardwicke) brought out a supplementary report that while not in any sense exculpatory was considerably more indulgent towards the Massachusetts House of Representatives than its predecessor and even affirmed "the freedom to which such Assemblies are by Law Entitled in their Debates and Resolutions." The Bay Colony was finally let off with an Explanatory Charter on one disputed point and a promise of amendment on the others.[124] In the later crisis, during the brief tenure of Governor William Burnett in 1728–29, Newcastle, as Secretary of State for the Southern Department, accepted the conclusion of the Board of Trade that the Bay Colony's misbehavior in not providing Burnett with a permanent salary justified referring the controversy to Parliament. Then he personally wrote to Burnett to abandon his demands for the sake of His Majesty's convenience and his own personal advancement.[125]

Newcastle and Hardwicke were durable politicians who knew when to push, when to yield, and when to resort to Parliament (only when there was no constitutional alternative and then only briefly). In the 1750s and early 1760s, however, this generation of Walpole-trained politicians mostly passed to its reward except for a very aged Newcastle, who had so little credit with the young men of the Rockingham ministry, the last in which he held office, that he was deliberately left out of policy meetings concerning the colonies.[126] Among the leading politicians of the post-1763 period the colonies could count on only William Pitt and his small band of adherents for some degree of restraint, but, except for taxation, Pitt held a very high view of Parliament's powers and, as the Americans were to discover, he was

[123] Pencak, *War, Politics, and Revolution in Provincial Massachusetts*, pp. 76–9; William Stevens Perry, *Historical Collections Relating to the American Colonial Church* ([Hartford, CT], 1870–78), III, pp. 121–6; BL Additional Manuscripts 35908, ff. 50–56, Additional Manuscripts 15486, ff. 1–8.

[124] BL, Additional Manuscripts 15486, ff. 25–40 (quotation at f. 26r.)

[125] Pencak, *War, Politics, and Revolution in Provincial Massachusetts*, pp. 80–3; Newcastle to Governor William Burnett, June 26, 1729, The National Archives, Public Record Office, CO5/10/ ff. 42r–43v.

[126] P.D.G. Thomas, *British Politics and the Stamp Act Crisis: The First Phase of the American Revolution, 1763–1767* (Oxford, 1975), pp. 181–2; Paul Langford, *The First Rockingham Administration, 1765–1766* (Oxford, 1973), pp. 33–8.

famously mercurial and unpredictable.[127] The story was much the same in the case of the Church of England: its presence in North America had been a source of recurrent tension since the 1680s, but the issues in dispute did not vary much from one decade to the next, and the controversy only reached crisis proportions after Thomas Secker became Archbishop of Canterbury in 1758.[128] In the course of the 1750s and early 1760s, in matters of church and state alike, the genie of colonial reform could at last be let out of the bottle, eligible for an old age pension. There was the same diagnosis as ever, decidedly grim, and the same heroic proposals for a remedy, now fueled by a sense of urgency and empowered with the reach and force of an Act of Parliament.

This kind of analysis, part constitutional, part political, has always been a little suspect because it seems too remote from the kinds of passions that lead to and sustain long nasty wars for high stakes. Undoubtedly, the ferocity with which the North American colonies tore themselves from the Empire can be traced to multiple causes, but not the least of them was the administratively inconvenient persistence of English liberties on the Imperial periphery. What is one to make, for example, of Lord Loudon during his American command complaining of society in colonial Pennsylvania as unnatural because insufficiently hierarchical: opposition to Imperial measures seemed "not to come from the *lower* People, but from the *leading* People, who raise the dispute, in order to have a merit with others, by defending their Liberties, as they call them."[129] Newcastle, the man who appointed Loudon as commander, and who was never happier than when electioneering, could have told him that superiors got their way by cultivating their clients and accepting them as equals. (They still knew that a duke was a duke.)[130] Alternatively, one may wonder what the draftsmen of the Stamp Act assumed about their right to engage in social engineering in the Empire, when, in the immediate aftermath of a great expansion of higher

---

[127] Thomas, *British Politics and the Stamp Act Crisis*, pp. 291–9; P.D.G. Thomas, *Tea Party to Independence: The Third Phase of the American Revolution, 1773–1776* (Oxford, 1991), pp. 84–5.

[128] James B. Bell, *A War of Religion: Dissenters, Anglicans, and the American Revolution* (Houndmills, 2008). See also the chapter by Jeremy Gregory in this volume.

[129] Loudon to Cumberland, December 26, 1756, in Pargellis (ed.), *Military Affairs in North America*, pp. 272–3.

[130] Browning, *The Duke of Newcastle*, pp. 31–4; Bob Harris, *Politics and the Nation: Britain in the Mid-Eighteenth Century* (Oxford, 2002), pp. 22–101; Frank O'Gorman, *Voters, Patrons, and Parties: The Unreformed Electoral System of Hanoverian England, 1734–1832* (Oxford, 1989).

education in the colonies, they casually slapped fees on college attendance and graduation that were much heavier than their English equivalents, primarily "in order to keep mean persons out of those situations in life which they disgrace."[131]

Forty-five years earlier, in 1720, the Bay Colony Chief Justice, Samuel Sewall, wrote to Agent Dummer to thank him for his efforts in defeating a bill in Parliament that would have forbidden the manufacturing of iron goods in the colonies. Sewall observed that "'twas one principle article of the forlorn Condition, our Aborigines were in, that they wanted the use of Iron: And to Deprive the Planters of it, would be to reduce them to the Miseries of the Iron Age."[132] Dummer responded that the London merchant community, a prime mover of the bill, "would be well enough content to see us reduced to the servile condition of the Jews, when under the tyranny of the Philistines, who were not permitted to have a smith throughout all their land."[133] Both men obviously resented the breezy indifference with which the Mother Country was willing to knock their colony down a notch or two on the civilization scale in response to the maneuvering of some special interest or another. Neither, however, was ready to make the issue a question of the rights of Britons wherever in the Empire they might reside. The effective incorporation of the Bay Colony within the Empire was still too new for them to feel a sense of betrayal at the sudden abrogation of what was not yet time-honored, and their inherent dependence on a power that could win great land victories on the Continent while they could barely hold their own against the French in North America was entirely obvious. Their descendants in 1765, having just shared in a hard won victory in a world war, were a good deal more sensitive about what was generally called "all *due* subordination" of the colonies to the metropole. A serious dispute about just what it meant to be British ensued.

In relatively short order, the Empire collapsed in on itself. Sophisticated grievance networks that had been used in the familiar business of petitioning

---

[131] Morgan and Morgan (eds), *The Stamp Act Crisis*, p. 80; Thomas, *British Politics and the Stamp Act Crisis*, p. 83n.; Edmund S. Morgan, *The Gentle Puritan: A Life of Ezra Stiles, 1727–1795* (Chapel Hill, NC, 1962), p. 326n.

[132] Samuel Sewall to Jeremiah Dummer, February 23, 1720, Mass. Hist. Soc., *Coll.*, 6th ser., II (Boston, 1889), p. 109.

[133] Jeremiah Dummer to Samuel Sewall, April 8, 1720, Mass. Hist. Soc., *Coll.*, 3rd ser., I (Boston, 1825), p. 140.

for redress from a Mother Country that was a little misinformed were redeployed to coordinate resistance to a corrupt tyranny.[134] Newspapers that had celebrated the triumph of British arms in the Seven Years' War were used to broadcast the misdeeds of the British army stationed in Boston to protect the commissioners of customs.[135] And the device of the intercolonial conference that had been pioneered at Albany in 1754 to aid in the war against France was brought into action at Philadelphia to run a war against Britain.[136]

Regardless of whether the Revolution was inevitable or contingent, when it finally came it drew on resentments of long standing in hypertrophied form and was accomplished by the selective use of some of the same devices that previously had sustained the Empire. In this special sense it can reasonably be said of British Empire in North America that its winding sheet was woven in its womb.

Select Bibliography

HUGH AMORY and DAVID D. HALL (eds), *The Colonial Book in the Atlantic World*, vol. I of *A History of the Book in America* (ed.), David D. Hall (Cambridge, 2000).

FRED ANDERSON, *The Crucible of War: The Seven Years' War and the Fate of Empire in British North America, 1754–1766* (New York, 2000).

DAVID ARMITAGE, *The Ideological Origins of the British Empire* (Cambridge, 2000).

BERNARD BAILYN, *The Ideological Origins of the American Revolution* (Cambridge, MA, 1967).

BERNARD BAILYN and PHILIP D. MORGAN (eds), *Strangers within the Realm: Cultural Margins of the First British Empire* (Chapel Hill, NC, 1991).

PATRICIA U. BONOMI, *The Lord Cornbury Scandal: The Politics of Reputation in British America* (Chapel Hill, NC, 1998).

TIMOTHY H. BREEN, *The Marketplace of Revolution: How Consumer Politics Shaped American Independence* (Oxford, 2004).

JOHN BREWER, *The Sinews of Power: War, Money, and the English State, 1688–1788* (New York, 1988).

---

[134] See the chapter by Daniel Hulsebosch in this volume.

[135] O.M. Dickerson (ed.), *Boston under Military Rule (1768–1769) as Revealed in a Journal of the Times* (Boston, 1936); Charles E. Clark and Charles Wetherall, "The Measure of Maturity: The Pennsylvania Gazette, 1728–1765," *WMQ*, 3rd ser., XLVI (1989), pp. 279–303.

[136] John Shy, "The American Colonies in War and Revolution, 1748–83," in Marshall (ed.), *OHBE*, II, pp. 304–5, 313–18.

STEVEN C. BULLOCK, *Revolutionary Brotherhood: Freemasonry and the Transformation of the American Social Order, 1730–1840* (Chapel Hill, NC, 1996).

CORNELIA HUGHES DAYTON, *Women before the Bar: Gender, Law, and Society in Connecticut, 1639–1789* (Chapel Hill, NC, 1995).

J. H. ELLIOTT, *Empires of the Atlantic World: Britain and Spain in America, 1492–1830* (New Haven, 2006).

JACK P. GREENE, *The Intellectual Construction of America: Exceptionalism and Identity from 1492 to 1800* (Chapel Hill, NC, 1993).

JACK P. GREENE, *Peripheries and Center: Constitutional Development in the Extended Polities of the British Empire and the United States, 1607–1788* (Athens, GA, 1986).

DAVID HANCOCK, *Citizens of the World: London Merchants and the Integration of the British Atlantic Community, 1735–1785* (Cambridge, 1995).

P. J. MARSHALL, *The Making and Unmaking of Empires: Britain, India, and America, c. 1750–1783* (Oxford, 2005).

JOHN J. MCCUSKER and RUSSELL R. MENARD, *The Economy of British America, 1607–1789*, 2nd edn (Chapel Hill, NC, 1991).

JANE T. MERRIT, *At the Crossroads: Indians and Empires on a Mid-Atlantic Frontier, 1700–1763* (Chapel Hill, NC, 1993).

EDMUND S. MORGAN, *Benjamin Franklin* (New Haven, 2003).

EDMUND S. MORGAN and HELEN M. MORGAN, *The Stamp Act Crisis: Prologue to Revolution*, 2nd edn (New York, 1962).

PHILIP D. MORGAN and SEAN HAWKINS (eds), *Black Experience and the Empire*, Oxford History of the British Empire Companion Series (ed.), Wm. Roger Louis (Oxford, 2004).

ALISON GILBERT OLSON, *Making the Empire Work: London and American Interest Groups, 1690–1790* (Cambridge, MA, 1992).

CARLA GARDINA PESTANA, *Protestant Empire: Religion and the Making of the British Atlantic World* (Philadelphia, 2009).

DANIEL K. RICHTER, *The Ordeal of the Longhouse: the Peoples of the Iroquois League in the Era of European Colonization* (Chapel Hill, NC, 1992).

TIMOTHY J. SHANNON, *Indians and Colonists at the Crossroads of Empire: the Albany Congress of 1754* (Ithaca, NY, 2000).

OWEN STANWOOD, *Empire Reformed: English America in the Age of the Glorious Revolution* (Philadelphia, 2011).

IAN K. STEELE, *The English Atlantic, 1675–1740: An Exploration of Communication and Community* (New York, 1986).

LAWRENCE W. STONE (ed.), *An Imperial State at War: Britain from 1689 to 1815* (London, 1994).

P. D. G. THOMAS, *British Politics and the Stamp Act Crisis: The First Phase of the American Revolution, 1763–1767* (Oxford, 1975).

RICHARD WHITE, *The Middle Ground: Indians, Empires, and Republics in the Great Lakes Region, 1650–1815* (New York, 1991).

KATHLEEN WILSON, *The Sense of the People: Politics, Culture and Imperialism in England, 1715–1785* (Cambridge, 1995).

SERENA R. ZABIN, *Dangerous Economies: Status and Commerce in Imperial New York* (Philadelphia, 2009).

NUALA ZAHEDIEH, *The Capital and the Colonies: London and the Atlantic Economy, 1660–1700* (Cambridge, 2010).

3

"Bound by Our Regal Office"

Empire, Sovereignty, and the American Colonies in the Seventeenth Century

Ken MacMillan

It has become commonplace to argue that the imperial connection between the metropolitan center and the American peripheries in the seventeenth century was weak. Various reasons have been offered for this attenuated relationship: an incoherent ideology of colonization that had, as yet, no imperial aspirations; a laissez-faire approach to colonial affairs at a time when these activities could yield little economic dividend or political power; the preference for a "weak state" model of national government that eschewed strong centralizing tendencies and instead delegated key state functions into private hands; the policy of (to quote Edmund Burke) "wise and salutary neglect," which benignly allowed the colonies to develop according to their unique needs; and the inability of central authorities, even if they wished, to exert power over the American peripheries because of limited coercive, financial, or administrative means.[1]

As a result of these various factors, it has been argued, a seventeenth-century English Atlantic emerged not through an act of central, imperial

---

[1] These themes are developed in Nicholas Canny (ed.), *The Origins of Empire: British Overseas Enterprise to the Close of the Seventeenth Century,* vol. I of *OHBE* (ed.), Wm. Roger Louis (Oxford, 1998), esp. in the introduction. See also the work of Charles M. Andrews, esp. *Our Earliest Colonial Settlements* (New York, 1933); K. R. Andrews, *Trade, Plunder, and Settlement: Maritime Enterprise and the Genesis of the British Empire, 1480–1630* (Cambridge, 1984); Jack P. Greene, *Peripheries and Center: Constitutional Development in the Extended Polities of the British Empire and the United States, 1607–1788* (Athens, GA, 1986), chap. 1; and J. R. Seeley, *The Expansion of England* (London, 1883). For Burke's position, see Warren M. Elofson (ed.), *Party, Parliament, and the American War, 1774–1780* (Oxford, 1996), vol. III of Paul Langford (ed.), *The Writings and Speeches of Edmund Burke,* p. 118 ("Speech on Conciliation with the Colonies," March 22, 1775).

will, but rather through the mundane process of "government by license." This was the franchising out of chartered enterprises, undertaken for profit at the risk and expense of trading companies and individual proprietors.[2] This method of dispensing favors and monopolies relieved the early Stuarts of the burden of overseas empire, while ultimately serving the public good by encouraging the spread of English subjects abroad and helping to ensure a thriving foreign and domestic economy. Some historians have noted a change in central control in the 1650s, when the republican government, in an effort to enforce acceptance of the new regime and bring about new national and liberal trade policies, woke to the concept of empire and began thinking in terms of a nascent imperial policy.[3] Others have suggested that this development of an imperial consciousness remained fitful and inchoate until at least 1675, when the appointment of an enduring conciliar committee of oversight, the development of a more coherent imperial policy, and the rise of the strong "fiscal-military state" model led to "some measure of stability, expertise, and direction" in the administration of the American colonies. By the time imperial policy was implemented in earnest circa 1696, the year that marked the creation of the durable Lords Commissioners of Trade and Plantations (Board of Trade), the colonies had become so used to autonomy and self-government through legislative assemblies, local court jurisdictions, and divergent colonial circumstances that this renewed effort at central control was begrudgingly negotiated, increasingly resented, and never fully accepted.[4] The ensuing struggle in the eighteenth century is well known.

---

[2] Michael Braddick, "The English Government, War, Trade, and Settlement, 1625–1688," in Canny (ed.), *OHBE*, I, p. 286. On the "logic of chartered enterprises," see Elizabeth Mancke, "Chartered Enterprises and the Evolution of the British Atlantic World," in Elizabeth Mancke and Carole Shammas (eds), *The Creation of the British Atlantic World* (Baltimore, 2005), pp. 238–40.

[3] This argument derives from the earlier work of Christopher Hill and Gerald Aylmer. On the empire specifically, see Robert M. Bliss, *Revolution and Empire: English Politics and the American Colonies in the Seventeenth Century* (Manchester, 1990); Robert Brenner, *Merchants and Revolution: Commercial Change, Political Conflict, and London's Overseas Traders, 1550–1653* (Princeton, 1992); Carla Gardina Pestana, *The English Atlantic in an Age of Revolution, 1640–1661* (Cambridge, MA, 2004), esp. chap. 6.

[4] In addition to the work cited earlier, see John Brewer, *The Sinews of Power: War, Money, and the English State, 1688–1783* (New York, 1989); Ian K. Steele, "The Anointed, the Appointed, and the Elected: Governance of the British Empire, 1689–1784," in P. J. Marshall (ed.), *OHBE*, II, *The Eighteenth Century* (Oxford, 1998); Stephen Saunders Webb, *1676: The End of American Independence* (Cambridge, MA, 1984); J. M. Sosin, *English America and the Restoration Monarchy of Charles II: Transatlantic Politics, Commerce, and Kinship* (Lincoln, NE, 1980) (quotation at p. 45).

This chapter challenges the notion of a weak seventeenth-century empire in America by demonstrating that from 1607 onward crown intervention in colonial affairs reflected a historically-based, ideologically principled, and broadly consistent (if generally un-intrusive) system of imperial governance. Sophisticated theories of empire and sovereignty that underpinned colonial American activities were well established before the seventeenth century, and had been applied and tested in various dominions of the English crown. While awarding significant levels of autonomy, which was consistent with how the crown historically ruled its wider composite monarchy, the colonial charters carefully, if not always explicitly, set out the rules of empire and the continuing relationship between American subjects, indigenous peoples, the crown, and other European powers. This relationship was reinforced by the administrative arm of the crown, the "imperially-minded" Privy Council (or, in the Commonwealth period, the Council of State). Beginning early in the seventeenth century, the council issued instructions to colonial governors, prepared royal proclamations that ensured the crown's sovereignty and prerogative was not derogated, reviewed colonial legislation and court decisions for elements repugnant to English sensibilities and liberties, and heard and determined private petitions and appeals that were received from the American colonies. All of these conciliar roles were within its sovereign responsibility to ensure that the subjects of England, wherever they resided and no matter how wide their chartered mandate, behaved and were treated according to the dictates of Christian reason, sovereign allegiance, natural rights, and traditional English liberties.[5] There were limits placed on colonial autonomy from the outset, which ensured that the crown's sovereign and imperial rights and obligations were respected by the colonies' administrators, inhabitants, and European competitors

✳✳✳✳

The notion of "empire," though quite distinct from the ideologically freighted term of later centuries, was already ancient by the seventeenth century. In the Roman republic, the Latin *imperium* referred to the executive power held by Roman military commanders and civilian magistrates over both people and territory. This power was vested in the holder of *imperium* by the people. It was temporary in that it was possessed only for a specified term, for

---

[5] For a fuller discussion of the crown's role, especially under the early Stuarts, see Ken MacMillan, *The Atlantic Imperial Constitution: Center and Periphery in the English Atlantic World* (Houndmills, 2011).

instance during a certain military campaign or by a general during his command. In the period of their investiture, possessors of *imperium* recognized no higher authority in the territory over which their rule was exercised, although they might recognize the authority of an extra-territorial ruler. As the Roman republic receded and the empire grew to incorporate various allied and conquered territories, *imperium* took on a broader, stronger definition that reflected the absolute rule of an individual over numerous, formerly independent states. This collection of states, identified by historians and legal commentators such as Sallust, Tacitus, Cicero, and Livy, as an "empire" (*imperii*), soon came under the permanent rule of the Roman Emperor, now the supreme holder of *imperium* in the entire western world. With the coming of Christianity this power was shared according to the Donation of Constantine, in which the emperor vested temporal authority over the "Western empire" in the Roman Catholic pope. Thereafter, these "twin swords of Christendom" were *domini mundi*, lords of the world, who together ruled a universal monarchy. Other Christian kings were recognized and awarded significant internal authority, but, in the age of feudal monarchies, all were inferior and all owed homage and obedience to the twin swords.[6]

Beginning in the thirteenth century, as feudal monarchies began to give way to the rise of the independent nation state, the universalist pretentions of emperor and pope suffered their first serious challenges. Many European princes, including those of Britain and France, were recognized as holding *plenitudo potestatis*, or complete power, within their territorial jurisdictions. This was both because they could claim predominance over internal competitors (many of whom were also styled "kings") and because they ruled more than one political territory in what is often referred to as "composite monarchy." When Pope Innocent III (1198–1216), for example, issued a decretal explaining why he would not interfere in a case that arose in France, he was respecting the Roman law maxim *rex imperator in regno suo est*, a king is

---

[6] David Armitage, *The Ideological Origins of the British Empire* (Cambridge, 2000), pp. 29–36; Armitage, "Literature and Empire," in Canny (ed.), *OHBE*, I, pp. 103–4; James Muldoon, *Empire and Order: The Concept of Empire, 800–1800* (New York, 1999), chap. 4; J.H. Burns, *Lordship, Kingship, and Empire: The Idea of Monarchy, 1400–1525* (Oxford, 1992), chap. 2; Thomas O. Hüglin, "The Idea of Empire: Conditions for Integration and Disintegration in Europe," *Publius*, XII (1982): pp. 12–19; Anthony Pagden, *Lords of All the World: Ideologies of Empire in Spain, Britain and France c. 1500–c. 1800* (New Haven, 1995), chaps. 1–2; J. S. Richardson, "*Imperium Romanum*: Empire and the Languages of Power," in David Armitage (ed.), *Theories of Empire, 1450–1800* (Aldershot, 1998), pp. 1–9.

emperor in his own kingdom. This notion of regional *imperium* harked back to the republican period in Rome.[7] In Britain, some form of imperial status had been claimed since at least the time of Athelstan (924–40), and was never seriously challenged by the universal monarchs throughout the period of the "first British empire," which reached its apogee in the reign of Edward I (1272–1307). In 1301, for instance, Edward successfully asserted his sovereign independence from Pope Boniface VII when the latter tried to intervene in Anglo-Scottish affairs.[8] These were not yet claims to equality with the emperor and pope but rather claims to supreme power where a single empire was affected, thereby rendering universal arbitration unnecessary.

By the early sixteenth century, European monarchs were in a position to assert supreme overlordship and writers such as Nicoló Machiavelli and Francisco de Vitoria clarified the absolute independent authority of kings. In a series of lectures delivered at the University of Salamanca between 1528 and 1539, Vitoria asserted that "the emperor is not master of the whole world."[9] In dismissing claims to universalism, Vitoria and his followers entrenched the idea that some monarchs held the brand of *imperium* claimed during the height of the Roman empire, which meant that they recognized no earthly authority higher than themselves.[10] This gained currency in England at the same time as Henry VIII was engineering his break with Rome, culminating in the Act in Restraint of Appeals (1533). In that Act, Henry claimed that "[w]here by divers sundry old authentic histories and chronicles, it is manifestly declared and expressed that this realm of England is an Empire."[11] The Act forbade clerical appeal to Rome, thereby making the king the final legal authority in all things spiritual and temporal. After the Act was in place, Henry and his council engineered the

---

[7] Kenneth Pennington, *Popes, Canonists, and Texts, 1150–1550* (Aldershot, 1993); Pennington, *The Prince and the Law, 1200–1600: Sovereignty and Rights in the Western Legal Tradition* (Berkeley, 1993).

[8] Armitage, *Ideological Origins*, p. 28; R. R. Davies, *The First English Empire: Power and Identities in the British Isles, 1093–1343* (Oxford, 2000), pp. 41–2; Julius Goebel, Jr., "The Matrix of Empire," in Joseph Henry Smith, *Appeals to the Privy Council from the American Plantations* (New York, 1950), pp. xiv–xv, xxi.

[9] Francisco de Vitoria, *Political Writings* (ed.), Anthony Pagden and Jeremy Lawrance (Cambridge, 1991), pp. 12, 85.

[10] Not all monarchs held *imperium*: the German princes, for example, held *dominium* over their lands, or the right to govern them, but did not hold *imperium*, or absolute rule, which was *de jure* retained by the Holy Roman Emperor until 1806.

[11] 24 Henry VIII, c. 12.

union of England and Wales into a single kingdom and sought advice about how to reassert imperial rule over the Stuart monarchy in Scotland (which, it was argued, held *dominium* but not *imperium*)—a relationship that had waned since Edward I's claims to overlordship in the late thirteenth century.

A resurgence of interest in Geoffrey of Monmouth's *Historia Regum Britanniae* (1136) provided the primary historical and legal evidence for the recovery of the medieval empire spanning the Atlantic. Grounding his claims in an apocryphal ancient Welsh book, Geoffrey narrated the tale of the Trojan soldier Brutus, who allegedly brought civility to Albion and founded an empire under the common name "Britain." Following his death, Brutus's three sons ruled England, Scotland, and Wales respectively, with the eldest holding *imperium* over the whole. Thereafter, Brutus's lineal descendant, the sixth-century Welsh king Arthur, who had gained control of the empire, conquered thirty kingdoms in the North Atlantic and Scandinavia, bringing these lands and peoples into the empire as well.[12] These conquests of Brutus and Arthur gained renewed attention from Elizabethan writers, including John Bale, John Leland, Humphrey Llwyd, and Edmund Spenser. According to these writers, although the empire of Arthur dissolved with its conquest by the Saxons, the return of the Welsh Tudors to the throne in 1485 revived the ancient empire fully intact. John Dee advanced this argument in the late 1570s, along the way developing an aggressive vision of a large "Imperiall British monarchy," headed by "our sovereign empress our most gracious Elizabeth." This empire included not only the nations of Albion and the Channel Islands, but also the British-discovered, Arthurian-conquered, and merchant-frequented "Collateral Islands" in the North Atlantic, such as Ireland, Iceland, Greenland, the Orkneys, and other "sundry foreign regions." These last included Florida (settled by the Welsh Lord Madoc), eastern Canada (discovered by John and Sebastian Cabot), and Meta Incognita (modern Baffin Island, discovered by Martin Frobisher).[13]

By the time the English expressed real interest in overseas travel and settlement, therefore, sophisticated theories of empire existed in England and throughout Europe. Specifically, this vernacular analogue of *imperium*

---

[12] Armitage, *Ideological Origins*, chap. 2.

[13] John Dee, *General and Rare Memorials Pertayning to the Perfect Arte of Navigation* (London, 1576) (quotations at pp. 31, 55); John Dee, *The Limits of the British Empire* (ed.), Ken MacMillan with Jennifer Abeles (Westport, CT, 2004), pp. 15–16, 43–9 (quotation at 48); Ken MacMillan, *Sovereignty and Possession in the English New World: The Legal Foundations of Empire, 1576–1640* (Cambridge, 2006), chap. 2.

implied the absolute and independent authority of a single individual (an emperor) over a diversity of territories (an empire) acquired through discovery, inheritance, cession (through treaty), or conquest. By the early Stuart period, this empire included England, Scotland, Wales, Ireland, various surrounding islands, and certain, largely incomplete, claims to parts of North America and the North Atlantic. This English empire was, however, far from the powerful entity that would become known as the "British Empire." While contemporaries such as Dee, Richard Hakluyt, and others were perfectly willing to see the Atlantic world as a new branch of the late medieval and early modern "British" empire, headed by an imperial crown, none assigned to this empire the ideological implications that the term and its ideological cousin *imperialism* came to be represent in the late eighteenth century.[14]

****

For authors such as Dee and Hakluyt, the concept of an English empire was closely related to contemporary ideas of sovereignty. As a juridical concept, sovereignty had been a topic of intense discussion since the recovery of Roman law in the twelfth century, and was related to the universalist challenges and the rise of the nation state of the late medieval period.[15] As defined by Jean Bodin in the most important statement of the subject written in the sixteenth century, "sovereignty is the most high, absolute, and perpetual power over citizens and subjects in a Commonwealth." To Bodin, this authority was absolute and perpetual because it was indivisible. Although authority might be delegated to agents of the crown—in England and its empire, to Privy Counsellors, regional lieutenants, palatine lords, and domestic parliaments—"the entire sovereignty belongs undivided to the kings of England," who alone held all of the power the state could wield. Bodin enumerated nine marks of "absolute" sovereignty: power to give laws as "sole legislator;" power of war and peace; right of final appeal; power to appoint and dismiss officers of state; power of taxation; power to pardon individuals and mitigate the severity of the law; power of life and death;

---

[14] David Armitage, "The Elizabethan Idea of Empire," *Transactions of the Royal Historical Society*, XIV (2004), pp. 270–2; generally, Armitage, *Ideological Origins*, chap. 1.

[15] Pennington, *Prince and the Law*, chaps. 2–4; generally, F. H. Hinsley, *Sovereignty* (Cambridge, 1986).

power to issue coinage; and the exclusive right to receive oaths of fealty and allegiance.[16]

Despite these wide-ranging marks of sovereignty, however, Bodin's definition of absolute and unlimited sovereignty should not be interpreted to mean an unrestricted and arbitrary rule that could degenerate into tyranny. Bodin (and many medieval civilians, from whom Bodin's illustrations are drawn) argued that although by the maxim *princeps legibus solutus* sovereign monarchs were not bound by the law, they were responsible "not so much out of necessity, as of courtesy," to apply the positive and customary laws of the realm, especially if they gave an oath to abide by such laws, as English kings did at their coronation ceremony. In two cases, however, the king could deviate from customary laws: either when these diminished the king's supreme authority in the realm; or when the law was "bad," meaning contrary to the fundamental laws of mankind. The king had an obligation to God and his subjects to extirpate "bad" law. Bodin privileged these fundamental laws of mankind over all local and customary laws and, generally, over the king's powers, in part because it was these laws to which the king and all mankind owed their existence. That is to say, the king was bound by the universal laws of God and nature, which no sovereign had the right to abrogate "without treason and rebellion against God."[17]

These laws had their foundation in the Bible and in the emperor Justinian's *Corpus Juris Civilis* (AD 533), a compilation of ancient Roman law that was deemed the *ratio scripta* (written reason) of natural law. They were subsequently glossed by Thomas Aquinas (who sought to fuse them together as a unitary system), by renowned civilians such as Accursius, Bartolus, and Ubaldis, and, in England, by the justice Henry de Bracton. These fundamental laws included natural rights to life, liberty, the enjoyment of personal property, and freedom from oppression, and even extended to limitations on how the king might tax his subjects and the requirement that, despite being absolute sovereign and *legibus solutus*, he was, like all men, bound by contracts and covenants once he entered into them. Only when there was universal consensus within the *jus gentium* (law of nations) did sovereigns have the authority to derogate from divine and natural law. Thus, for instance, although these laws prohibited killing and

---

[16] Jean Bodin, *The Six Bookes of a Commonweale*, trans. Richard Knolles (London, 1606), book I, chaps. 8–10 (quotations at pp. 84, 96–7, 103).

[17] Bodin, *Six Bookes*, pp. 103–12.

degradation into slavery, the law of nations sometimes bestowed these powers on sovereigns when there was seen to be sufficient cause.[18] It was largely the Bodinic view of sovereignty that would become central to the Tudor "cult of kingship," which reached its apogee under Elizabeth, and would be espoused in writing by James VI and I in his *Trew Law of Free Monarchies* (1598).[19]

In England, the application of sovereignty was governed by the royal prerogative, which further mitigated any potential for arbitrary rule found in the language of Bodin and James VI and I. Prerogatives in England were recognized as central components of sovereignty circa 1300, around the time Edward I secured imperial overlordship, in a treatise entitled *Prerogativa Regis*. Discussions of prerogative, and especially the distinction between ordinary and absolute powers (known in Roman law as *potestas ordinata et absoluta*), were further developed by Sir John Fortescue in his *De Laudibus Legum Angliae* (1470) and by several important Elizabethan and early-Stuart legalists.[20] These interpretations of prerogative suggested that, within national boundaries, the king's sovereignty was limited by local laws in the same manner that Bodin had argued it was restricted by customary laws. In England, for example, the king had an "ordinary" (or limited) prerogative obligation to conform to laws made by the sovereign "king in parliament" (*lex scripta*), though he might choose to veto a bill before it was enacted or to vitiate it in individual circumstances, and to the customary laws of the realm (*lex terrae*), as determined by historical usage and court precedents. In theory, though not always in practice, especially under the early Stuarts, the limitations on prerogative meant that the king was not allowed to issue

[18] Pennington, *Prince and the Law*, chap. 4; Peter Stein, *Roman Law in European History* (Cambridge, 1999); Stein, *The Character and Influence of Roman Civil Law: Historical Essays* (London, 1988).

[19] Glenn Burgess, *Absolute Monarchy and the Stuart Constitution* (New Haven, 1996); Johann P. Sommerville, "English and European Political Ideas in the Early Seventeenth Century: Revisionism and the Case of Absolutism," *JBS*, XXXV (1996), pp. 168–94; Joyce Lee Malcolm, "Doing No Wrong: Law, Liberty, and the Constraint of Kings," *JBS*, XXXVIII (1999), pp. 161–86.

[20] Glenn Burgess, *The Politics of the Ancient Constitution: An Introduction to English Political Thought, 1603–42* (University Park, PA, 1992), chap. 5; Margaret McGlynn, *The Royal Prerogative and Learning in the Inns of Court* (Cambridge, 2003); Thomas Egerton, "A Copy of a Written Discourse ... Concerning the Royal Prerogative (c. 1604)," in Louis Knafla, *Law and Politics in Jacobean England: The Tracts of Lord Chancellor Ellesmere* (Cambridge, 1977), tract 9; D. E. C. Yale (ed.), *Sir Matthew Hale's The Prerogatives of the King* (London, 1976).

proclamations that arbitrarily revoked, changed, or conflicted with legislation (that is, he held limited "suspending and dispensing powers"); or to
infringe the liberties of Parliament (such as freedom from arrest) or tax his
subjects without consent; or to interfere with the due process of law,
including the decisions of royal judges even in cases where the crown was
concerned.

In other areas of the empire, although the domestic English common law
did not apply, the king was still required to conform to local laws, unless
these infringed his sovereignty. In Scotland, the king had to respect the
historical usage of civil law, just as in Ireland he recognized the Brehon law,
and in Wales (until the English common law was extended under Henry
VIII), the Welsh law, and so on. These expectations for the use of local laws
by the king were entrenched in the thirteenth and fourteenth centuries as
the result of the development of the Roman law mechanism of appeal to the
holder of *imperium*, and the recognition that the English common law could
not service the needs of subjects within the wider empire.[21] One of the
leading proponents of this notion in the early seventeenth century was,
surprisingly, Sir Edward Coke, who argued in various writings that the
common law and its courts had no jurisdiction in royal territories outside
England, in part because it was not designed for such circumstances and
because other parts of the empire had their own customary laws.[22] For this
reason, the king's "ordinary" (also known as remedial or domestic) writs,
initiated from Chancery, did not operate throughout the empire.

In keeping with his rights of sovereignty and *imperium*, however, the king
was also recognized to have broad-ranging "extraordinary," or unlimited
prerogatives, which were not restricted by customary laws. These prerogatives were employed where there was a lacuna in customary laws, where they
failed to be equitable, where they were "bad law" and derogated from the
king's sovereignty, or when more than one political territory was involved,
in which case no single customary system was relevant. In all of these
instances, the king possessed vast powers, which allowed him to create
laws *ex nihilo* (from nothing) through proclamation, to employ his residual

---

[21] Mary Sarah Bilder, "The Origins of Appeal in America," *Hastings Law Journal*, XLVIII
(1997), pp. 913–68; Goebel, "Matrix of Empire," pp. xxv–lii; Hale, *Prerogatives*, chap. 3.

[22] Daniel J. Hulsebosch, "The Ancient Constitution and the Expanding Empire: Sir Edward
Coke's British Jurisprudence," *Law and History Review*, XXI (2003), pp. 439–82; see also Matthew
Hale, *The History of the Common Law of England* (ed.), Charles M. Gray (Chicago, 1971), chaps.
9–10; and Yale (ed.), *Hale's Prerogatives*, chap. 2.

judicial powers to show mercy through the royal pardon, and to ensure that the laws of natural equity, to which all persons under the king's sovereignty were entitled as part of their allegiance, took precedence over written or customary laws. This power allowed the king to override inequitable or unreasonable statute legislation and court precedent, both within England and within the wider composite monarchy. To ensure that this power could not be employed arbitrarily, the king when applying his extraordinary prerogatives, was expected to conform to the laws of God, nature, and nations. This is why, despite the renowned supremacy of the common law in England in the early modern period, civil and canon lawyers with training in "universal" legal systems were frequently employed by the crown as personal advisors and in various civil law and equity court jurisdictions, such as Chancery, Requests, and Star Chamber, whose mandate was to "give natural equity" regardless of the procedural or substantive strictures of local laws.[23]

Absolute sovereignty also implied, in the words of Sir Edward Coke, "a dual and reciprocal tie" between monarchs and subjects.[24] Not unlike the medieval feudal relationship between lords and vassals, the king, as the indivisible and divine-right holder of sovereignty, had the right to demand perpetual homage and allegiance from his subjects. Those who failed to give these to the king could be subjected to such remedies as civil or criminal punishments, proactive steps taken to reacquire allegiance, or even the withdrawal of sovereignty itself, essentially sending them into exile. In exchange, subjects had the right to expect royal protection from the illegal or immoral actions of all aggressors, whether foreign or domestic, in theory (as Bodin implied) including the king himself. In such cases, subjects could exercise their right to petition the king for redress. This could involve the king complaining to other princes on behalf of his subjects, or using his

---

[23] J. H. Baker, *The Oxford History of English Law, VI: 1483–1558* (Oxford, 2003), chaps. 9–11; Brian Levack, *The Civil Lawyers in England, 1603–41: A Political Study* (Oxford, 1973); Burgess, *Politics of the Ancient Constitution*, pp. 121–6.

[24] The phrase appears in Coke's argument in Calvin's Case (1608). See: Hulsebosch, "Ancient Constitution," pp. 655–7; David M. Jones, "Sir Edward Coke and the Interpretation of Lawful Allegiance in Seventeenth-Century England," in Allen D. Boyer (ed.), *Law, Liberty, and Parliament: Selected Essays on the Writings of Sir Edward Coke* (Indianapolis, IN, 2004); Mark L. Thompson, "'The Predicament of Ubi': Locating Authority and National Identity in the Seventeenth-Century English Atlantic," in Mancke and Shammas (eds), *The Creation of the British Atlantic World*, esp. pp. 72–3.

superior judicial powers to override, through pardon, prerogative, or the laws of natural equity, illicit actions—a process that was usually followed by some form of reparation and restitution. This notion of reciprocal sovereignty was not territorially static or, in the words of Coke, not "within the predicament of *ubi* [location]." It travelled with subjects of the monarch wherever they went, including Europe and the Americas. Neither the king nor his subjects lost or relinquished their rights and responsibilities because of geographical distance or even political, religious, or ideological attenuation.[25]

Partly because of this doctrine of reciprocal sovereignty, and because kings no longer recognized the authority of the emperor and pope to arbitrate supranational disputes, possessors of sovereignty also had certain obligations toward other European monarchs of equal status. In England, this sovereign responsibility was within the ambit of the extraordinary prerogative, which obliged the king to send and receive foreign ambassadors, engage in supranational trading relationships, declare war and peace, and, especially in an age of heightened New World activities, enter into diplomatic negotiations regarding disputes over land and the treatment of subjects abroad. To be effective, all of this demanded some coordination among European legal systems, such that by the sixteenth century sovereign princes were conforming to a universal *jus commune*. This "common law" (not to be confused with English common law) was developed and employed as needed by civil lawyers and monarchs and used to solve problems within the broader European community. This system, only much later called "international law," allowed holders of *imperium* to function within a corpus of recognized, universal legal languages. These included the fundamental laws of God, nature, and nations, and also the associated laws of war, peace, prize, and the seas, as defined and digested by, for instance, Justinian, and interpreted by contemporary civilian lawyers. Although, in the era before the Peace of Westphalia (1648), the *jus commune* was neither formal, consistent, codified, nor legally binding, it was nonetheless an important body of laws that allowed European monarchs to negotiate supranationally.[26]

The royal body most directly responsible for ensuring that the king's rights and obligations associated with his *imperium* and absolute sover-

---

[25] These ideas have benefited from discussions with Elizabeth Mancke. See also Paul D. Halliday and G. Edward White, "The Suspension Clause: English Texts, Imperial Contexts, and American Implications," *Virginia Law Review,* XCIV (2008): pp. 575–714, section II.

[26] MacMillan, *Sovereignty and Possession,* esp. pp. 41–7 and chap. 6.

eignty were applied and respected was the Privy Council. Headed by the Lord Chancellor or Keeper, who controlled the use of the great and privy seals of England, this body comprised the major officers of state and the royal household, averaging twenty members during the late Tudor and early Stuart periods. As its name implies, the council was appointed at the king's personal discretion and its function was to give private advice to the king. It was, thus, an appendage of the imperial crown rather than of the domestic, political nation. Its actions were, both literally and figuratively, stamped with the imprimatur of the king.

By the time of Elizabeth, the council had already developed a number of imperial functions that contributed to the development of state formation in early modern England.[27] It was responsible for initiating the king's "extraordinary" writs (*brevia mandatoria*), which extended beyond England into the wider empire. These writs, including those of *mandamus, quo warranto,* and *habeas corpus,* applied throughout the entirety of the monarch's dominions to command the actions of magistrates and subjects.[28] The council also enforced crown decisions by means of official letters and instructions signed by a majority of Counsellors (usually seven or more). Through the attorneys and solicitors general, also members of the Council, it drafted royal proclamations, which were the principal legal devices used to engage the extraordinary prerogative and had the force of law, and letters patent (charters), the "contractual" royal documents ultimately used to authorize the American colonies. The council also provided oversight for the appendage councils in the Marches of Wales and the North created to administer English borderlands, approved Irish parliamentary legislation (under Poynings' Law, 1494), and received petitions from subjects of the empire. In the last case, the Council could compel the attendance of involved parties, issue commissions to demand that local authorities review the case and report back, and when necessary turn itself into the Court of Star Chamber (until its abolition by statute in 1642) to hear and determine the cause.[29] Finally, the Council had numerous foreign functions, including advising the king on matters of trade and diplomacy and, frequently, appointing its own members to lead treaty

---

[27] Michael Braddick, *State Formation in Early Modern England, c. 1550–1700* (Cambridge, 2000), chap. 1; John Guy, *Tudor England* (Oxford, 1988), pp. 310–19.

[28] See, eg., L. S. Goodman, "Mandamus in the Colonies," *American Journal of Legal History* [*AJLH*], I (1957), pp. 308–35, II (1958), pp. 1–34, 129–47; and Paul D. Halliday, *Habeas Corpus: From England to Empire* (Cambridge, MA, 2010).

[29] Smith, *Appeals,* esp. pp. 12–45.

negotiations with other sovereign states. It was, in short, the administrative arm of royal *imperium* and the practical source of sovereign authority for the English imperial state. As we shall see, the council invoked all of these roles and responsibilities when overseeing the American colonies.

****

Contemporary European and English theories of empire and sovereignty were expressed in the colonial charters issued to trading companies and proprietors throughout the seventeenth century.[30] The process of acquiring a charter began with individuals or corporations submitting petitions to the King-in-Council. These petitions were reviewed and either allowed or disallowed, depending on the position put forth by the petitioners, the king's pleasure, and the current state of domestic and foreign policy. Once approved in principle, the charters would be drafted by the attorney or solicitor general, who would submit them to the review of the king and council, process revisions, and ensure that the instrument was engrossed and ultimately stamped with the Great Seal.[31] Though often regarded by historians as documents in which the crown absent-mindedly relinquished its sovereign powers to trading companies and proprietors, the charters were, instead, rife with imperial, sovereign, and prerogative force, and very much acts of central will.[32] They were not in any sense an abandonment of imperial authority and sovereign responsibility by the crown. Rather, they were affirmations of these rights by virtue of the crown's ability to determine and devolve the powers enumerated therein, to examine abuses of these delegated powers when it was deemed necessary, and—in the face of abuse that derogated the king's sovereignty or the fundamental rights of subjects—to recall the charter by *quo warranto* proceedings.

The preamble of all colonial charters clearly asserted the crown's continued imperial and sovereign rights. They all included a variant of the phrase "James,

[30] For context, see Viola F. Barnes, "L and Tenure in English Colonial Charters of the Seventeenth Century," in Viola F. Barnes, et al., *Essays in Colonial History* (New Haven, 1931), pp. 1–40; Elizabeth Mancke, "Chartered Enterprises," pp. 237–62; Christopher Tomlins, "Law's Empire: Chartering English Colonies on the American Mainland in the Seventeenth Century," in Diane Kirkby and Catherine Colebourn (eds), *Law, History, Colonialism: The Reach of Empire* (Manchester, 2001), pp. 26–45.

[31] On this process, see MacMillan, *Sovereignty and Possession*, pp. 80–5.

[32] The argument that the overseas empire was not an act of central will—that it was created "in a fit of absence of mind"—derives from historiographical engagement with Seeley, *Expansion of England* (quotation at p. 8).

by the grace of God, King of England, Scotland, France and Ireland." This passage invoked the imperial power of James I, not merely as king of England but also as undisputed ruler of the larger composite monarchy over which *imperium* was asserted.[33] This imperial power was intertwined with absolute sovereign authority by the inclusion of the passage, "our especial grace, certain knowledge, and mere motion." These were personal traits bestowed by God on absolute sovereigns.[34] This passage also implicitly denied the right to establish sovereignty in the New World to anybody who did not hold *plenitudo potestatis*. This is the same authority that was assumed by Pope Alexander VI when he issued the bull *Inter caetera* (which awarded Spain all new lands west of a line of demarcation), under his "*mera liberalitate, et ex certa scientia, ac de Apostolicae potestatis plenitudine.*"[35] By drawing upon the same authority and phraseology for English patents, the crown both emphasized its independent status and ensured that its colonial charters held the same legal authority as the papal bull and similar documents issued by the other European colonizing powers.[36] This authority was communicated to the supranational world by the passage "to all whom these presents shall come, greeting." The charters, or patents, were not intended solely for internal reading, but rather were "open" (Old French *patente*) documents, which were to be shown to other English and British subjects and Europeans in order to prove that the activities described therein had the express, written authority of a sovereign prince.

One of the central purposes of the colonial charters was to claim sovereignty over extra-territorial land in a manner that would gain recognition within the wider European community. These criteria were to be found, principally, in Justinian's *Corpus*, specifically an important chapter of the

---

[33] English overlordship of France derived from the claims of Edward III. Though long in desuetude, these claims were not abandoned until the Treaty of Westphalia in 1648. For context, see David Green, "Lordship and Principality: Colonial Policy in Ireland and Aquitaine in the 1360s," *JBS*, XLVII (2008), pp. 3–29.

[34] Patricia Seed, "Taking Possession and Readings Texts: Establishing the Authority of Overseas Enterprises," *WMQ*, 3rd ser., XLIX (1992), pp. 183–209.

[35] Frances G. Davenport (ed.), *European Treaties Bearing on the History of the United States and its Dependencies* (Gloucester, MA, 1967), I, p. 62.

[36] See esp. the works of James Muldoon: "Discovery, Grant, Charter, Conquest, or Purchase: John Adams on the Legal Basis for English Possession of North America," in Christopher L. Tomlins and Bruce H. Mann (eds), *The Many Legalities of Early America*. (Chapel Hill, NC, 2001) pp. 25–46; "The Contribution of the Medieval Canon Lawyers to the Formation of International Law," *Traditio*, XXVIII (1972), pp. 483–97; "Papal Responsibility for the Infidel: Another Look at Alexander VI's *Inter caetera*," *Catholic Historical Review*, LXIV (1978), pp. 168–84.

Digest, entitled "Acquisition of ownership of things," parts of which were also abstracted in the briefer *Institutes.* Justinian's writings were, of course, never intended to be used in the context of the extra-European world, but in the absence of newer precedents they were frequently employed within the *jus commune* because of their status as *ratio scripta* of natural law. In addition, Justinian's arguments could be effectively used to delegitimize Iberian claims. Although the Spanish and Portuguese justified their sovereignty over the extra-European world on the basis of the discoveries of Columbus and the papal bulls of 1493, in the eyes of the English this was not sufficient to claim possession. Specifically, the English did not accept that discovery, coupled merely with the intention to occupy the land at some future time, was sufficient to create a possessory title in Roman law.[37] Rather, Justinian emphasized that possession required both mental intention (*animus*) and physical control (*corpus*): "there can be no acquisition of possession by intent alone, unless there be a physical holding of the thing." Because possession was only completed through territorial control, discovery and written authorizations fulfilled only the mental intention, but the title remained inchoate. "[I]f you are holding land," as the Spanish asserted they were doing through the pope's grant, "and nevertheless intend not to possess it, you will at once lose possession. Possession can therefore be lost by mere mental act, although it cannot be so acquired." Furthermore, "if an owner abandons a thing the property passes straight away to anyone who takes possession of it."[38] Thus, at least to the English, regardless of Spain's mental possession of the New World through the Columbian voyages and the papal bull, and even their occasional ceremonies of possession in the New World, it was the present state of the territory that determined rights of sovereignty and possession. Both Richard Hakluyt and John Dee, among others, had developed this argument, and the Queen herself had employed it to challenge Portuguese claims in Africa in the 1560s and Spanish claims in America in the 1580s. By the early seventeenth century, as English colonization in the New World got underway in earnest, this argument was well entrenched in English legal thought.[39]

---

[37] R. Y. Jennings, *The Acquisition of Territory in International Law* (Manchester, 1963), chap. 2.

[38] References to Justinian will be given using original book, chapter, and section numbers, which can be accessed in any edition. Justinian, *Digest,* 41.2.3.1–6; *Institutes,* 2.1.47, 4.6.4.

[39] Dee, *Limits of the British Empire,* doc. 3; Peter C. Mancall, *Hakluyt's Promise: An Elizabethan's Obsession for an English America* (New Haven, 2007), chaps. 7, 9; Ken MacMillan,

The Justinianic viewpoint regarding effective occupation was emphasized in the Virginia Company charter of 1606, in which the colonists were allowed to settle those lands "not now actually possessed by a Christian prince or people."[40] By explicitly challenging any notion that mental claims secured sovereignty, James I and his successors emphasized the importance of physical control of territory and, implicitly, denied the rights of any other claimants who, regardless of their knowledge of the land's existence, had allowed the territory to remain unoccupied. "[B]y the law of nature and nations," reads the Newfoundland Company charter of 1610, "We may of our royal authority possess our selves ... without doing wrong to any other prince ..., considering they cannot justly pretend any sovereignty ... in respect that the same remaineth so vacant and not actually possessed and inhabited by any Christian."[41] This viewpoint was nuanced in the New England patent of 1620: "[T]here is no other the subjects of any other Christian King ... by any authority from their sovereign lords or princes actually in possession."[42] The implication of this passage is that even if other Europeans were sporadically planted in patches of the territory, which was true of both the Dutch and the French in early America, unless these planters could prove though a document of similar legal status to a charter that they had settled on the authority of a sovereign prince, there was no legal claim to the territory. This position was also supported by Justinian.[43]

Of course, expressing the Roman viewpoint regarding the acquisition of sovereignty in the charters was, in itself, nothing more than a mental claim unless it was followed up by physical possession. In order to retain rights of possession, English presence had to be visible, permanent, and unassailable, for which reason the colonists were instructed to "hold, occupy, and enjoy" the territory, to make "habitation and plantation," and to "inhabit and remain there, to build and fortify." They were also ordered to erect physical

---

"Exploration, Trade, and Empire," in Norman Jones and Susan Doran (eds), *The Elizabethan World* (London, 2010), pp. 646–62.

[40] Virginia, 1606; most colonial charters are to be found online at the Avalon Project at Yale Law School (Pre-18th Century Documents), ⟨http://www.yale.edu/lawweb/avalon/pre18.htm⟩, hereafter "Yale Avalon Project."

[41] David B. Quinn and others, *New American World: A Documentary History of North America to 1612*, IV (New York, 1979), p. 133.

[42] New England, 1620, Yale Avalon Project.

[43] Justinian, *Institutes*, 2.9: "Property passes to us ... through those [acts] of the people within our authority." See also Justinian, *Digest*, 41.1.10, 41.2.1.2–3, 41.2.4, 41.2.11.

fortifications and equip the forts and the colonists with "ordnance, powder, shot, armor, and all other weapons, ammunition, and habiliments of war, both for defense and offence whatsoever."[44] Once all of these charter obligations of physical settlement were accomplished in America, the *corpus* of settlement was added to the *animus* of discovery and the charter to complete the claim to sovereignty. The territorial limits of the claim were usually specified using latitude and longitude references. Even though many of these geographical references were so vast as to be untenable (the New England patent granting land "from sea to sea"), they were legally important in isolating the boundaries of the claim. Justinian noted that it is not necessary to visit every parcel of an estate to possess it; rather "it is enough to enter any part of the estate, provided one has the purpose and intention of taking possession of the whole estate to its utmost boundaries."[45] Thus, in defining in the charter a specific area, followed by the ceremonial and physical act of settling within that region, the colonists fulfilled Justinianic requirements for possession of the whole region "to its utmost boundaries." The means by which possession was acquired were often mundane, involving building houses and fences, cultivating land, and emulating traditional English village life. Other methods that strengthened English claims included ceremonies of possession, building forts as "images of dominance," and printing maps for international dissemination.[46] All of these methods communicated both sovereignty over and "certain knowledge" of the land and its peoples and an intention to remain in and effectively use the territory, which collectively conferred a virtually unassailable right of possession in Roman law.

The litany of phrases justifying absolute sovereignty over discovered and settled New World territories also had implications for North America's first peoples. In various passages, the charters made it clear that the crown expected new-found lands to be possessed by Christians and ultimately under the sovereign authority of Christian princes. To these pregnant phrases were added more explicit claims, derived from the same early modern theories, which denied that indigenous peoples could have absolute

---

[44] Providence Island charter (1630), The National Archive of the UK [TNA]: PRO CO 124/1, fol. 5v.

[45] Justinian, *Digest*, 41.2.3.1.

[46] Patricia Seed, *Ceremonies of Possession in Europe's Conquest of the New World, 1492–1640* (Cambridge, 1995), chap. 1; MacMillan, *Sovereignty and Possession*, chaps. 4–5; MacMillan, "Center and Periphery in English Maps of North America, 1590–1685," in Martin Brückner (ed.), *Early American Cartographies* (Chapel Hill, NC, 2011), pp. 67–92. On "images of dominance," see A. P. Thornton, *Doctrines of Imperialism* (New York, 1965).

sovereignty (*imperium*) on the basis of breaches of the laws of God and nations, such as their alleged cannibalism, their supposed polygamy, and their general failure to emerge out of a "state of nature." The Virginia Company patent of 1606 cites the natives as those who "live in darkness and miserable ignorance of the true knowledge and worship of God," and who were needful of "human civility" and "settled and quiet government."[47] These concerns reflected the fundamental expectation of divine and natural law that "Godly societies," especially those that were heirs to the "universal monarchy" and thus held *imperium*, had an obligation to convert non-Christians in order to force conformity with the laws of God and nature.[48] Although the English were often ambivalent about pressing religious arguments for dispossession, they frequently defended their claims to sovereignty on the grounds that the king, as "defender of the faith" and head of a new branch of Protestantism, possessed powers and obligations of conversion equal to those of the pope.

To some writers, the natives' refusal to allow Europeans to travel through or trade in North America, or occupy empty parcels of it as neighbors, meant that they broke the natural law theory of *filiis hominum*, which held that God bestowed the entire world "to the sons of men" for the purpose of interdependency and communication.[49] Other writers in the seventeenth century justified dispossession through a rather crude interpretation of the Roman law concept of *res nullius*. This principle held that "nobody's things" remained common until they were privatized and their full potential realized, generally through placing them under man's control. In the case

---

[47] Virginia, 1606, Yale Avalon Project.

[48] Jörg Fisch, "Law as a Means and as an End: Some Remarks on the Function of European and Non-European Law in the Process of European Expansion," in W. J. Mommsen and J. A. de Moor (eds), *European Expansion and Law: The Encounter of European and Indigenous Law in 19th- and 20th-Century Africa and Asia*, (Oxford, 1992), pp. 15–38; Richard Tuck, *The Rights of War and Peace: Political Thought and the International Order From Grotius to Kant* (Oxford, 1999).

[49] See especially the work of Andrew Fitzmaurice and Anthony Pagden. Fitzmaurice: *Humanism and America: An Intellectual History of English Colonisation, 1500–1625* (Cambridge, 2003), chap. 5; "Moral Uncertainty in the Dispossession of Native Americans," in Peter C. Mancall (eds), *The Atlantic World and Virginia, 1550–1624*, (Chapel Hill, NC, 2007), pp. 383–409. Pagden: "Dispossessing the Barbarian: The Language of Spanish Thomism and the Debate over the Property Rights of the American Indians," in A. Pagden (ed.), *The Languages of Political Theory in Early-Modern Europe* (Cambridge, 1987), pp. 79–98; "The Struggle for Legitimacy and the Image of Empire in the Atlantic to c. 1700," in Canny (ed.), *OHBE*, I, pp. 34–54; *Lords of All the World*, chaps. 2–3.

of wild animals (*ferae bestiae*), this involved domestication or at least restriction of their freedom using fences. In the late sixteenth century, the *res nullius* argument was extended to land by a civilian lawyer working in England, Alberico Gentili.[50] This new principle held that realizing the potential of land involved either agricultural production or regular use as common or public property. Whether because of a nomadic hunter-gatherer lifestyle or because they were living in a "state of nature" (which provided sustenance without labor), first peoples allowed much of the land in North America to remain, in the words of several charters, "untilled." By failing to fulfill Biblical injunctions to "replenish the earth, and subdue it" (as drawn from Genesis 1:28 and 9:1), first peoples allowed the Americas to remain wilderness and failed, therefore, to establish sovereignty and possession.

Though a fiction associated with limited English understanding of the indigenous peoples' methods of land use, this "agriculturalist argument" developed throughout the seventeenth century and was expressed most aggressively by John Locke in his *Second Treatise on Government* (1689–90). To Locke, possession was acquired only when a man "mixed his labour" with the land and "joined to it something that is his own."[51] In certain regions of North America, where the land appeared to be used effectively by indigenous peoples, colonists and royal officials secured title through purchase.[52] Locke argued, however, that even when effective possession or a certain degree of civilization and political organization was demonstrated by first peoples, they nonetheless possessed only "a very moderate sovereignty," and were not equal to European absolute sovereigns.[53] Instead, they were petty kings under the *imperium* of, in the case of England, the Stuart crown. Thus,

[50] Tuck, *Rights of War and Peace*, pp. 47–50; Ken MacMillan, "Benign and Benevolent Conquest?: The Ideology of Elizabethan Expansion Revisited," *Early American Studies*, IX (2011), pp. 68–70.

[51] Pagden, *Lords of All the World*, pp. 76–80; Duncan Ivison, "The Nature of Rights and the History of Empire," in David Armitage (ed.), *British Political Thought in History, Literature, and History, 1500–1800* (Cambridge, 2006), chap. 10.

[52] Stuart Banner, *How the Indians Lost Their Land: Law and Power on the Frontier* (Cambridge, MA, 2005), chaps. 1–3, esp. pp. 44–8; William Cronon, *Changes in the Land: Indians, Colonists, and the Ecology of New England*, rev. edn (New York, 2003), chap. 3; Patricia Seed, *American Pentimento: The Invention of Indians and the Pursuit of Riches* (Minneapolis, 2001), chap. 1.

[53] Paul Corcoran, however, has argued that Locke's position on native land has been misunderstood, and that Locke saw treating with natives as the only "natural law" method of gaining possession: "John Locke on the Possession of Land: Native Title vs. the "Principle" of Vacuum

when Powhatan was "crowned" king and given a royal scarlet cloak by Captain Christopher Newport, his superiority within his native confederacy was recognized, but this same act, which matched closely the submission ceremonies in England and the various palatine jurisdictions under the Normans, Scotland under Edward I, and Ireland under Henry VIII, conferred a level of vassalage on Powhatan and, subsequently, other native kings.[54]

The charters also extended the reach of absolute sovereignty by making provision for the redress of illegal acts committed by English colonists against the subjects of other Christian princes. Until the 1660s, the charters declared "to all Christian kings ... that if any person or persons ... of the said several colonies and plantations ... shall at any time or times hereafter rob or spoil ... or do any act of unjust and unlawful hostility to any the subjects of any king ... being then in league or amity with us ... the said person ... [shall] make full restitution ..., so as the said princes ... may hold themselves fully satisfied or contented." In addition to asserting the monarch's absolute prerogative to deal with foreign matters, this passage recognizes that the subjects of other sovereign monarchs had the right to travel the seas unassailed, and to land in ports and harbors for the express purpose of trade and friendship, or as the result of shipwreck. This hostility clause did not apply in those instances when the colonists were forced to repel usurpers, or when such entrants were the king's enemies, but rather protected allies from activity deemed contrary to the laws of nature and nations, or to the laws of war, peace, prize, merchant, and the seas. If an illegal act occurred, the English crown was responsible to foreign princes for providing for satisfactory restitution. If such was not made in the prescribed time, then "the said [colony] ... shall be out of our allegiance and protection, and free for all Princes ... to pursue with hostility, as being not our subjects, ... nor to be holden ... to our protection, or dominion, or allegiance."[55] This clause was consistent with the theory

---

Domicilium," Proceedings of the Australasian Political Studies Association Annual Conference, 2007.

[54] Karen Ordahl Kupperman, *Indians and English: Facing Off in Early America* (Ithaca, NY, 2000), pp. 71–3; Nicholas Canny, "England's New World and the Old, 1480s–1630s," in Canny (ed.), *OHBE*, I, pp. 156–8. On Scotland, e.g., see Dee, *Limits of the British Empire*, pp. 72–81 (with Baliol's vassalage recorded at p. 76).

[55] E.g., Virginia, 1606, Yale Avalon Project. The absence of this passage after 1660 can probably be attributed to the fact that, in the post-Westphalian era, these provisions were assumed among sovereign powers.

of reciprocal sovereignty. The crown accepted its sovereign responsibility to protect its colonists from harm, both through continued oversight and by engaging in diplomatic disputes with other sovereign powers. In this case, however, the withdrawal of protection was precipitated by the belief that the colonists had withdrawn their allegiance by committing insurgent acts, and the mental component of possession, without which sovereignty could not be sustained, was in consequence revoked, in effect leaving the territory *de iure* if not *de facto* abandoned, and free for settlement by any other Christian prince. This passage is a pre-eminent example of the perpetual sovereign authority and right of oversight claimed by the English crown over its American plantations.

****

In addition to claiming title to extra-territorial land, the promulgation of charters was used as an opportunity to enumerate the various legal rights and powers of the crown (the center) and the colonies and colonists (the peripheries). The ability to exercise this authority differed according to the type of colony established. In the first type, the "body politic and corporate," established for trading companies, governing councils were either appointed by the king or elected by shareholders and headed by a company director. In the second type, proprietary colonies, which dominated in the Restoration period, "true and absolute lords and proprietors" with the same privileges as "any Bishop of Durham, within the Bishopric or County Palatine of Durham" were awarded vice-regal powers equal to those held in other palatine jurisdictions within the composite monarchy.[56] The proprietors thereby held a limited or regional sovereignty (*dominium*), not as expansive as the absolute sovereignty possessed by the holder of *imperium* but more powerful than the typical feudal landlord. The crown was careful to emphasize this relationship by demanding certain forms of homage from the proprietors, such as two white horses or a gold coronet, whenever the king visited the territory. These gifts were, of course, never delivered, and were never intended to be. Instead, they were symbolic demands that emphasized the superior status of the imperial prince. In the third type of

---

[56] In an exception, the last chartered seventeenth-century colony, Pennsylvania (1681), though proprietary, was not palatine, presumably because the crown wished to assert greater degrees of authority.

colony, the royal colony—which was the result not of chartered design but of perceived necessity following the conquest of Jamaica (1655) and the revocation of the charters for Virginia (1625), New Hampshire (1679), Massachusetts Bay, and Bermuda (both in 1684)—authority was exercised by crown-appointed governors general, usually individuals with military experience, who represented royal power and answered to the Privy Council.[57]

In the charters, the colonists were authorized to "make, ordain, and establish all manner of orders, laws, directions, instructions, forms and ceremonies of government and magistracy, fit and necessary for and concerning the government of the said colony." They were also permitted to "abrogate, revoke, or change" laws "as they in their good discretion, shall think to be fittest for the good of the inhabitants there," and to "correct, punish, pardon, govern, and rule all such the subjects of us."[58] Colonial officials appointed legal officers, such as judges, sheriffs, and coroners, to maintain law and order and to deliver sentences on legal matters both civil and criminal. They also introduced laws and ordinances, which, though rarely provided for explicitly in the charters, came to be accomplished by bicameral colonial assemblies comprised of elected delegates in a lower house and the governor and his council in the upper house.

To guide the legislative process and impose restraint on excessive legal innovation, the charters included the well-known "non-repugnancy" and "divergency" clauses. Though assemblies could create laws that were consistent with "the nature and constitutions of the place and people there," and thus diverge from English laws, these laws were always to be "consonant to reason, and be not repugnant or contrary, but as near as conveniently may be agreeable to the laws and statutes, and rights of this our kingdom of England."[59] As recent historians have suggested, these passages should not be interpreted as referring to the common law of England, which as Coke pointed out had no efficacy in non-domestic realms. Rather, they referred to several "brands of law, [and] types of legal reasoning, an expansive but not infinite range of legal sources."[60] This could include, for instance, the impressive range of canon, natural, civil, and equity laws operative in

---

[57] Stephen Saunders Webb, *The Governors-General: The English Army and the Definition of Empire, 1569–1681* (Chapel Hill, NC, 1979); chaps. 1, 7, Conclusion.

[58] Virginia, 1609, Yale Avalon Project.

[59] Pennsylvania, 1681, Yale Avalon Project.

[60] William Offutt, "The Atlantic Rules: The Legalistic Turn in Colonial British America" in Mancke and Shammas (eds), *Creation of the British Atlantic World*, p. 164.

England, legal systems that were appropriate for all "reasonable creatures" and could not be abrogated in preference for laws repugnant to English and Christian sensibilities. The bodies that could determine the issues of repugnancy were, presumably, both local colonial courts and assemblies, who were responsible for ensuring legislation was consonant with reason and English liberties, and the King-in-Council, who had superior powers of oversight.[61]

In order to emphasize the continued *imperium* of the English crown over these largely self-governing regions, and the application of reciprocal sovereignty, most of the colonies were expected to administer the oaths of allegiance and supremacy to new emigrants and male colonists and were strictly enjoined not to "withdraw any of the subjects or people of those lands or places from the allegiance of us . . . as their immediate Sovereign under God." Colonial subjects, whether born in England or the colonies, were also to have "liberties, franchises, and immunities, within any of our other dominions, . . . as if they had been abiding and born, within this our realm of England, or any other of our said dominions." These passages on law, allegiance, and liberties ensured that the colonists continued to recognize the sovereignty of the king, which was a personal, natural law relationship between individuals and the monarch. In exchange for their allegiance, those living in the colonies retained basic natural and civil liberties that all subjects enjoyed as part of English subjecthood. As Sir Matthew Hale wrote in the 1650s, the colonists retained "those English liberties that are incident to their persons."[62] Colonists were to be treated in the same fashion as all English subjects, which included certain customary English "liberties, franchises, and immunities," and the right to be treated according to the dictates of Christian reason (that is, the laws of God and nature).

These natural liberties were described by Coke in the second book of his *Institutes of the Laws of England* (1628), Locke in the second of his *Two Treatises on Government* (1690), and Blackstone in the first volume of his *Commentaries* (1765). To Blackstone, these liberties were the "absolute and

---

[61] Mary Sarah Bilder, *The Transatlantic Constitution: Colonial Legal Culture and the Empire* (Cambridge, MA, 2004), chap. 2; D. O. McGovney, "The British Origins of Judicial Review of Legislation," *University of Pennsylvania Law Review* [*UPLR*], XLIII (1944), pp. 1–49; McGovney, "The British Privy Council's Power to Restrain the Legislatures of Colonial America," *UPLR*, XLIV (1945), pp. 59–93.

[62] Yale (ed.), *Hale's Prerogatives*, pp. 42–3; Halliday and White, "The Suspension Clause," pp. 633–44.

subordinate rights of every Englishmen ... founded on nature and reason."[63] They included rights of *personal security*, which involved the protection of life, limb, health, and reputation, and, generally, the right not to be deprived of these except by the due process of law, which included the right to trial by jury for legal cases of a certain severity. Next were the rights of *personal liberty*, including freedom of association and locomotion, and freedom from "honourable exile" (being forced from the realm without a just sentence at law), arbitrary arrest, imprisonment, and oppression (the latter subsumed under *habeas corpus*). The third absolute right was that of *property*, specifically the free use, enjoyment, and disposal of acquisitions according to set forms of law and the right not to be taxed except by common consent through legislative representation. Subordinate rights included, for example, limitations set on royal prerogatives, the right to appeal to the king for redress of injuries (both misprision of the law and gaining relief through equity when the law was inequitable), and the right to bear arms in order to protect all of these natural rights. It is these historical natural rights, of course, that would be interpreted and defended in the Petition of Right (1628), the Bill of Rights (1689), and the Declaration of Independence (1776), and would be codified in the United States Constitution.[64] Though conformable to the dictates of nature and reason, these were "English liberties" because they were forged in England (in, for example, Magna Carta and *Prerogativa Regis*) and reflected historical English usage. Such rights might be interpreted differently in other parts of the empire, where custom and usage, though not contrary to nature, diverged. Because, as Hale noted, the colonies were acquired by the king "under his great seal of England," they were "parcel of the dominions though not the realm of England."[65] Thus, while the common law and parliamentary legislation did not apply, English liberties (to Blackstone, "the birthright of every subject" and the unique marker of

---

[63] William Blackstone, *Commentaries on the Laws of England, Vol. I: Of the Rights of Persons* [1765] (ed.), Stanley N. Katz (Chicago, 1979), pp. 121–41.

[64] On the "international" nature of the Declaration of Independence, see David Armitage, *The Declaration of Independence: A Global History* (Cambridge, MA, 2008). See also Jack P. Greene, "Empire and Identify from the Glorious Revolution to the American Revolution," in Marshall (ed.), *OHBE*, II, pp. 208–30; and Burke, "Speech on Conciliation with America," in Elofson (ed.), pp. 119–21, 156–8.

[65] Yale (ed.), *Hale's Prerogatives*, p. 43.

English identity) did, because the acquests were made by James and Charles in their position as king of England.[66]

****

One of the more contentious issues in Anglo-American relations in the seventeenth century is the extent to which, following the issuance of the colonial charters and all of the delegated powers they enumerated, the King-in-Council retained oversight in the colonies. This relationship was made explicit in only a few of the early charters. The short-lived 1606 Virginia Company charter provided for a "royal council" comprised of privy councilors, who had "the superior managing and directing...of the said several colonies." Likewise, Sir Robert Heath's palatine charter for Carolina, never in fact executed, required him to conform "to instructions and directions signed by our royal hand," which would involve the council applying the privy seal to royal instructions. Beyond these brief passages in, as it turned out, transient charters, no pre-Restoration charters specified the continuing role of the King-in-Council in these affairs, especially regarding review of legislation, and none granted colonists the right of appeal. Instead, it took until the New York charter of 1664 for the crown's role in appeal and review to be explicitly mentioned, after which such language became standard. In the Pennsylvania charter of 1681, for instance, the king, through his council, reserved the "receiving, hearing, and determining of the appeal sovereignty or lawful prerogative of us,... or contrary to the faith and allegiance due [to us]...the said laws shall be adjudged and declared to be void."[67]

The absence of these passages prior to the Restoration charters caused a prominent early-twentieth-century historian of colonial America to observe that "the superintendence of colonial affairs by the Privy Council was not the outcome of deliberate policy," but rather was an ad hoc, reactive, and consequently heavily disputed system that developed in the Restoration period.[68] Many other historians have sustained this argument, generally accepting that the pre-Restoration period was the "pre-history" of imperial administrative oversight. In turn, some putative "end of American independ-

---

[66] Blackstone, *Commentaries*, I, p. 105.

[67] Pennsylvania, 1681, Yale Avalon Project.

[68] H.E. Egerton, "The Seventeenth and Eighteenth Century Privy Council in Its Relations with the Colonies," *Journal of Comparative Legislation and International Law*, 3rd ser., VII (1925), p. 1.

ence" is attributed to the creation of an enduring, largely commercially-directed colonial council in 1675 under the control of the imperial secretary, William Blathwayt, or the suppression of Nathaniel Bacon's rebellion in Virginia in 1676, or the aftermath of the Glorious Revolution of 1688, which led, in 1696, to the imperially-minded Board of Trade.[69]

Perhaps the best way to evaluate the argument for ineffectual imperial control before about 1660 is to re-examine the instance usually assigned a central role in the development of the empire after that date, the crown's struggles with Massachusetts Bay. Beginning in the 1630s, the Massachusetts General Court frequently challenged any claims of the Privy Council to oversight, as well as the right of colonists to appeal to England, on the grounds that these were not privileges granted by the crown in the charter. Instead, in the Court's interpretation, the charter awarded security from outside interference, including from the king himself, a position it believed to be consistent with fundamental English liberties. Their recalcitrance was tangibly demonstrated when, in contravention of normal practice, the charter (and, thus, the company) was physically carried to America, thereby preventing the Privy Council from calling company officials to respond to important matters. The situation was exacerbated when the colonists were required to swear fidelity to the commonwealth instead of allegiance to the king, and appeals to the King-in-Council were routinely forbidden. In response, the council issued a proclamation that all emigrants to America had to take the oath of allegiance before departing, in the process staying several ships. It also attempted to vacate the charter in 1637 because of these infringements of the king's sovereignty, although the mid-century constitutional struggles meant that the resumption of this conflict had to await the Restoration. In 1661, the alleged abuses of the charter were formally protested by those aggrieved by the actions of the Massachusetts Bay government, and the Privy Council committed itself to bringing the colony to heel. This lengthy process involved sending numerous commissions to America, particularly under the auspices of the crown customs officer Edward Randolph, and was only completed with the cancellation of the charter in 1684. The colony was subsequently drawn into the royal Dominion of New England the following year and a new charter, issued in 1691, clarified explicitly the rights of the crown, using virtually the same language

---

[69] See the work by Jack P. Greene, J. M. Sosin, Ian K. Steele, and Stephen Saunders Webb cited above in notes 1 and 4.

as that in the Pennsylvania charter of a decade earlier.[70] This episode is often used to prove that the crown's effective commitment to imperial control emerged only after the Restoration.

This received version of the origins of imperial control overlooks the important and historic role of empire and sovereignty in these affairs. Even though there were few direct passages in the early charters that specified crown supervision of the colonies, there was no need (and little historical precedent) for making such overt statements. Instead, the various passages associated with law, liberty, allegiance, and supranational relations, present from the 1606 Virginia charter onward, all provided for this oversight. The passages on allegiance and liberty implicitly awarded the right of appeal to the king, else colonial subjects would be denied the privileges associated with their imperial subjecthood and the doctrine of reciprocal sovereignty derogated. Similarly, consistent with the crown's absolute prerogative role in ensuring that no inequitable or unreasonable law was created or in force anywhere in the empire, the repugnancy and divergency clauses implicitly allowed for conciliar review of colonial legislation, else these clauses would have served no practical function. In short, "it probably did not even occur to the granting authorities that a patent appeal reservation was necessary... [because] there was probably a consciousness that... the crown retained supervisory jurisdiction."[71] The same can be said of the crown's ability to review colonial legislation for repugnant elements, since the continued Englishness of colonists guaranteed that the king could be relied upon to extirpate unnatural, unreasonable, or inequitable laws. Furthermore, as the crown had the sole legal responsibility for dealing with foreign affairs, its role was paramount from the beginning of colonial activities.[72]

Even though it took until the Restoration period for these rights and responsibilities to receive explicit formulation in the charters, the relevant passages merely codified centuries of historical and decades of colonial practice. Under the early Stuarts, the council heard French complaints over English claims to exclusive rights over the Newfoundland fisheries,

---

[70] Bliss, *Revolution and Empire*, pp. 227–36; Egerton, "Privy Council," pp. 6–8; Smith, *Appeals*, pp. 45–63; Sosin, *English America and the Restoration*, chap. 13.

[71] Smith, *Appeals*, p. 42.

[72] The remainder of this section is based on MacMillan, *Atlantic Imperial Constitution*. For primary materials, see W. L. Grant, J. Munro, and A. W. Fitzroy (eds), *Acts of the Privy Council, Colonial Series* [*APCC1*], I (1613–1680) (Hereford, 1908); W. Noel Sainsbury (eds), *Calendar of State Papers, Colonial Series, 1574–1660* [*CSPC*] (London, 1860).

which had led to the capturing of a French ship. Providing reparations to the French involved turning the matter over to the civilian Court of Admiralty for a decision, instructing the Lord Deputy of Ireland (in whose harbour the ship currently resided) to restore the ship to its owners, and later regulating, for the benefit of both English subjects and foreigners, how the Grand Banks would be governed in the "Western Charter" (1634). In 1613, the French also complained of English depredations committed by Samuel Argall, on orders from Virginia, against their settlements in Nova Scotia and Maine. Further complaints came after the brothers David and Thomas Kirke razed several French settlements in 1629. This dispute ultimately led to protracted discussions over who held sovereignty over Canada, a question that was resolved by treaty in 1632 with England's recognition of French claims to Acadia, though not to Maine. Similar complaints were brought over English actions by the Spanish. In 1620, the Spanish ambassador complained of English plans to settle Guiana, which he claimed was part of Spain's possessions. The council suspended by proclamation any English actions until the claims could be investigated, and saw to the imprisonment of Captain Roger North in the Tower of London, and the impounding of his cargo, when he did not heed these orders. The following year, settlers in Bermuda were accused of taking as a prize a Spanish shipwrecked vessel, a claim that was investigated by the council and admiralty before restitution was authorized. The council deemed it "expedient to give the ambassador all due content," who subsequently "acknowledged the speedy justice they had done to him." These incidents also caused James I to deny merchants a Caribbean charter, which instead had to await the reign of Charles I, when relations with Spain had deteriorated.

Conciliar activities were not restricted to, nor even dominated by, matters of external relations. The council through proclamation also authorized the Virginia lottery and later revoked it because of abuses; allowed for the transportation of women, children, and convicts to Virginia and Bermuda; issued numerous proclamations to the effect that Virginia was to be the sole importer of tobacco into England; and instructed the colony not to rely on tobacco monoculture to the exclusion of other activities, such as building ironworks, preserving trees that produced fruits and spices, and ensuring a wide variety of crops were planted in arable land. It also routinely issued instructions to the governors of Virginia, inquired into the defensive ability of the colonies, and established policies about the transportation of tobacco, including an early suggestion that plantation commodities should only be shipped in "English bottoms" and should first land in London. It also heard and determined a host of disputes between private individuals, considered overlapping charter claims (in Canada, the Caribbean, and Maryland), and, of course, busied itself with the recalcitrant colony of Massachusetts Bay. All of this was part of the King-in-Council's responsibility to assist the colonies in establishing self-sufficient, defensible, and economically viable societies, while also protecting the crown's interests in trade and other prerogatives.

The crown also showed interest in the legal and governmental makeup of the colonies. In 1620, the Virginia Company wrote of its intention to submit to the king and council for their "view and approbation" its abstract of "the laws of England proper for the use of that plantation," so that these laws would "receive the influence of their life" from that body.[73] Whether this was done before Virginia became a royal colony is unclear, but it does show some early recognition of the crown's role in reviewing laws. In a very well known series of events, beginning in 1622 the council received a number of complaints from John Bargrave, Nathaniel Butler, and other planters in Bermuda and Virginia, who complained of the "popular" (democratic) form of government, the poor defensibility of Virginia, and the abuses caused by wealthy landowners against lesser planters. In response to these petitions, and to the news that the Virginia colony had recently been attacked by the Powhatans, the king issued a "commission under the great seal" for a committee of "sufficient and sincere" men to "inquire of the true estate of... Virginia and the Summer Islands [Bermuda]." The first in a long line of conciliar commissions and committees that would be created to oversee the American colonies, this body worked with considerable diligence, sending investigators to Virginia, calling company officials to answer, and ultimately recommending the revocation of the Virginia Company patent, accomplished through *quo warranto* proceedings in 1624.[74]

The process was completed in May 1625, when Charles I issued a proclamation that clarified the imperial relationship between the center and periphery. He declared that he held the "territories of Virginia and the Somers Island, as also that of New England... to be part of our royal empire,

---

[73] Council for Virginia, *A Declaration of the State of the Colonie and Affaires in Virginia* (London, 1620), p. 8.

[74] See Wesley Frank Craven, *Dissolution of the Virginia Company: The Failure of a Colonial Experiment* (Gloucester, MA, 1932).

descended upon us and undoubtedly belonging and appertaining unto us."
The king asserted that he was "bound by our regal office, to protect, maintain,
and support the same...as any part of our dominions."[75] In this proclamation, Charles asserted *imperium* and its associated rights and responsibilities
not merely over Virginia, whose government the king assumed, but also over
the other American plantations, presumably including those that would
be founded subsequently, such as Massachusetts Bay (1629) and Maryland
(1632). It was under the guise of his "regal office" that other proclamations
soon followed, including ones ensuring that emigrants, particularly to New
England and Maryland, take the oaths of allegiance and supremacy before
departing England, and several prohibiting colonists from trading weapons
with the indigenous peoples of America, which both threatened the security
of the colonies and had potential to incur the complaints of other European
colonizing powers.[76] In 1641, Charles also issued a proclamation expressing
his concern that certain colonial officials were refusing to allow colonists to
leave the plantations. Aware that his subjects were thereby "deprived not only
of that due liberty of free subjects...but also of those opportunities of
advancing their estates," the king ordered that all who were free of "debt,
service, or otherwise" were free to remove themselves to other places.[77] This
proclamation ensured that those English natural rights to liberty and property incident to the person of the king's subjects were not derogated by
deputies of the crown.

Much of this activity was handled not by the council of the whole but
rather by conciliar sub-committees, the creation of which serves as an index
of the efficiency and seriousness with which colonial affairs came to
be managed by the center. In 1632, a "Committee on the New England
Plantations" was formed, and from its impetus emerged, in 1634, the
"Committee for Foreign Plantations." The committee was charged with
"making laws and orders for government of English colonies planted in
foreign parts," with powers to "remove governors, and require an account of
their government; to appoint judges and magistrates and establish courts; to
hear and determine all manner of complaints from the colonies...[and] to
have power over all charters and patents." Although this would appear

[75] Charles I, *A Proclamation for Settling the Plantation of Virginia* (London, 1625).

[76] On the oath of allegiance, see Alison Games, *Migration and the Origins of the English Atlantic World* (Cambridge, MA, 1999), pp. 19–20.

[77] Quoted in Games, *Migration*, p. 201.

contrary to the charter privileges that allowed for self-government and the creation of laws relevant to colonial circumstances, in practice the committee was expected to review colonial laws for repugnancy, and to hear appeals from the colonies and protect the sovereign interests of the crown. When the commission was reappointed in 1636, it was further instructed to govern the colonies "according to the laws and constitutions there," which accorded better with the original charter privileges. This committee, comprised of a dozen or so Privy Counsellors, of which a quorum was five, continued to exist until the Privy Council went into abeyance in 1642.[78]

The imperial policies of the early Stuarts were, generally, carried into the Commonwealth period, modified as necessary for a republican form of government. One of the more significant policies initiated during this period was the Navigation Act of 1651. This parliamentary Act, sometimes seen as the watershed moment in imperial policy-making, was designed to ensure that goods being transported to or from English territories were carried either in English ships or in ships of the country of production, which would first land in England, to the benefit of both English merchants and the government.[79] While unique in that its terms reflected republican free-trade principles rather than royal monopolies, the Navigation Act and its implementation by the Council of State was, in fact, little different from the various trade policies designed to benefit England and its American colonies initiated under the early Stuarts. Although the use of legislation, rather than proclamation, would appear to represent a shift in how colonial governance was conceived from the center, this simply embodied how a republican, rather than a monarchical, government could regulate matters of imperial trade. Another role of the Council of State during this period was "reducing" the colonies, particularly royalist-leaning ones such as Virginia, to obedience to the central government. Though undertaken more actively than Charles I's engagement with Virginia and Massachusetts between 1625 and 1637, the principle behind these claims to authority was based on the same historical theories of empire and liberty.[80] Finally, during the interregnum, sub-committees of the Council of State heard petitions,

---

[78] Charles M. Andrews, "Committees, Commissions, and Councils of Trade and Plantations, 1622–1675," *Johns Hopkins University Studies in Historical and Political Science*, ser. 26, nos. 1–3 (1908), pp. 15–17; Egerton, "Privy Council," p. 4.

[79] Braddick, *State Formation*, pp. 411–13.

[80] See Pestana, *English Atlantic in an Age of Revolution*, esp. chaps. 3, 5.

referred matters to the admiralty, remonstrated and instructed colonial governors, and reviewed claims to overlapping parcels of property, much as the committees of 1634 and 1636 had done.[81]

The responsibilities of the Council of State shifted back to the Privy Council after 1660. Although the various commissions and committees of trade and plantations that came and went in the first fifteen years of the Restoration suggest that the council was struggling to find a sustainable administrative mechanism for the empire, these bodies, which were either sub-committees of, or answered to, the Privy Council, nonetheless bustled with activity, particularly regarding affairs of the royal colonies and the actions taken against Massachusetts Bay.[82] The two salaried committees of trade and plantations that were created in 1670 and 1672, for instance, met a total of 208 times, averaging approximately two meetings each week during the working months of the year, a figure that does not take into account meetings of the council as a whole.[83] The committee of 1670 was given a lengthy commission from Charles II. Its members were instructed to inquire into the "condition of all and every of our said respective colonies"; to consider and determine any "neglect, or miscarriage" committed by govern-ors or deputies that "tend to the abuse of our authority"; to "ensure the due observance and preservation of justice"; to hold a "continual correspond-ence" with all plantations; to acquire and examine all charters and determine whether the "privileges, rights, or properties" therein were infringed; and to inform themselves how the colonies were "fortified" and "possessed." Charles also reminded the members that, "as you are not to permit any of our loving subjects to be oppressed ... you are carefully to examine ... all such laws, as have been at any time made ... [and] if any of the said laws be found inconvenient or contrary to the laws of this land, or to the honour and justice of our government, all such laws may be immediately nulled."[84] These instructions were based on the passages on sovereignty and prerogative within the early Stuart charters (to become more explicit in the Restoration charters), Charles I's proclamation of 1625, his commissions to the 1634 and

[81] *CSPC*, pp. 328–479; Andrews, "Committees," chap. 2; Bliss, *Revolution and Empire*, chaps. 3–4.

[82] Egerton, "Privy Council," pp. 4–6.

[83] Andrews, "Committees," chap. 5; R. P. Bieber, "The British Plantation Councils of 1670–4," *English Historical Review*, XL (1925), pp. 93–106; E. E. Rich, "The First Earl of Shaftesbury's Colonial Policy," *Transactions of the Royal Historical Society*, 5th ser., VII (1957), pp. 47–70.

[84] Andrews, "Committees," Appendix II, pp. 117–26.

1636 committees, and the practical activities of the Privy Council and republican Council of State throughout the seventeenth century. The same general instructions would be issued to the 1672, 1675, and 1696 standing conciliar committees, the last of which would exist until 1782, revealing the overall continuity of imperial governance in the seventeenth century.

****

The theories of empire and sovereignty that gained currency in the late medieval and Tudor period shaped England's American colonies in several key ways. They were embedded in the colonial charters, which explained to Europeans and, less directly, American indigenous peoples, how lawful possession was being claimed and sustained by a sovereign and imperial prince who recognized no higher earthly authority. Through passages about law, allegiance, and liberty, the charters set the rules of empire and ensured that colonies and colonists maintained an historical relationship between the crown and English subjects abroad. The crown applied these theories in its engagement with other European colonizing powers, initially in the promises made in the charters, and subsequently in dispute resolution and, when appropriate, formal treaty negotiation. To facilitate these claims to sovereignty and possession against competing powers, various principles of Roman law were accessed in the charters and afterward, which accorded with the *jus commune* (a combination of the laws of nature, nations, war, peace, prize, and the seas) used to adjudicate supranational relations.

Perhaps most saliently, crown powers of review, appeal, and sovereign oversight were exercised in a manner consistent with how they were carried out throughout the "British" composite monarchy of diverse political territories. Though often unspecified in the colonial charters, the crown's right to provide such oversight was never abandoned by that imperial body. Instead, the mere existence of the charters, issued at the discretion of the crown and stamped with the Great Seal of England, together with the imperial and sovereign statements in their preambles, and the devolution of the powers they subsequently enumerated, emphasized this perpetual role. Using a combination of imperial authority, independent sovereignty, royal prerogatives, and domestic and natural laws, the crown, through the administrative body of the Privy Council, maintained regular, though generally non-interventionist, oversight over the American empire. In the pre-Restoration period the crown recognized that the colonies (as other dominions of the English imperial crown) had comprehensive, self-regulating powers based on unique circumstances. Its interventions usually involved matters associated with assisting in the success of colonial endeavors, regulating monopoly rights and foreign and domestic trade, the derogation or abrogation of the king's sovereignty, disputes between separate colonies (in which superior judicial powers were required), and concerns that subjects be treated according to the dictates of reason and nature. The powers of review, appeal, and oversight that were conferred upon the Board of Trade in 1696 did not signal new imperial policy, but rather reflected already existing or evolving practice, within both the American colonies and the wider composite monarchy. Crown intervention in colonial affairs throughout the seventeenth century was not intermittent, reactive, absent-minded, and reflective merely of a fitful "colonial and commercial" rather than active "imperial" policy. Instead, it was the product of the historical, principled, and broadly consistent (though hardly perfect nor uncontested) imperial relations forged in the medieval and early modern composite monarchy headed by the English crown.

This is not to dispute the general argument that imperial administration after about 1675 became more "vigorous and systematic" in strictly enforcing trade policies, strengthening the powers of colonial governors and, consequently and not without contest, weakening the authority of colonial representative assemblies.[85] Instead, it is to suggest that the rights and responsibilities of the crown to exercise those mechanisms of imperial oversight that were applied throughout the seventeenth century were consistent with English historical and contemporary theories of empire and sovereignty. This imperial oversight must, however, be seen in a different light from that which would come to characterize metropolitan involvement and the consequent center–periphery relationship in the eighteenth century. That relationship, dominated by a powerful English Parliament that assumed new imperial responsibilities against the backdrop of an increasingly impotent Privy Council and a casual Hanoverian crown, was the one being contested by John Adams, James Otis, and others in the period after 1760. It was this novel imperial relationship, and not its historical predecessor, that would ultimately lead to colonial rebellion. To properly understand the historical and functional center–periphery relationship in America in the seventeenth century, we must cast our glance

---

[85] Greene, *Peripheries and Center*, p. 13.

backward to the English empire of the Tudors, not forward to the British Empire of the Hanoverians.

Select Bibliography

CHARLES M. ANDREWS, *The Colonial Period of American History: The Settlements* (New Haven, 1934).

DAVID ARMITAGE, *The Ideological Origins of the British Empire* (Cambridge, 2000).

ROBERT M. BLISS, *Revolution and Empire: English Politics and the American Colonies in the Seventeenth Century* (Manchester, 1990).

ANDREW FITZMAURICE, *Humanism and America: An Intellectual History of English Colonization, 1500–1625* (Cambridge, 2003).

JACK P. GREENE, *Peripheries and Center: Constitutional Development in the Extended Polities of the British Empire and the United States, 1607–1788* (Athens, GA, 1986).

KEN MACMILLAN, *The Atlantic Imperial Constitution: Center and Periphery in the English Atlantic World* (Houndmills, 2011).

KEN MACMILLAN, *Sovereignty and Possession in the English New World: The Legal Foundations of Empire, 1576–1640* (Cambridge, 2006).

CARLA GARDINA PESTANA, *The English Atlantic in an Age of Revolution, 1640–1661* (Cambridge, MA, 2004).

J. M. SOSIN, *English America and the Restoration Monarchy of Charles II: Transatlantic Politics, Commerce, and Kinship* (Lincoln, NE, 1980).

STEPHEN SAUNDERS WEBB, *1676: The End of American Independence* (Cambridge, MA, 1984).

4

Toleration and Empire

The Origins of American Religious Pluralism*

Evan Haefeli

> ... another benefit, which accrues to the monarchy by a toleration,
> and that is a balance at home: For though it be improbably, it may so
> happen, that either the conforming or non-conforming party may be
> undutiful; the one is then a balance to the other.[1]

Denominational pluralism and religious toleration are arguably more
closely associated with the United States of America than with any other
nation. The Dutch, of course, claim an affinity for toleration, but not the
pluralism—the open coexistence of multiple faiths, Christian or not—that
is widely believed to be essential to the creation of the United States.
American pluralism has evolved, been challenged, theorized, and theolo-
gized, but never questioned as a fundamental hallmark of American society.
The concept of pluralism often provides something of a nationalist cultural
bridge across the Revolution, uniting the American colonies with the independent United States. Critical studies of religion in early America may
focus on pluralism's limitations but they never doubt either its existence or
its intrinsic value and feel no very great need to explain just how and why

* Earlier versions of this chapter were presented at the University of Hamburg, Harvard
University, the University of Chicago, the Massachusetts Historical Society, the annual confer-
ences of the American Historical Association and the Omohundro Institute for Early American
History and Culture as well as the "Rethinking Religion in India" conference in New Delhi. The
author would like to thank the participants at these events, as well as the following individuals
for their comments on earlier drafts: Christopher L. Brown; Martha Minow; David Como;
Stephen Taylor; Scott Sowerby; Sam Haselby; Owen Stanwood; Jon Butler; and Peter Marshall.
Last but not least, I thank Stephen Foster's meticulous and relentless editorial work.

[1] William Penn, *A Perswasive to Moderation to Dissenting Christians* (London, 1685), p. 32.

America became a land of many churches instead of just one (as in the Latin American colonies).[2]

When historians have tried to explain why the thirteen colonies that declared independence in 1776 were so religiously diverse their accounts never extend beyond the boundaries of the future United States.[3] Instead they invoke, jointly or severally: the North American environment; the logical imperatives of colonizing a new land; the influence of a particular ethnic group (such as the Dutch); the brilliance of a particular advocate of toleration, be he (it is always a he) Roger Williams, William Penn, James Madison, or Thomas Jefferson; the influence of a particular denomination such as the Quakers; or the compelling example of a particular colony.[4] The question is never "why" toleration and pluralism, but "when," "where," and, occasionally, "how much."[5] The fundamental assumption that toleration and pluralism are America's distinctive destiny is always axiomatic, even in the current debate about the role of religion in American public life.[6]

---

[2] For examples, see: Carla Gardina Pestana, *Liberty of Conscience and the Growth of Religious Diversity in Early America, 1636–1786* (Providence, RI, 1986); Mark Häberlein, *The Practice of Pluralism: Congregational Life and Religious Diversity in Lancaster, Pennsylvania, 1730–1820* (University Park, PA, 2009); William R. Hutchinson, *Religious Pluralism in America: The Contentious History of a Founding Ideal* (New Haven, 2003); Chris Beneke, *Beyond Toleration: The Religious Origins of American Pluralism* (Oxford, 2006). Ned Landsman, "Roots, Routes, and Rootedness: Diversity, Migration, and Toleration in Mid-Atlantic Pluralism," *Early American Studies*, II (2004), pp. 267–309 is an excellent introduction to aspects of colonial pluralism.

[3] Some notable examples: Thomas J. Curry, *The First Freedoms: Church and State in America to the Passage of the First Amendment* (Oxford, 1986); James H. Hutson, *Church and State in America: The First Two Centuries* (Cambridge, 2008); William G. McLoughlin, *New England Dissent, 1630–1833: The Baptists and the Separation of Church and State* (Cambridge, MA, 1971); James Lowell Underwood and W. Lewis Burke (eds), *The Dawn of Religious Freedom in South Carolina* (Columbia, SC, 2006).

[4] Some examples: Thomas E. Buckley, *Church and State in Revolutionary Virginia, 1776–1787* (Charlottesville, VA, 1977); Paul Finkleman, "The Soul and the State: Religious Freedom in New York and the Origin of the First Amendment," in Stephen L. Shechter and Richard B. Bernstein (eds), *New York and the Union* (Albany, NY, 1990), pp. 78–105; J. William Frost, *A Perfect Freedom: Religious Liberty in Pennsylvania* (University Park, PA, 1993), pp. 1–9. Among colony founders, Roger Williams has gotten more attention on this issue than William Penn. Important studies include: Edmund S. Morgan, *Roger Williams: The Church and the State* (New York, 1987); Edwin S. Gaustad, *Liberty of Conscience: Roger Williams in America* (Grand Rapids, MI, 1991); Mary Maples Dunn, *William Penn: Politics and Conscience* (Princeton, 1967).

[5] For example, Frank Lambert, *The Founding Fathers and the Place of Religion in America* (Princeton, 2002).

[6] This assumption frames the current debate about religion in America. Some examples: Jon Meacham, *American Gospel: God, the Founding Fathers, and the Making of a Nation* (New York,

In actual fact, American religious freedom was less an intrinsic national virtue than the default option for those who sought to forge a new country out of a baker's dozen of provinces torn out of the British Empire.[7] The American colonies had not been founded with the intention of creating an independent United States, nor were toleration and religious diversity restricted to the thirteen that eventually did so. Several colonies with some sort of pluralism remained within the British Empire (Quebec, Nova Scotia, and the Leeward Islands being notable cases), while several of the newly independent states retained a religious establishment. It was the variety of colonial religious arrangements, not a shared ideal of religious freedom, which made American pluralism possible if not necessary. For the United States, religious liberty is a post-colonial necessity turned into a national virtue.

The religious history of England and its emerging empire provided the vital context for the emergence of American pluralism. The nature of the connection between American religious pluralism and English religious politics has been obscured by the tendency, on the one hand, of British Imperial historians to conflate the religious history of the Empire with that of the Church of England,[8] and on the other, of American historians to study religion only in relation to a particular place (usually New England) or particular denomination (such as the Quakers). Events in England are usually treated as little more than the source of persecution that drove religious dissidents to seek freedom in America. However, to view America as a refuge from England misreads the colonial dynamic. The colonies were not refuges from English power. They were extensions of it in the first instance, the possessors of privileges granted and protected by English authorities until,

---

2006); Martha Nussbaum, *Liberty of Conscience: In Defense of America's Tradition of Religious Equality* (New York, 2008); Steven Waldman, *Founding Faith: How our Founding Fathers Forged a Radical New Approach to Religious Liberty* (New York, 2008).

[7] Various aspects of this dilemma are treated in Chris Beneke and Christopher S. Grenda (eds), *The First Prejudice: Religious Tolerance and Intolerance in Early America* (Philadelphia, 2011).

[8] Rowan Strong, *Anglicanism and the British Empire, c. 1700–1850* (Oxford, 2007), and Andrew Porter, *Religion versus Empire: British Protestant Missionaries and Overseas Expansion, 1700–1914* (Manchester, 2004), identify Anglicanism with British imperialism by beginning their studies when the Society for the Propagation of the Gospel in Foreign Parts was created (1701) and overlooking the previous hundred years.

unexpectedly and not without bitter resistance, they became independent.[9] The tumultuous series of changes in church and state in early modern Britain coincided with the establishment of most of the North American colonies and one way or another produced a hodgepodge of conflicting arrangements in America, only some of them favoring pluralism.

To discuss the early religious history of the British Empire is to confront a complex situation that varied substantially over time and place.[10] Both at the Imperial center and throughout its dependencies there were competing, contradictory visions of the way the state should treat the church, each favoring certain groups while disadvantaging others. Contention, dissension, and efforts at reform were regular features of religious life from the foundation of the colonies up through the American Revolution. The proudly "Protestant Empire" of the eighteenth century was the cumulative composite product of the ambiguities of the Reformation in England in its first century, the abolition of episcopacy and the emergence of new sects (especially Quakerism) during the Interregnum of 1642–1660, and the makeshift religious settlements of the Restoration and Glorious Revolution, along with the failure of various schemes of "comprehension" to make the national church fit the heterogeneous religious complexion of the nation, the Union of England and Scotland (in 1707), immigration from France and Germany, successive attempts to provide relief for the civil disabilities of British Catholics, and a long series of military conquests that incidentally and haphazardly expanded the religious diversity of those denominated British subjects.

Ironically, the misleading idea that America was a place of religious refuge from England's stormy religious and political history, not an active participant in it, is a product of that self-same history. Robert Cushman, a founder of Separatist Plymouth, claimed that, "If it should please God to punish his people in the Christian countries of Europe ... here is a way opened for such as have wings to fly into this wilderness."[11] Anglicans of all sorts took his

---

[9] Indeed, this chapter can be seen as an effort to insert the colonies into the increasingly sophisticated literature on toleration in early modern England. See especially John Coffey, *Persecution and Toleration in Early Modern England, 1558–1689* (Harlow, 2000), and Alexandra Walsham, *Charitable Hatred: Tolerance and Intolerance in England, 1500–1700* (Manchester, 2006).

[10] Carla Pestana's overview *Protestant Empire: Religion and the Making of the British Atlantic World* (Philadelphia, 2009) is a rare attempt to tell this story.

[11] Robert Cushman, *A Sermon Preached in Plimouth in New-England* (London, 1622), (sig. A2v).

point in their own way: they understood that only one part of North America, New England, could be considered a refuge, though they saw its foundation as an act of disloyalty. The historian White Kennett, a Tory turned Whig, observed in 1706 "that it was the Unhappiness of New-England and the adjoyning Parts, to be first planted and inhabited by Persons who were generally disaffected to the Church by Law establisht in England, and had many of them taken Refuge or Retirement in those Parts, on Account of their Suffering for Non-conformity here at home."[12] Kennett's remark echoes the 1638 complaint of Archbishop William Laud (the man whose church reforms the Puritans were fleeing), about the "universal running to New England, and god knows whither," which concluded, "this it is, when men think nothing is their advantage, but to run from government."[13] In 1699, the High Church Tory, Edward Ward, mocked the pretensions of Separatists and Puritans to have fled the mother country for reasons of conscience in his satirical account of New England, which opens with the tongue-in-cheek claim that "Bishops, Bailiffs, and Bastards, were the three Terrible Persecutions which chiefly drove our unhappy Brethren to seek their Fortunes in our Forreign Collonies."[14] And in 1776, Thomas Paine effectively tied the trope of religious refuge to American nationalism when he wrote that the "reformation was preceded by the discovery of America, as if the Almighty graciously meant to open a sanctuary to the persecuted in future years, when home should afford neither friendship nor safety."[15]

Despite the consensus of such disparate individuals as Laud and Paine, it is clear that only some colonists embraced the idea of America as a religious refuge. Even those who did, as in New England, did so in very restricted ways. Most Americans, as the histories of both Massachusetts and Virginia demonstrate, strove to reduce religious diversity and favored some sort of religious establishment. Indeed, the Church of England, supported by the

---

[12] White Kennett, *An Account of the Society for Propagating the Gospel in Foreign Parts* (London, 1706), p. 10.

[13] Laud to Wentworth, May 14, 1638 in James Bliss (ed.), *The Works of Archbishop Laud* (New York, 1975), VI, p. 523.

[14] Edward Ward, *A Trip to New England with a Character of the Country and People, both English and Indian* (London, 1699), p. 3. This is a satirical account. Ward never actually visited New England, which makes his published impressions all the more telling about the region's reputation.

[15] Thomas Paine, *Common Sense Addressed to the Inhabitants of America* (Philadelphia, 1776), p. 29.

Society for the Propagation of the Gospel in Foreign Parts (SPG) and many of its adherents among the colonists, first began to lay effective claim to an empire-wide degree of strength and influence only *after* 1689, at the purported dawning of the age of toleration. It took nothing less than the advent of the American Revolution to bring this "counter-revolution" to an end.[16]

There was nothing intrinsic to colonization in the New World that made a Rhode Island or a Pennsylvania particularly likely. What made America exceptional was its English context.[17] Scotland and Ireland also played a role, although their influence was more on the later content rather than the actual legal and political structure of colonial American religion. Religious diversity in colonial America owed far more to the ambivalent attitude of England's rulers to the national church than it did to any legacy of persecution or tolerance as an ideal. The various possibilities for a religious settlement in the colonies were much greater than in the metropole precisely because the executive, whether monarch, Parliament, or Protector, had more ability to determine the framework of religious life overseas than at home, where it confronted entrenched institutional interests ranging from Parliament to elements of the national church itself. What is most striking about how England's rulers used their greater power to affect religion in the colonies is their *un*willingness to promote the national church there, especially in the Restoration era (1660–1688). In their overseas dominions, unburdened by an established church or vengeful parliaments, England's rulers could and did at certain times (but not always) encourage pluralism at the expense of conformity.

From an international perspective, England's failure to fully establish its national church overseas is remarkable. France, Spain, and Portugal relied heavily on the Catholic Church and its missionaries to control and expand their territory.[18] The Protestant Dutch and Swedes did as

---

[16] For the implementation of the Church of England establishment in the colonies, see Jeremy Gregory's chapter in this volume.

[17] One recent work that moves in this direction is Andrew R. Murphy, *Conscience and Community: Revisiting Toleration and Religious Dissent in Early Modern England and America* (University Park, PA, 2001).

[18] Cornelius J. Jaenen, *The Role of the Church in New France* (Toronto, 1976), surveys French Canada. The literature on religion in Latin America is vast, but there is no doubt that Catholicism was the only permitted faith. Stuart Schwartz, *All Can Be Saved: Religious Tolerance and Salvation in the Iberian Atlantic World* (New Haven, 2008) is an account of popular attitudes, not legal or official policy and practice.

well.[19] In Brazil, Dutch Reformed toleration of Jews and Catholics derived from very specific circumstances (no other Dutch colony did the same). Once the Dutch were expelled, the Catholic Church was restored to its privileged position, and Judaism and Protestantism (a.k.a. heresy) prohibited.[20] Initially, it seemed as if the Church of England would similarly preside uncontested over the English colonies. To understand why the English colonial situation eventually turned out to be so different, one must track colonial and metropolitan events simultaneously across the whole period of British involvement with North America, from the sixteenth century through the 1780s. Then it will become clear that tolerance and religious pluralism in America were the cumulative effect of various influences rather than the direct product of any single all-conquering force.

The First Colonies (c. 1580–1640)

When the English first ventured to colonize America, in the 1580s, Queen Elizabeth's national church already differed significantly from its Reformed counterparts in the rest of Europe. A largely Calvinist institution, it nonetheless retained much of its pre-Reformation governance, giving Anglican bishops more ecclesiastical authority and institutionalized prominence and influence in both politics and religion than either Lutheran bishops or Reformed synods.[21] At the same time, Roman Catholics retained a not insignificant presence in certain areas and among the gentry and aristocracy, albeit in constrained and at times clandestine circumstances. Nonetheless, committed adherents of the state church dominated colonizing activities during Elizabeth's reign.[22] The Elizabethan legacy to America, however, was

---

[19] Evan Haefeli, "The Pennsylvania Difference: Religious Diversity on the Delaware before 1683," *Early American Studies*, I (2003), pp. 28–60, contrasts Swedish and Dutch with English colonial religious arrangements. For more on Dutch tolerance see Evan Haefeli, *New Netherland and the Dutch Origins of American Religious Liberty* (Philadelphia, 2012).

[20] F. L. Schalkwijk, *The Reformed Church in Dutch Brazil (1630–1654)* (Zoetermeer, 1998).

[21] For Calvinism in the Elizabethan church, see Peter Lake, *Moderate Puritans and the Elizabethan Church* (Cambridge, 1982), and the works of Patrick Collinson, *Archbishop Grindal, 1519–1583: The Struggle for a Reformed Church* (Berkeley, 1979) and *The Religion of Protestants: The Church in English Society, 1559–1625* (Oxford, 1982).

[22] Douglas Bradburn, "The Eschatological Origins of the English Empire," in Douglas Bradburn and John C. Coombs (eds), *Early Modern Virginia: Reconsidering the Old Dominion* (2011), 15–56.

not the founding of colonies—none that were attempted succeeded—but the emergence of religious tensions within the national church that ultimately undermined England's ability to create a religiously homogeneous empire.[23]

By the 1580s an increasingly vocal portion of the Church of England was growing unhappy with the anomalous condition of their church and the still incomplete reformation of their nation. Their aspirations earned them the sobriquet of "Puritans." As a force for further reform in the church and religious life of England (and, later, America), they would remain an important factor up through the 1630s. What exactly a Puritan was or wanted has become even more controversial in recent scholarship than it was at the time, and the very use of the term has been called into question. Once the individuals labeled "Puritans" had the opportunity to act on their religious visions in New England in the 1630s and in England itself during the Interregnum from 1642 to 1660, they developed a wide range of theological and ecclesiastical options, from Antinomianism to rigorous Calvinism, and from Presbyterianism to Congregationalism, Baptism, and eventually Quakerism. At root they shared a preference for scriptural reasoning and sermons over traditional rites and ceremonies as the true path to salvation.[24]

The Puritan movement was crucial to the subsequent profusion of Protestant sects after 1640, but this outcome was the unforeseen result of the upheavals, religious and political, that defined the history of England in the seventeenth century. Puritans *qua* Puritans were committed to a single national church and simply wanted to remodel it according to their own rigorous conception of what a true reformation should be. In the event, however, they found themselves under pressure to conform to a national church that increasingly moved away from its Reformed roots. A few Protestants responded by separating themselves from the national church, denying that it was a True Church with any authority over them or they any

---

[23] For an overview of this period see Diarmaid MacCulloch, *The Later Reformation in England, 1547–1603* (London, 1990).

[24] A useful overview of the problems with the term "Puritan," especially in relation to America, is Michael P. Winship, "Were there any Puritans in New England?" *The New England Quarterly*, LXXIV (2001), pp. 118–38. Other helpful contributions to this tangled question include Diarmaid MacCulloch, "The Myth of the English Reformation," *JBS*, XXX (1991), pp. 1–19, and Peter Lake, *Anglicans and Puritans? Presbyterianism and English Conformist Thought from Whitgift to Hooker* (London, 1988).

spiritual kinship with it. By their very act of separation they left Puritanism no less than the established church behind them.[25]

Upon the accession of the committed Calvinist, James VI of Scotland, to the throne of England as James I in 1603, Puritan hopes for further reformation of the national church revived. Catholics for their part hoped he would grant them greater toleration. Both groups were soon disappointed. James I was content to continue Elizabeth's church essentially as he had found it. He even encouraged the careers of a number of English churchmen who were turning against Calvinism and embracing the ambiguities of the English church as a defining virtue.[26]

To some extent, the tensions within the Jacobean church were carried across the Atlantic when the colony of Virginia was founded in 1607. Robert Hunt, the first clergyman in Virginia, was praised by the president of the colony's council as "a man not any waie to be touched with the rebellious humors of a popish spirit, not blemished with the least suspicion of a factious Schismatik." The Privy Council in 1628 admonished its appointed governor, Sir John Harvey, to ensure that every congregation had a "conformable" minister and to "suffer no innovation in matters of Religion."[27] Much the same can be said of the Caribbean islands settled in the 1610s (Bermuda), 1620s (Barbados, St. Kitts, Nevis), and 1630s (Antigua). All of these colonies conformed to the Church of England and made no formal provision for religious toleration of Catholics, Protestant dissidents, or any other group. This paper uniformity, however, did not keep colonists of Puritan sympathies out of most of the colonies, while some of the Separatists also went to Virginia and a significant number of the early Caribbean settlers were Irish Catholics. These colonies are often described as having been founded for "economic" reasons as opposed to the putatively "religious" origins of New England, but such distinctions are anachronistic. The economy mattered to all the colonies, as did religion. The conformist

---

[25] The classic work on the English Puritans under Elizabeth is Patrick Collinson, *The Elizabethan Puritan Movement* (Berkeley, 1967). On the early Separatists, see Barrington Raymond White, *The English Separatist Tradition: From the Marian Martyrs to the Pilgrim Fathers* (Oxford, 1971).

[26] Kenneth Fincham (ed.), *The Early Stuart Church, 1603–1642* (London, 1993); Nicholas Tyacke, *Anti-Calvinists: The Rise of English Arminianism, c. 1590–1640* (Oxford, 1987).

[27] Quoted in James B. Bell, *The Imperial Origins of the King's Church in Early America, 1607–1783* (Houndmills, 2004), pp. 6, 8. See also Edward L. Bond, *Damned Souls in a Tobacco Colony: Religion in Seventeenth-century Virginia* (Macon, GA, 2000).

colonies simply lacked the resources, the printing press, and institutional depth (including sufficient ministers for their parishes) that made religion such a tangible aspect of life in early New England.[28]

Separatists and Catholics posed a threat to the religious (and thus potentially) political unity of England. Both were persecuted early in the reign of James I, especially in the aftermath of the 1605 Gunpowder Plot to blow up James and his Parliament. The Separatists, who would eventually settle Plymouth, initially found shelter in Holland. Soon they dreamed of establishing a church their own way, without interference from existing European churches. This was the religious liberty they sought when, in 1620, they sailed for America. They received permission to settle in Virginia only by masking their radical views. Circumstances took them to New England instead, where their vision persuaded the thousands of Puritans migrating to the Massachusetts Bay colony, beginning in 1629, to become Congregationalists (a church system still largely unknown in England at the time).[29] The religious overlap between the two colonies facilitated Plymouth's absorption into Massachusetts in 1691. Plymouth has long served as an exemplum for the story of America as a refuge for those persecuted for their faith in Europe, but their refuge was for Congregationalists only.[30]

The subsequent large-scale Puritan migration that created New England was first and foremost a statement of opposition to the political policies of Charles I in the 1630s and to the direction the Church of England was taking under Archbishop William Laud. It was also, in its own way, like the establishment of the colony of Providence Island off the coast of Nicaragua at the same time, part of the effort to commit the nation to a Protestant foreign policy and especially to confrontation with Catholic Spain.[31] In England during the 1630s, as Charles attempted to rule his domains without Parliament, and Laud, now Archbishop of Canterbury, sought to remodel the Church of England around ceremonialism rather than doctrine,

---

[28] On the connection between wealth and piety even in New England see Mark A. Peterson, *The Price of Redemption: The Spiritual Economy of New England* (Stanford, 1997).

[29] Michael Winship, *Godly Republicanism: Puritans, Pilgrims, and a City on a Hill* (Cambridge, MA, 2012).

[30] John Michael Bumsted, *The Pilgrim's Progress: The Ecclesiastical History of the Old Colony, 1620–1775* (New York, 1989). On Plymouth's long-term symbolic appeal, see John D. Seelye, *Memory's Nation: The Place of Plymouth Rock* (Chapel Hill, NC, 1998).

[31] Karen Ordahl Kupperman, *Providence Island, 1630–1641: The Other Puritan Colony* (Cambridge, 1995).

Puritan-minded subjects expressed their dissent either through emigration themselves or by supporting the colonies to which their fellows migrated.[32]

In America, wherever Puritans governed they established their version of a True Church and expected everyone in the colony to adhere to it. Congregationalism was usually the form of church they opted for, but not without some conflict and dissent. Without their shared opposition to the Laudian church to unite them, their differences in religious and ecclesiastical inclinations suddenly loomed much larger. Hundreds of colonists left Massachusetts for Connecticut (1634), New Hampshire (an overgrown fishing settlement since the 1620s which fell intermittently under Massachusetts rule), New Haven (1638), and Maine (occasionally a separate colony but generally a part of Massachusetts after 1652), allowing for a limited range of variations within what was essentially a single Congregational order, the New England Way.[33]

Historians have done an excellent job in analyzing the subtle differences and conflicts between the various New England colonies but it needs to be remembered that there was a greater degree of uniformity and conformity throughout New England than in most parts of England. The comparative religious diversity of the northern New England settlements, whose population included Episcopalians, Baptists and, after 1655, Quakers, was balanced by the success of Connecticut and New Haven in keeping out the latter two groups. Whatever the larger implications of apparently minor conflicts within the prescribed orthodoxy, toleration of overt differences was never an option. Those who could not conform either fled to live among Native Americans, like Roger Williams (who left in 1636 for what later became Rhode Island), or, like Anne Hutchinson, found shelter among the comparatively more indulgent Dutch in New Netherland. (Religious

---

[32] Kevin Sharpe, *The Personal Rule of Charles I* (New Haven, 1993) discusses the policies of Charles and Laud that so distressed the Puritans. Tom Webster, *Godly Clergy in Early Stuart England: The Caroline Puritan Movement, c. 1620–1643* (Cambridge, 1997), and Francis J. Bremer, *John Winthrop: America's Forgotten Founding Father* (Oxford, 2003), examine the motives and means of those who migrated to Massachusetts Bay or at least seriously considered doing so. For an introduction to the nature of Laud's reforms, and Puritan opposition to them, see Peter Lake, "The Laudian Style: Order, Uniformity and the Pursuit of Holiness in the 1630s," in Kenneth Fincham (ed.), *The Early Stuart Church, 1603–1642* (Houndmills, 1993), pp. 161–85, and Peter Lake, " 'A Charitable Christian Hatred': The Godly and Their Enemies in the 1630s," in Christopher Durston and Jacqueline Eales (eds), *The Culture of English Puritanism, 1560–1700* (Houndmills, 1996), pp. 145–83.

[33] On the New England establishment, see Jeremy Gregory's chapter in this volume, pp. 749–51.

differences on Providence Island, as deep as elsewhere, were abruptly rendered moot by the Spanish conquest of the colony in 1641.)[34]

Maryland, begun shortly after Massachusetts, was the great exception to early Stuart colonial policy. Granted as a personal proprietary colony to the Catholic Calvert family in 1633, this act of royal patronage speaks volumes about the religious conditions in England that so upset the Puritan migrants. Scholars regularly refer to it as a "Catholic refuge" or "haven"[35] in the face of the inconvenient fact that very few Catholics actually migrated there. Those who did were usually of a particular sort: younger sons of Catholic gentry—precisely those men denied gainful employment suitable to their station by the penal laws in England. In Maryland, they could become landowners and grandees. Otherwise, English Catholics, mostly left in peace in the reign of Charles I, had little reason to seek refuge in a distant and vulnerable colony.[36] Maryland also never served as a refuge for persecuted *foreign* Catholics in the way the colonies attracted Protestants from France and Germany from the late seventeenth century onwards. Irish Catholics tended to go to the Caribbean. Scottish and Dutch Catholics mostly stayed at home. Maryland might be a land of opportunity of sorts for a few comparatively well off English Catholics and for the Society of Jesus, but most of its population at any point in the seventeenth century belonged to the Church of England.[37]

---

[34] Stephen Foster, *The Long Argument: English Puritanism and the Shaping of New England Culture, 1570–1700* (Chapel Hill, NC, 1991) provides an overview of the evolution of religious life and politics in New England. Michael Winship, *Making Heretics: Militant Protestantism and Free Grace in Massachusetts, 1636–1641* (Princeton, 2002), makes the point that Puritans in America resolved important differences through migration to new colonies. For the emigration to the Dutch, see Haefeli, *New Netherland*, and Simon Middleton, "Order and Authority in New Netherland: The 1653 Remonstrance and Early Settlement Politics," *WMQ*, 3rd ser., LCVII (2010), pp. 31–68.

[35] Most recently Jon Butler, *New World Faiths: Religion in Colonial America* (Oxford, 2008), pp. 50, 64–5.

[36] For the combination of Catholic confidence and favorable attitudes among at least some Laudian churchmen in the 1630s, see Michael C. Questier, *Catholicism and Community in Early Modern England: Politics, Aristocratic Patronage and Religion, c. 1550–1640* (Cambridge, 2006), and Anthony Milton, *Catholic and Reformed: Roman and Protestant Churches in English Protestant Thought, 1600–1640* (Cambridge, 1994).

[37] On early Maryland, see three chapters in David B. Quinn (ed.), *Early Maryland in a Wider World* (Detroit, 1982): David B. Quinn, "Why They Came," pp. 119–48, John Bossy, "Reluctant Colonists: The English Catholics Confront the Atlantic," pp. 149–64, and Russell R. Menard and Lois Green Carr, "The Lords Baltimore and the Colonization of Maryland," pp. 167–215.

Religious toleration in Maryland amounted to little more than a series of laws prohibiting religious quarrels between the Catholic few and the Protestant majority. Non-establishment, however, was not religious neutrality. Since only those who could afford to pay for their own religious ministry could properly practice their faith, the few wealthier and well-connected Catholics had a distinct advantage over their poorer Protestant neighbors. Until 1689, Protestant religious services were very rare. Toleration in Maryland effectively prevented English Protestants from exercising the social, political, and religious dominance they were accustomed to elsewhere.[38] Neighboring Protestants objected to the Privy Council that Virginia's Governor, who had helped Maryland's early colonists, "countenances the [Popish] religion in Maryland, and that there is public mass there."[39]

If there was a colonial American refuge for Catholics, it was on the island of Montserrat. Begun informally in the 1630s by Irish Catholic servants fleeing the harshness of life on St. Kitts and Nevis, Montserrat's official church was the Church of England, although it retained an Irish Catholic majority into the eighteenth century. There was never any formal arrangement for toleration on the island. Catholic services were rarely performed, and then only clandestinely by visiting priests. Catholicism was largely confined to the domestic realm, as it would be in Maryland after 1689.[40]

As the case of Montserrat indicates, the Church of England could have been established in all the English colonies, even if many of the inhabitants in actual practice failed to conform to it. Archbishop Laud did indeed aspire to extend religious uniformity (as he understood it) over all English subjects overseas. By 1638, Laud's offensive had reached even the traditional Puritan refuges in the Netherlands and Ireland, and he was drawing up plans to take over New England when the English Civil War intervened. Without the

[38] On religion in Maryland see Michael James Graham, "Lord Baltimore's Pious Enterprise: Toleration and Community in Colonial Maryland, 1634–1724" (Ph.D. diss., University of Michigan, 1983), and John D. Krugler, English and Catholic: The Lords Baltimore in the Seventeenth Century (Baltimore, 2008). Bell, Imperial Origins, pp. 13–14.

[39] Notes on Privy Council meeting, December 11, 1635, Noel Sainsbury (ed.), Calendar of State Papers, Colonial Series, I, America and West Indies, 1574–1660 (London, 1860), p. 216.

[40] Donald Harman Akenson, If the Irish Ran the World: Montserrat, 1630–1730 (Montreal, 1997); Kristen Block and Jenny Shaw, "Subjects without an Empire: The Irish in the Early Modern Caribbean," Past & Present, 210 (February, 2011), pp. 33–60. Ronald Hoffman with Sally D. Mason, Princes of Ireland, Planters of Maryland: A Carroll Family Saga (Chapel Hill, NC, 2000) provides a close study of how wealthy colonial planters preserved their Catholicism through the eighteenth century.

resulting confusion of metropolitan political and religious authority, the story of Anglo-American religion would have been more about conformity than diversity.[41]

Civil War and Interregnum (1639–1660)

The polarization of religious and political attitudes that had brought about the almost simultaneous creation of Catholic Maryland and Puritan Massachusetts came to a head in England in the 1640s. In a civil war that became a revolution, the established church was overthrown, the king executed, and the monarchy abolished in favor of a republic. Presbyterians, Congregationalists (under the title Independents), and Baptists openly advocated their distinctive church orders. By the 1650s, several new sects, most notably the Quakers, had also emerged.[42] American pluralism was effectively born here, in the religious chaos of the Interregnum, during which toleration formally became a tool of English colonial policy.

In North America, the response to the political turmoil at home was the consolidation of the various local religious establishments. Virginia expelled Puritan sympathizers (who moved to Maryland, where they caused difficulties). Massachusetts and Connecticut fleshed out their new Congregational church order in the Cambridge Platform. Plymouth joined its Congregational neighbors in the political and religious alliance of the United Colonies. On the other hand, Rhode Island, Maryland, and the Caribbean islands declared for "liberty of conscience," in an effort (not always successful) to damp down the religious conflict provoked by the growing number of challengers to the local religious status quo.[43]

Rhode Island, the only English colony that publicly opposed religious persecution, became a place of refuge in the 1640s. However, the refugees in question were fleeing the other New England colonies, not Europe, and many moved on to New Netherland, which offered better trading opportunities as

---

[41] Peter Heylyn, *Cyprianus Anglicus* (London, 1668), pp. 275–6. For the Laudian impact on the English churches in the Netherlands, see Keith L. Sprunger, *Dutch Puritanism: A History of English and Scottish Churches of the Netherlands in the Sixteenth and Seventeenth Centuries* (Leiden, 1982), pp. 91–377.

[42] The new sects were famously catalogued and denounced by the Presbyterian, Thomas Edwards, in his *Gangraena: or a Catalgoue and Discovery of many of the Errours, Heresies, and Blasphemies and Pernicious Practices of the Sectaries of this Time* (London, 1646).

[43] Carla Pestana, *The English Atlantic in an Age of Revolution* (Cambridge, MA, 2004).

well as liberty of conscience. Weak and without official support, Rhode Island's hopes for survival rested on Europe, not America. The political upheaval of the Civil War had brought to power men sympathetic to Roger Williams's cause. Returning to England by way of New Amsterdam, he made adroit use of his connections to obtain a Parliamentary charter for his colony in 1644.

While in England, Williams published the books attacking persecution in Massachusetts and advocating a radical separation of church and state that have made him famous. However, the separation that Williams proposed never quite took hold in colonial Rhode Island, where his writings carried less weight than in contemporary England or present-day history texts. Rather, like Maryland, the colony simply avoided any sort of established church and prohibited the coercion of individuals in religious matters. As with Maryland, Rhode Island was only able to secure a form of toleration in America with the blessing of the English executive power, although Rhode Island's toleration favored Baptists, Quakers, Jews, and Congregationalists over Catholics.[44]

The English Civil War brought to power a new set of men who moved beyond the comparatively conservative Puritan consensus of the 1630s and favored more radical action, including religious toleration.[45] The most significant figure for colonial history in this respect was Roger Williams's patron, Robert Rich, Earl of Warwick. Heavily involved in colonial and privateering schemes since the 1610s, he became head of the Parliamentary commission to govern the American colonies—the entity that gave Rhode Island its charter—in 1643. Warwick was also influential in securing the first general proclamation of religious toleration in America. This extraordinary act was a response to events in Bermuda, where Presbyterian and Congregationalist-minded Puritans had been struggling with each other for control of the island's religious life, a conflict that mirrored clashes among the revolutionaries in England. In response, the Long Parliament passed an

---

[44] On Rhode Islanders' early religious struggles, see Philip F. Gura, *A Glimpse of Sion's Glory: Puritan Radicalism in New England, 1620–1660* (Middletown, CT, 1984), pp. 185–214, Timothy L. Hall, *Separating Church and State: Roger Williams and Religious Liberty* (Urbana, IL, 1998), and Sydney V. James, *John Clarke and His Legacies: Religion and Law in Colonial Rhode Island, 1638–1750* (ed.), Theodore Dwight Bozeman (University Park, PA, 1999).

[45] John Coffey, "Puritanism and Liberty Revisited: The Case for Toleration in the English Revolution," *The Historical Journal*, XLI (1998), pp. 961–85 provides a good overview of the toleration debates.

Act "for the establishment of freedom of worship in the American Plantations and especially in Bermuda" on November 4, 1645. As long as colonists
obeyed the civil authority, they were not to suffer "trouble & molestation
by & for any ceremony or imposition in the matters of Gods worship" but
were to be allowed "quietly, freely, & peaceably to worship God accordingly
in those Islands, and also in all other parts & through out the coasts of
America" and to settle where they desired.[46]

The Act precluded the imposition of any sort of religious uniformity on
the colonial churches apart from a liberally defined Protestantism, protected
by liberty of conscience. Such then was the ecclesiastical environment in
which the next phase of English expansionism took place, all of it in the
Caribbean. First, in 1647, Puritan-minded men from Bermuda began settlements on Eleuthera and then New Providence in the Bahamas. Then, in 1651,
some Barbadians began to settle in Suriname. After an unsuccessful effort to
capture New Netherland during the First Anglo-Dutch War, England gained
its next colony with the subsequent Western Design of 1655. The expedition
failed to conquer Hispaniola, but did take Jamaica from the Spanish—and
immediately prohibited Catholicism in its new conquest.[47] Cromwell's
empire was not relentlessly anti-Catholic. The Catholic Lords Baltimore
were restored to power in Maryland, while the acquisition of Dunkirk in
1658 required an agreement to allow Catholics to continue to worship there.
However, in both cases, restrictions were placed on Catholics, and Protestant worship was deliberately encouraged.[48]

There is very little information available about religious life on the
Caribbean islands in the seventeenth century. Their reputation for things
spiritual has not been strong. The Bahamas, for example, a small, impover-
ished colony dependent on wrecking, privateering, and smuggling, has been
dismissed as "a relatively ungodly place until the end of the eighteenth

[46] *Oxford Dictionary of National Biography*, s.v. "Rich, Robert, second earl of Warwick
(1587–1658)," online edn, January 2008 <http://www.oxforddnb.com/view/article/23494>,
accessed June 10, 2010. John Henry Lefroy, *Memorials of the Discovery and Early Settlement of
the Bermudas or Somers Islands, 1515–1685* (London, 1877–1879), I, pp. 600–2.

[47] A Spanish account noted that "No priest nor book might remain in the island," Julian de
Castilla, *The English Conquest of Jamaica: An Account of What Happened in the Island of Jamaica,
from May 20 of the Year 1655, when the English Laid Siege to it, up to July 3 of the Year 1656*, trans.
Irene A. Wright, Camden Miscellany, XIII (London, 1924), 3rd ser., XXIV, p. 12.

[48] The Restoration regime would prove notably friendlier to Catholic religious practice in
both Dunkirk and Maryland. For Dunkirk, see Clyde L. Grose, "England and Dunkirk," *AHR*,
XXXIX (1933), pp. 1–27, esp. pp. 15–17, 20.

century." This verdict echoes the contemporary assessment of Barbados by Henry Whistler, who visited the island as part of the expedition carrying out the Western Design. He noted that in Barbados "they haue that Libertie of contienc [conscience] which wee soe long haue in England foght for: But they doue abuse it." Whistler immediately followed with the observation that the "Island is inhabited with all sortes: with English, French, Dutch, Scotes, Irish, Spaniards they being Iues: with Ingones and miserabell Negors borne to perpetuall sluery thay and thayer seed." Regardless of the actual quality of island piety, what it is clear is that pluralism of one sort or another had become a fixture of English Caribbean life.[49]

Indeed, in one important respect the Caribbean took a lead over the metropole in expanding toleration: this was in the readmission of Jews to the English world. Cromwell in 1655 famously considered allowing Jews back in to England for the first time in almost four hundred years. The so-called readmission, however, was unofficial, small scale, and opposed by a number of Cromwell's advisors. Effectively Cromwell did no more than allow the handful of Jews living in London as Spanish and Portuguese Catholics to remain, but as Jews. No open acknowledgement of this toleration was made until after the Restoration.[50] By contrast, a handful of Jews, who were recognized and accepted as such, began settling in the English Caribbean in the late 1640s. Jews were in Barbados by 1647 and in Jamaica by 1655, while at some point in the 1650s they moved to Suriname and possibly Nevis as well.[51]

[49] Michael Craton and Gail Saunders, *Islanders in the Stream: A History of the Bahamian People*, (Athens, GA, 1992), I, p. 131; Henry Whistler, "Extracts from Henry Whistler's Journal of the West India Expedition," Appendix E, in C. H. Firth (ed.), *The Narrative of General Venables: with an Appendix of Papers Relating to the Expedition to the West Indies and the Conquest of Jamaica, 1654–1655* (London, 1900), p. 146. For religion in the Leewards, see Natalie Zacek, *Settler Society in the English Leeward Islands, 1660–1776* (Oxford, 2010), pp. 121–68.

[50] David S. Katz notes in *Philo-Semitism and the Readmission of the Jews to England, 1603–1655* (Oxford, 1982) that those who favored readmission hoped that it would facilitate the "calling" (conversion) of the Jews that was to herald the arrival of the millennium.

[51] For the emergence of Jews in the Caribbean between the 1640s and 1660s, see Jonathan I. Israel, "Menasseh Ben Israel and the Dutch Sephardic Colonization Movement of the Mid-seventeenth Century (1645–1657)," in Yosef Kaplan, Henry Méchoulan, and Richard H. Popkin (eds), *Menasseh Ben Israel and his World* (Leiden, 1989), pp. 139–63. Richard Ligon mentions a Jew on Barbados in 1647, in *A True & Exact History of the Island of Barbados* (London, 1657) (p. 42). See also Mordechai Arbell, *The Jewish Nation of the Caribbean: The Spanish-Portuguese Jewish Settlements in the Caribbean and the Guianas* (Jerusalem, 2005).

The spectacular growth of religious diversity and the increasing support for toleration both notwithstanding, the impulse to create a single national church in Cromwellian England was as strong as ever. Circumstances, however, compelled a greater degree of latitude in the establishment to be created in so volatile a polity as the Commonwealth. The suppressed diversity within the Puritan movement had at last issued in a cacophony of sects: Congregationalists, Presbyterians, Baptists, Quakers, and other radicals and Seekers of uncertain affiliation. The Commonwealth's church accommodated many of them through a combination of preferential treatment for the "Godly" and toleration for most everyone else. The 1653 Instrument of Government endorsed "the Christian religion" but only "as contained in the Scriptures." (In other words the national church was Protestant.) In an important break with prior laws, it forbade punishing those who did not attend the "Public Profession." Nevertheless, the official church "endeavour" was to win over those who refused to attend church "by sound doctrine and the example of a good conversation."[52]

In the long-standing debate between persuasion and persecution, the Commonwealth came down on the side of persuasion with important qualifications. Those tolerated were not to abuse "this liberty to the civil injury of others, and to the actual disturbance of the public peace on their parts."[53] This proviso eventually justified the use of force against Levellers, Diggers, Fifth Monarchists, and, most famously, the Quaker James Naylor. In the Instrument, and in all future acts of toleration, new sects received protection (to different degrees in different places) but a single official church protected by law remained, reaffirming the traditional ideal of national unity in religion. Consequently, the majority of pre-Revolutionary clergy (about three-fourths) found themselves able to conform and coexist with the new regime.[54]

Though vague on what this national religion was, the Instrument of Government was clear on what it was not. It explicitly excluded toleration

---

[52] "Instrument of Government," in J. P. Kenyon (ed.), *The Stuart Constitution: Documents and Commentary* (Cambridge, 1986), pp. 312–13. Cf. also Barry Coward, *The Cromwellian Protectorate* (Manchester, 2002), pp. 14–17, 39–47, 58–62, 80–5, and Alan G. R. Smith, *The Emergence of a Nation State: The Commonwealth of England, 1529–1660* (London, 1997), pp. 341–7.

[53] Kenyon (ed.), *Stuart Constitution*, p. 313.

[54] Kenneth Fincham and Stephen Taylor, "Episcopalian Conformity and Nonconformity, 1646–60," in Jason McElligott and David L. Smith (eds), *Royalists and Royalism during the Interregnum* (Manchester, 2010), pp. 18–43.

of "popery" or "Prelacy" (meaning by the latter term the government and liturgy of the Church of England under the Elizabethan settlement).[55] Additionally, by allowing freedom and protection to "such as profess faith in God by Jesus Christ (though differing in judgment from the doctrine, worship, or discipline publicly held forth)" the Commonwealth implicitly excluded Jews and Socinians from its pledge of toleration. This latest religious settlement was both evangelically Protestant and unashamedly Erastian.

Had the Commonwealth survived another generation or so, transatlantic religion might have looked very different. Where religious arrangements were at all uncertain or contested—in the Caribbean islands, in Rhode Island—the endorsement of liberty of conscience allowed Protestantism to prevail without quibbling over church forms or particulars of belief. Staunch Episcopalians, without a Restoration to resuscitate them, might have faded away or, at best, coexisted alongside Catholics and Jews at the level of a manageable minority. The loose structure but clear boundaries of the Instrument of Government certainly had a better chance of laying the foundation for a unified Imperial church than anything that came after. By the end of the Commonwealth period, Reformed priorities seem to have displaced particular ecclesiastical loyalties. Many preferred hearing sermons (whether or not the preacher was a duly licensed minister) to the ritual life of their community church.[56]

Restoration (1660–1688)

The Restoration of the monarchy in 1660 brought dramatic political and religious changes. England possessed a national church once again, though one occupying a narrower base than its pre-Civil War incarnation. The Church of England, as defined by the Uniformity Act of 1662 and a series of

[55] Kenyon (ed.), *Stuart Constitution*, p. 313.

[56] My argument here draws on Jeffrey R. Collins, "The Church Settlement of Oliver Cromwell," *History*, LXXXVII (2002), pp. 18–40; Albert J. Loomie, S. J., "Oliver Cromwell's Policy toward the English Catholics: The Appraisal by Diplomats, 1654–1658," *Catholic Historical Review*, XC (2004), pp. 29–44; Blair Worden, "Toleration and the Cromwellian Protectorate," in W. J. Sheils (ed.), *Persecution and Toleration, Studies in Church History*, XXI (1984), pp. 199–233; W. K. Jordan, *The Development of Religious Toleration in England: From the Convention of the Long Parliament to the Restoration, 1640–1660* (Cambridge, MA, 1938); John Spurr, "Religion in Restoration England," in Lionel K. J. Glassey (ed.), *The Reigns of Charles II and James VII & II* (London, 1997), pp. 90–124.

other Acts over the next twenty years, now sought to suppress both Protestant nonconformists and Catholicism. The new Episcopalianism in England (and Scotland and Ireland) marks both the beginning of Anglicanism as later generations experienced it and a definitive break with the majority of the American churches, which could no longer pretend to fellowship with the churches of Virginia and the Caribbean or with the Church of England at home. Quakers, Baptists, Congregationalists, and Presbyterians, whatever their differences, were lumped together as "Dissent," the term for all Protestants who would not conform to the Church of England.[57]

It is important to acknowledge that the Restoration settlement, which coupled exclusion with legal disabilities for the excluded, was a policy of the restored Parliament far more than of Charles II. Personally, Charles II inclined towards pluralism over uniformity. He had made his preferences clear before he returned to the throne, in his 1660 Declaration of Breda. He would allow Parliament the authority to determine the composition of the new Church of England, but he also expected an "act of parliament . . . for the full granting of that indulgence," that is, "a liberty to tender consciences, and that no man shall be disquieted or called in question for differences of opinion in matter of religion which do not disturb the peace of the kingdom."[58] Charles hoped that this liberty would extend to Catholics. When Parliament did not grant him "that indulgence" in England, Charles ensured that it would exist overseas, even in Massachusetts. Complaining that the Bay Colony's rulers "doe in truth deny that liberty of conscience to each other, which is equally provided for and granted to every one of them by their charter," he ordered a halt to the colony's murderous persecution of Quakers. Versions of the wording of the Breda Declaration found their way into the laws of all the new Restoration colonies, from Carolina to New York, and into the laws of those colonies whose charters were re-granted, such as Rhode Island. Moreover, Charles encouraged a wider range

---

[57] For an overview see John Spurr, *The Restoration Church of England, 1646–1689* (New Haven, 1991). The split within Protestantism was not easy for contemporaries to accept. Scholars emphasize that elements on both sides hoped for reunion until the Toleration Act of 1689 confirmed the division. John Spurr, "Schism and the Restoration Church," *Journal of Ecclesiastical History*, XLI (1990), pp. 108–24 describes the national church's reluctance to accept other churches within its jurisdiction. John D. Ramsbottom shows nonconformists' reluctance to be left out of the national church in "Presbyterians and 'Partial Conformity' in the Restoration Church of England," *Journal of Ecclesiastical History*, XLIII (1992), pp. 249–70.

[58] Declaration of Breda reprinted in Kenyon (ed.), *The Stuart Constitution*, pp. 331–2.

of tolerance in the Empire than the Revolutionary regime had, from Tangiers and Bombay to the creation of Pennsylvania.[59]

Political obedience and stability, not religious conformity, was Charles's prime concern. In his opinion, the "principall busynesse is by all good expedients, to unite and reconcile persons of very different judgments and practice in all things, at least which concerne the peace & prosperity of those people and their joint submission and obedience to us and our government."[60] The lack of metropolitan support in the colonies for the newly re-established Church of England, most particularly the absence of a bishop in America, was a crucial legacy of the Restoration era. Not until the 1670s would efforts be made to strengthen the position of the colonial Church, and even then little was actually accomplished.[61]

Charles II's willingness to re-authorize royal charters for Rhode Island and Connecticut bespeaks both his ability to come to terms with a fait accompli and his comfort with religious pluralism.[62] In 1663, this policy reached its fullest expression in the first new colony of his reign, Carolina (which did not split into North and South Carolina until the early eighteenth century). The Fundamental Constitutions of Carolina, drafted by one of its proprietors, the Earl of Shaftesbury, and his secretary, John Locke, combined a remarkably flexible attitude towards religion with an aristocratic vision of society. They allowed for the public exercise of any religion on which "seven or more persons" could agree. They encouraged the settlement of "Jews, heathens, and other dissenters from the purity of Christian religion," even if only in the hopes that "by good usage and persuasion" they might "be won over to embrace and unfeignedly receive the truth." Only three conditions were imposed. First, everyone had to belong to a church and every church had to keep a strict record of its membership. Second, no one could "use any

---

[59] For the Asian context, see Glenn J. Ames, "The Role of Religion in the Transfer and Rise of Bombay, c. 1661–1687," *The Historical Journal*, XLVI (2003), pp. 317–40.

[60] Charles II to Col. Nicolls, April 23, 1664, in Edmund B. O'Callaghan and Berthold Fernow (eds), *Documents Relative to the Colonial History of the State of New York* (Albany, NY, 1853–1887), III, pp. 58–9.

[61] On efforts to strengthen the church's position in America before 1688, see William Gibson, "A Bishop for Virginia in 1672: A Fragment from Bishop Ward's Papers," *Archives*, XXIV (2009), pp. 36–41; Bell, *Imperial Origins*, pp. 10–40. For the strength of establishment even without a bishop, see the chapter in this volume by Jeremy Gregory.

[62] For the politics that made Rhode Island's religious disestablishment possible, see Alison Gilbert Olson, *Anglo-American Politics, 1660–1775: The Relationship between Parties in England and Colonial America* (Oxford, 1973), pp. 15–37; James, *John Clarke and His Legacies*, pp. 59–83.

reproachful, reviling, or abusive language against any religion of any church or profession." Finally, allowance was made for the eventual establishment of the Church of England in the colony by act of its assembly. Though the provisions of the Fundamental Constitutions were never approved, their spirit regulated the colony's religious life until the establishment of the Church of England in 1706. Restoration religious policy in the colonies continued the Interregnum commitment to toleration but visibly retreated from the Commonwealth's enthusiasm for a unified national church, however liberal its boundaries.[63]

In terms of American religious history, the most significant development of the Restoration period was the conquest of New Netherland in 1664. The middle colonies (New York, Pennsylvania, and New Jersey) were carved out of this extensive territory between Connecticut and Maryland. Then, instead of taking advantage of the chance to establish a strong basis for the Anglican church in the new colonies, the Restoration government oversaw the expansion of the forms of religious toleration already available elsewhere within the empire. In addition to Swedish Lutherans and Dutch Reformed (who were already present in some numbers in the area), the new denominations, particularly Quakers, Presbyterians, and Baptists, acquired a foothold otherwise denied them in the older colonies, as would German Pietist and French Huguenot immigrants too at a later date. Thanks to the middle colonies, North America quickly became the vibrant center of religious pluralism in the English world.[64]

New York was the first. The Duke's Laws, promulgated in 1665 (though not extended over all the colony until 1674), divided the settlements into

---

[63] "Fundamental Constitutions of Carolina, March 1, 1669/70," in Mattie Erma Edwards Parker (ed.), *North Carolina Charters and Constitutions* (Raleigh, 1963), pp. 181–3; Charles H. Lippy, "Chastized by Scorpions: Christianity and Culture in Colonial South Carolina, 1669–1740," *Church History*, LXXIX (2010), p. 269; L. H. Roper, *Conceiving Carolina: Proprietors, Planters, and Plots, 1662–1729* (New York, 2004), pp. 128–31; Robert M. Weir, "'Shaftesbury's Darling': British Settlement in the Carolinas at the Close of the Seventeenth Century," in Nicholas Canny (ed.), *OHBE*, I (Oxford, 1998), pp. 375–97; James Lowell Underwood and W. Lewis Burke (eds), *The Dawn of Religious Freedom in South Carolina* (Columbia, SC, 2006).

[64] Cf. Jon Butler, *Becoming America: The Revolution before 1776* (Cambridge, MA, 2000); Ned C. Landsman, *From Colonials to Provincials: American Thought and Culture, 1680–1760* (Ithaca, NY, 2000). My argument sets the date of the move away from a national church in the colonies in the 1660s and emphasizes the English political context, as in Mary K. Geiter, "The Restoration Crisis and the Launching of Pennsylvania, 1679–81," *English Historical Review*, CXII (1997), pp. 300–18.

parishes and allowed each parish to choose the sort of church it wanted by a majority vote. Crucial qualifications, however, effectively excluded anyone other than Protestants, as well as Quakers and Baptists, from the possible choices.[65] The intended beneficiaries of this limited toleration were Presbyterians, Lutherans, the Dutch Reformed, Congregationalists, and Anglicans, who together made up the majority of the colony's population. Beyond these legal provisions, Jews received special support from New York's governors (against the inclination of many of the Protestant colonists). Compared to the religious situation under the Dutch, these arrangements were a significant expansion of toleration.

The remainder of New Netherland was split into three Quaker-dominated colonies, East Jersey, West Jersey, and Pennsylvania, each of which opened up religious liberty to an extent unimaginable in Europe and the other colonies. New Jersey began as a single colony shared between two proprietors. Its 1665 "Concessions and Agreements of the Lords Proprietors of the Province of New Jersey" echoed the Declaration of Breda. Individuals and groups could "at all times truly and fully have and enjoy his and their Judgements and Conciences in matters of Religion throughout all the said Province." As long as they behaved "themselves peaceably and quietly and" did not use "this liberty to Licentiousness, nor to the civill injury or outward disturbance of others," none could be "any waies molested punished disquieted or called in Question for any difference in opinion or practice in matters of Religious concernments."[66]

The division of New Jersey into two colonies in 1674 prompted the drafting of new constitutions. Reaching a new level of reasoning in favor of toleration, more principled and more explicit than anything to be found earlier, West Jersey's 1676 Concessions and Agreements affirmed that "no Men nor number of Men upon Earth hath power or Authority to rule over mens consciences in religious matters." If any member of the colony's Assembly should "designedly willfully and Malitiously move or excite any to move any matter or thing whatsoever that contradicts or any wayes subverts any fundamentall of the said Laws...they shall be proceeded

---

[65] Edward T. Corwin (ed.), *Ecclesiastical Records: State of New York*, (Albany, NY, 1901–16), I, pp. 570–2.

[66] William A. Whitehead, et al. (eds), *Archives of the State of New Jersey*, 1st ser. (Newark, NJ, 1880–1949), I, p. 30.

against as Traitors to the said Government."[67] These principles were reiter-ated in a toned down form in the Fundamental Agreement of 1681. Liberty "of conscience in matters of faith and worship towards God" was granted to all "who shall live peaceably and quietly therein." The right of Quakers to hold colonial office was expressly guaranteed with the provision that "none of the free people of the said province shall be rendered uncapable of office in respect of their faith and worship."[68] The 1683 Fundamental Constitution for the Province of East New Jersey similarly required officials to swear that they would not "endeavor alteration in the government" or seek "the turning out of any in it or their ruin or prejudice, either in person or estate, because they are, in his opinion, heretics or differ in their judgment from him."[69]

Pennsylvania's religious provisions exhibited a more overtly ecumenical spirit while eschewing the radical sounding language of the Jersey consti-tutions. William Penn wanted the government of his colony to be in the hands of committed Christians but carefully avoided implying a preference for any given denomination. All officers and all electors were to "be such as profess faith in Jesus Christ, and that are not convicted of ill fame or unsober and dishonest conversation." All colonists likewise had to be persons "who confess and acknowledge the one almighty God to be the creator, upholder, and ruler of the world." If they held "themselves obliged in conscience to live peaceably and justly in civil society," they would "in no ways be molested or prejudiced for their religious persuasion or practice in matters of faith and worship." Finally, none shall "be compelled at any time to frequent or maintain any religious worship, place, or ministry what-ever."[70] Generous as these terms were, their implied limitations were entirely clear: there is no evidence of Jews living in either the Jerseys or Pennsylvania before the eighteenth century.

The closing years of the Restoration period saw one final innovation in the colonies: the creation between 1683 and 1686 of the Dominion of New

---

[67] Richard S. Dunn and Mary Maples Dunn (eds), *The Papers of William Penn* (Philadelphia, 1981–1987), I, pp. 396–7.

[68] "Fundamental Agreement of the Governor, Proprietors, Freeholders, and Inhabitants of West New Jersey, November 25, 1681," in W. Keith Kavanagh (ed.), *Foundations of Colonial America: A Documentary History* (New York, 1973), II, p. 1101.

[69] Kavanagh (ed.), *Foundations of Colonial America*, II, p. 1107.

[70] "Laws Agreed Upon in England," in Jean R. Soderlund (ed.), *William Penn and the Founding of Pennsylvania: A Documentary History* (Philadelphia, 1983), p. 132.

England, a short-lived amalgamation of the New England colonies, to which New York and the Jerseys were eventually added. The Dominion's provision for liberty of conscience provided a legal basis for its governor, Sir Edmund Andros, to set up an Anglican congregation in Boston. Though it provoked the indignation of many a Congregationalist, King's Chapel was a far cry from an attempt to establish the Church of England in New England. Its foundation merely added a dash of denominational diversity to what remained a Congregational hegemony.[71]

One could say that the common denominator of Restoration religious policy in the colonies was a presumption in favor of toleration. However, these assorted tolerations sprang from different motives and had different results. Jews were welcome in New York and (later) Rhode Island and Carolina, but not in the Quaker colonies. The toleration on offer in the Quaker colonies, by militating against the establishment of any sort of church, favored Catholics, Quakers, Baptists, and other smaller sects (such as the Scots Covenanters in New Jersey). Contemporaries understood the subtleties of the matter: Huguenots, the first and most famous group of Protestant religious refugees to come to America, shunned the Quaker colonies for New York, Carolina, and Massachusetts, where they could recreate a Reformed church and ministry with the hope of some governmental support. Though victims of persecution, Huguenots did not seek religious diversity. They wanted an establishment friendly to Reformed churches.

Perhaps the most distinctive aspect of Restoration-era colonial charters was the absence of language that explicitly excluded Catholics from the general promise of toleration, even as new forms of anti-Catholic legislation, especially the Test Acts of 1673 and 1678, were passed in England. The ecumenical spirit of the charters, however, was not matched by many of the colonists. After New York's proprietor, James, Duke of York, converted to Catholicism, some of the offices in the colony went to his co-religionists, which made them an object of suspicion to the Protestant majority, and once he became king as James II in 1685 the same kinds of anxiety spread to other colonies. As this chapter's epigraph demonstrates, some, like William Penn, saw a positive connection between pluralism and a Catholic monarch.

---

[71] Viola Barnes, *The Dominion of New England: A Study in British Colonial Policy* (New Haven, 1923), pp. 122–34.

Many more joined in the anti-popish frenzy that marked the colonists' participation in the Glorious Revolution.[72]

The Rise of the Church of England (1689–1707)

The Glorious Revolution of 1688–89 encouraged the growth of pluralism in some ways but restricted it in others, primarily by giving a strong boost to the Church of England overseas. The final failure to come up with some sort of comprehension for Protestant nonconformists within the Church of England put the last nail in the coffin of the ideal of religious unity both in England and in America. The Toleration Act of 1689 relieved most Dissenters of penalties for practicing their religion while also denying them full rights. Toleration for certain forms of Dissent was now combined with an assertion of the primacy of the established church. Everywhere, even in Pennsylvania, laws were rewritten to establish formal discrimination against Catholics and strengthen the position of the Church of England.[73] Across the empire only Protestants could hold office, inherit property without difficulty, and worship relatively unmolested. These restrictions did not suppress Catholicism, but left it in a state of legal subjection, much as in Ireland. Jews, by contrast, took advantage of a lighter degree of discrimination than Catholics to expand out from their initial enclaves in the Caribbean, London, and New York to carve out communities in the diverse trading ports of Newport, Rhode Island, Charleston, South Carolina, and Philadelphia.[74]

The foundation of the Society for the Propagation of the Gospel in Foreign Parts (SPG) in 1701 ensured that the Church of England overseas became stronger than ever before. From the 1690s to the 1740s, the Church of England was the fastest growing denomination in British America. By the time of the Revolution, it had achieved an unprecedented degree of predominance in the colonies. In one form or another it was established in parts of New York and the Caribbean, both Carolinas, Nova Scotia, New

[72] Owen Stanwood, *The Empire Reformed: English America in the Age of the Glorious Revolution* (Philadelphia, 2011). For the alternative possibility advocated by James II, see Scott Sowerby, "Of Different Complexions: Religious Diversity and National Identity in James II's Toleration Campaign," *English Historical Review*, CXXIV (2009), pp. 29–52.

[73] Patricia U. Bonomi, *Under the Cope of Heaven: Religion, Society, and Politics in Colonial America* (Oxford, 1986), p. 36.

[74] William Pencak, *Jews and Gentiles in Early America, 1654–1800* (Ann Arbor, 2005).

Jersey, Maryland, and Prince Edward Island, all colonies in which non-Anglicans were subject to legal disabilities. Even where it did not enjoy the advantage of establishment, Anglicanism made noticeable inroads, particularly in Connecticut and Quebec. Anglican ministers began appearing in new places, such as the Bahamas (in 1721). The Church also proved adept at absorbing non-English immigrants, such as the Huguenots.[75]

Britain's eighteenth century empire proudly identified itself as Protestant, a deliberately ambiguous term suitable for a polity without a single all-inclusive imperial church.[76] This ideological stance allowed the existing toleration of Dissent in Britain and its colonies to be extended to a number of non-English Protestants immigrants from France, Germany, Scotland, and Ireland. However, given the ever more numerous French and Spanish Roman Catholics incorporated into the British Empire as it expanded (not to mention the Irish Catholics at home and in the colonies), alongside the many thousands of non-Christian Africans, Native Americans, and Asians, the claim to be a Protestant empire was something of a misnomer or, rather, a fierce statement of ideological priorities. Overall, after 1689, the Empire restricted the dramatic possibilities for religious liberty opened up during the Restoration period. Yet in important ways it continued to promote pluralism in colonial America, though often inadvertently.

The Bi-Confessional Empire (1707–1783)

Just as the Church of England seemed on the verge of gaining the hegemonic status in the Empire that had eluded it in the seventeenth century, changes in British religious life undermined its pretensions. The Union of Scotland and England in 1707 introduced a second nationally established church into the Imperial equation. Presbyterian in structure and unambiguously Calvinist in doctrine, the instance of the Church of Scotland was ammunition for the claims of Presbyterians and Congregationalist apologists that the

---

[75] See: Jeremy Gregory's chapter in this volume, pp. 159–61; Bell, *Imperial Origins*, pp. 41–164; Jon Butler, *The Huguenots in America: A Refugee People in New World Society* (Cambridge, MA, 1983); Peter Doll, *Revolution, Religion, and National Identity: Imperial Anglicanism in British North America, 1745–1795* (Madison, NJ, 2000) for Nova Scotia and Quebec.

[76] David Armitage emphasizes Protestantism's ideological significance to the eighteenth century in *Ideological Origins of the British Empire* (Cambridge, 2000), as does Pestana, *Protestant Empire*. Both works draw on Linda Colley, *Britons: Forging a Nation, 1707–1837* (New Haven, 1992).

Church of England had no automatic right to be considered the established church of the Empire. A nice talking point, it never really silenced Anglican pretensions. Over time, however, Presbyterians mobilized and expanded their influence, especially in the middle colonies where they benefited from the existing grants of toleration, although they never gained the full rights of establishment.[77]

Broadly speaking, the progress of religion in the colonies in the eighteenth century favored the growth of one or another of the Protestant churches that were already established in Europe, whether Lutheranism among the German immigrants or Presbyterianism among the Scots and Irish immigrants, at the expense of both the Protestant radicals and the Catholics who had gained footholds in the colonies in the seventeenth century. Emblematic of the reduced pluralism of the new order was the case of Georgia (established in 1732), where toleration was a Protestants-only affair and the Anglican church retained a favored position. In the course of the perennial competition for members and influence, denominations on the defensive regularly invoked tolerationist principles to fend off the aspirations of other churches, but the establishmentarian ideal generally remained noticeably more potent after 1689 than it had before.[78]

Even the rise of Methodism can be seen as a potential source of strength for Anglicanism in the Anglo-American world. Methodism originated within the Church of England as an emotional, evangelical movement with the capacity to fill the growing gaps in the Church's pastoral coverage: expanding cities; mining areas; new industrial regions; and (from the 1760s on) colonial America. If the Methodist movement could have been contained within the church of its origin (and it did in fact avoid outright schism until the 1780s) it would have been a potent weapon to extend Anglican influence in North America. As it was, American independence enabled (or compelled) Methodism to evolve into a church of its own, first

---

[77] Ned C. Landsman, "The Episcopate, the British Union, and the Failure of Religious Settlement in Colonial British America," in Beneke and Grenda (eds), *First Prejudice*, pp. 75–97, and his "Roots, Routes, and Rootedness, *Early American Studies*," II (2004), pp. 267–309.

[78] See also Richard W. Pointer, *Protestant Pluralism and the New York Experience: A Study of Eighteenth-Century Religious Diversity* (Bloomington, IN, 1988), and Joyce Goodfriend, "The Limits of Religious Pluralism in Eighteenth-Century New York City," *European Contributions to American Studies*, LIX (2005), pp. 67–86.

in America—where it became the fastest growing church in the new nation—then in Britain.[79]

Immigration from outside the British Isles, as well as the denominational schisms of the Great Awakening, added to the religious diversity of the colonies without reversing the growth of establishmentarianism. Though American scholars like to locate the emergence of something new and distinctly American in both phenomena, what is more impressive in the long run is the effectiveness and determination of local establishments in restricting and absorbing these challenges. The existing laws and practices governing religious tolerance remained largely unchanged, and there was no second Maryland or Pennsylvania in the eighteenth century to give any of the new religious groupings a bastion of their own. The Church of England at home experienced comparable challenges to its established status in the same period, mostly for reasons similar to the colonies, and weathered them all. The great difference in America was the way in which the different colonial arrangements shaped a range of contrasting responses rather than producing a single overall result.

If there was a distinct expansion of pluralism in the eighteenth century British Empire, then it was taking place outside of the Thirteen Colonies. Ironically, Britain's vaunted Protestant empire was becoming less Protestant. Apart from the growing number of non-Christians brought into the Empire's ambit in Africa, Asia, and the Americas (not least through the rapidly expanding transatlantic slave trade), the number of Catholics was increasing for several reasons: natural population growth, especially in Ireland and Maryland (in Montserrat their numbers were actually decreasing); immigration (some of the Germans moving to Pennsylvania were Catholics); but, most importantly, the fruits of war. Thousands of Catholics were added to the British Empire thanks to an ambitious series of conquests: Minorca, Gibraltar, and Acadia in 1713; and New France, Grenada, Dominica, and Tobago in 1763.

The changing situation transformed Parliament from the protector of the endangered Church of England against the threat of Catholics, schismatics, and fanatics to the leading advocate of toleration in the Empire. As the Jewish population in America and Britain continued to grow, Parliament almost granted Jews in the colonies rights as British subjects through the

---

[79] For the beginnings of Methodism in America, see Dee E. Andrews, *The Methodists and Revolutionary America, 1760–1800: The Shaping of an Evangelical Culture* (Princeton, 2000).

so-called Jew Bill of 1753–54. Popular opposition within Britain forced the repeal of this liberal measure but could not stop the British government from turning to Catholic Relief in its efforts to hinder the growth of opposition in the colonies and then to prosecute the war against America once independence was declared. Indeed, Parliament's willingness to grant Roman Catholics a degree of official tolerance under the Quebec Act of 1774 was cited as a grievance by the American revolutionaries.[80]

Ultimately, for the Thirteen Colonies, the single most decisive influence in securing religious freedom was not the founding of any particular colony or the spread of any given idea but the American Revolution. The Revolution broke the standing ties between church and state and put nothing in its place. While American Independence had not originated as a struggle for religious freedom, the close connection between the Church of England and the British monarchy meant that it was impossible to imagine separating from the one without separating from the other. From 1776 onwards, the Church of England lost its established status in colony after colony. The process culminated in Virginia in 1786 with the passage of the Statute for Religious Freedom drafted by Thomas Jefferson.[81] The statute defied the commonplaces of the late eighteenth century, well expressed by Lord North's half-brother, the Bishop of Worcester, in 1778: "History hath put it beyond doubt, that an equality of sects under one government, without any established church at all, is a chimerical idea, and totally inconsistent with religious order and peace."[82] The Virginia Statute was genuinely audacious; it was also, however, really a reversion to the policies of the Restoration Empire—policies that Virginia had once rejected.

---

[80] Stephen Taylor, "Sir Robert Walpole, The Church of England, and the Quakers Tithe Bill of 1736," *The Historical Journal*, XXVIII (1985), pp. 51–77; G. A. Cranfield, "The *London Evening-Post* and the Jew Bill of 1753," *The Historical Journal*, VIII (1965), pp. 16–30; P. J. Marshall, "British North America, 1760–1815," in P. J. Marshall (ed.), *OHBE*, II, *The Eighteenth Century* (Oxford, 1998), pp. 378–80; Robert Kent Donovan, "The Military Origins of the Roman Catholic Relief Programme of 1776," *The Historical Journal*, XXVIII (1985), pp. 79–102.

[81] Nancy Lee Rhoden, *Revolutionary Anglicanism: The Colonial Church of England Clergy During the American Revolution* (New York, 1999); Jon Butler, *Awash in a Sea of Faith: Christianizing the American People* (Cambridge, MA, 1992), pp. 194–256.

[82] Brownlow North, *A Sermon Preached before the Incorporated Society for the Propagation of the Gospel* (London, 1778), p. 17.

The Virginia Statute had little direct impact on the other original states, but it ensured that there could be no single unified American religion. By the time the Constitution was drafted in 1787 there was no real basis on which to build a national church. Had Virginia maintained a commitment to some form of established church, that institution might well have crossed the Appalachian Mountains under that state's aegis and flourished in its new homeland. Instead, a variety of churches mushroomed in the West. Most were Protestant but none enjoyed the ability to enforce conformity, and this impromptu marketplace of faiths would eventually become the national state of affairs. The First Amendment, prohibiting Congress from ever establishing such an institution, reflects the fact that no denomination was strong enough to bid for national hegemony while all of them had reason to wish for protection should any group subsequently make a bid for the tarnished prize.

Curiously, the Revolution also made possible what had hitherto been virtually inconceivable: the creation of an Anglican bishop for America. Once the thirteen North American colonies finally achieved their independence in 1783, bishops began to appear left and right: first in Connecticut (1784); then New York and Pennsylvania (1787); Nova Scotia (1787); and Quebec (1791), though only the Canadian bishops enjoyed the privileges of establishment. While the old hostility to a local bishop lingered into the nineteenth century in the Caribbean, in the United States "prelacy" was no longer an object of fear.

The Revolution put an end to the expansion of established churches in the United States but the path to an American form of religious freedom was still not straightforward. The degree of liberty legally allowed in the independent United States varied over time and place, just as the emergence of toleration in the Empire had. Religious tests for office remained in many states excluding (variously) non-Christians, Catholics, and Unitarians. In Massachusetts and Connecticut established churches persisted into the nineteenth century. Not until 1840 did the logic of religious liberty and pluralism reign undisputed across the entire United States. Even then, it was not understood equally everywhere. While the cumulative effect was impressive, it was not inevitable, consistent, or coordinated.

America's exceptional religious situation was the product of an exceptional period of English history. In considering the place of pluralism in America, one cannot take Pennsylvania or the middle colonies to be representative of the whole nation, as enlightenment writers like Thomas Paine did for polemical and political purposes. The dilemmas and possibilities of religious pluralism certainly distinguish American history almost from the earliest days of European settlement, but they are not intrinsic or necessary aspects of the American experience or even symptomatic of the democratic possibilities of colonialism. The maneuverings and motives of a handful of men at the highest levels of power made toleration in the colonies possible. England's rulers, in different ways and at different times, felt that a religiously diverse population, deprived of the unity of an established church, could be a reliable instrument of empire.

They were right. Pluralism produced more Loyalism than religious unity did. In the American Revolution, the colonies with the strongest church establishments and greatest degree of conformity, such as Massachusetts and Virginia, overthrew British authority with remarkable ease. The middle colonies—ostensibly the most American by virtue of their pluralism—were bitterly divided over the Imperial crisis, and many of their inhabitants ended up either loyalists or neutrals. If one extends the analysis to Canada and the Caribbean, a startling picture emerges. The colonies with the most pluralism were least likely to separate from Britain. And if pluralism is what makes America distinctive, then this is a paradox worthy of more thought.

Select Bibliography

CHRIS BENEKE and CHRISTOPHER S. GRENDA (eds), *The First Prejudice: Religious Tolerance and Intolerance in Early America* (Philadelphia, 2011).

PATRICIA U. BONOMI, *Under the Cope of Heaven: Religion, Society, and Politics in Colonial America* (Oxford, 2003).

JOHN COFFEY, *Persecution and Toleration in Protestant England, 1558–1689* (Harlow, 2000).

THOMAS J. CURRY, *The First Freedoms: Church and State in America to the Passage of the First Amendment* (Oxford, 1986).

AARON SPENCER FOGLEMAN, *Jesus is Female: Moravians and Radical Religion in Early America* (Philadelphia, 2007).

WILLIAM FROST, *A Perfect Freedom: Religious Liberty in Pennsylvania* (University Park, PA, 1993).

JOYCE GOODFRIEND, "The Limits of Religious Pluralism in Eighteenth-Century New York City," *European Contributions to American Studies*, LIX (2005), pp. 67–86.

MARK HÄBERLEIN, *The Practice of Pluralism: Congregational Life and Religious Diversity in Lancaster, Pennsylvania, 1730–1820* (University Park, PA, 2009).

WILLIAM R. HUTCHINSON, *Religious Pluralism in America: The Contentious History of a Founding Ideal* (New Haven, 2003).

JAMES H. HUTSON, *Church and State in America: The First Two Centuries* (Cambridge, 2008).

SYDNEY V. JAMES, *John Clarke and His Legacies: Religion and Law in Colonial Rhode Island, 1638–1750* (ed.), Theodore Dwight Bozeman (University Park, PA, 1999).

NED LANDSMAN, "Roots, Routes, and Rootedness: Diversity, Migration, and Toleration in Mid-Atlantic Pluralism," *Early American Studies*, II (2004), pp. 267–309.

CHARLES H. LIPPY, "Chastized by Scorpions: Christianity and Culture in Colonial South Carolina, 1669–1740," *Church History*, LXXIX (2010), pp. 253–70.

WILLIAM G. McLOUGHLIN, *New England Dissent, 1630–1833: The Baptists and the Separation of Church and State* (Cambridge, MA, 1971).

ANDREW R. MURPHY, *Conscience and Community: Revisiting Toleration and Religious Dissent in Early Modern England and America* (University Park, PA, 2001).

CARLA PESTANA, *Protestant Empire: Religion and the Making of the British Atlantic World* (Philadelphia, 2009).

RICHARD W. POINTER, *Protestant Pluralism and the New York Experience: A Study of Eighteenth-Century Religious Diversity* (Bloomington, IN, 1988).

JAMES LOWELL UNDERWOOD and W. LEWIS BURKE (eds), *The Dawn of Religious Freedom in South Carolina* (Columbia, SC, 2006).

ALEXANDRA WALSHAM, *Charitable Hatred: Tolerance and Intolerance in England, 1500–1700* (Manchester, 2006).

The interested reader is also advised to consult the bibliography of the next chapter, "'Establishment' and 'Dissent' in British North America: Organizing Religion in the New World," pp. 168–9. Titles listed there are not repeated here.

5

"Establishment" and "Dissent" in British North America

*Organizing Religion in the New World**

Jeremy Gregory

For most of the nineteenth century and almost all of the twentieth, historians paid little attention to the existence of religious establishments in colonial British North America. The usual way to organize religion in the polities of early modern Europe had been to give a church an exclusive, or at least a privileged, position and government support, including funding, normally through some kind of endowment or taxation system. This had cemented an alliance between church and state, customarily with the state having some control over who was appointed to religious posts, and sometimes over doctrine and church governance. Typically, (male) ministers preached on public occasions, church attendance was mandatory, and full political participation was often limited to members of that church.[1] Historians have viewed the New World, by contrast, as being characterized by voluntary religion and denominational pluralism, a state of affairs that would be achieved in full only in the antebellum period but which was perceived as having had its roots firmly planted in the colonial era. The institution of a state-supported church in the American colonies was thus looked on as an anachronism which went against the grain of the "true" American experience and which was seen as irrelevant to "real" American history. In this scenario, religious establishments were regarded as relics of

* In writing this chapter, I have benefited hugely from the advice of Stephen Foster and Evan Haefeli.

[1] James D. Tracy and Marguerite Ragnow (eds), *Religion and the Early Modern State: Views from China, Russia and the West* (Cambridge, 2004).

the Old World, which the voluntaristic and pluralistic New World had largely—and thankfully—left behind.[2]

For these historians, the clearest example of a meaningful colonial religious establishment—Congregationalism in New England—was regarded in the darkest of terms as a repressive and unwholesome force, especially in its seventeenth-century formulation, but this was often presented as an oddity and an anomaly in the development of a nation that aspired to freedom in religious matters.[3] In any case, "Puritan New England" came to be celebrated more for its dissenting stance with respect to English/British religious establishments in the 1620s and 30s and in the 1760s and 70s than for the establishment it itself created in the years in between.[4] Edmund Burke famously remarked that the New England Congregationalists exemplified "a refinement on the principle of resistance ... the dissidence of dissent ... and the protestantism of the protestant religion."[5] From the standpoint of other religious groups trying to make headway in New England, they could be said also to have demonstrated the essence of establishmentarianism.

For the rest of British North America, establishments have usually been described as being too weak to merit much consideration. Above all, the Anglican establishment in Virginia was thought of as being so under the thumb of the gentry that it had supposedly fostered a debased form of

[2] William Warren Sweet, *Religion in Colonial America* (New York, 1942). More recently, see Carla Gardina Pestana, *Liberty of Conscience and the Growth of Religious Diversity in Early America, 1636–1786* (Providence, RI, 1986), Thomas J. Curry, *The First Freedoms: Church and State in America to the Passage of the First Amendment* (New York, 1986), Boyd Stanley Schlenther, "Religious Faith and Commercial Empire," in P. J. Marshall (ed.), *OHBE*, II (Oxford, 1998), *The Eighteenth Century*, pp. 128–50, Mark Noll, *America's God: from Jonathan Edwards to Abraham Lincoln* (Oxford, 2002), Philip Hamburger, *Separation of Church and State* (Cambridge, MA, 2002), and Chris Beneke, *Beyond Toleration: The Religious Origins of American Pluralism* (New York, 2006). For a scintillating overview, see Carla Pestana, *Protestant Empire: Religion and the Making of the British Atlantic World* (Philadelphia, 2009).

[3] M. Louise Green, *The Development of Religious Liberty in Connecticut* (Boston, 1905). Even Susan M. Reed, *Church and State in Massachusetts, 1691–1740* (Urbana, IL, 1914) tends to emphasize the development of toleration.

[4] Carl Bridenbaugh, *Mitre and Sceptre: Transatlantic Faiths, Ideas, Personalities and Politics, 1689–1775* (London, 1962).

[5] Warren M. Elofson (ed.), *Party, Parliament and the American War, 1774–1800* (Oxford, 1996), vol. III of Paul Langford (ed.), *The Writings and Speeches of Edmund Burke*, p. 122 ("Speech on Conciliation with the Colonies," March 22, 1775).

religion, lacking any theological or spiritual dimension.[6] Historians often accepted uncritically the views of the Virginian establishment's opponents and presented a perhaps unfair contrast between the "secularity" of Virginian church life and New England religiosity, confirming the verdict that a religious establishment (and particularly an Anglican one) was necessarily detrimental to "real" religious ends.[7] Overall, historians have usually highlighted challenges to religious establishments and have emphasized those factors that allowed religious pluralism and toleration to thrive in some parts of the colonial world. These instances of *de facto* pluralism were often regarded as a precursor to the growth of a fully-fledged nineteenth-century voluntaristic religious marketplace, and as such were frequently viewed as representing the ideals of an "American" approach to the place of religion in society.

Yet, in the mid-eighteenth century, three quarters of the British colonies in North America (echoing their European past) had a clearly defined religious establishment. Indeed, more colonies had religious establishments in the eighteenth than in the seventeenth century, and most pre-Revolutionary ministers preached from the pulpit of a church established by law. Not surprisingly, then, modern historians such as Jon Butler and J.C.D. Clark have paid increasing attention to what Butler has termed "state churches" in colonial America.[8] As Butler has argued, eighteenth-century developments "made North America more establishmentarian and coercive, often intensifying rather than jettisoning its European state church heritage."[9] By the 1750s, there was roughly one church for every 600 New Englanders, one for every 470 people in the middle colonies, and one for every 1,050 white colonists in the south, and at that date over half of all churches in these colonies were established: 423 being Congregational and 246 Anglican.[10] The trajectory that runs from a concern with religious establishments in the early seventeenth century to a more tolerant and diverse situation in the eighteenth

---

[6] Rhys Isaac, *The Transformation of Virginia, 1740–1790* (Chapel Hill, NC, 1982).

[7] Jon Butler, *Awash in a Sea of Faith: Christianizing the American People* (London, 1990), p. 55; Nancy L. Rhoden, *Revolutionary Anglicanism: The Colonial Church of England Clergy during the American Revolution* (New York, 1999), pp. 32–3.

[8] Butler, *Sea of Faith*, p. 105; J.C.D. Clark, *The Language of Liberty, 1660–1832: Political Discourse and Social Dynamics in the Anglo-American World* (Cambridge, 1994).

[9] Butler, *Sea of Faith*, pp. 165.

[10] Mark A. Noll, "British and French North America to 1765," in Stewart J. Brown and Timothy Tackett (eds), *The Cambridge History of Christianity*, VII (Cambridge, 2006), p. 404.

century is misleading at best: establishments were still being vigorously upheld when the period covered by this volume ends. As some recent historians have emphasized, issues surrounding the nature of those establishments continued to shape political and social, as well as religious, life throughout the colonial period, and beyond. John and Samuel Adams, who certainly knew the people of Massachusetts better than Burke, ruefully observed that "we might as soon expect a change in the solar system as to expect they would give up their establishment."[11] Furthermore, not only were two of the events most often cited as contributing to the build-up to the American Revolution—"The Parsons' Cause" in Virginia (1758)[12] and "The Bishop Controversy" in New England (c. 1761 to c. 1776)[13]—explicitly triggered by issues connected with the existence of religious establishments, but, more broadly, the different dogmatic and doctrinal positions (particularly perhaps the divisions between Calvinists and Arminians), liturgical patterns, and modes of worship entrenched in the distinctions between establishment and dissent, were the stuff of much heated controversy at the time. At the very least, all these "anomalous" arrangements suggest that we need to use models other than that of the free market or religious pluralism if we are to understand the place of religion in British North America. This chapter accordingly begins by examining the nature of religious establishments in the American Colonies in general.[14] It then focuses on the position of the Church of England, which was established in some parts of the British Imperial world but suffered as a dissenting denomination in others. The discussion will concentrate in particular on the way in which, after a difficult start in the seventeenth century, Anglicanism had become by 1776 the most pervasive religious denomination in British North America, as well as the second largest denomination in the British colonies.

****

[11] Isaac Backus, *The Diary of Isaac Backus* (ed.), William G. McLoughlin (Providence, RI, 1979), II, p. 917.

[12] Rhys Isaac, "Religion and Authority: Problems of the Anglican Establishment in Virginia in the Era of the Great Awakening and the Parsons' Cause", *WMQ*, 3rd ser., XXX (1973), pp. 3–6.

[13] See Bridenbaugh, *Mitre and Sceptre*, Clark, *Language of Liberty*, and, more recently, James B. Bell, *A War of Religion: Dissenters, Anglicans, and the American Revolution* (Houndmills, 2008).

[14] I am indebted for some of the details of the nature of the religious establishments in various colonies to Michael W. McConnell, "Establishment and Disestablishment at the Founding, Part 1: Establishment of Religion," *William and Mary Law Review*, XLIV (2003), pp. 2105–2108.

How colonies should be organized religiously, and how ministers should be supported, was frequently stipulated, often quite precisely, in their foundation documents. What at first seems most striking are the differences in the ways religious life was organized within the assorted colonies, or groups of colonies, and the variety of religious denominations who could claim to have the status of an "establishment." In broad terms, British North America can be regarded as being divided ecclesiastically into three "regions" by the early eighteenth century: the south, where the Church of England was increasingly established; the north-east, where Congregationalism was the effective establishment; and the middle colonies, which were more pluralistic, thanks to their convoluted religious history from their foundation in the seventeenth century onwards. By the mid-eighteenth century most of the non-established churches in the thirteen colonies could be found in this third region. In order, by number of churches, they were: Presbyterian (160); German and Dutch Reformed (129); Baptist (96); Lutheran (95); Quaker (50); Mennonite and Moravian (c. 30); and Roman Catholic (27).[15] "Established" religious denominations ranged from Anglicans (in Virginia) to Congregationalists (in Massachusetts), and arguably until 1691, Roman Catholics (in Maryland), while those who were considered to be, and were treated as, "dissenters" from those establishments, ranged from Anglicans (in Connecticut) to Quakers (in Maryland) and Baptists (in Virginia). However, this broad-brush categorization is too static and too sweeping, failing to register both variations within regions and changes over time within individual colonies.

From their founding in the seventeenth century onwards most colonies harbored simultaneously those who adhered to the Church of England (as they understood it), to the reformed Protestant tradition, and to a more sectarian version of Christianity,[16] while the homogeneity of even "Puritan" New England can be exaggerated, as evidenced by the recurring religious controversies there. The ways in which religion was legislated for in the first British Empire thus appear rather unusual when compared to how religion was dealt with in other empires, and certainly in those empires—both historical and contemporary—with which it most frequently compared itself and which had usually attempted to organize and impose some kind

---

[15] Noll, "British and French North America," p. 404.

[16] Carla Pestana, *The English Atlantic in an Age of Revolution, 1640–1661* (Cambridge, MA, 2004), p. 2.

of uniformity on their various peoples.[17] From this perspective, religion in British North America certainly looks remarkably de-regulated, each colony effectively patterning its religious organization in its own way (within certain parameters). It seems, indeed, a model of "subsidiarity," in which central authority is limited to intervening in ecclesiastical affairs only on such relatively rare occasions as the peculiarities of the local situation warrant.

To explain the oddity of the British case, it is necessary to understand the religious situation in Britain itself, especially during the seventeenth century. Patterns of thought, behavior, and organization inherited from the Old World helped to shape and determine their articulation in the New, perhaps even to a greater extent in the case of religion than for other topics covered in this volume, since many emigrated to British North America (from both Britain and Europe) expressly to either escape from, implement, or further a particular form and brand of religious organization. As Butler has observed, "religion was a learned habit of the mind, and for English-speaking settlers, the religion they learned came from Europe."[18] One could go even further and argue that for many who either migrated to or were born in North America, their understanding of how their religious rivals had operated in Britain and Europe were fixed in particular historical moments—to the extent that some debates between religious denominations in eighteenth-century America were a literal replay of seventeenth-century English debates.[19] Yet religion was not simply transplanted from across the Atlantic entirely intact. British expansion to North America also created opportunities for novel ways of structuring religion, although even these may better be seen as modifications of the European heritage than as anything peculiarly "North American."

Catholic or Protestant, all early modern European polities agreed on the need for some kind of religious establishment as a safeguard for political and social order and as a way of maintaining and furthering what was considered true religion in the territory in question.[20] Nevertheless, the

---

[17] For late eighteenth-century readers, the seminal discussion of the place of religion in the Roman Empire before Christianization was Edward Gibbon's *The Decline and Fall of the Roman Empire*, the first volume of which, ironically, was published in 1776. For the drive to uniformity in the contemporary French empire, see Cornelius J. Jaenen, *The Role of the Church in New France* (Toronto, 1976), and for the Spanish empire, see Susan Schroeder and Stafford Poole (eds), *Religion in New Spain* (Albuquerque, NM, 2007).

[18] Butler, *Sea of Faith*, p. 5.

[19] See Bell, *War of Religion*, pp. 35–9.

[20] For European confessionalization, cf. Heinz Schilling, *Konfessionskonflikt und Staatsbildung: eine Fallstudie über das Verhältnis von religiösem und sozialem Wandel in der Frühneuzeit am Beispiel der Grafschaft Lippe* (Gutersloh, 1981).

religious history of Britain in the early modern period was marked by a number of distinctive complexities and tensions not found elsewhere in Europe. First, in the late 1620s and 30s, the broadly inclusive Calvinist consensus of the Elizabethan and Jacobean periods was challenged by a more exclusive Laudian vision, which meant that many who emigrated to North America and elsewhere in the 1630s saw themselves as members of the Church of England in flight from novel and unwarranted changes.[21] Second, from 1660 until 1689 definitions of "establishment" and "dissent" were the stuff of severely contested national politics.[22] Government policy veered between outright persecution of dissenters and either some form of comprehension (by which the majority of the nonconformists would be "comprehended" into a more relaxed version of the establishment), or toleration, which would permit the carefully delimited practice of certain forms of nonconformity.

Of crucial importance, in 1689 the "Toleration Act" guaranteed freedom of worship to all Protestant Trinitarian groups. An older historiography saw the Act, along with a second measure in 1712 that gave some freedoms to Episcopalians in Scotland, as a major turning point, marking the winning of religious liberty, a step on the road to Enlightenment, and, in some accounts, a move towards the growth of a secular society where religious issues were increasingly marginal. More recent interpretations, however, have emphasized the continuing pertinence of religious divisions to political life throughout the eighteenth century and have downplayed the two Toleration Acts as markers of human rights, recognizing that the English Act in particular, originally entitled "an act for exempting their majesties Protestant subjects dissenting from the Church of England from the penalties of certain laws," was merely a grudging grant of an incomplete, legally precarious, license to worship to certain specified nonconformist groups.[23] J.C.D. Clark has indeed argued that from 1660 until 1828/1832 England should be seen as a "confessional state," where allegiance to the Church of England (now largely Arminian in its theology) was a defining factor of

---

[21] The literature here is vast. Some landmark contributions include Patrick Collinson, *The Religion of Protestants: The Church in English Society, 1559–1625* (Oxford, 1982) and Nicholas Tyacke, *Anti-Calvinists: The Rise of English Arminianism, c. 1590–1640* (Oxford, 1987).

[22] John Spurr, *The Restoration Church of England, 1646–1689* (New Haven, 1991).

[23] John Coffey, *Persecution and Toleration in Protestant England, 1558–1689* (London, 2000); Ole Peter Grell, et al. (eds), *From Persecution to Toleration: The Glorious Revolution and Religion in England* (Oxford, 1991).

English political life.[24] Other historians, such as James Bradley, emphasize the continuing tensions between the English religious establishment and Protestant dissenting groups throughout the eighteenth century, particularly in times of political crisis, highlighting the capacity for those differences to be reflected in political allegiances, most notably in the debates over the American War of Independence.[25]

Nonetheless, however tentative, tenuous, and unsystematic the legitimacy allowed to Protestant groups outside the establishment, however potent the Tory cry of "the Church in danger" proved at intervals for the rest of the eighteenth century, the arrangement cobbled together early on after the overthrow of James II in 1689 endured as the Revolution "settlement." Moreover, England, and in particular London, was home to a diverse range of foreign Protestants from abroad,[26] while the Union in 1707 made Britain a bi-confessional state, since it admitted two religious establishments (the Church of England in England and Presbyterianism in Scotland).[27] To complicate matters further, there were accommodations at both theoretical and practical levels among the various religious denominations in England throughout the entire period[28] and in Scotland from 1660 to 1690, when moderate Episcopacy and moderate Presbyterianism found some common ground.[29] Linda Colley, in particular, has been impressed by a common Protestantism defining itself against a foreign Catholic "other," which she argues enabled a sense of Britishness to emerge after the Union with Scotland.[30] The maintenance of this "Protestant interest" would, in fact, be a central plank of religious life in British North America, enabling

[24] J.C.D. Clark, "England's Ancien Regime as a Confessional State," *Albion*, XXI (1989), pp. 450–74, and his "Great Britain and Ireland" in Brown and Tackett (eds), *The Cambridge History of Christianity*, VII, pp. 54–71.

[25] James Bradley, *Religion, Revolution, and English Radicalism: Nonconformity in Eighteenth-Century Politics and Society* (Cambridge, 1990).

[26] Robin D. Gwynn, *Huguenot Heritage: the History and Contribution of the Huguenots in Britain* (London, 1985); C.J. Podmore, *The Moravian Church in England, 1728–1760* (Oxford, 1998).

[27] For some of the implications see James J. Caudle, "James Boswell and the Bi-Confessional State," in William Gibson and Robert G. Ingram (eds), *Religious Identities in Britain 1660–1832* (Aldershot, 2005), pp. 119–46.

[28] Colin Haydon, *Anti-Catholicism in Eighteenth-Century England, c. 1714–80: A Political and Social Study* (Manchester, 1993).

[29] Clare Jackson, *Restoration Scotland, 1660–1690: Royalist Politics, Religion and Ideas* (Woodbridge, Suffolk, 2003).

[30] Linda Colley, *Britons: Forging the Nation, 1707–1837* (New Haven, 1992).

successive regimes to back and support a variety of colonial establishments as long as they maintained the Protestant cause.[31] This defining ambiguity—a dual establishment with a circumscribed but still permitted freedom for nonconformist denominations—along with a revived sense of Britain as the home of a pan-Protestant bulwark against the Catholic menace was carried across the Atlantic to the plantations, with all its tensions and contradictions intact. The colonists, in their turn, were able to appeal to the variegated establishments of Great Britain to promote either "establishmentarian" or "tolerationist" claims as it suited them.

Perhaps the first and most significant consequence of North American colonies being British was that they were part of a Christian empire, one with a distinctive religious message that would have enormous implications for European migrants and their descendants and also for the Native Americans and African slaves who lived within its dominion.[32] Almost as important, the British colonies, with the exception of Maryland,[33] were almost the only Protestant polities in a world of Catholic empires. The anti-Catholicism that provided the ideological and emotive undergirding for much of the emerging British identity took the form of an intense antipathy towards the neighboring colonies of France and Spain. If anything, the fear of the foreign Catholic "other" had even more bite behind it overseas where, after the third Anglo-Dutch War (1672–74), the colonial theatres of successive Imperial wars always pitted a Protestant Britain directly against the Catholic forces of Spain and France. The anti-Catholic spirit allowed colonists and metropolitan Britons to combine together in support of a shared Protestant interest and engaged the colonists as active participants in the century-long Anglo-French conflict that rocked both Europe and the New World.[34] In 1698, a Congregationalist minister (showing his knowledge of European history) described New England's interest as being with "the Protestant people and [God's] witnesses in Germany,

---

[31] Thomas S. Kidd, *The Protestant Interest: New England after Puritanism* (New Haven, 2004).

[32] Eliga H. Gould, "Prelude: The Christianizing of British America," in Norman Etherington (ed.), *Missions and Empire, OHBE* Companion Series (Oxford, 2005), pp. 19–39; James Axtell, *The Invasion Within: The Contest of Cultures in Colonial North America* (New York, 1985); Philip D. Morgan, "The Black Experience in the British Empire, 1680–1810," in Marshall (ed.), *OHBE*, II, pp. 465–86.

[33] See the essays in David B. Quinn (ed.), *Early Maryland in a Wider World* (Detroit, 1982).

[34] Kidd, *Protestant Interest.*

Bohemia, Hungarra [*sic*], France, the valleys of the Piedmont, and any other places in Europe where for his Names and Gospel sake they have been killed all day long."[35] This kind of sentiment helps explain the outrage and distrust felt by Protestant British North Americans over the passing of the Quebec Act in 1774, which appeared to establish Roman Catholics in Canada and was sufficiently provocative to be listed as a grievance in the Declaration of Independence.[36]

From the start, then, issues of establishment and dissent were intimately bound up with the progress of the British colonies in America. Even in those colonies where religion was not necessarily the prime mover behind their foundation, colonial leaders had, at least eventually, to work out some kind of a public religious strategy. Colonial charters laid down the respective frameworks for the religious constitution of each colony, which were then developed in general assemblies (or the like). Nevertheless, during the one and three-quarter centuries under review in this chapter, English/British legislators clearly did not have a single and coherent colonial religious policy. Given the remarkable changes in the religious life of the Mother Country in the same period, from the reign of James I to that of George III, it could hardly have been otherwise. Indeed it would be difficult to maintain that there was a colonial "policy" at all until the Interregnum.[37] Issues of religion were dealt with on a piecemeal basis, with a mixture of ideology, pragmatism, and opportunism. What also has to be borne in mind is the difference between legislation and implementation, so that while this chapter focuses largely on ecclesiastical laws, these were not always strictly adhered to nor put into practice. The remarkable variety of colonial governments in the New World—company colonies, proprietary governors, and more locally controlled colonies—by and large managed their own religious affairs in their own peculiar ways. Even when a more coherent religious policy did emerge

---

[35] Quoted in Thomas S. Kidd, "'Let Hell and Rome Do Their Worst': World News, the Catholic Threat, and International Protestantism in Provincial Boston," *New England Quarterly*, LXXVI (2003), p. 270.

[36] Peter Doll, *Revolution, Religion, and National Identity: Imperial Anglicanism in British North America, 1745–1795* (Madison, NJ, 2000); P. J. Marshall, "British North America, 1760–1815," in Marshall (ed.), *OHBE*, II, pp. 378–80.

[37] On the importance of the Interregnum in creating a colonial policy, see Pestana, *English Atlantic*. However, the readers should take note of Ken MacMillan's chapter in this volume, which argues that the Jacobean and Carline governments did have a reasonably well-worked out notion of sovereignty and imperial responsibility. Be that as it may, I would argue that this was not translated into a coherent vision for the church in the colonies as a whole.

during the Cromwellian regime, plantations reacted in different ways to the somewhat contradictory religious directives coming from home—ranging from the suppression of the Church of England to the promotion of godly reform or the toleration of all non-Anglican Protestants. Individual colonies generally pursued a combination of any two of these goals, but not all three. Although, after the Restoration, all the colonies had to acknowledge the established church, no less than the monarchy, as a central feature of the nation of which they were a dependency, how they did so was still largely left up to them. At the same time, the creation of new colonies without any link to an established British church, like West Jersey and Pennsylvania, ensured that not every colony would have a formal establishment.

****

The full range of the implications of setting up establishments of religion in North America can be seen in the cases of Virginia, on the one hand, and the New England colonies, on the other. As the first colonies to be settled, they offered two conflicting, but complementary, types of religious establishment, which mirrored the differing, and at times competing, religious sensibilities of those who emigrated from England to the New World. In the preamble to the first charter establishing Virginia, James I indicated that he expected the early rulers of the colony to "provide that the word and Science of God be preached, planted, and used... according to the rites and doctrines of the Church of England," and barred all other forms of worship.[38] The religious order of the Mother Country was to be replicated overseas, albeit in a very much pared down form, without the bishops, dioceses, archdeaconries, and church courts which were crucial to the functioning of the Anglican church at home. By the outbreak of civil war in England in 1642, however, the selection of clergy, which had originally been claimed by the governor, was firmly under the control of the local vestries, and strict adherence to the Church's doctrine, liturgy, and polity was not totally enforced.[39] The largest problem was not dissent but the challenge of transferring church structures to the colonies.[40] Even the Laudian governor of Virginia, William Berkeley, initially held back from prosecuting

---

[38] Quoted in Sanford H. Cobb, *The Rise of Religious Liberty in America: A History* (New York, 1902, reprint 1970), p. 418.

[39] George Maclaren Brydon, *Virginia's Mother Church and the Political Conditions under Which it Grew,* (Richmond, VA, 1947–1952), I, p. 259.

[40] Pestana, *English Atlantic,* p. 21.

those who did not conform, although in the late 1630s he allowed parishioners to refuse to pay tithes to a nonconforming minister (which encouraged Puritans to migrate to nearby Maryland).[41] During the Commonwealth and Protectorate, the English authorities were similarly pragmatic: they insisted on toleration for all forms of Protestants but in 1646 allowed the use of the Book of Common Prayer—which had been prohibited in England—for one year longer providing the prayers for the king were left out.[42] There is some indication that this arrangement lasted until 1660.[43]

At the restoration of the monarchy, Virginia quickly formulated a set of canons in 1661 which included the fundamental components of an established church[44] and which anticipated the English 1662 Act of Uniformity in a number of ways.[45] They mandated a publicly-funded church or chapel in every parish and a fixed salary for the clergy (with recourse to law for non-payment). They also laid down regulations for parish vestries, restricted induction to clergy who had been episcopally ordained and approved by the governor and vestry, and stipulated that services had to be performed according to the Book of Common Prayer. The canons also decreed that only Church of England ministers could perform marriage ceremonies and required vestries to deal with those found swearing, breaking the Sabbath, missing church, committing slander or back-biting, or the "foule and abominable sins of drunkenness, fornication and adultery." Under a follow-up law in 1662, "scismaticall persons" who did not have their children baptized were to be fined, and other laws barred Quakers from coming to live in the colony and made Quaker meetings unlawful.[46] Taken together, this legislation created a religious establishment for Virginia. They are also indicative of the ways in which post-Restoration Anglicanism, both at home and in the plantations, was able to bring the Puritan program of godliness and reformation of manners under its own auspices.[47]

[41] Pestana, *English Atlantic*, pp. 61–5.

[42] Brydon, *Virginia's Mother Church*, II, p. 123.

[43] Cobb, *The Rise of Religious Liberty*, p. 89.

[44] William Waller Hening, *The Statutes at Large, Being a Collection of all the Laws in Virginia* (New York, 1823), II, pp. 41–2.

[45] For the English Act of Uniformity, see Carl Stephenson and Frederick George Marcham (eds), *Sources of English Constitutional History*, rev. edn (New York, 1972), II, pp. 543–6.

[46] Hening, *Statutes at Large*, II, pp. 165–6; Brydon, *Virginia's Mother Church*, I, pp. 474–7.

[47] Cf. Jonathan Barry, "Bristol as a 'Reformation City', c. 1640–1780," in Nicholas Tyacke (ed.), *England's Long Reformation, 1500–1800* (London, 1998), pp. 261–84.

Theoretically, Virginia's religious establishment lasted the entire length of the colonial period. On occasion, the powers that be even sought to deny that the 1689 Toleration Act had any force in the colony.[48] But, in practice, as early as the mid-eighteenth century, partly as a result of a growth in numbers, Presbyterians were allowed to worship publicly.[49] Baptists, however, were still treated so harshly that, after witnessing such treatment, the young James Madison, although raised in the Church of England, was moved to denounce the "diabolical, hell-conceived principle of persecution."[50] Despite their mistreatment, Baptists were able to make some headway in the colony in numerical terms after 1750 and began to contest the Anglican church's legal privileges.[51]

As was often the case with religious establishments, tensions arose in Virginia over the ways in which ministers were paid. The legislature had fixed the salary of the parish minister at 16,000 pounds of tobacco per year, a measure of weight only. The fluctuating prices of the commodity led, not surprisingly, to conflict between clergy and taxpayers. In 1758, when tobacco prices were rapidly rising, the Virginia assembly countered with the "Two-penny Act," fixing clerical salaries at two—pence per pound. In the ensuing legal battles, the Presbyterian Patrick Henry emerged as an anti-clerical leader. His forceful anathema against the "greed" of the clergy crystallized sentiment of a more general nature around the notion that the Anglican church in Virginia was a byword for pastoral indifference, entrenched sloth, and a near total absence of genuine spiritual commitment.[52] The stereotype was then made gospel by nineteenth-century evangelicals, hostile on principle to anything established and looking for a convenient state of decline in need of the revivals that were their trademark. Only recently has less partisan research begun to rectify this disguised polemic.[53]

---

[48] Isaac, "Religion and Authority," *WMQ*, 3rd ser., XXX (1973), p. 28.

[49] Cobb, *The Rise of Religious Liberty*, pp. 97–107.

[50] James Madison to William Bradford, January 24, 1774, in Gaillard Hunt (ed.), *The Writings of James Madison*, 10 vols. (New York, 1900–1910), I, p. 18.

[51] Rhys Isaac, "Evangelical Revolt: the Nature of the Baptists' Challenge to the Traditional Order in Virginia, 1765–1775," *WMQ*, 3rd ser., XXXI (1974), pp. 345–68.

[52] Cobb, *The Rise of Religious Liberty*, p. 108; Isaac, *Transformation of Virginia*, chap. 7.

[53] Edward L. Bond (ed.), *Spreading the Gospel in Colonial Virginia: Preaching Religion and Community* (Lanham, MD, 2004), and Lauren F. Winner, *A Cheerful and Comfortable Faith. Anglican Religious Practice in the Elite Households of Eighteenth-Century Virginia* (New Haven, 2010). See also Joan Gundersen, *The Anglican Ministry in Virginia, 1723–1766: A Study of a Social*

If, in England's first colony, the Church of England enjoyed the same legal security as its counterpart at home (although endowed with few of metropolitan Anglicanism's institutional strengths), further north in New England its opponents were creating their own religious laboratories. Plymouth (1620), Massachusetts Bay (1630), Connecticut (1636), and New Haven (1639) were founded by Calvinist groups who came to be regarded as "dissenters" from the English establishment. The creation of these colonies can be seen in large measure as a religious act, an effort to fulfill the ideals of the Reformation, which the migrants felt had been betrayed in Old England.[54] Congregationalism, the denomination established by law in these colonies, resembled its counterpart in Virginia, but instead of privileging the national church and transatlantic centralization, the New England establishment was based on the religious beliefs of the majority in each town.[55]

Distinctions can be made between the Plymouth "pilgrims," who were separatists, and the Massachusetts Bay settlers who, though they believed that the church needed to be purified, never formally renounced their membership of the Church of England.[56] The Plymouth pilgrims had little hope of reforming the world and focused instead on their own lives without interfering much with those who disagreed with them, even drifting towards a "closet royalism" in the 1640s and 50s.[57] The Massachusetts Bay settlers, by contrast, wanted to reform the world, and persecuted anyone within their jurisdiction (as they defined it) who resisted them. Even during the Interregnum, when the suspension of any sort of establishment in most of the Anglophone world permitted new religious groups such as the Quakers and Baptists to proselytize with success,[58] "Puritan" New England's establishments survived intact. Only Rhode Island, founded in 1636 by Roger

Class (New York, 1989), and John K. Nelson, A Blessed Company: Parishes, Parsons and Parishioners in Anglican Virginia, 1690–1776 (Chapel Hill, NC, 2001).

[54] For example, see Frank J. Bremmer, John Winthrop: America's Forgotten Founding Father (New York, 2005). But also note those disillusioned migrants who returned to England during the 1640s and 50s: Susan Hardman Moore, Pilgrims: New World Settlers and the Call of Home (New Haven, 2008).

[55] Cobb, The Rise of Religious Liberty, p. 156. New England establishments did, however, make use of occasional colony-wide synods and official "platforms" to effect significant changes in their religious life. See Richard P. Gildrie, The Profane, the Civil and the Godly: The Reformation of Manners in Orthodox New England, 1679–1749 (Philadelphia, 1994).

[56] Cobb, The Rise of Religious Liberty, pp. 150–1.

[57] Pestana, English Atlantic, p. 45.

[58] Carla Gardina Pestana, Quakers and Baptists in Colonial Massachusetts (Cambridge, 1991).

Williams after his expulsion from Massachusetts Bay, was, in European terms, a remarkable experiment in religious liberty, although the meeting at Newport which ratified the newly-approved charter in 1663 added the rider that Roman Catholics could not be freemen.[59]

After 1660, the New England establishment was in an inherently uncomfortable situation in dealing with the metropolitan authorities: in England, nonconformists were excluded by law from the established church, while in New England, Anglicans were treated as nonconformists.[60] Three decades of failed initiatives on both sides led to the new Massachusetts charter of 1691, which required some degree of toleration for all varieties of Protestant in the Bay Colony but said nothing of what, if anything, could be established.[61] To finesse the continuing dilemma, religious legislation in Massachusetts after that date did not refer by name to any denomination, and instead demanded that all towns outside Boston maintain "an able, learned and orthodox minister," elected by the vote of the male members of the church, approved by the congregation, and provided for by taxation.[62] In every case but one this maneuver resulted in a Congregationalist establishment, but notoriously in Swansea, where Baptists were the largest group, the result was the only Baptist establishment anywhere on the globe.[63]

It is seriously misleading to suggest, as some historians have done, that in the more relaxed atmosphere of the eighteenth century New England developed a "multiple religious establishment."[64] In both Massachusetts and Connecticut prior to the Revolution all inhabitants were presumptively Congregationalists and thereby liable for the support of the church in their parish. Concessions were given grudgingly and only to named dissenting groups. When the first Anglican church was built in Connecticut in 1723, its members tried unsuccessfully to retain the taxes that they were forced to pay to support a Congregationalist minister in order to maintain a clergyman of

---

[59] Conrad Henry Moehlman, *The American Constitutions and Religion: Religious References in the Charters of the Thirteen Colonies and the Constitution of the Forty-Eight States, A Source Book on Church and State in the United States* (Berne, IN, 1938), p. 28.

[60] Pestana, *English Atlantic*, pp. 213–19.

[61] Moehlman, *American Constitutions and Religion*, p. 23.

[62] Reed, *Church and State in Massachusetts*.

[63] Leonard W. Levy, *The Establishment Clause: Religion and the First Amendment* (New York, 1986, 2nd edn, 1993), p. 17.

[64] Levy, *Establishment Clause*, ch. 2–3.

their own denomination.[65] In 1727, Connecticut (under An Act for the Ease of such as Soberly Dissent) and Massachusetts (under the Five Mile Act, which granted the concession to those who lived no more than five miles from a church of their denomination) legalized Anglican worship. Later this same indulgence was extended to Quakers and Baptists.[66] But non-named groups had no protection whatsoever in either colony. In New Hampshire, "conscientious" dissenters were ostensibly let off paying ministerial taxes from 1692 as long as they "constantly attend the publick worship of God on the Lord's day according to their own persuasion."[67] The resulting situation contained so many anomalies as to generate overlapping chains of local wrangles, appeals to the crown, and suits at law pretty regularly throughout the eighteenth century, both in the colonial and British courts. It would take the Revolution and the subsequent decline in the numerical strength of Congregationalism to put an end to this rigged "marketplace," first by making establishment more equitable and then ultimately by abolishing it entirely.

New England's rather tangled history in the eighteenth century is just the confused situation in the colonies in general in particularly vivid form. Where New England reluctantly liberalized its establishment, other colonies were, however, in the process of going in the opposite direction, towards narrowing what had been achieved previously. Butler has noted that the power of the state church tradition came from three principal features: "coercion, territoriality and public ceremonialism"; and that, although the different religious denominations that had establishment status in the various colonies wielded these three weapons in their own distinctive ways, they were neverthless, from the perspective of the laity, "a remarkably similar product."[68]

Overall, kings of England in the seventeenth century had allowed much more liberal religious arrangements in America than many colonists themselves were willing to endorse in the first half of the eighteenth. Nicholas Trott's *The Laws of the British Plantations in America, relating to the Church and the Clergy, Religion and Learning* illustrated graphically on its publica-

---

[65] Cobb, *The Rise of Religious Liberty,* pp. 268–70.

[66] Cobb, *The Rise of Religious Liberty,* pp. 234–5, 270–1. On New England Baptists, see William G. McLoughlin, *New England Dissent, 1630–1833: The Baptists and the Separation of Church and State* (Cambridge, MA, 1971).

[67] Cobb, *The Rise of Religious Liberty,* pp. 298–9.

[68] Butler, *Sea of Faith,* p. 165.

tion in 1721 the ways in which the legislatures of the various colonies after 1685 effectively reversed the relatively liberal measures that had earlier been imposed upon them by an interventionist crown.[69] Royal charters were far more likely than parliamentary statutes to indicate the personal sympathies and inclination of an individual monarch. It is highly unlikely, for example, that in the early 1630s, Parliament—if it had met—would have created an English colony as a retreat for Catholics as Charles I did when he issued the Maryland charter. Similarly, if later monarchs and their immediate advisors were generally more concerned with the maintenance of the Protestant interest than simply with the defense of the Church of England, then the pan-Protestant world of North America could be seen as a necessary counter to the French and Spanish colonies. What is particularly noticeable is the way that a number of charters issued by Charles II, well before the 1689 Toleration Act, built in some form of religious toleration. In the Declaration of Breda of April 1660, Charles II had promised "a liberty to tender consciences...that no man shall be disquieted or called in question for differences of opinion in matter of religion which do not disturb the peace of the kingdom,"[70] and it is striking how far the Breda formulation became a template for the charters which were issued during his reign, in direct opposition to the sharply punitive measures his parliaments inflicted on nonconformity in England.[71] Ironically, in the colonies, the absence of the kinds of constitutional and political constraints that made Charles anything but an absolute monarch at home allowed him (in effect, arbitrarily) to do such things as order the High-Church Governor of Virginia "not to suffer any man to be molested, and disquieted in the exercise of religion."[72] In a similar vein, the charter for Carolina, issued in 1663, gave the colonial proprietors control over the religious complexion of the colony with "such indulgences and dispensations and with such limitations as... [they] shall think fit and reasonable,"[73] and the 1665 charter went further in

[69] Nicholas Trott, *The Laws of the British Plantations in America: Relating to the Church and the Clergy, Religion and Learning, Collected in One Volume* (London, 1721).

[70] The text of the Declaration of Breda is printed in J.P. Kenyon (ed.), *The Stuart Constitution: Documents and Commentary* (Cambridge, 1986), pp. 331–2.

[71] See, for example, the very similar language of the Rhode Island charter of 1663, quoted in Moehlman, *American Constitutions and Religion*, p. 27. For the religious attitudes of the parliaments of Charles II's reign see I.M. Green, *The Re-Establishment of the Church of England, 1660–1663* (Oxford, 1978).

[72] Quoted in Pestana, *English Atlantic*, p. 223.

[73] John Wesley Brinsfield, *Religion and Politics in Colonial South Carolina* (Easley, SC, 1983).

ordering that "no person . . . be molested . . . for any differences in opinion or practice in matters of religious concernments who do not actually disturb the civil peace" allowing them to act according to their "judgements and conscience," "any law, statute or clause contained or to be contained, usage or custom of our realm of England, to the contrary thereof, in any-wise notwithstanding."[74] The "Fundamental Constitutions of Carolina" (1669/70), never fully put into operation, did grant public maintenance for the Church of England alone, but they also recognized the Amerindians, who were deemed "utterly strangers to Christianity, [but] whose idolatry, ignorance or mistake give us no right to expel them or use them ill," and acknowledged as well the need to attract others to the colony who "will unavoidably be of different opinions concerning matters of religion," an offer extending to "Jews, heathens, and other dissenters from the purity of the Christian religion."[75] The Constitutions even allowed for any seven or more people "agreeing in any religion" to worship together as long as they acknowledged there was a God who should be publicly worshipped in some external way, and provided they did not use abusive language against other religions.[76]

Despite this lofty rhetoric, the Anglican religious establishment in both Carolinas came to have the same legal features as in Virginia over the course of the eighteenth century. Although the relevant measures were by no means wholly implemented, they were a marked reversal of what had been permitted earlier. In the late seventeenth century, almost 50 percent of North Carolina's inhabitants were nonconformist (generally Presbyterians or Quakers), as were several of the governors.[77] Yet rather than foster religious liberty, the South Carolina assembly in 1704 passed legislation (very similar to that adopted in Virginia in 1661) which made the Anglican Church the sole establishment, required the use of the Book of Common Prayer, banned

---

[74] Quoted in Moehlman, *American Constitutions and Religion*, p. 29.

[75] Quoted in Moehlman, *American Constitutions and Religion*, p. 30. Cf. David Armitage, "John Locke, Carolina, and the Two Treatises of Government," *Political Theory*, XXXII (2004), pp. 602–27, and Vicki Hsueh, "Giving Orders: Theory and Practice in the Fundamental Constitutions of Carolina," *Journal of the History of Ideas*, LXIII (2002), pp. 425–46.

[76] Charles H. Lippy argues for the remarkable level of religious pluralism in South Carolina in the late seventeenth and early eighteenth centuries: "Chastized by Scorpions: Christianity and Culture in Colonial South Carolina, 1669–1740," *Church History*, LXXIX (2010), pp. 253–70.

[77] Brinsfield, *Religion and Politics*, pp. 6–9. See also Robert M. Weir, "'Shaftesbury's Darling': British Settlement in the Carolinas at the Close of the Seventeenth Century," in Nicholas Canny (ed.), *OHBE*, I, *The Origins of Empire* (Oxford, 1998), pp. 375–97.

nonconformists from any role in government, and supported clergy and church buildings from the public purse.[78] North Carolina, after debates about tax support and church power, adopted an Anglican establishment in 1715.[79] Dissenters in both Carolinas were treated far more leniently than they were in Virginia; nevertheless, in all three colonies in the early eighteenth century there was such a thing as establishment and dissent in a form that would have been entirely recognizable to an inhabitant of the Mother Country.

The same consolidation of the position of the Church of England in the southern colonies after 1689 was continued in the cases of Maryland and Georgia. Maryland became officially Anglican in 1691 after the Catholic Calvert family lost the proprietorship in the aftermath of the Glorious Revolution, and the exclusive position of the established church was re-enforced by further legislation passed between 1697 and 1707.[80] In their former refuge, Maryland Catholics were obliged to pay double taxes and were barred from political office, while their religious services were forbidden outright.[81] In Georgia, the last of the thirteen colonies to be settled, the Church of England was also given a privileged position from its foundation and was accorded full establishment status in 1758, although the Trustees encouraged immigration by welcoming a wide variety of Protestant dissenters from throughout Britain and Europe.[82]

Standing somewhat apart from the South and New England, the middle colonies, founded in the Restoration period, provided an anti-establishment model of sorts. Both Anglicans and Congregationalists were under-represented in the region, partly because in addition to the Scots and Scots-Irish, these colonies attracted large numbers of immigrants from Germany.[83] Pennsylvania, founded in 1681 as a grant to William Penn from Charles II, was envisaged as a refuge for Penn's fellow Quakers, subject to some of the

---

[78] Brinsfield, *Religion and Politics*, pp. 23–4. See also S. Charles Bolton, *Southern Anglicanism: The Church of England in Colonial South Carolina* (Westport, CT, 1982).

[79] Butler, *Sea of Faith*, p. 103.

[80] Nelson Waite Rightmyer, *Maryland's Established Church* (Baltimore, 1956), pp. 14–54.

[81] Thomas O'Brien Hanley, *The American Revolution and Religion: Maryland, 1770–1800* (Washington, 1971), p. 10.

[82] Reba Carolyn Strickland, *Religion and the State in Georgia in the Eighteenth Century* (New York, 1939), pp. 36–43.

[83] Stephen L. Longenecker, *Piety and Tolerance: Pennsylvania German Religion, 1700–1850* (New York, 1994).

most severe bouts of persecution that seventeenth-century England would witness, and as a "holy experiment" in religious liberty.[84] The "Frame of Government" Penn wrote for Pennsylvania in 1682 was one of the most comprehensively tolerant of all of the founding documents of the colonies: all who acknowledged God to be the creator and who saw themselves "obliged in conscience to live peaceably and justly" could believe what, and worship how, they wanted: "nor shall they be compelled, at any time, to frequent or maintain any religious worship, place or ministry whatsoever."[85]

The middle colonies were home to a collection of religious traditions and faith communities so various as to be unlikely to be found in the same profusion anywhere in Europe.[86] But it would be wrong to equate their religious diversity with a mutually tolerant pluralism. Instead, the sheer variety of religious alternatives on display in the middle colonies could foster a sharp sense of denominational rivalry.[87] When Michael Schlatter, a German Reformed Church minister, first came to Philadelphia in 1746 he found a rich array of religious groupings: Church of England; Swedish; Lutheran; Presbyterian; German Reformed; Roman Catholic; Quaker; Anabaptist; and Moravian. But, instead of being impressed by the range of faith options on offer, he was more concerned with the "poison" his congregations could imbibe from their religious rivals.[88] This mutual hostility was not a peculiarity of presumptively inbred, parochial German immigrants (Franklin's "Boors"): the British groups were, if anything, worse in their infighting. In Pennsylvania, for example, there was often bitter sectarian conflict between Quakers and Presbyterians. However much we might regard the middle colonies as the future United States in embryo, to an eighteenth-century sensibility they were an object lesson in why an

---

[84] Edwin B. Bronner, *William Penn's Holy Experiment: The Founding of Pennsylvania, 1681–1701* (New York, 1962).

[85] Quoted in Moehlman, *American Constitutions and Religion*, p, 33.

[86] See J. William Frost, *A Perfect Freedom: Religious Liberty in Pennsylvania* (University Park, PA, 1993); Richard W. Pointer, *Protestant Pluralism and the New York Experience: A Study of Eighteenth-Century Religious Diversity* (Bloomington, IN, 1988); Sally Schwartz, *A Mixed Multitude: The Struggle for Toleration in Colonial Pennsylvania* (New York, 1987).

[87] Clark, *Language of Liberty*.

[88] Quoted in Clark, *Language of Liberty*, p. 211. See also Aaron Fogleman, *Jesus is Female: Moravians and the Challenge of Religion in Early America* (Philadelphia, 2007).

establishment of religion (albeit a generally tolerant one) was a necessity for a decently ordered society.

To a large extent, then, the anti-establishment ethos of the middle colonies (and Rhode Island) has perhaps loomed disproportionately large in discussions of religious life in colonial America.[89] In their own day, they were regarded with suspicion by the inhabitants of the other colonies, and they were not quite the unqualified bastions of religious liberty that we sometimes imagine. They had no hesitation in enacting religious tests for office holders, as well as laws against blasphemy, echoing the 1698 Blasphemy Act in England which penalized those who denied the Trinity, believed in more gods than one, denied that Christianity was true, or denied the divine authority of Scripture.[90] Presbyterians, strongly represented in the middle colonies, were keen to attack the Church of England but cited the Scottish precedent to demand an establishment for themselves.[91] And while most of the colony of New York did not have a religious establishment, in metropolitan New York successive attempts to gain government support for the Church of England were relatively successful in the main. After the Dutch ceded power to the English in 1664, the new government agreed to tolerate the Dutch Reformed Church, and gave religious freedoms to Protestant nonconformists. Nevertheless, the authorities demanded that each parish should choose overseers who were to select a minister and to raise taxes as well as supporting the Dutch church, thereby in effect creating a binary establishment.[92] Then, during the governorship of the Anglican Benjamin Fletcher, the assembly passed the Ministry Act in 1693, which created parishes in metropolitan New York (New York, Richmond, Westchester and Queens), and authorized the salaries of "a good, sufficient Protestant minister."[93] The governor took this to mean a Church of England cleric, although this interpretation was contested by other Protestant groups. But, to all intents and purposes, metropolitan New York had a Church of England establishment throughout the colonial period.

---

[89] See Ned C. Landsman, *From Colonials to Provincials: American Thought and Culture, 1680–1760* (New York, 1997), and Jon Butler, *Becoming America: the Revolution before 1776* (Cambridge, MA, 2001).

[90] Levy, *Establishment Clause*, p. 5.

[91] Landsman, *From Colonial to Provincials*, p. 21, and see his "Nation, Migration, and the Province in the First British Empire: Scotland and the Americas, 1600–1800," *AHR*, CIV (1999), pp. 471–2.

[92] Michael Kammen, *Colonial New York: A History* (New York, 1975), pp. 220–1.

[93] Hugh Hastings (ed.), *Ecclesiastical Records, State of New York* (Albany, NY, 1901), I, p. 570.

The colonial government even sought an opinion in 1766 to determine whether the 1662 English Act of Uniformity applied in the colonies and refused to charter a Presbyterian congregation as late as 1775.[94]

By the mid 1730s, religious establishments in the colonies seemed to be approaching maturity. The New England colonies had made their minimal and grudging concessions to their own versions of dissent, the Church of England had been established where it was going to be established, and in the new colony of Georgia, its pre-eminence was taken for granted, showing just how much of a given it had become in the South. Then, very suddenly, during the late 1730s and 40s, the whole arrangement was widely and fiercely contested in much of British North America by the massive religious revival known as the "Great Awakening." Often associated with the evangelical preaching of the Anglican turned Calvinist Methodist George Whitefield, the Great Awakening put pressure on all religious establishments, perhaps most severely in both Virginia and New England, where the respective establishments were most securely entrenched.[95] While there is no space for a detailed account of the Great Awakening here, its importance for the position of religious establishments in North America is worth drawing out. At one level, the Great Awakening can be seen as a challenge to religious authority, pitting the impulses of sectarian purity against apparently formalistic establishments. The raw emotive force of the movement fuelled repeated calls for a voluntary religion based on a personal apprehension of the Spirit. Whitefield himself emphasized religion as a matter for the individual and criticized established churches of all hues, while the revival over which he presided attracted a heterogeneous collection of adherents of all classes and races, even finding room on occasion for black, Indian, and women preachers.[96] The result was a series of schisms and divisions within congregations as true believers were invited to break free from what were

---

[94] Cobb, *The Rise of Religious Liberty*, pp. 342–3.

[95] For Virginia, see Isaac, "Religion and Authority," and Wesley M. Gewehr, *The Great Awakening in Virginia, 1740–1790* (Durham, NC, 1930). For New England, see C.C. Goen, *Revivalism and Separatism in New England, 1740–1800: Strict Congregationalists and Separate Baptists in the Great Awakening*, 2nd edn (Hamden, CT, 1969).

[96] Harry S. Stout, *The Divine Dramatist: George Whitefield and the Rise of Modern Evangelicalism* (Grand Rapids, MI, 1991); Frank Lambert, *"Pedlar in Divinity": George Whitefield and the Transatlantic Revivals, 1737–1770* (Princeton, 1994), and his *Inventing "The Great Awakening"* (Princeton, 1999); and Thomas S. Kidd, *The Great Awakening: The Roots of Evangelical Christianity in Colonial America* (New Haven, CT, 2007).

seen as the lifeless government-supported churches. In New England alone, the revival resulted in more than 200 schisms[97] and caused permanent divisions between the "Old Lights" who attempted to keep traditional Congregationalism intact and "New Lights" who responded to the revivalist message of Whitefield and Jonathan Edwards. Others were encouraged to seek refuge in a more rationalistic religion, while some found a safe haven in the ordered liturgy of the Church of England. Inspired by the revival, the New England Baptist leader, Isaac Backus, chided Congregationalists for attacking "taxation without representation" while themselves taxing Baptists and other non-Congregationalists. He himself saw all religious establishments as morally wrong,[98] as did many other Baptists and Methodists. Similar divisions and debates occurred throughout colonial British North America, so much so that recurring speculation in the secondary literature about the relationship between the Great Awakening and the Revolution has become a regular feature of early American historiography.[99]

Yet, on the eve of the Revolution, more than thirty years after Whitefield's first itinerancy, the colonial religious establishments were on the whole still pretty secure. Congregationalists remained the majority denomination in New England, while the Baptists had made only moderate headway there and less still in the Southern backcountry. Methodism, eventually the big winner in the antebellum period, was as yet a tiny sect, and much of the original insurgency in the middle colonies had been accommodated, absorbed, and to a degree pre-empted. The Revolution itself would, of course, alter power relations within the colonies, and make the courting of popular support a necessity, with significant consequences for religious freedoms. But arguably it was the post-Revolutionary Second Great Awakening (1790–1840) which

---

[97] Butler, *Sea of Faith*, p. 179.

[98] William G. McLoughlin, "Isaac Backus and the Separation of Church and State in America," *AHR*, LXXIII (1968), pp. 1392–413.

[99] Jerome Mahaffey, *Preaching Politics: the Religious Rhetoric of George Whitefield and the Founding of a New Nation* (Waco, TX, 2007), and Dee E. Andrews, *The Methodists and Revolutionary America, 1760–1800: The Shaping of an Evangelical Culture* (Princeton, 2000). See also Alan Heimert, *Religion and the American Mind: From the Great Awakening to the Revolution* (Cambridge, MA, 1966), Harry S. Stout, "Religion, Communications, and the Ideological Origins of the American Revolution," *WMQ*, 3rd ser., XXXIV (1977), pp. 519–41, and Philip Goff, "Revivals and Revolution: Historiographic Turns since Alan Heimert's *Religion and the American Mind*," *Church History*, LXVII (1998), pp. 695–721. For an excellent overview, see Thomas S. Kidd, *God of Liberty: A Religious History of the American Revolution* (New York, 2010).

would accomplish far more change, and in much shorter time, than its colonial namesake.[100]

****

Thus far, this chapter has demonstrated that the issue of religious establishment in colonial America is less straightforward in both its nature and in its development over time than the usual narrative of progress towards liberty would have it. The remainder of the discussion will be a short case study of the Church of England in British North America. Given the prominent role of the Church within Britain, its position within the colonies can shed some light on links with, and relations between, Britons on both sides of the Atlantic. Equally, given the Anglican church's mix of established and dissenting status in the colonies, its place in North America gives some insight into what being established or dissenting could mean in practice.

It has often been (rightly) claimed that the Church of England in the seventeenth century had been rather slow at conceiving of North America as either a mission field or an opportunity for enlarging the territories under its charge.[101] Although Anglican clergy did accompany settlers to Virginia and elsewhere in the early seventeenth century, and Archbishop Laud as early as 1634 had handed the responsibility of overseeing the interests of the Church of England in the colonies to the bishops of London, nothing significant was accomplished during the disruptions of the 1640s and 1650s. The Restored Stuart church, however, was more aware of the opportunity the colonies offered for spreading its brand of Protestantism to a far wider world than had been dreamt of in the first century of the Reformation. The 1662 Book of Common Prayer, for example, included a new baptism service "for those of riper years," added in part because it was hoped that it "may be always useful for the baptizing of Natives in our Plantations and others converted to the Faith." Moreover, from his appointment as Bishop of London in 1675 until his death in 1713, Henry Compton took a more active line in the colonies than his predecessors, and aided the cause of Anglicanism there through two crucial appointments: James Blair,

---

[100] Charles Hambrick-Stowe, *Charles G. Finney and the Spirit of American Evangelicalism* (Grand Rapids, MI, 1996).

[101] Hans Cnattingius, *Bishops and Societies: A Study of Anglican Colonial Missionary Expansion, 1698–1850* (London, 1952), pp. 1–12.

rector of Henrico parish in Virginia from 1685, and, from 1689 until his death in 1743, commissary in the colony; and Thomas Bray, commissary in the newly Anglican Maryland from 1695.[102]

Blair could claim much of the credit for the Anglican renewal in Virginia during his long residence in the colony. Under his stewardship, clergy were better educated and undertook their duties more diligently, while the College of William and Mary, an unabashedly Anglican institution from its founding in 1693, was very much his handiwork. The much-increased Anglican presence in the colony had a physical dimension as well in the handsome new brick buildings (paid for by public revenues), which increased the number of churches in Virginia from 35 in 1680 to 61 in 1724.[103]

Bray was behind the organization and institutionalization of the Anglican missionary impulse through the founding of the Society for the Promotion of Christian Knowledge [SPCK] (1698) and, even more pertinently, the Society for the Propagation of the Gospel [SPG] in 1701. Endowed with a royal charter, and supported by significant funding, the charge of the SPG in the colonies extended to Native Americans, African slaves, and, most pertinently, European colonists who lived in places where the Church was not established. By 1776, over 100 clergy and schoolmasters were funded by the SPG, which also sent over books, paid for catechists, and through an annual fundraising sermon in London publicized the Church's colonial project.[104]

By the mid 1730s, the Church was established throughout the South and in parts of New York, and Anglican numbers had grown to the point where they were the second largest denomination in the colonies. Anglicans were also easily the most ubiquitous colonial denomination because their main rival, the numerically larger Congregationalists, were to be found almost exclusively in

---

[102] James B. Bell, *The Imperial Origins of the King's Church in Early America, 1607–1783* (Houndmills, 2004), pp. 10–73, and G. Yeo, "A Case without Parallel: The Bishops of London and the Anglican Church Overseas, 1660–1748," *Journal of Ecclesiastical History*, XLIV (1993), pp. 450–75. For biographies of Blair and Bray, see *Oxford Dictionary of National Biography*, s.v. (A commissary was an episcopal officer who, acting on delegated powers from his bishop, was charged with oversight of the clergy in some part of his diocese).

[103] Nelson, *Blessed Company*, and Gundersen, *Anglican Ministry in Virginia*.

[104] Standard histories of the SPG are H.P. Thompson, *Into All Lands: The History of the Society for the Propagation of the Gospel in Foreign Parts* (London, 1951), and Daniel O' Connor, et al., *Three Centuries of Mission: The United Society for the Propagation of the Gospel, 1701–2000* (London, 2000). See also Rowan Strong, *Anglicanism and the British Empire, c. 1700–1850* (Oxford, 2006), and Andrew Porter, *Religion Versus Empire?: Protestant Missionaries and Overseas Expansion, 1700–1914* (Manchester, 2004), pp. 16–28.

New England, the most densely populated region of British North America. But Anglicans had begun to have a presence even in Congregational New England as early as 1686 with the foundation of a small congregation which would soon become King's Chapel, Boston, while the building of Christ Church, Philadelphia in 1696 indicated that the Church was also beginning to make inroads in Pennsylvania, the one-time haven for Quakers.[105]

For all these successes, where the Church of England was not established, it suffered from a lack of resources. Robert Jenney, the commissary in Pennsylvania, moaned to London officials in 1749 that "the members of our Church are not the Richest in the place, the Riches generally centring in the Quakers and High Dutch who are very numerous and carry all before them."[106] He also pointed to a wider problem: "our Church labours under very great discouragement as we have no legal Establishment (as they have at New York) not so much a Charter of Incorporation to enable us to manage our Business to the best advantage." Even where the Church was established, it lacked the administrative and organizational structures and apparatus (most crucially bishops) which were integral to its functioning, including the primary means for the pastoral oversight of the Church in Old England, the episcopal visitation process.[107] From Philadelphia, William Sturgeon acknowledged that "the Church of England without a Bishop is left to the care only of a few private Clergymen who have no person to oversee or call them to account upon their misbehavior, nor to encourage and support them in their best cause. This leaves them and their respective congregations to do the best they can and indeed sometimes it is bad enough."[108]

Efforts to procure a bishop for North America preoccupied leading Church of England clergy in England from the late seventeenth century onwards.[109] In one of the most influential pleas for an American episcopate,

---

[105] See Bell, *Imperial Origins*. For a survey of the developing position of the Church throughout the British Colonies, see John Frederick Woolverton, *Colonial Anglicanism in North America* (Detroit, MI, 1984).

[106] Rev. Dr Robert Jenney to Secretary of the SPG, October 26, 1749, in William Stevens Perry (ed.), *Historical Collections Relating to the American Colonial Church* ([Hartford, CT.], 1870–78), II, p. 260.

[107] For a discussion of the eighteenth-century visitation process in England, see Norman Sykes, "The Primary Visitation of William Wake of the Diocese of Lincoln, 1706," *Journal of Ecclesiastical History*, II (1951), pp. 190–206.

[108] Rev. William Sturgeon to the Archbishop of Canterbury, November 29, 1758, in Perry (ed.), *Historical Collections*, II, p. 268.

[109] Rhoden, *Revolutionary Anglicanism*, p. 39.

a sermon before the SPG in 1741, Thomas Secker, a future archbishop of Canterbury, admitted that a strengthened Church in the colonies would save souls in its own very distinct way: "We acknowledge it, where is taught Christianity by our care, will be taught it as professed in the Church established here by Law. There can be no Teaching at all, but in some particular Form. We think our own the Best."[110] Therefore, a bishop needed to be sent to the colonies so that "the primitive and most useful Appointment of Confirmation might be restored, and an Orderly Discipline exercised in the Church," although Secker was careful to stress that such a bishop would not "encroach at all on the present Right of the Civil Government in our colonies or bring their Dependence into any Degree of that Danger."[111] Leading politicians at home were afraid that these proposals would encourage the higher-flying Tories among the English clergy and antagonize colonists of all varieties, and so they came to nothing.[112] For some Anglicans in America the lack of a bishop demonstrated the profound and inequitable disadvantages that the Church was under when compared with other denominations in the colonies. Henry Caner, the rector of King's Chapel in Boston from 1747 until he fled America in 1776, expressed his sense of unfairness: "we are a Rope of Sand; there is no union, no authority amongst us; we cannot even summon a Convention for united Counsell and advice, while the Dissenting Ministers have their Monthly, Quarterly and Annual Associations, Conventions, &c., to advise, assist, and support each other in any Measures which they shall think proper to enter into."[113] Caner was, of course, writing from what might be considered the inhospitable terrain of New England, but even Anglicans in those southern colonies where the Church was established were unable to procure a bishop. Indeed, some Anglican clergy in Virginia were amongst the most vociferous opponents of having a bishop in America, concerned as they were about episcopal meddling in their affairs.[114]

---

[110] Thomas Secker, *A Sermon Preached before the Incorporated Society for the Propagation of the Gospel in Foreign Parts...* (London, 1741), p. 29.

[111] Secker, *Sermon*, p. 28.

[112] Stephen Taylor, "Whigs, Bishops and America: The Politics of Church Reform in Mid-Eighteenth-Century England," *Historical Journal*, XXXVI (1993), pp. 331–56. See also Doll, *Revolution, Religion and National Identity*, pp. 166–7, 193–4.

[113] Caner to Archbishop Thomas Secker, January 7, 1763, in Perry (ed.), *Historical Collections*, III, p. 489.

[114] Frederick V. Mills, *Bishops By Ballot: An Eighteenth-Century Ecclesiastical Revolution* (New York, 1978).

What is noteworthy is that the Church in North America managed to function at all in the face of all these difficulties. It could re-supply and expand its own ranks only through clergy sent over from Britain or, increasingly, by American-born ordinands making the sometimes perilous sea crossing to London and back. Given the time lags involved, a parish might be left empty after the death of a minister for several years, as letters had to be sent over requesting a replacement. The lack of effective oversight of the clergy could also seriously retard the Church's mission. Philip Reading moaned in 1747 of the behavior of the incumbent of Duck Creek, Pennsylvania, "one irregular Clergyman...will pull down more in six months than a diligent missionary can build up in almost as many years." But as Reading also noted, the Church of England could "obtain a preference only by the purity of our doctrine and the testimony of our own good lives and examples,"[115] and there are ample testimonials to the growth of congregations in the colonies through the respect earned by individual Anglican clergy.[116]

In the absence of formal ecclesiastical structures, the Church was heavily reliant on lay members for leadership. This dependence can be seen most obviously in Virginia, where the laity had much control over day to day activities through the powers of the General Assembly (which framed legislation for the Church as a whole) and vestries (which had oversight of individual churches, including the right to elect ministers). Historians have traditionally viewed the "laicization" of the American Church in negative terms, confusing laicization with secularization, but in fact it can be seen more positively as members of the laity taking their religious duties seriously. Throughout North America, the Church was reliant on lay members in other ways, not only for contributing to the upkeep of the fabric, serving as lay readers and, in areas such as New England where the Church was on an unsure footing, providing spaces in private houses for meetings before a church could be built.[117]

[115] Rev. Philip Reading to SPG, March 26, 1747, in Perry (ed.), *Historical Collections*, II, pp. 244–5.
[116] For an account of the viability of the Church even in arguably the most hostile territory in the colonies, see Jeremy Gregory, "Refashioning Puritan New England: the Church of England in British North America, c. 1680–c. 1770," *Transactions of the Royal Historical Society*, 6th ser., XX (2010), pp. 85–112.
[117] Gregory, "Refashioning Puritan New England," *Trans. Royal Hist. Soc.*, 6th ser., XX, pp. 99–109.

The Church was able to make advances in other areas of its operation as well. The clerical training already provided by the College of William and Mary in Virginia was augmented in the 1750s by the foundation of both the College of Philadelphia in 1750 and King's College, New York in 1754. Archbishop Secker himself was instrumental in getting senior staff such as Myles Cooper, a fellow of Queen's College, Oxford, to a position at King's College.[118] And in a period when transatlantic influence was still highly valued, the colonial Church showed off its long reach in successfully lobbying the Privy Council to scotch a Congregationalist-inspired missionary society for the Indians, as well as in scuppering—with Secker's backing—George Whitefield's plan to change the orphanage in Bethesda, Georgia, into a ministerial training college (which it was feared would have privileged dissenters).[119]

Colonial Anglican clergy have generally received a bad press, in particular for their dull formalism and supposed indifference to pastoral opportunities. Nevertheless, there were some who, in their different ways, could be considered model clergy, such as Francis Le Jau (1665–1717)[120] in South Carolina, Charles Woodmason (1720–1789)[121] in North Carolina, and Devereux Jarratt (1733–1801) in Virginia and the borders with North Carolina.[122] Le Jau spent much of his time as a missionary among the Native Americans and African Americans at Goose Creek, Woodmason was employed in itinerating in the backcountry and denouncing followers of the Great Awakening, and Jarrett was an Anglican evangelical, embracing the revivalist message, yet keeping within the bounds of the colonial Anglican church. All three were operating in regions of the country where the Church was established, and their careers indicate how establishment could work with, rather than against, pastoral vitality.

Conceiving of colonial Anglicanism this way, as integral and effective in the religious life of the colonies at mid-century, rather than alien and

---

[118] Robert G. Ingram, *Religion, Reform and Modernity in the Eighteenth Century: Thomas Secker and the Church of England* (Woodbridge, Suffolk, 2007), p. 221.

[119] Ingram, *Religion, Reform and Modernity*, pp. 232, 223–6.

[120] F. Klingberg (ed.), *The Carolina Chronicle of Dr Francis Le Jau, 1706–1717* (Berkeley, CA, 1956).

[121] Richard J. Hooker (ed.), *The Carolina Backcountry on the Eve of Revolution: The Journal and Other Writings of Charles Woodmason, Anglican Itinerant* (Chapel Hill, NC, 1953).

[122] David L. Holmes (ed.), *The Life of the Reverend Devereux Jarratt: An Autobiography* (Cleveland, OH, 1995).

vestigial, necessarily calls into question all those claims, old and new, that the ensuing Revolution was actually a "war of religion," fuelled by anti-Anglican ideology.[123] In this account, denominational rivalry has been viewed as a crucial ingredient in the build-up to war, and sectarian hatred rather than toleration amongst religious groups has been seen as a hallmark of the colonial period. To be sure, historians of the Revolution in New England are no doubt right to stress the ways in which Congregational fears of an aggressive Imperial Anglicanism could inflame other forms of discontent in the later 1760s. However, to dismiss Anglicanism as a metropolitan intrusion is to take the polemics of the time at face value. Rather, the Church of England enjoyed genuine local support even in the apparently forbidding environment of eighteenth-century New England.[124] If there was denominational competition as a result, some of it unedifying in the extreme, polemical exchanges, celebrity conversions, and recurrent disputes over enforced support of religion do not in themselves add up to a war of religion. They were just part and parcel of colonial life in New England and elsewhere in America long before the Revolution and well after.

In any case, early American historiography now comes with a standard warning to historians against taking the New England experience as normative.[125] Certainly, in the case of colonial Anglicanism, it has been commonplace to read New England hostility to the Church as representative of a more general American experience. Equally, while New England Anglicans tended to take the position "that the Protection, Support and encouragement of the Church in the American Colonies" was "the best security of this peoples Allegiance and Attachment to the Mother country"[126] and accordingly to tend to loyalism at the onset of the War of Independence, in other parts of North America Anglican political allegiance was more varied and

---

[123] Notably Bridenbaugh, *Mitre and Sceptre*; Clark, *Language of Liberty*; Bell, *War of Religion*.

[124] Gregory, "Refashioning Puritan New England," *Trans. Royal Hist. Soc.*, 6th ser., XX, pp. 85–112.

[125] J.P. Greene, *Pursuits of Happiness: The Social Development of Early Modern British Colonies and the Formation of American Culture* (Chapel Hill, NC, 1988) and Trevor Burnard, "The British Atlantic," in J. P. Greene and Philip D. Morgan (eds), *Atlantic History: A Critical Appraisal* (Oxford, 2009), pp. 111–36, esp. pp. 123–4.

[126] Ebenezer Dibblee to SPG, October 28, 1765, quoted in Ingram, *Religion, Reform and Modernity*, p. 233.

nuanced.[127] Indeed the majority (two thirds) of the signatories of the Declaration of Independence in 1776 were at least nominally Anglican.[128] The nearly 400 Church of England congregations in the thirteen colonies at the same date testify equally to how entrenched the Church had become in British North America at the very moment of the Empire's dissolution.[129]

Religious establishment in British America was a major force in the development of most of the colonies. Nevertheless, it differed in nature and history from its equivalent in other European overseas empires. In a genuinely unique twist, there was more than one establishment within the Empire after 1707: that of England, Wales, and all the colonies south of Pennsylvania; that of Ireland; that of Scotland; that of New England (outside of Rhode Island). Religious pluralism in colonial America, therefore, rather than stemming from a comprehensive vision of a tolerant diversity was often simply the only feasible means of controlling competing establishments. Such holes in this establishmentarian phalanx as were to be found in colonial America can be traced back pretty much entirely to the unusual policies of the Restoration period, which worked against the expansion of the Church of England and in favor of the privileges of religious minorities. The religious freedom to be found in Pennsylvania was the most durable legacy of this period. In the eighteenth century, the colony became the primary entry point for most European immigration, enhancing an already extensive degree of religious diversity but without seriously challenging the strength of established churches where they already existed. When colonial establishments *were* subject to serious challenges in the eighteenth century, they gave ground grudgingly with precisely the sort of limited, conditional grants of tolerance familiar to the Dissenting inhabitants of Britain, rather than embracing religious pluralism in anything like the ways that had been encouraged in the colonies established during the Restoration period. In the end, while the hold of establishment was never complete or uniform in British America, its effective expansion was the major trend in the evolution of colonial American religion, especially after the Revolutionary settlement

---

[127] David L. Holmes, "The Episcopal Church and the American Revolution," *Historical Magazine of the Protestant Episcopal Church*, XLVII (1978), pp. 261–91; Rhoden, *Revolutionary Anglicanism*.

[128] W.S. Perry, "The Faith of the Signers of the Declaration of Independence," *The Magazine of History* (Tarrytown, NY, 1926), pp. 215–37.

[129] Frederick V. Mills, "Anglican Expansion in Colonial America, 1761–1775," *Historical Magazine of the Protestant Episcopal Church*, XXXIX (1970), pp. 315–24.

of 1689 put an end to the conflicts within and without the Church of England, which had previously undercut any chance of it gaining the dominant position in the British colonies that the nationally established church had in all the other European empires.

****

Religious establishments in North America did not end with Independence. The eventful year 1776 did however did see a significant attack on the Virginian establishment in the colony's Declaration of Rights. "All men," it proclaimed in language which anticipated the First Amendment, "are equally entitled to the free exercise of religion, according to the dictates of conscience; and . . . it is the mutual duty of all to practice Christian forbearance, love, and charity towards each other."[130] In itself this did not mean the instant downfall of the established Church, or of the establishment principle. The Assembly in Virginia carried on legislating for the Church and raised taxes for its support. In the heated debates over the place of religion in Virginia, Patrick Henry, who had led the attack on Anglican clergy in 1758 during the "Parsons' Cause" furor, backed a scheme that would have entailed all taxpayers contributing to a Christian denomination of their choosing or, alternatively, paying the same tax to support Virginia's schools.[131] However, in the course of the 1780s mandatory taxes for the Church in Virginia were done away with and, in 1786, the new commonwealth passed an Act for Establishing Religious Freedom,[132] which prohibited any state support of churches and thereby put an end in the Commonwealth of Virginia to the church–state relationship which had been in place in most parts of the Christian world since the age of Constantine.

Virginia's radical stance was not immediately the norm. In addition to New England, where establishment ideas not only survived but were arguably strengthened after 1776, Georgia, South Carolina, Maryland, Delaware and New York continued to support some form of establishment during the 1780s. In other colonies, there were moves to give equal support either to all denominations of Christianity or at least to all brands of Protestantism

---

[130] The Virginia Declaration of Rights (1776) is reprinted in Michael W. McConnell, et al. (eds), *Religion and the Constitution* (New York, 2002), pp. 58–9. See also Thomas E. Buckley, *Church and State in Revolutionary Virginia, 1776–1787* (Charlottesville, VA, 1977), pp. 10–19.

[131] Buckley, *Church and State*, p. 18.

[132] See D. Peterson and R.C. Vaughan (eds), *The Virginia Statute for Religious Freedom: Its Evolution and Consequences in American History* (New York, 1988).

under a "multiple establishment."[133] Nevertheless, during the course of the Revolution, and even more so in the decades that immediately followed, the need to bid for political support from a wide spectrum of religious denominations, and the explosive growth of new evangelical denominations opposed to establishment on principle, undermined the establishmentarian cause.[134] The end result was such that an institution that had been regarded as central to the colonial religious landscape in 1740 would by 1840 seem unthinkable, or at the most an archaism that must have been withering in the free air of the New World before the Revolution. The precise ways by which anti-establishment ideals were taken up in the rest of the new United States is the subject of American history proper and not of the history of the British Empire. Due attention, no doubt, must be given to the transformation of popular politics and the rise of evangelicalism. But ultimately, perhaps, the vital explanation lies in an increasing willingness on the part of the powers that be to exploit alternative ways of placing their stamp on the politics and culture of their day without having to resort to state supported and state protected religion. In this process, allegiance to an established church was supplanted by allegiance to the idea of "America."[135]

Select Bibliography

JAMES B. BELL, A War of Religion: Dissenters, Anglicans, and the American Revolution (Houndmills, 2008).

JAMES B. BELL, The Imperial Origins of the King's Church in Early America, 1607–1783 (Houndmills, 2004).

CARL BRIDENBAUGH, Mitre and Sceptre: Transatlantic Faiths, Ideas, Personalities and Politics, 1689–1775 (London, 1962).

JON BUTLER, Awash in a Sea of Faith: Christianizing the American People (London, 1990).

J. C. D CLARK, English Society, 1660–1832: Religion, Ideology and Politics during the Ancien Regime (rev. edn, Cambridge, 2000).

J. C. D CLARK, The Language of Liberty, 1660–1832: Political Discourse and Social Dynamics in the Anglo-American World (Cambridge, 1994).

[133] Butler, Sea of Faith, p. 259. See also Colin Kidd, 'Civil Theology and Church Establishments in Revolutionary America,' Historical Journal, XLII (1999), pp. 1007–26.

[134] See M. D. McGarvie, One Nation under Law: America's Early National Struggle to Separate Church and State (DeKalb, IL, 2004), and Andrews, Methodists and Revolutionary America. See also the older study by Philip Schaff, Church and State in the United States; or, the American Idea of Religious Liberty and its Practical Effects (New York, 1888).

[135] Cf. Peter Bellah, "Civil Religion in America," Daedalus, 96 (1967), pp. 1–21.

PETER DOLL, *Revolution, Religion, and National Identity: Imperial Anglicanism in British North America, 1745–1795* (Madison, NJ, 2000).

ELIGA H. GOULD, "Prelude: The Christianizing of British America," in *Missions and Empire. Oxford History of the British Empire* Companion Series (ed.), Norman Etherington (Oxford, 2005), pp. 19–39.

THOMAS S. KIDD, *The Great Awakening: The Roots of Evangelical Christianity in Colonial America* (New Haven, 2007).

NED C. LANDSMAN, *From Colonials to Provincials: American Thought and Culture, 1680–1760* (New York, 1997).

MARK A. NOLL, "British and French North America to 1765," in *The Cambridge History of Christianity,* VII: *Enlightenment, Reawakening, and Revolution* (ed.), Stewart J. Brown and Timothy Tackett (Cambridge, 2006), pp. 392–410.

ANDREW PORTER, *Religion Versus Empire? Protestant Missionaries and Overseas Expansion, 1700–1914* (Manchester, 2004).

NANCY L. RHODEN, *Revolutionary Anglicanism: The Colonial Church of England Clergy during the American Revolution* (New York, 1999).

BOYD STANLEY SCHLENTHER, "Religious Faith and Commercial Empire," in Peter Marshall (ed.), *The Oxford History of the British Empire,* II (Oxford, 1998), pp. 128–50.

NICHOLAS TROTT, *The Laws of the British Plantations in America, Relating to the Church and the Clergy, Religion and Learning. Collected in One Volume* (London, 1721).

LAUREN F. WINNER, *A Cheerful and Comfortable Faith: Anglican Religious Practice in the Elite Households of Eighteenth-Century Virginia* (New Haven, 2010).

JOHN FREDERICK WOOLVERTON, *Colonial Anglicanism in North America* (Detroit, 1984).

The interested reader is also advised to consult the bibliography of the previous chapter, "Toleration and Empire: The Origins of American Religious Pluralism," pp. 134–5. Titles listed there are not repeated here.

6

Periphery as Center

Slavery, Identity, and the Commercial Press in the British Atlantic, 1704–1765

Robert E. Desrochers, Jr.

In late April 1704, when postmaster and printer John Campbell began publication of the *Boston News-Letter*, the first successful weekly newspaper in the British American colonies, he was gambling on a form of enterprise whose profitability was anything but certain.[1] It is thus a matter of some significance that the *News-Letter* had been in business barely a month when the first advertisements offering slaves for sale appeared in its pages. Over the next sixteen years, on average one new "slave for sale" notice appeared in every second issue, so that by 1720 the newspaper had helped broker the sales of more than five hundred slaves. Campbell's *News-Letter* may have been "very, very dull," but at a time when no more than about four hundred slaves and free people of color resided in the vicinity of Boston, the human traffic Campbell sponsored amounted to a lively trade indeed, and the revenue generated by slavery-related advertisements helped keep his fledgling operation afloat.[2] In the half century after 1720, "slave for sale"

---

[1] Isaiah Thomas, *The History of Printing in America, With a Biography of Printers and an Account of Newspapers* (ed.), Marcus McCorison (New York, 1970), p.15; Carol Sue Humphrey, *"This Popular Engine": New England Newspapers during the American Revolution, 1775–1789* (Newark, DE, 1992), pp. 26, 150–6; Patricia Crain, "Print and Everyday Life in the Eighteenth Century," in Scott E. Casper, Joanne D. Chaison, and Jeffrey D. Groves (eds), *Perspectives on American Book History: Artifacts and Commentary* (Amherst, MA, 2002), pp. 47–78.

[2] Charles E. Clark, *The Public Prints: The Newspaper in Anglo-American Culture, 1665–1740* (New York, 1994), pp. 132 (quotation), 204–6. Cf. Eric Burns, *Infamous Scribblers: The Founding Fathers and the Rowdy Beginnings of American Journalism* (New York, 2006), p. 4. David Wald-streicher estimates that a quarter to a fifth of advertising in the *Pennsylvania Gazette* "directly concerned unfree labor" (servants and slaves). Waldstreicher, *Runaway America: Benjamin*

ads in New England newspapers appeared with such frequency and regularity that they became a normal part of everyday life.[3] Fugitive notices were equally commonplace, so much so that in 1768 the owner of one runaway, desperate to catch the public's attention, convinced the editors of the *Connecticut Courant* to run his ad with the word "RUN-AWAY" printed upside down.[4]

The advent of print capitalism fundamentally changed the way people thought about slavery in Britain's far northern colonies, underwriting its growth, expanding its purview, and enforcing its boundaries. In the process, the early and abiding marriage of slavery and print also changed the way white New Englanders thought about themselves and their place in the English Atlantic world, replacing the traditional transatlantic connections built on shared religion with new and (initially) strange alliances. One such strategic realignment began in December 1705 when William Pepperrell, a wealthy merchant of Kittery, Maine, took out an ad in the still-new *Boston News-Letter* to advertise the flight of a twenty-year-old "Negro Man-Slave" named Peter, who went off wearing what Pepperrell described as a pair of stylish "French fall shoes." Pepperrell's notice caught the eye of a fellow slaveholder in faraway South Carolina, Sir Nathaniel Johnson, the proprietary governor of the province. Four months later, Johnson sent word to Pepperrell (via the *News-Letter*) that he had in fact "secured" Peter and a traveling companion in a southern jail a thousand miles from Maine. Pepperrell was a poor fisherman who had made good in America. Johnson, one generation ahead of him—his *grand*father was a blacksmith—was the son of a member of the ruling oligarchy of Newcastle during the Interregnum with pretensions to gentry status, and himself a Tory and high-flying Anglican. Anomalous as the pairing of the two men was, slavery and print

Franklin, Slavery, and the American Revolution (New York, 2004), pp. 23–4. Ads routinely cost at least half as much as annual subscriptions, which patrons rarely seem to have paid in any case if we are to believe the frequent laments of the printers. See Charles G. Steffen, "Newspapers for Free: The Economies of Newspaper Circulation in the Early Republic," *Journal of the Early Republic*, XXIII (2003), pp. 381–419.

[3] Not counting repeats, more than 3,100 "slave for sale" advertisements appeared in Boston newspapers in the eighteenth century. More than one thousand separate advertisements marketing 2,500 slaves appeared in the pages of the *Boston Gazette* alone. See Robert E. Desrochers, Jr., "Slave-For-Sale Advertisements and Slavery in Massachusetts, 1704–1781," *WMQ*, 3rd ser., LIX (2002), pp. 623–64.

[4] *Connecticut Courant*, August 1, 1768.

culture had created a community of interest between them. As it proclaimed a politics of mutual recognition across the miles their remarkable exchange effectively transformed one New Englander's attempt to recoup a missing slave into the production of space and identity in the English Atlantic.[5]

To use Winthrop Jordan's formulation, "the question with New England slavery is not why it was weakly rooted," but why "it existed at all." To be sure, slavery came to assume a more prominent role in New England in the four or five decades before the American Revolution chiefly because slaves performed productive work in most aspects of the region's local economies. But this transformation was always more than an uncomplicated economic reflex. In an era marked by economic growth, rising consumerism, and strident British patriotism, the regularity and sheer ordinariness of the appearance of slavery in print brought New Englanders' ways of thinking closer to the mindset of the slaveholding British Atlantic generally.[6] To the extent that this phenomenon—part neurotic fantasy, part cost–benefit analysis—offset the regional peculiarities that for so long marked New England's experience as atypical and possibly sinister, slavery's discursive existence in the public prints and in the intra- and inter-regional conversations among slaveholders was a form of "official nationalism" whose repetitions, distortions, and omissions came to define the purported commonality they ostensibly only described.[7] This print-based culture of

[5] *Boston News-Letter*, December 10, 17, 31, 1705, April 22, 1706; Peter Wood, *Black Majority: Negroes in South Carolina from 1670 through the Stono Rebellion* (New York, 1974), p. 47; Byron Fairchild, *Messrs. William Pepperrell: Merchants at Piscataqua* (Ithaca, NY, 1954), pp. 19–20; Roger Howell, *Newcastle upon Tyne and the Puritan Revolution: A Study of the Civil War in North England* (Oxford, 1967), pp. 175–6, 186 note 2; Basil Duke Henning (ed.), *The History of Parliament: The House of Commons, 1660–1690*, II (London, 1983), s.v. "Johnson, Nathaniel"; M. Eugene Sirmans, *Colonial South Carolina: A Political History, 1663–1763*, (Chapel Hill, NC, 1966), pp. 80, 86–9. Cf. also Ian Baucom, *Specters of the Atlantic: Finance Capital, Slavery, and the Philosophy of History* (Durham, NC, 2005), pp. 145–6; Paul Gilroy, *The Black Atlantic: Modernity and Double Consciousness* (Cambridge, MA, 1993); Gretchen Holbrook Gerzina, "Mobility in Chains: Freedom of Movement in the Early Black Atlantic," *South Atlantic Quarterly*, C (2001), pp. 41–59.

[6] Winthrop Jordan, *White Over Black: American Attitudes Toward the Negro, 1550–1812* (Chapel Hill, NC, 1968; reprinted New York, 1977), p. 66; John J. McCusker and Russell R. Menard, *The Economy of British America, 1607–1789* (Chapel Hill, NC, 1985); T.H. Breen, *The Marketplace of Revolution: How Consumer Politics Shaped American Independence* (New York, 2004); Linda Colley, *Britons: Forging the Nation, 1707–1837* (New Haven, 1992).

[7] David Waldstreicher, *In the Midst of Perpetual Fetes: The Making of American Nationalism, 1776–1820* (Chapel Hill, NC, 1997), pp. 33, 51. Benedict Anderson, *Imagined Communities: Reflections on the Origin and Spread of Nationalism* (rev. edn, London, 1991), p. 101.

slavery was a world made largely by slaveholders and their ideological allies, men of commercial wealth in the colonies who shared in the world view of the English upper classes and who stood to gain the most from slavery's broad acceptance in New England as both social practice (a way of living in the world) and cognitive structure (a way of thinking about it).[8] Their success in accomplishing both of these undertakings is demonstrable.

****

New Englanders had been employing African slaves since the 1640s, but slavery's rapid and visible expansion in the eighteenth century was something new that at first provoked both skepticism and outright hostility.[9] New England's slave population continued to grow anyway and at a faster rate than the region's white population in every decade but one from 1690 to 1770. By mid-century, slaves, whether imported from the West Indies or directly from Africa, comprised 10 to 20 percent of the population in the region's larger seacoast towns, and slavery was making inroads into the countryside as well.[10] Ministers, military men, lawyers, and other self-styled gentlemen remained those most likely to own slaves. Increasingly, however, farmers, tradesmen, artisans, sea captains, and middling families could also aspire to the status and by implication the lifestyle associated with slaveholding. If economic factors and a budding middle class made slavery's extension feasible, a growing sensibility that "the presence of slaves" signified "healthy, wealthy empires and viable colonies" provided an important added incentive for New Englanders to lay aside their reservation and embrace slavery as a pathway to prosperity.[11] In the first half of the eighteenth century, new

---

[8] Clark, *The Public Prints*, p. 221.

[9] Samuel Sewall, "The Selling of Joseph: A Memorial" (Boston, 1700), in George H. Moore, *Notes on the History of Slavery in Massachusetts* (New York, 1866), pp. 83–87. See also Mark A. Peterson, "The Selling of Joseph: Bostonians, Antislavery, and the Protestant International, 1689–1733," *Massachusetts Historical Review*, IV (2002), pp. 1–22; and Lawrence W. Towner, "The Sewall-Saffin Dialogue on Slavery," *WMQ*, 3rd ser., XXI (1964), pp. 40–52.

[10] For population figures, see Greene, *The Negro in Colonial New England*; William D. Piersen, *Black Yankees: The Development of an Afro-American Subculture in Eighteenth-Century New England* (Amherst, MA, 1988); Edgar McManus, *Black Bondage in the North* (Syracuse, NY, 1973); Robert K. Fitts, *Inventing New England's Slave Paradise: Master/Slave Relations in Eighteenth-Century Narragansett, Rhode Island* (New York, 1998), p. 83; and Philip D. Morgan, "Black Experience in the British Empire, 1680–1810," in Morgan and Sean Hawkins (eds), *Black Experience and the Empire*, OHBE Companion Series (Oxford, 2004), p. 88.

[11] Quoted passages from Waldstreicher, *Runaway America*, p. 18.

understandings of consumer behavior in an emerging "empire of goods" turned the (mostly) economic decision to invest in slaves into a political and cultural act that heightened "colonists' shared sense of identity with each other and with Great Britain." As T. H. Breen has observed, the emergence of this conceptual framework fueled "new perceptions of empire" rooted in "mutual imagining, the product of rumor and exaggeration, fantasy and fact." For New England provincials, anxious to prove that they "really counted for something in the larger imperial scheme," it also turned slave-holding—already a leading indicator of material success and an effective means of inflating one's sense of individual self-worth—into a symbol of collective identity in the British Atlantic.[12]

Some colonists continued to balk at these transformations, sensing that a smaller scale version of what worked for Virginians or Jamaicans might prove unsustainable in New England. A cheeky piece signed "ANTHONY FALLSHORT," attributed to the controversial printer James Franklin, Sr. (Benjamin's brother) and published in his own *New England Courant* in March 1722, derided the aspirations of "*New-England Gentry*" whose "Estates are for the most part imaginary" but whose "Expences" were "real" and too often included "a Chamber-Maid" to wait on their wives, "a Cook-Maid to wait on the Chamber-Maid, and a Negro to wait on the Cook-Maid." A newspaper report from 1740 similarly mocked the polite culture that rising consumerism had helped to introduce, noting that three slaves convicted of breaking into a Boston sugar manufactory had been "tickled" at the whipping post "in a very easy and genteel Manner, to the Praise of the polite Executioner, and Encouragement of other Negroes to deserve the like Honour." In pointing up the ineffectiveness of a slave regulatory system that took its cues from habits of gentility, the piece also anticipated the social tensions that over time would lead to more direct critiques of slavery itself. Writing on behalf of the Salem town meeting in September 1755, an anonymous contributor to the *Boston Evening-Post* asked why "common people who have no Slaves" should be expected to act as "a continual Safeguard" for "Gentlemen's" servants. If "every Family [had] Slaves," Massachusetts would "be in as much or more Danger" from them "than we are from the French," who would not dare "trouble us" in the first

---

[12] Breen, *Marketplace of Revolution*, pp. 21, 75–6. My understanding of "collective memory" as a shared understanding of the past follows Maurice Halbwachs, *On Collective Memory* (ed.), Lewis A. Coser (Chicago, 1992), p. 40.

place if "all the Slaves in . . . America were instead free Men." The author concluded that perhaps New Englanders "had better be without" slaves rather than "be exposed to Danger and fill'd with Terror by Reason" of their presence.[13]

All this would have sounded familiar to Samuel Sewall, who as early as 1700 had compared slavery in the Bay Colony to the unjust sale of the Biblical patriarch Joseph into Egyptian bondage. Even staunch Puritans of Sewall's generation, however, had to confront Oliver Cromwell's old charge, much repeated, that New England was a "poor, cold, and useless place," a commercial and cultural backwater that did not quite measure up to what Britain expected of its overseas possessions. Newer ideas associated slaveholding with civility, refinement, and improvement and stamped slavery itself with what Breen has called "a seal of imperial patriotism." Personifying the collective ambivalence over slavery's increasing entanglement in the very fabric of New England society, another Samuel Sewall, nephew and namesake of the diarist and author, went on to place no fewer than eight ads offering a total of seventeen slaves for sale in the Boston News-Letter between 1714 and 1722.[14]

The print culture of slavery ultimately revolved to a large degree around slaves doing things. But the overwhelming majority of printed accounts, predicated upon an unswerving egotism that sought to inscribe race, circumscribe black identity, and replicate social processes that transformed human beings into slaves, also reduced the enslaved to nameless ciphers: a "Negro Man" coughs up a giant worm; a "Negro Woman" smothers her baby and hides it in a cellar; a "Negro Boy," too careless with an open flame, burns down the barn.

The language of commodification carried over all too easily from slave ships and auction rooms to city streets, a process of linguistic debasement

---

[13] *New England Courant*, March 26, 1722; *Boston Evening-Post*, July 28, 1740; September 8, 1755. (James Franklin is identified as the author of the Fallshort piece by Leo Lemay: <http://www.english.udel.edu/lemay/franklin/1722frame.html> [accessed May 18, 2011].) Cf. William Douglass, *A Discourse Concerning the Currencies of the British Plantations in America* (Boston, 1740), pp. 4, 55.

[14] Sewall, *Selling of Joseph* in Moore, *History of Slavery in Massachusetts*, p. 86; Breen, *The Marketplace of Revolution*, p. 93; Cromwell quoted in Mark A. Peterson, "Life on the Margins: Boston's Anxieties of Influence in the Atlantic World," in Wim Klooster and Alfred Padula (eds), *The Atlantic World: Essays on Slavery, Migration, and Imagination* (Upper Saddle River, NJ, 2005), p. 45. Sewall advertised slaves for sale in the *Boston News-Letter* on September 13, 1714; April 18, 1715; April 9, June 18, December 17, 1716; September 2, 1717; May 25, 1719; and June 25, 1722. See also Eve LaPlante, *Salem Witch Judge: The Life and Repentance of Samuel Sewall* (New York, 2007), p. 225.

epitomized in "slave for sale" notices by the word "parcel," a term that was used ubiquitously to describe incoming shipments of imported slaves. So, in January, 1738, the *Boston Evening-Post* reported that "a parcel of Negroes" gathered together in a warehouse "to make merry" had neglected to clear the chimney before cooking their victuals and nearly burned down the Boston waterfront.[15] Except in the case of runaways, when the fear of losing property temporarily disrupted the language of white dominance, and to a lesser extent in instances where slaves stood accused of acts of violence, the project of representing slavery in print imposed near-universal anonymity on its subjects.[16] Only two of roughly 2,500 slaves advertised for sale in the *Boston Gazette* from 1719 to 1781 were mentioned by name. By way of contrast, only fourteen of 321 fugitive slave advertisements in the *Boston Gazette* failed to name the escapee. Reduced to affirmations of the ties that bound, black lives became in the imagination of whites largely so many contentless effigies.[17] Barely heard of and very seldom heard from, like so many others in their condition, they remained trapped in a kind of limbo that Patricia Williams has aptly called "the pornography of living out other people's fantasies."[18]

For many New Englanders, slaveholding remained just that—a fantasy lived out by other people, a commonly accepted practice but never an exceedingly common one. Just one in four wills inventoried in Boston in the thirty years after 1725 included slaves, a substantial increase over the

---

[15] *Boston Evening-Post*, July 24, 1758; *Boston Gazette*, April 15, 1723; *Boston Evening-Post*, January 16, 1738.

[16] Richard Slotkin, "Narratives of Negro Crime in New England, 1675–1800," *American Quarterly*, XXV (1973), pp. 4, 16. On liminality and the process by which enslaved people were stripped of their identities, marked as socially and figuratively dead, and ritually resurrected as extensions of their masters, see Baucom, *Specters of the Atlantic*, pp. 11–14; Alex Bontemps, *The Punished Self: Surviving Slavery in the Colonial South* (Ithaca, 2001); Saidiya Hartman, *Scenes of Subjection: Terror, Slavery, and Self-Making in Nineteenth Century America* (New York, 1997); and Orlando Patterson, *Slavery and Social Death: A Comparative Study* (Cambridge, MA, 1982).

[17] Cf. James Clifford, "Introduction: Partial Truths," in Clifford and George Marcus (eds), *Writing Culture: The Poetics and Politics of Ethnography* (Berkeley, CA, 1986), pp. 1–26; Dana D. Nelson, *The Word in Black and White: Reading "Race" in American Literature, 1638–1867* (New York, 1993), p. 27. There was little to distinguish press and pen when it came to white attempts at imposing anonymity on slaves. Cf. Trevor Burnard, *Mastery, Tyranny, and Desire: Thomas Thistlewood and His Slaves in the Anglo-Jamaican World* (Chapel Hill, NC, 2004); Natalie Zacek, "Voices and Silences: The Problem of Slave Testimony in the English West Indian Law Court," *Slavery and Abolition*, XXIV (2003), pp. 24–39.

[18] Patricia Williams, *The Alchemy of Race and Rights* (London, 1993), p. 177.

preceding years (and a higher percentage than the comparable figures for Philadelphia over the same period), but nonetheless an indicator that slave ownership remained somewhat anomalous even in the region's largest cities and towns. Similarly, just 42 percent of Newport taxpayers owned at least one slave around 1760, and the comparable figure for Providence stood at around 25 percent.[19] Of course, one did not have to own slaves in order to profit materially by any number of subsidiary economic activities that slavery helped support: shipping; insurance; provisioning; and, not least, the distilling industry that underwrote the participation of New England merchants and sailors in the African slave trade.[20] Nor did the ability to parlay slavery into social capital necessarily depend on actual slave ownership. In the late 1730s a patron of the *New England Weekly Journal* took to carrying printed advertisements for runaways in the leather case where he also kept his pocket money—a fitting reminder, first, that the physical artifact of print made slavery a constant companion for some white New Englanders, and second, that the rewards offered for fugitives gave everyone a stake in the system.[21] The essential parasitism of British Atlantic slavery—its reduction to the "calculus of profit and risk," which allowed Boston sailors to throw the body of a newly imported slave overboard while docked in port rather than pay "the Charge of burying her"—had taken root in New England.[22]

Newspaper stories of slaves who fenced stolen goods, stayed out past curfew, or plotted the deaths of their masters contextualized personal experience even for those New Englanders who did come into regular contact with slaves and slavery. For the rest, those who lacked the kinds of experiential frameworks that shaped slavery's primary social meaning, the

[19] Gary Nash, *The Urban Crucible: The Northern Seaports and the Origins of the American Revolution* (Cambridge, MA, 1986), p. 401; Lynne Withey, *Urban Growth in Colonial Rhode Island: Newport and Providence in the Eighteenth Century* (Albany, NY, 1984), pp. 130–1.

[20] In 1770, New England boasted half of the twenty-six sugar refineries, and nearly one hundred of the 140 working rum distilleries on the British North American mainland. The seven refineries and thirty-six distilleries in Boston made the city the center of sugar processing on the mainland. Newport similarly accounted for another four refineries and twenty-two distilleries. Lester J. Cappon, et al. (eds), *Atlas of Early American History: The Revolutionary Era* (Princeton, NJ, 1976), p. 26; McCusker and Menard, *Economy of British America, 1607–1789*, pp. 290–93; Greene, *Negro in Colonial New England*, pp. 25–6; "Remonstrance of the Colony of Rhode Island to the Board of Trade," in Elizabeth Donnan, *Documents Illustrative of the Slave Trade to America* (Washington, 1930–35; reprinted New York, 1969), III, p. 205.

[21] *New England Weekly Journal*, January 2, 1739.

[22] Baucom, *Specters of the Atlantic*, p. 11; *New England Weekly Rehearsal*, June 4, 1733.

store of images accumulated in print possessed an even greater capacity to create its own reality and to make the imagined community of slavery "vivid and legible" to large numbers of white New Englanders.[23] In either case, print collated and packaged slavery's rituals and local performances, wrapping them for the most part in the rhetoric of shared belonging among whites, whether they were slaveholders or not. The result was a cultural palimpsest: a new, racialized understanding of regional identity overwritten onto an older one that traced its genealogy to an atavistic Puritan founding myth.[24] This regional discourse invented a shared slaveholding tradition where one had not really existed before for a people who were becoming more self-consciously British after about 1720 and who also increasingly measured themselves against fellow colonials elsewhere in North America. And (as the slave Peter learned) print's spatial reach transcended circumscribed localities: masters who resided outside a given newspaper's colony of publication placed nearly a quarter of all runaway slave notices in eighteenth-century New England newspapers.[25]

Nearly universal white male literacy had been achieved in New England by the middle of the eighteenth century, extending the "open communion" of readership well beyond the social elite. A conservative estimate places the number of newspapers produced by New England presses at about 6,660 per week by 1765, but promiscuous circulation patterns meant that at a bare minimum three people probably read each dog-eared paper published in the region.[26] Printers openly encouraged potential customers to share

[23] George Lipsitz, *Time Passages: Collective Memory and American Popular Culture* (Minneapolis, 1990), p. 42. The quoted phrase is from Cora Kaplan, "Imagining Empire: History, Fantasy, and Literature," in Catherine Hall and Sonya O. Rose (eds), *At Home with the Empire: Metropolitan Culture and the Imperial World* (Cambridge, 2006), p. 191.

[24] On the invention of a New England identity rooted in a myth of the fathers, see esp. Robert Middlekauff, *The Mathers: Three Generations of Puritan Intellectuals, 1596–1728* (New York, 1971); and David Cressy, *Coming Over: Migration and Communication Between England and New England in the Seventeenth Century* (Cambridge, 1987), esp. pp. 213–62.

[25] E. Jennifer Monoghan, "Reading for the Enslaved, Writing for the Free: Reflections on Liberty and Literacy," American Antiquarian Society, *Proceedings*, CVIII (1998), pp. 309–41; Jill Lepore, "Literacy and Reading in Puritan New England," in Casper, et al. (eds), *Perspectives on American Book History*, p. 38; Crain, "Print and Everyday Life in the Eighteenth Century," in ibid., p. 69.

[26] Timothy M. Barnes, "The Loyalist Press in the American Revolution, 1765–1781" (Ph.D. diss., University of New Mexico, 1970), pp. 3–4. Analysis of circulation figures similarly suggests an expanding audience for printed news. While it has been estimated that John Campbell sold three hundred copies per issue of the *Boston News-Letter* in 1719, by 1754 each of Boston's four weeklies

subscriptions, and newspapers were also exchanged regularly in taverns and coffeehouses. Samuel Sewall gave copies of the *Boston News-Letter* to the string of widows he courted in the 1720s and routinely sent the paper to distant friends such as Edward Taylor, the longtime minister and closet poet of Westfield, Massachusetts.[27] Archival forms of usage were also to be found from an early date: when John Campbell reported in October 1706 that New Yorkers had received the official journal of a joint French and Spanish invasion of South Carolina, he noted that an account of the attack had been "Printed in our *Boston News-Letter*, Numb. 130, to which we refer you." For New Englanders who dutifully annotated and bound local newspapers in chronological order, print acted as a secular counterpart to sacred modes of communication, serving to preserve elements of the "community's collective experience."[28]

Those who could not or did not read the news often heard it repeated aloud in churches and meeting houses, town squares, on waterfronts, and at hearthsides. In March 1762, the *Newport Mercury* reported that an aged patriarch from Wethersfield, Connecticut, "expired in an instant" while "reading a Newspaper to his Family." One wonders how many times the

---

averaged about six hundred regular subscribers and, on the eve of the Imperial crisis, the weekly output of a number of papers was higher still. The editor of the *Connecticut Courant* was probably exaggerating in 1778, when he put weekly production at near eight thousand copies; a recent study has estimated that the wartime subscription list of that paper numbered not much more than about 700. More reliably, Isaiah Thomas's *Massachusetts Spy* may have boasted the largest subscription list of all New England weeklies by 1775, nearly 3,500. But other papers easily topped one thousand subscribers, including Boston's *News-Letter* and *Chronicle*, each of which claimed about 1,500 subscribers in the 1760s. Weekly runs of the *Boston Gazette* amounted to around two thousand copies just prior to the skirmish at Lexington and Concord. See Humphrey, *"This Popular Engine,"* pp. 72–3; Mary Ann Yodelis, "Who Paid the Piper?: Publishing Economics in Boston, 1763–1775," *Journalism Monographs*, XXXVIII (February 1975), p. 35; Frank Luther Mott, *American Journalism, A History: 1690–1960*, 3rd edn (New York, 1962), p.13; and Arthur M. Schlesinger, *Prelude to Independence: The Newspaper War on Britain, 1764–1776* (New York, 1958), pp. 303–4 (appendix A).

[27] Print had begun to bridge the distance between rural and urban well before mid-century. Moreover slaveholders, who quickly came to incorporate print into their arsenal of control, did much to encourage this phenomenon. See Richard Brown, *Knowledge is Power: The Diffusion of Information in Early America, 1700–1865* (New York, 1989), p. 38, Brown, "Emergence of Urban Society in Rural Massachusetts, 1760–1820," *Journal of American History*, LXI (1974), pp. 31–3, 49.

[28] *Boston News-Letter*, October 21, 1706; Clark, *The Public Prints*, p. 245. The quotation is from William J. Gilmore, *Reading Becomes a Necessity of Life: Material and Cultural Life in Rural New England, 1780–1835* (Knoxville, TN, 1993), p. 382. Gilmore is referring primarily to the keeping of public records, but newspapers served the same purposes, arguably in an enhanced form.

family had shared stories like the two that appeared on the same page of the very issue that reported this man's unexpected demise. The first anecdote noted the apparent suicide of a "Negro Fellow" from Hartford who reportedly "put the Muzzle" of a loaded gun into his mouth and blew his "Head to Pieces." In the second, a slave named Fortune received sentence of execution from Rhode Island's Superior Court for "setting Fire to a Warehouse on the Long Wharf." Resistance confirmed, order restored, violent death made routine: the repetition over time of these and other kinds of voyeuristic accounts made slavery's plotlines a family affair for all ranks and ages.[29]

****

It is hardly surprising that, in a commercial economy, printers and publishers cultivated the public's appetite for slave news in part to promote their own entrepreneurial endeavors. *The Boston Gazette,* New England's second news-paper, from its inception in 1719 included a wide array of materials related to slaves and slavery, amounting by 1784 to more than 3,300 references, if "slave for sale" advertisements and fugitive slave notices are included. Routine burial figures appeared alongside sensationalized accounts of slave insurgencies, real and imagined. Expressions of consternation over slaves' behavior mingled with slave-trade boosterism. Poetic ruminations on the consequences of slave girls courting "fair" young men gave way to unusual instances of reproductive "Prolifickness." In the *Gazette,* as in other New England newspapers, slaves were to be found at the center of many of British imperialism's most noted accomplishments, abject failures, and intractable problems. Duplicitous or loyal slaves aided or averted French, Spanish, and Indian intrigues at the edge of British settlement. Hanoverian proclamations and accounts of assembly battles over governors' salaries shared space with stories of black pirates and murderous slaves who turned tidy conceptions of ordered English liberty upside down. Shipping news weighed the successes of the coasting trade and the African slave trade in the same scales. Currency crises and economic downturns incidentally raised questions of the efficacy of slave oversight, as amateur and professional Jeremiahs chastised the masters of idle slaves, whose lack of employment and of proper supervision alike allegedly encouraged crime and sinister cabals. Slaves could even be involved in the running

---

[29] Brown, *Knowledge is Power,* p. 38; Barnes, "Loyalist Press in the American Revolution, 1765–1781," pp. 3–4; *Newport Mercury,* June 19, 1758, March 16, 1762.

conflicts with Parliament: in 1736, when crown agents seized "two Hogsheads of Molasses," imported in violation of the unpopular Molasses Act, rumor had it the "Informer" was a "Negro Man Servant" from Boston's South End.[30]

Inevitably, the Boston printers ended up competing with one another over so interesting a "commodity." Consider the execution of Julian, a twenty-year-old Native American slave convicted and hanged in Boston in March 1733 for an act of arson that killed his master. *The Last Speech and Dying Advice of Poor Julian* appeared first, published by Thomas Fleet. Allegedly "Written with" the offender's "own Hand and delivered to" Fleet on "the Day before his Execution," it depicted Julian (who died maintaining his innocence) as the latest instance of a stock type, the unfaithful servant. Forsaking his master's moral instruction, Julian fell into a spiral of sin, which led to the crime for which he paid with his life.[31] However, at the very end of the narrative, the *Last Speech* abruptly deviated from the traditional tropes of gallows literature and Julian designated "Mr. *Fleet*" as his publisher of choice and "utterly disown[ed] and disclaim[ed] all other Speeches, Papers, or Declarations that may be printed" in his name. The target of this supposed disavowal was a broadside poem published by Benjamin Gray and Alford Butler entitled *Poor Julleyoun's Warnings to Children and Servants*. Fleet then followed up with a broadside of his own, *Advice from the Dead to the Living; Or, a Solemn Warning... Occasioned by the Untimely Death of Poor Julian*. In a game of one-upmanship, Fleet's *Solemn Warning* contained twenty stanzas of stilted verse where *Poor Julleyoun's Warnings* consisted of nineteen, and where some construction of the word "warning" appeared five times in Gray and Butler's piece, there were six such in Fleet's broadside. Fleet defended his exclusive rights to the story by including a "*Note*" to "certify" that the "foolish Paper" called "*Julian's Advice to Children and Servants*" had been "disowned by the said Julian in the Presence of" three witnesses. Gray and Butler's "false and spurious" tract could boast only two.[32] This feud between

[30] *Boston Gazette*, December 21, 1719; February 10, 1735; *Newport Mercury*, December 31, 1764, November 22, 1762; *Boston News-Letter*, February 5, 1736.

[31] *The Last Speech and Dying Advice of Poor Julian, Who Was Executed the 22d of March, 1733, for the Murder of Mr. John Rogers of Pembroke* (Boston, 1733). The last speech also appeared in its entirety in Fleet's *New England Weekly Journal*, 26 March 26, 1733.

[32] *Poor Julleyoun's Warnings to Children and Servants to Shun the Ways of Sin, and Those Particularly Which Hath Brought Him to His Doleful End* (Boston, 1733); *Advice From the Dead to the Living; Or, A Solemn Warning to the World. Occasioned by the Untimely Death of Poor Julian, Who was Executed on Boston Neck, on Thursday the 22d. of March, 1733, for the Murder of Mr. John*

rival printers ultimately had little to do with content, for in that regard the competing productions are barely distinguishable. Rather, the controversy centered solely on who had the authority to tell, and more importantly to sell, Julian's story.

Selling slavery was a role for which New England printers were exceptionally well qualified. A peripatetic lot, the "typographical fraternity" was as steeped in the affairs of the English Atlantic as anyone in America, and only New England's largest human traffickers could claim deeper involvement in brokering slaves. Many printers owned slaves themselves, sometimes employing them as pressmen and hawkers. For an additional fee, printers and publishers held captured runaways for the patrons who placed runaway ads. And the vast majority of all "slave for sale" advertisements in New England newspapers required customers to "inquire of the printer" in order to complete a transaction, transforming newspaper offices into slave marts.[33] Printers also appointed themselves to the role of slavery's watchdog. Thomas Fleet could not "but think" that his long-winded account of a slave conspiracy discovered near Burlington, East Jersey, in 1734 had rendered a "great Service to the Country in general," and "especially" to Bostonians, if they were "wise enough take the Hints therein given, and in Time provide for our Safety." John Boydell of the *Boston Gazette* in July of that same year reported that authorities in Portsmouth, New Hampshire, had apprehended a "Gang of Negroes" suspected of organizing a theft ring, whom he hoped would be made public examples in order to deter those "of the black Tribe which now pour in upon us from the like Crimes."[34]

A certain amount of ambivalence always inhered in providing delinquent slaves with this degree of publicity. Stories of local slaves trafficking in stolen goods suggested that slave oversight might be lax, while slaves might draw conclusions of their own from accounts of other slaves plotting against their masters. Such concerns never reached the level of panic that prompted the *South-Carolina Gazette* to omit all slave news in the immediate aftermath of

Rogers of Pembroke, the 12th of September, 1732 (Boston, 1733). Reproductions of the three broadsides discussed in this and the preceding note can be found in Lawrence W. Towner, "True Confessions and Dying Warnings in Colonial New England," in *Sibley's Heir: A Volume in Memory of Clifford Kenyon Shipton,* Colonial Society of Massachusetts, *Publications,* LIX (Boston, 1982), pp. 523–39.

[33] Schlesinger, *Prelude to Independence,* p. 55; Desrochers, "Slave-For-Sale Advertisements," *WMQ,* 3rd ser., LIX, pp. 634–5.

[34] *New England Weekly Rehearsal,* April 8, 1734; *Boston Gazette,* July 1, 1734.

the Stono Rebellion in 1739.[35] But white New Englanders did know that slaves found ways to acquaint themselves with the content of newspapers. In August of 1757, James Dwyer pinned his hopes for recovering a runaway named Scipio upon the slave reading his own fugitive advertisement in the *Boston Gazette*, which promised that if he returned "of his own Accord" and without putting his master to the charge of a reward, he would "be kindly received" and "forgiven." Eighteen years later, in 1775, two Georgians admitted to John Adams that "the negroes have a wonderful art of communicating intelligence among themselves; it will run several hundreds of miles in a week or fortnight."[36]

If, in actuality, slaves like Scipio—a three time runaway—made a habit of contravening their masters' authority, it can still be argued that, by organizing slavery into tidy, purposive narratives reaffirming the existing racial order, the New England press served the same cultural purposes as the (ineffectual) southern-style media blackouts. Newspaper reports of wrongdoings committed by slaves were as standardized and pre-packaged as execution sermons and dying speeches from the scaffold, but where the conventions of gallows literature also explored the nature of sin and sought to establish the moral identification of the condemned criminal with an assembled crowd or readership, the newspaper accounts of slave malefactors contented themselves solely with a single-minded focus on the familiar, reassuring moral "that excesse in wickedness doth bring untimely Death." In February, 1718, the report in the *Boston News-Letter* of the attempted rape of a white woman from western Connecticut ended with a passer-by overpowering and castrating the alleged assailant on the spot. The editor, John Campbell, then added that he intended the story "as a caveat" to dissuade "all Negroes" from "meddling with any White Women, least they fare with the like Treatment."[37] Printers, publishers, and editors made every effort to endow suitable events with appropriate and timely morals to ensure that (for the white reading public, at least) transgression always met with condign punishment. When the Boston firm of Kneeland and Green adver-

---

[35] David A. Copeland, *Colonial American Newspapers: Character and Content* (Newark, DE, 1997), 147–8.

[36] *Boston Gazette*, August 8, 1757; Sidney Kaplan and Emma Nogrady Kaplan, *The Black Presence in the Era of the American Revolution* (Amherst, MA, 1989), p. 25.

[37] Increase Mather, *The Day of Trouble is Near: Two Sermons Wherein is Shewed, What are the Signs of a Day of Trouble Being Near* (Cambridge, MA, 1674); *Boston News-Letter*, February 24, 1718.

tised the publication in 1738 of the *Faithful Narrative of the Wicked Life and Remarkable Conversion* of Patience Boston, an Indian woman who was executed in York, Maine three years earlier for drowning her master's grandson, they assured readers in the title that it contained "an account of the Reason for its being Published at this Time."[38] And on numerous occasions, where initial news reports of transgressions such as murder, arson, rape, and rebellion failed to bring the controlling narrative to an acceptable denouement (for example, in the case of accused criminals who eluded capture), follow-ups that sometimes appeared many months after the fact noted that the malefactors had finally been detained, killed, subdued, or otherwise made to answer to British justice.

No amount of careful manicuring, however, could prevent these stories from calling attention to slavery's violent underbelly and the costs associated with its maintenance. Slave executions and the printed accounts that accompanied them were, at one and the same time, moral exempla for the enforcement of a racist institution, and documents of the "literature of social insurgency." The paradox was unavoidably visible in the executions themselves. White New Englanders routinely claimed that most of the slave problems they encountered stemmed from "the bad Effects of Negroes too freely consorting together," as the *Boston Evening-Post* observed upon the execution in 1763 of a slave named Bristol in Taunton, Massachusetts. If so, one wonders if Sylvanus Conant, the New Light minister who preached at the event, grasped the irony of the mixed race audience assembled to hear his sermon. As they scanned the sizable collection of black faces in the crowd at the occasion itself, or read the account that accompanied the sermon in published form, Conant's white audience might have taken cold comfort from his declaration that "the grand Source of all the Evils" concocted by slaves in Massachusetts owed in the first place to "their companying together."[39]

---

[38] *A Faithful Narrative of the Wicked Life and Remarkable Conversion of Patience Boston, alias Samson; who was Executed at York, in the County of York, July 24, 1735, for the Murder of Benjamin Trot of Falmouth on Casco Bay, a Child of about Eight Years of Age, whom she drowned in a Well. With a Preface by the Rev. Messrs. Samuel and Joseph Moody, Pastors of the Churches in said Town; giving an account of the Reason of its being Published at this Time* (Boston, 1738).

[39] Daniel Cohen, *Pillars of Salt, Monuments of Grace: New England Crime Literature and the Origins of American Popular Culture, 1674–1860* (New York, 1993), esp. pp. 115–63; *Boston Evening-Post*, June 13, 1763; Sylvanus Conant, *The Blood of Abel, and the Blood of Jesus Considered and Improved, in a Sermon Delivered at Taunton, December the First, 1763. Upon the Day of the Execution of Bristol, a Negro Boy of about Sixteen Years Old, for the Murder of Miss Elizabeth*

Inherently, the production and reproduction of these highly stylized "scenes of subjection" pulled in two different directions at once. When a Massachusetts slave named Arthur was executed for the alleged rape of a white woman in 1768, his *Life and Dying Speech* recounted such a long string of repeated instances of "*stealing, lying, uncleanness, prophanness, and drunkenness*" that it placed him squarely in the first rank of New England rogues. Indeed, before his final capture, he had busted out of a jail in Worcester, Massachusetts (not his first jailbreak) in league with the "celebrated" Isaac Frasier, at the time the most notorious burglar in all New England. In typical fashion, Arthur's *Dying Speech* served to justify his execution but also provided a richly empirical description (as opposed to the kind of truncated account that often appeared in the newspapers) of one man's utter refusal to act the part of a slave. If such well-publicized defiance clearly raised serious questions about the community's ability to control its most indomitable slaves, it also hinted at a deeper problem: what lesson might other slaves draw from a picaresque tale of a man who had an uncommon ability to avoid capture, making him something of a local legend throughout western Massachusetts? Did they resolve to "*hear and fear, and do no more so wickedly,*" as preacher Aaron Hutchinson sermonized a week after Arthur's death? Had they "been led to see what an infinite evil sin is," as Reverend Thaddeus Maccarty chided on the day Arthur died? Or would they seek to emulate the sorts of actions for which "I have since been famous," as Arthur half-bragged from his prison cell? Inevitably, Arthur's "official" memory—the holding up of his effigy as a symbol of God's wrath—was shadowed by the ominous residue of counter-memories of his all but gleeful transgressions.[40]

Inter-colonial newspaper exchanges encouraged the frequent reprinting of news items of this type, a practice that helped make slavery a powerful (if anxious) bellwether of common identity throughout the Atlantic world. When a slave from Kittery, Maine, tossed his master's child down a well

---

McKinstry (Boston, 1764), p. 33. A newspaper account of Bristol's execution in the *Boston Evening-Post* (June 13, 1763) also noted "the bad Effects of Negroes too freely consorting together."

[40] *The Life, and Dying Speech of Arthur, a Negro Man Who Was Executed at Worcester, October 20th 1768, for a Rape Committed on the Body of One Deborah Metcalfe* (Boston, 1768); Thaddeus Maccarty, *The Power and Grace of Christ Display'd to a Dying Malefactor. A Sermon Preached at Worcester October the Twentieth, 1768. Being the Day of the Execution of Arthur, a Negro of about 21 Years old, for a Rape* (Boston, 1768); Aaron Hutchinson, *Iniquity Purged by Mercy and Truth; A Sermon Preached at Grafton, October 23d, 1768. Being the Sabbath after the Execution of Arthur, a Negro Man, at Worcester, aged about 21, For a Rape* (Boston, 1769).

"where it perished" in August 1755, the news traveled south from Boston to newspapers in New Haven, New York, Philadelphia, and Annapolis within three weeks. It had taken roughly the same amount of time in 1750 for word to reach the same cities that a group of slave rebels from Curaçao had been racked and executed by having "their hearts taken out and dash'd in their faces."[41] Year after year, stories like these refracted slavery through a lens that tended to blend, blur, and flatten the particulars of any given incident, reducing the cognitive distance between slavery in New England and slavery elsewhere in the Atlantic to a point where regional differences could be understood as distinctions of degree rather than kind. Whether these accounts held up an accurate mirror to social reality is of secondary importance to this discussion. What is of primary significance is that these products fabricated for and by the commercial press functioned as the Wedgewood china of British Atlantic slavery on its periphery: as commodities the consumption of which both provided New Englanders with entrée to the desideratum of empire and signaled assent to its practices.

****

Perhaps the single most important event in the history of slavery in the northern colonies of British America occurred in New York in 1741. The alleged slave conspiracy that kept white New Yorkers frenzied throughout the spring and summer of that year commanded space in Boston's five weeklies from April through October. In late July, the *Boston Gazette* observed that New Yorkers had already executed seventeen slaves, ordered forty-two out of the colony, and jailed about another hundred. A "further Account from New York" in the same issue observed that a slave "call'd Willmos" (or Will) at his execution confessed his prior involvement in slave revolts on the Danish island of St. John in 1734, during which he claimed to have killed "several White People with his own Hands," and at Antigua in 1736.[42] Jittery accounts of the "hellish Conspiracy" in Antigua and of the plans of the colony's "subtil and crafty" slaves had already filled New

---

[41] *Boston Gazette*, August 11, 1755; Copeland, *Colonial American Newspapers*, pp. 139–40, 147; *New York Gazette*, August 6, 1750; *Boston Evening-Post*, August 13, 1750; *Boston Weekly Post-Boy*, August 13, 1750; *Pennsylvania Gazette*, August 9, 1750; *Pennsylvania Journal, or Weekly Advertiser*, August 9, 1750; *Maryland Gazette* (Annapolis), September 5, 1750.

[42] *Boston Gazette*, July 20, 1741. For newspaper coverage of the New York conspiracy, see: *Boston Gazette*, April 20, June 8, 22, 29; July 6, 13, 20, 27, and August 10, 1741; *Boston News-Letter*, April 9; May 7; June 4, 18; July 2, 16, 23, August 6, 27, September 3, October 8, 1741. The best recent

England newspapers in late 1736 and early 1737. At the time the *Boston Gazette* had taken the unprecedented step of reprinting the names and manners of death of all sixty-four Antiguan slaves convicted as conspirators, along with the names of their masters. Now, five years later, Will's last words confirmed white New Englanders' worst fears that the chronic servile revolts in the island plantations had been imported into the Northern cities of the American mainland.[43]

In the past, New Englanders had reacted to reports of collective slave resistance from other colonies by enacting and tightening restrictive legislation, enforcing curfews, and taking other precautionary measures. Following an insurrection scare in New York in 1712, which implicated Indian servants along with Africans, Massachusetts lawmakers moved to prohibit the further "importation or bringing into this province [of] any Indian servants or slaves."[44] Again, in the summer of 1740 in the aftermath of the Stono Rebellion in South Carolina, amid rumors that blacks "intending to revolt" had set fire to Charleston, several "sober and substantial Housekeepers" in Boston revived the town's moribund slave patrol and asked other "lovers of Peace and good Order" to "join their Endeavours for preventing the like Disorders for the future." A year later, responding to news of the New York conspiracy, Judge Robert Auchmuty of the Bay Colony's Court of Admiralty implored the General Court to adopt "some further Act" to "correct the Licentious Behaviour" of Boston's "black Crew." Himself the exasperated owner of an incorrigible slave named Cesar, Auchmuty urged Bostonians to ship their unruly slaves out of the colony if they hoped to "avert what a neighboring Government providentially escaped."[45]

The overcharged atmosphere of the summer months of 1741 led to paranoid acts of pre-emptive violence. In Roxbury, located just outside Boston, a group of vigilantes stopped an aged black man named London

study of the New York plot is Jill Lepore, *New York Burning: Liberty, Slavery, and Conspiracy in Eighteenth-Century Manhattan* (New York, 2005).

[43] *Boston Gazette*, November 29, 1736, March 7, 28, 1737. Cf. *Boston Evening-Post*, November 29, 1736; *Boston News-Letter*, April 8, 1737. On the Antigua conspiracy, see David Barry Gaspar, *Bondmen and Rebels: A Study of Master-Slave Relations in Antigua, With Implications for Colonial British America* (Baltimore, 1985).

[44] *Boston News-Letter*, April 14, 21, 1712; Kenneth Scott, "The Slave Insurrection in New York in 1712," *New York Historical Society Quarterly*, XLV (1961), p. 46.

[45] *Boston Post-Boy*, January 19, 1741; *Boston News-Letter*, January 15, 1741; *Boston Evening-Post*, January 12, 1741; *New England Weekly Journal*, January 13, 1741; *Boston Evening-Post*, July 14, 1740; *Boston News-Letter*, July 16, 1741; *New England Weekly Journal*, September 23, 1734.

for being out past the nine o'clock curfew. The fraught scene that followed was fueled by newspaper reports that the New York conspirators had been involved in theft and the fencing of stolen goods. The patrollers found a bill of exchange in London's pocket, which they insisted came from a slave woman who had recently confessed to taking a sizable amount of cash from her master. Discounting London's claims to have come by the bill honestly, they tied him and tried to "make him confess" to the existence of a slave plot in Boston. When London remained unyielding, his attackers finally cut him down, but he had been "whipped" to "such a degree" that he perished not long after being carried back to his master's house. A hastily conducted coroner's inquest ruled London's death an "Accidental Murder."[46]

In death, London—like Arthur, Julian, Patience Boston, and any number of other New England slaves—marked and questioned the boundaries of white New Englanders' claims to identity in the eighteenth-century British Atlantic. A local act of ritual violence enabled the members of the Roxbury crowd to feel a sense of shared Englishness with New Yorkers, Antiguans, South Carolinians, and other British colonials who had faced down recalcitrant slaves in the middle decades of the eighteenth century. Then an act of ritual storytelling in the press turned social practice into a cultural artifact that affirmed this shared identity to others.[47] Both performances—the initial murder and its subsequent remembrance in print—seared events like the New York conspiracy into a collective memory that informed and disturbed English colonial identity for many years afterward.[48]

****

It may be that Herbert Aptheker had it right when he described colonists throughout the British Atlantic reacting in common to an unprecedented wave of slave unrest that crested in the middle decades of the eighteenth century. It may also be the case that "throughout the Americas, slavery presented more significant similarities than differences," as David Brion Davis has argued. The

---

[46] For London's murder, see *Boston Gazette, Boston Post-Boy, Boston Evening-Post*, July 20, 1741; New *England Weekly Journal*, July 21, 1741; *Boston News-Letter*, July 23, 1741.

[47] Cf. Joseph Roach, *Cities of the Dead: Circum-Atlantic Performances* (New York, 1996), pp. 36, 39, 55, 279–80; Waldstreicher, *In the Midst of Perpetual Fetes*, p. 274.

[48] For instances of the continuing effect of the New York conspiracy see *Boston Evening-Post*, January 2, 1744, *Boston Gazette*, January 3, 1744, *Boston News-Letter*, January 5, 1744, *Boston Evening-Post*, March 4, 1745.

point to be stressed here, however, is that the print culture of the period gave both of these claims *every* appearance of *subjective* truth—a "truth," that is, that would have been accepted as such by the New Englanders of the time— and thus in its own strange way contributed to the phenomenon of cultural convergence in colonial British America.[49] It is not, however a "truth" we have to endorse in our turn. In the end, as slavery's detractors liked to point out, New England's commitment to slavery never reached the same level as that of the colonies to the south. Instead, it was a "tolerable falsehood" built up over half a century, which no sooner coalesced than it began to implode, a casualty of an imperial crisis that forced New Englanders to begin imagining the contours of a new nation, neither British nor colonial.[50]

Prior to the mid-1760s, the pretense of inclusion as a member in good standing in a slave-holding empire protected the white inhabitants of the New England colonies from the unacceptable alternative of exposing their region as a social, cultural, and economic dead end within an otherwise triumphant Empire. But Whitehall's new attempts at large-scale reform of the Empire abruptly pulled the metropole and the colonies in opposite directions on the matter of slavery. In Britain itself, a diffuse, long-standing dislike of the institution crystalized into the more explicit claim that slavery had no legal standing at the Imperial center but was confined to the presumptively less developed periphery. Dependence on so barbaric, if necessary, a form of labor was proof positive, in turn, of the hypocrisy of colonial protests in the name of liberty and effectively debarred the colonists from any presumption of equality with the inhabitants of the Mother Country.[51] In New England, by contrast, resistance to the new taxation schemes and other restrictive measures emanating from Parliament set off a wide-ranging critical discussion of the habits and practice of consumerism that eventually came to implicate slavery in the growing sense of dissatisfaction with all things Imperial. In a response to the Sugar Act, an essayist in

---

[49] Herbert Aptheker, *American Negro Slave Revolts* (New York, 1943); David Brion Davis, *The Problem of Slavery in Western Culture* (Ithaca, NY, 1966), p. 262. For a sustained exposition of the concept of cultural convergence see Jack P. Greene, *Pursuits of Happiness: The Social Development of Early Modern British Colonies and the Formation of American Culture* (Chapel Hill, NC, 1988), as well as the chapter by Nancy Rhoden in this volume.

[50] Anthony Appiah, "Tolerable Falsehoods," in Jonathan Arac and Barbara Johnson (eds), *Consequences of Theory* (Baltimore, 1991), pp. 63–90.

[51] Christopher Leslie Brown, *Moral Capital: Foundations of British Abolitionism* (Chapel Hill, NC, 2006), pp. 44–101, esp. pp. 91–101, 117–34.

the *New Hampshire Gazette* in 1764 traced "the Source" of New England's "Misfortunes and Hardships" to "our own past Behaviour and Management...for these thirty years past," and chided the heirs of the thrifty Puritans for vying "with the Sugar Islands and Southern Colonies in Splender & Luxury, without possessing their Wealth." In a particularly cruel irony, "*an exhausted Country*" perversely persisted in the habits of consumption that had enabled wealthy West Indian planters to secure passage in London of a molasses duty that threatened to derail the economy of New England (and along with it, as Rhode Islanders were especially keen to point out, a growing trade in African slaves) and that depended on the production of "several thousand Hogsheads" of cheap rum per year. To continue on this way was to risk becoming "as much" the "*Servants*" of metropolitan officials and their powerful Caribbean allies "*as their Negroes are.*"[52]

Passage of the Stamp Act the following year endowed this rhetoric with still greater power. In an article in the *New Hampshire Gazette,* the colonial distributors of the stamps were likened to West Indian "Negro Overseers" who, "in order to please their Master, and hold their Posts, are more severe to their own Colour in their Exactions and Whippings." A second article in the same newspaper (reprinted from the *Boston Gazette*) plainly asserted "we won't be their negroes. Providence never designed us for negroes." A third piece, echoing Samuel Sewall's rhetoric of some six decades earlier, challenged supporters of the Stamp Act to consider "whether it is lawful for any Numbers of Men to sell another Number as free as themselves for Slaves? Let them prove that the Sale of *Joseph* into *Egypt,* was lawful, and then they may doubt on."[53] In the subsequent run up to the Revolution, "PHILANDER" made the link between resistance to Britain and anti-slavery explicit. "At a time when many among us, who call themselves SONS OF LIBERTY, are asserting the natural Rights of Mankind, and their peculiar privileges as Englishmen," the piece inquired, "is it not surprising to find many of those very Persons tyrannizing over some of their fellow Creatures, and making them SLAVES in the fullest sense of the Word?" To indulge in so glaring an inconsistency was to render "Robbery and Murder, consistent with Equity."[54]

---

[52] *New Hampshire Gazette*, November 16, 23, 1764.

[53] *New Hampshire Gazette*, June 7, 1765, October 18, 1765, October 31, 1765.

[54] *New Hampshire Gazette*, August 19, 1768.

Even the foundational narratives about slavery that New England printers had been propagating for years suddenly began to merit a critical gloss at the very same time that runaway slave advertisements in New England newspapers were reaching their peak. On August 22, 1766, the *New Hampshire Gazette* printed two fairly typical accounts of local slave resistance. In the first, a slave from the seacoast community of Newington, "being in Liquor," struck his master "on the Head with a Hatchet, and cut him across the Thigh," a crippling blow for which the slave was "sold out of the Country." The second story, directly below the first, concerned a man from New Ipswich, New Hampshire, who had been beaten "senseless and speechless" by two runaway slaves when he attempted to take them up in Dover, some fifty miles from their home. After duly noting that "the Villains" had subsequently been "taken and bro't to their Masters," printer and publisher Daniel Fowle exclaimed: "These are the *blessed* Effects of bringing Negro Slaves into the Country! Scarce one in a hundred proves good for any Thing, and yet the Guinea Trade is continued in Spight of Reason and Humanity. Quid Domini facient, *audent cum talia Fures?*" (Lifted from Virgil's *Eclogues*, this last line means "what would the masters do, when their slaves dared such things?")[55]

The libertarian rhetoric of resistance to English "enslavement" revolutionized discussions of slavery and the slave trade in New England and ultimately put both on the road to extinction. Abandoning so essential a component of a common transatlantic identity required an enormous psychological adjustment, but British actions in the 1760s and 1770s made taking the step seem a matter of survival. In November 1768, a British army captain stationed in Boston had to answer the shocking charge that he and other troops under his command had advised "several Negro Slaves in the Town to beat, abuse and cut their Masters Throats, promising them as a Reward, if they would appear at the Place of Parade to make them free." In 1774, Abigail Adams wrote husband John, then a Massachusetts delegate attending the Continental Congress in Philadelphia, that another "conspiracy" had been "discovered" in Boston, wherein slaves had written to British military governor Thomas Gage offering to fight for the British if only he would arm them. After fearing for decades that external influences might

---

[55] *New Hampshire Gazette*, August 22, 1766. This piece, including the editorial comment, also appeared in the *Boston Gazette*, August 25, 1766 (from which the quoted passages are taken).

tempt their slaves to revolt, disillusioned New Englanders had learned that the enemy turned out to be Britain itself.[56]

****

In a draft passage subsequently expunged from the final version of the Declaration of Independence, Jefferson charged the British crown with thwarting colonial attempts to "prohibit" or "restrain" that "execrable commerce" the slave trade. The polemicists of New England had in fact anticipated him: by blaming the British for the existence of slavery in the colonies, they bracketed the institution with the assorted post-1763 Imperial reform measures as proof of the sinister nature of British intentions generally. A Massachusetts tax on the slave trade in the early 1730s, it was pointed out, had been overruled by the Board of Trade, and efforts to suspend the African slave trade in the late 1760s, adopted as part of a coordinated non-importation movement through which Americans sought to put pressure on the British, had similarly been vetoed by the Bay Colony's royal governor.[57] By the end of the 1700s, one myth, slavery's exaggerated significance as a marker of shared social identity within the Empire, was well on its way to being replaced by another in which New Englanders sought to deny that slavery had ever existed in their region.[58]

For all these efforts, a revenant of their slave-holding past would survive as a visible and graphic rebuke to their pretensions to be the wellspring of American freedom. On September 18, 1755, "the greatest Number of Spectators ever known on such an Occasion" had gathered outside the Middlesex County Court in Cambridge, Massachusetts to watch two slaves named Mark and Phyllis pay with their lives for the death by poison of their master, John Codman.[59] Phyllis was "burnt to Death" in accordance with the capital

---

[56] *New Hampshire Gazette*, November 11, 1768; Abigail Adams to John Adams, September 22, 1774, in Lyman H. Butterfield (ed.), *Adams Family Correspondence* (Cambridge, MA, 1963), I, p. 162.

[57] *Boston News-Letter*, May 11, 1732; *American Weekly Mercury* (Philadelphia), June 29, 1732; *Boston Gazette*, July 17, 1732; Brown, *Moral Capital*, pp. 115–53 (esp. 138–9, 148).

[58] Joanne Pope Melish, *Disowning Slavery: Gradual Emancipation and "Race" in New England, 1780–1860* (Ithaca, NY, 1998). Other important studies of memory, myth, and regional identities in New England include Joseph A. Conforti, *Imagining New England: Explorations of Regional Identity from the Pilgrims to the Mid-Twentieth Century* (Chapel Hill, NC, 2001); John Seelye, *Memory's Nation: The Place of Plymouth Rock* (Chapel Hill, NC, 1998); David Jaffee, *People of the Wachusett: Greater New England in History and Memory, 1630–1860* (Ithaca, NY, 1999); and Stephen Nissenbaum, "New England as Region and Nation," in Edward L. Ayers, et al. (eds), *All Over the Map: Rethinking American Regions* (Baltimore, 1996), pp. 38–61.

[59] *Boston Evening-Post*, September 8, 1755; *Boston Gazette*, September 22, 1755.

penalty for women; Mark was hanged until dead on a gallows just thirty feet away. Afterwards, the crowd took down his body and conveyed it some thirteen miles to Charlestown Common, closer to the scene of the alleged crime. There it dangled in chains from a "Gibbet" that had been "erected" precisely "for that Purpose," as Thomas Fleet's *Boston Evening-Post* noted with grim austerity. Fleet also sold a broadside poem commemorating the event.[60] For decades afterward, Mark's slowly mummifying corpse continued to serve as a grisly reminder of white vengeance, spiritual terrorism, and territorial power to anyone who traveled the busy road to the ferry that connected Charlestown to Boston. In time, the site became a local landmark and then a place of deep and conflicted memory when Paul Revere, on his famous ride to alert patriot leaders about the movements of British regulars in April 1775, rendezvoused with other alarm riders at the spot "opposite where *Mark*" still "*hung in chains.*"[61] One would be hard pressed to imagine a more fitting juxtaposition to this iconic scene than another enjoying the same hagiographic status, Revere's own endlessly reproduced and reprinted engraving of the so-called Boston Massacre. Appropriately, Revere had deliberately whitewashed out of the scene Crispus Attucks, the mixed-race former Massachusetts slave who became one of the first to die in the struggle for American liberty on that night in March 1770. Gone but not forgotten, forgotten but not gone; the legacy of slavery in New England remained to haunt the region's—and the country's—independence.

Select Bibliography

BENEDICT ANDERSON, *Imagined Communities: Reflections on the Origin and Spread of Nationalism* (1983; rev. edn, New York, 1991).

T. H. BREEN, *The Marketplace of Revolution: How Consumer Politics Shaped American Independence* (New York, 2004).

---

[60] Abner Cheney Goodell, Jr., *The Trial and Execution, for Petit Treason, of Mark and Phillis, Slaves of Capt. John Codman, Who Murdered Their Master at Charlestown, Mass., in 1755; for which the Man was Hanged and Gibbeted, and the Woman was Burned to Death, Including, also, Some Account of Other Punishments by Burning in Massachusetts* (Cambridge, MA, 1883), reprinted in Paul Finkelman (ed.), *Slavery, Race, and the American Legal System, 1700–1872,* (New York and London, 1988) I, pp. 3–39; *Boston Gazette*, August 25, 1755; *Boston Evening-Post*, September 11, 1755; *A Few Lines on Occasion of the Untimely End of Mark and Phillis...* (Boston, 1755).

[61] Goodell, "Trial and Execution of Mark and Phillis," p. 30. As Vincent Brown has observed, "[p]lacing the bodies of the condemned along well-traveled paths served to haunt those places with memories and narratives of crime and punishment." *The Reaper's Garden: Death and Power in the World of Atlantic Slavery* (Cambridge, MA, 2008), p. 136.

NICHOLAS CANNY and ANTHONY PAGDEN (eds), *Colonial Identity in the Atlantic World, 1500–1800* (Princeton, 1987).

JOSEPH A. CONFORTI, *Imagining New England: Explorations of Regional Identity from the Pilgrims to the Twentieth Century* (Chapel Hill, NC, 2001).

JACK P. GREENE, *Pursuits of Happiness: The Social Development of Early Modern British Colonies and the Formation of American Culture* (Chapel Hill, NC, 1988).

ERIC HOBSBAWM and TERENCE RANGER (eds), *The Invention of Tradition* (New York, 1983).

JOANNE POPE MELISH, *Disowning Slavery: Gradual Emancipation and "Race" in New England, 1780–1860* (Ithaca, NY, 1998).

PERRY MILLER, *The New England Mind: From Colony to Province* (Boston, 1953).

JOSEPH ROACH, *Cities of the Dead: Circum-Atlantic Performances* (New York, 1996).

IAN K. STEELE, *The English Atlantic, 1675–1740: An Exploration of Communication and Community* (New York, 1986).

DAVID WALDSTREICHER, *In the Midst of Perpetual Fetes: The Making of American Nationalism, 1776–1820* (Chapel Hill, NC, 1997).

7

Colonial Identity and Revolutionary Loyalty

The Case of the West Indies

Sarah Yeh

The American Revolution marked not only a separation of thirteen rebellious colonies from Britain, but also a historiographical fissure that has long shaped our understanding of British America. The future United States has loomed large in the minds of historians on both sides of the Atlantic, with geographic borders often forming the bounds of historical inquiry. Admittedly, this divide can be exaggerated. Imperial and economic historians as well as scholars of the transatlantic slave trade have often embraced a broad definition of North America, for in these fields the Caribbean plays far too vital a role to be ignored. But for many others, British America was a clearly defined entity, comprised of the hallowed thirteen mainland colonies and their western frontiers, together with the future loyalists of the Canadian north. The picture now, however, has grown wonderfully more complicated. In recent decades, the literature of the ever-growing field of Atlantic history has reminded us that "America" did not stop at the shores of the East Coast, but also encompassed Britain's substantial empire in the Caribbean. Furthermore, historians of North America have come to routinely include in their analysis not only the British Caribbean, but also the equally significant non-British colonies of the region. How much richer the story of North America has become now that the revolution in St. Domingue is studied alongside the evolution of the early American republic!

With our minds freed from old boundaries, we now find ourselves faced with the question of just where the Caribbean colonies do fit into the picture of colonial British America. There is no question that they are inextricably linked to the history of the mainland. As Atlantic historians have shown us, it is impossible to understand the colonial American South

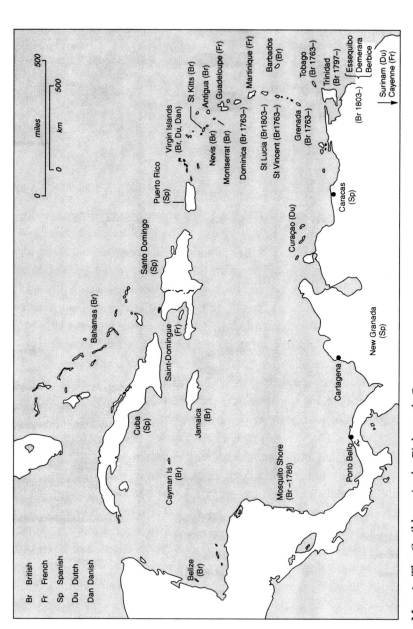

Map 4. The Caribbean in the Eighteenth Century

Br British
Fr French
Sp Spanish
Du Dutch
Dan Danish

Belize
(Br)

Mosquito Shore
(Br ~1786)

Cayman Is
(Br)

Cuba
(Sp)

Jamaica
(Br)

Bahamas (Br)

Saint-Domingue
(Fr)

Santo Domingo
(Sp)

Puerto Rico
(Sp)

Virgin Islands
(Br, Du, Dan)

St Kitts (Br)
Antigua (Br)
Nevis (Br)
Montserrat (Br)
Guadeloupe (Fr)
Dominica (Br 1763→)
Martinique (Fr)
St Lucia (Br1803→)
St Vincent (Br1763→)
Barbados
(Br)
Grenada
(Br 1763→)
Tobago
(Br 1763→)
Trinidad
(Br 1797→)

Curaçao (Du)

Caracas
(Sp)

Cartagena

Porto Bello

New Granada
(Sp)

Essequibo
Demerara
Berbice
(Br 1803→)

Surinam (Du)
Cayenne (Fr)

miles
km

0   500

0   500

without reference to its Caribbean origins. After all, West Indian planters were the leading force in the settlement of South Carolina, bringing with them all they had learned about plantation slavery in the Caribbean. Britons traveled frequently between the Caribbean and mainland colonies: Alexander Hamilton was born and raised in Nevis; Benjamin Franklin and Hugh Meredith bought the *Pennsylvania Gazette* from Samuel Keimer, who then ventured to Barbados and published the *Barbados Gazette*; John Adams bought his Georgian home in Quincy from Leonard Vassall, a wealthy West Indian planter; and countless others of lesser name and note traveled back and forth with extended family and business on all sides of the Atlantic. In an era when land was often a greater barrier to travel and communication than sea, the waters between the islands and the mainland represented far less of a divide to early modern Britons than to later historians. Having recognized these links, however, one must also be cautious not to overlook important differences for the sake of stressing commonality. In fact, reintegrating the Caribbean into the history of early America has served not only to point out the similarities between the islands and the mainland, but also to highlight the different directions the two regions were taking over the course of the long eighteenth century. The political unity of British America officially fractured after 1783, but the process of cultural differentiation was already well underway.

A number of differences had emerged between the regions over the colonial period, differences ranging from demography, geography, and ecology, to economics and politics (to name a few). This chapter explores one such key fracture in the Atlantic empire: a diverging sense of identity. Colonists throughout the empire faced the challenge of balancing life in the periphery with their connections to Britain; but in the Caribbean the struggle proved particularly acute in that Caribbean Britons were simultaneously the most integrated and most alienated members of the British Atlantic Empire. The Caribbean islands produced the most valuable commodity of the American colonies and they were the news centers of the colonial world. The planters were the richest of the American colonists and they maintained a much stronger presence (either as permanent absentee planters or part-year residents) in London and Britain than did their mainland counterparts. They could also prove a powerful political force, with returnees forming the prominent West-India interest, a group of MPs whose influence over colonial policy, particularly duties on molasses and sugar, frequently proved vexing to mainland colonists. The West Indian settlers conceived of themselves as the Atlantic settlers most deeply connected to Mother Britain. Yet there proved to be a striking disconnection between how the planters viewed themselves and how they were viewed (or perceived themselves as being viewed) by the people at home whose opinion and high regard they valued most. This disconnection proved particularly problematic as the West Indian colonists struggled to find their place in the Atlantic empire, unable to find the acceptance they craved in Britain, uncertain about their relationship with the American mainland colonies, and reluctant to embrace a distinct sense of island identity.

The problem began early. Proud of the lives they had created for themselves in a new and challenging environment, the early settlers were surprised that visitors remained unimpressed by planter efforts to recreate British civilization in the Caribbean wilderness. Quite the contrary, from the mid-seventeenth century onwards, reports from the islands painted a picture of the West Indian planter that was anything but that of a British gentleman or lady. The more the West Indians failed to convince British observers of their genteel civility, the more desperately they clung to an idealized sense of Britishness to which they were ultimately unable to conform. While they initially echoed the political fractiousness of their mainland neighbors during the upheaval of the Glorious Revolution, the Caribbean colonists of the eighteenth century increasingly worked to emphasize their close connection to and dependence upon Britain. Even here they faltered, making dubious claims of poverty at one moment, and flaunting their vast wealth on visits to London the next, prompting British observers to conclude that the colonies had gone from barbarism to decadence in the West Indies, without much evidence of civilization in between. In the Imperial crisis after 1763, the West Indians were uncertain what line to take. When British policy decisions turned against them, they shared the frustrations of the mainland colonists but could not bring themselves to match the intensity of mainland resistance. The failure of the Caribbean islands to join in the American Revolution had many causes, the most frequently noted being the threat of slave rebellions and the need for British naval protection from European rivals in the region. To these must be added the colonists' complex crisis of identity and the fact that their imperative to remain "British" despite metropolitan scorn prevented them from developing any form of strong coherent identity, be it British, Creole, or West Indian.

The question of identity and what it meant to be a Briton in the early modern period has been a matter of fierce debate in British historiography.[1] Studies on the question of identity in the British world have suggested a range of organizing principles, from notions of race and gender held in common, shared religious commitments, and distinctive sets of manners, to a sense of common descent and of the concept of liberty as a defining birthright. There is no longer a simple answer to the question of what defined the early modern Briton, for identities must be understood as complex, multi-layered, and fluid.[2] Well before the rise of nineteenth-century nationalism, however, there was a sense among Europeans generally that particular "group identities" bonded various individuals together and provided a "sense that the people belong together by virtue of the characteristics that they share."[3] Though contemporaries did not necessarily speak in terms of

[1] A partial list of relevant titles would include: Kathleen Wilson, *The Sense of the People: Politics, Culture and Imperialism in England, 1715–1785* (Cambridge, 1995); Nicholas Rogers, *Crowds, Culture, and Politics in Georgian Britain* (Oxford, 1998); Jeremy Black, *British Foreign Policy in the Age of Walpole* (Edinburgh, 1985); Jeremy Black (ed.), *British Politics and Society from Walpole to Pitt, 1742–1789* (New York, 1990); P. J. Marshall, "The Eighteenth-Century Empire," in *British Politics* (ed.), Black, pp. 177–200; Eliga Gould, *The Persistence of Empire* (Chapel Hill, NC, 2000); Alexander Murdoch, *British History, 1660–1832: National Identity and Local Culture* (New York, 1998); Raphael Samuel (ed.), *Patriotism: The Making and Unmaking of British National Identity* (London, 1989); Tony Claydon and Ian McBride (eds), *Protestantism and National Identity: Britain and Ireland c. 1650–1850* (Cambridge, 1998); Stephen Conway, *The British Isles and the War of American Independence* (Oxford, 2000), pp. 167–8; J. C. D. Clark, *The Language of Liberty 1660–1832: Political Discourse and Social Dynamics in the Anglo-American World* (Cambridge, 1994); David Armitage, *The Ideological Origins of the British Empire* (Cambridge, 2000); Colin Kidd, *British Identities Before Nationalism: Ethnicity and Nationhood in the Atlantic World, 1600–1800* (Cambridge, 1999); Kathleen Wilson, *The Island Race: Englishness, Empire, and Gender in the Eighteenth Century* (London, 2003).

[2] Stephen Conway, "From Fellow-Nationals to Foreigners: British Perceptions of the Americans, circa 1739–1783," *WMQ*, 3rd ser., LIX (2002), pp. 65–100; Jack P. Greene, "Empire and Identity from the Glorious Revolution to the American Revolution," in P. J. Marshall (ed.), *OHBE, II, The Eighteenth Century*, pp. 208–30; Claydon and McBride, *Protestantism and National Identity*; Kathleen Wilson (ed.), *A New Imperial History: Culture, Identity, and Modernity in Britain and the Empire, 1660–1840* (Cambridge, 2004); Lawrence Brockliss and David Eastwood (eds), *A Union of Multiple Identities: The British Isles, c. 1750–c. 1850* (Manchester, 1997); Brendan Bradshaw and Peter Roberts (eds), *British Consciousness and Identity: The Making of Britain, 1533–1707* (Cambridge, 1998); Paul Langford, *Englishness Identified: Manners and Character, 1650–1850* (Oxford, 2000); John D. Garrigus and Christopher Morris (eds), *Assumed Identities: The Meaning of Race in the Atlantic World* (College Station, TX, 2010).

[3] David Miller, *On Nationality* (Oxford, 1995), p. 25; for extended discussions of the theories and historiography of national identity and nationalism see Hans Kohn, *Nationalism: Its Meaning and History*, rev. edn (Malabar, 1982), pp. 9–10; Adrian Hastings, *The Construction of Nationhood: Ethnicity, Religion and Nationalism* (Cambridge, 1997), pp. 3–4, 11, 36–55; Hugh

the "nation" in the eighteenth century, they increasingly discussed the differing characteristics associated with particular kingdoms, states, or peoples, referring to what we might today consider "national" traits (sometimes viewed as innate and sometimes believed to have been shaped by historical, social, and cultural circumstances).[4]

Here, Britain was no exception. Great Britain did not formally exist as a political unit until 1707, and both before and after this date English and Scottish culture collided on many levels. Nonetheless, over the course of the eighteenth century, the two regions were drawing increasingly closer together, such that contemporaries did speak of such a thing as "British" traits.[5] Admittedly, something described here as "British" might not capture the sentiments of all Scots, the Protestant Irish, or the English for that matter; but in many cases to use the term "English" or "Scottish" alone, implying that other groups in the British Isles were excluded from the description, would be equally misleading, if not more so.

Early modern Britons did not divide the world's population into British and non-British in so many words, but if one looks beneath the surface of their words and actions, distinct patterns of inclusion and exclusion emerge. These patterns represented a sense of collective social and cultural identity that Britons associated with an idealized version of their own society and which shaped their self-perceptions and judgments of others. Several subcategories contributed to this collective identity (gentility, morality, femininity, masculinity, and Christianity, among others) and fostered a particular vision of Britishness. The settlers of the Caribbean islands aspired to replicate this vision of Britain in their new environments, only to be regularly rebuffed

Seton-Watson, *Nations and States: An Enquiry into the Origins of Nations and the Politics of Nationalism* (Boulder, CO, 1977), p. 3; Patrick Kelly, "Nationalism and the Contemporary Historians of the Jacobite War in Ireland," in Michael O'Dea and Kevin Whelan (eds), *Nations and Nationalisms: France, Britain, Ireland and the Eighteenth-Century Context* (Oxford, 1995), pp. 89–90; Craig Calhoun, *Nationalism* (Minneapolis, 1997), p. 29; Anthony Smith, *The Nation in History: Historiographical Debates about Ethnicity and Nationalism* (Hanover, NH 2000); John A. Armstrong, *Nations Before Nationalism* (Chapel Hill, NC, 1982), p. 3.

[4] Pierre Lurbe, "John Toland, Cosmopolitanism, and the Concept of Nation," in Michael O'Dea and Kevin Whelan (eds), *Nations and Nationalisms: France, Britain, Ireland and the Eighteenth Century Context* (Oxford, 1995), pp. 253, 257–8; Anthony D. Smith, *National Identity* (Reno, NV, 1991), pp. 85–6; Langford, *Englishness Identified*, pp. 7–8.

[5] Linda Colley, *Britons: Forging the Nation, 1707–1837* (New Haven, 1992); Colin Kidd, *Subverting Scotland's Past: Scottish Whig Historians and the Creation of an Anglo-British Identity, 1689–1830* (Cambridge, 1993).

by the British upper classes whose ranks they fruitlessly attempted to join. Examining the standards by which Britons found the societies of their West Indian colonies wanting in Britishness, therefore, can tell us a great deal about how they constructed the borders of, to borrow Benedict Anderson's phrase, their "imagined communities,"[6] and why the West Indians went to such lengths in their quixotic efforts to measure up to metropolitan opinion. When applied to the question of identity in British North America, this cultural approach helps highlight a growing divergence between mainland Americans who, without repudiating their claim to Britishness, had begun to embrace distinct regional identities, and the British West Indians who increasingly eschewed the conscious creation of a Caribbean identity.[7]

In discussing the British settlers of the Caribbean, this chapter focuses primarily on those who were not only literate, but who could afford paper, ink, and postage costs and who believed the details of their lives, property, or businesses needed to be recorded and preserved. Planters, the landed elite, figure heavily in the discussion, as do the people who often represented them to the metropole: lawyers, doctors, ministers, etc. Precisely because they maintained for public consumption an idealized vision of the country squire, or the lord and lady of the manor, the landed elite often bore the most scrutiny when contemporaries assessed the "Britishness" of a region. At the same time, the evidence here also considers public perceptions of Caribbean culture, relying on books, prints, plays, sermons, pamphlets, newspapers, and accounts that integrate the voices and actions of a range of figures, sorts, and orders—from journalists, clergymen, and local officials to merchants, sailors, tenants, and slaves.

****

To understand these West Indian societies, it is important to begin with patterns of settlement. At the same time that people of Old World descent were creating colonies on the mainland of North America, a similar scenario emerged in the British West Indies, led by a familiar mix of English, Scottish, Irish, and (to a lesser degree) Continental immigrants. There were, of course, also significant differences. The rapid spread of disease during the Columbian Exchange of the late fifteenth and sixteenth centuries meant that the

---

[6] Benedict Anderson, *Imagined Communities*, rev. edn (London, 1991).
[7] For a detailed discussion of the problematic nature of British Caribbean identity, see Sarah E. Yeh, "'In an Enemy's Country': British Culture, Identity, and Allegiance in Ireland and the Caribbean, 1688–1763" (Ph.D. diss., Brown University, 2006).

British settlers of the West Indies did not have to contend with indigenous populations to the same extent that mainland settlers did. While both regions increasingly had to come to terms with the growing presence of slavery in their societies, the sheer magnitude of coerced immigrants from West Africa to the Caribbean, and the staggering ratios of slave to free populations in the islands by the eighteenth century (in some cases as high as 10:1), made the Caribbean distinct. Moreover, in the course of the development of the sugar economy in the seventeenth century, large planters gained control of the bulk of island land. In 1680, 175 planters (7 percent of property holders) controlled 54 percent of Barbadian land and, by 1729, 30 estates in Barbados held 80 percent of the land. In Jamaica, 467 planters (each with a plantation in excess of 1,000 acres) owned close to 78 percent of patented land in 1754.[8] The lack of available land discouraged the migration of families to the region, a fact that further exacerbated the skewed gender ratios that had plagued several of the islands from the outset. Such families as there were on the islands were fragile units frequently disrupted by the high mortality rates. Equally, disease and piracy, combined with the constant threat of invasion or slave rebellion, made the islands less attractive to precisely those settlers who might have been most capable of reproducing a "British" society.

Under these circumstances, Caribbean colonial life had developed a negative image almost from its inception: in 1692, for example, one British visitor described Jamaica as "a sink of all filthiness."[9] What proved surprising was the persistence of this low opinion long after the islands had achieved a degree of stability and enviable prosperity. In the seventeenth century, the islands genuinely had been an Imperial backwater where settlers faced a daily struggle against disease, squalor, hurricanes, and pirates. By the mid-eighteenth century, however, planters were living on vast plantations in elaborate manor houses filled with the most luxurious imported consumer goods money could buy. Yet the planters' ostentatious displays of their new gentry lifestyle did little to convince British visitors that much had changed. Rather than being impressed by the aristocratic lifestyle of the planters and their lavish displays of hospitality, visitors found the attempts at displays of luxury somewhat ridiculous, pathetic, or vain. As one such visitor put it,

---

[8] Hilary Beckles, *A History of Barbados: From Amerindian Settlement to Nation-State* (Cambridge, 1990), p. 24; Andrew Jackson O'Shaughnessy, *An Empire Divided: The American Revolution and the British Caribbean* (Philadelphia, 2000), p. 27; Richard B. Sheridan, "The Formation of Caribbean Plantation Society, 1689–1748," in Marshall (ed.), *OHBE*, II, p. 403.

[9] *A True and Perfect Relation of that most Sad and Terrible Earthquake, at Port Royal in Jamaica, which Happened on Tuesday the 7th of June, 1692...* (London, [1692]).

there was not much pleasure to be taken in the generosity and hospitality of a people characterized by "great boorishness & rusticity."[10] When observers looked beyond the superficial trappings of genteel, civilized society, they found much of substance lacking.

One particular complaint was the fractured family life of the Caribbean. Members of both sexes in the islands were accused of sexual licentiousness, but the male West Indian planters were especially notorious for the liberties they took with their own slaves as well as with the wives of fellow planters. In their turn, West Indian women were sometimes seen as subverting proper gender roles in taking on control of the estates of deceased or absent husbands, as plantation management required a stern, presumptively masculine hand over one's slaves. The planters' children reportedly ran wild in the islands, with liberty to give full vent to every form of self-indulgence. Turned loose in the streets of London, Cambridge, and Oxford with vast sums of wealth at their disposal, they rapidly fell into profligacy and ruin. The parents were held to be little better, fond of drinking, dueling, gambling, blood sports, cards, dancing, and various other violent or frivolous pastimes. These social vices were of course common enough among the inhabitants of Britain proper, but for London society they quickly became the *defining* features of the Caribbean lifestyle. Many Britons were convinced that the Caribbean planters had degenerated through their close contact with the black slaves who formed an overwhelming majority of the colonial population.[11]

As abolitionist literature spread through Britain in the course of the eighteenth century, the harsh slave master of the plantation came to seem a hideous parody of the benevolent English lord of the manor he so idolized. If, prior to the Revolution, the British public proved reluctant to view slavery itself as a sin,[12] they found it easy (and much less costly) to cast the planters as the sinners. Eighteenth-century Britain was undergoing dramatic change, both in terms of rising urbanization and nascent industrialization, but a powerful vision persisted of the idealized manor as the heart of British society. Land remained the primary source of support for the ruling elite well into the nineteenth century, and it is estimated that as

---

[10] Delacherois correspondence, Department of Records, National Army Museum (hereafter NAM), London, 1978-05-63, pp. 44, 65.

[11] Sarah Yeh, "'A Sink of All Filthiness': Gender, Family, and Identity in the British Atlantic, 1688–1763," *The Historian*, LXVIII (2006), pp. 66–88.

[12] Christopher L. Brown, *Moral Capital: Foundations of British Abolitionism* (Chapel Hill, NC, 2006).

late as the mid-eighteenth century, some 45–50 percent of the British labor force continued to earn a living through agriculture. Moreover, those living in areas most affected by the changes in the economy were often the ones to cling to and cherish an idyllic past. Wealth from trade and manufacture brought new men and money into the countryside, but local country servants preferred to work for the "real gentry" who knew the traditions and ties of manorial life rather than the upstart newcomers.[13] In an age when British poets and artists like Goldsmith, Thomson, Stubbs, Lambert, and Gainsborough were writing and painting nostalgic tributes to a lost era of rural social harmony, the Caribbean islands looked like exactly what many feared might be the fate of rural England: a land full of arrogant, heartless grandees and an exploited, degraded labor force, devoid of happy cottagers, sturdy yeomen, and loyal tenants. Hostility toward returnee planters who settled in the English countryside only accentuated this stereotype. Rightly or wrongly, the planters were often seen as vulgar, arrogant types who flaunted their wealth, bid up the cost of seats in Parliament with little intention of showing up after election, and brazenly displayed their African slaves and illegitimate children.

Again, while patterns and customs were certainly changing, notions such as deference and reciprocal benevolence remained strongly rooted in British hearts and minds. The realities of life on the slave plantations of the West Indies collided violently with this image. The planters, who ruthlessly and repeatedly imported fresh slaves to replace those who had not survived the brutal conditions of Caribbean plantation agriculture, were a disturbingly extreme version of the new "improving" landlords in rural Britain who callously hired and fired tenants and laborers according to their needs without any sense of obligation or responsibility to those beneath them. British visitors to the West Indies often had no theoretical or moral objections to slavery, but found themselves troubled how to interpret the actions of their hosts, who maintained their estates with violence and chains rather than through the bonds of loyalty, tradition, and proverbial mutual respect.

It could be argued, in reply to this dark picture of a descent into barbarism, that the islands appealed to a different, more entrepreneurial and "modern" set of Britons than those who shaped the cultural and moral standards of Britain proper. The diverse demands of sugar cultivation and

---

[13] G. E. Mingay, *Land and Society in England, 1750–1980* (London, 1994), pp. 49, 119, 130; Alun Howkins, *Reshaping Rural England: A Social History, 1850–1925* (London, 1991).

production made the planters essentially the heads of small factories. In their capitalistic desire to exploit land and labor with an eye to profit rather than human costs, the early modern planters can be presented as anticipating the values and visions of industrial modernity. Those most adept at adapting to this new form of society and economy, the successful planters and merchants, became the wealthiest subjects in the Empire in the eighteenth century.[14] Moreover, the relaxed morality and the excesses of colonial life might have been a welcome relief to settlers who chafed against religious intolerance, social rigidity, or the restrictions of polite British culture. In this sense, the planter lifestyle could be viewed as exciting, liberating, and rewarding to some, just as it appeared debauched and degenerate to others.

The difficulty with this approach lies in the fact that the Caribbean settlers did not particularly embrace an identity in which they heralded themselves as modernizing and progressive, or convince Britons this was the case (one cannot help but wonder how the development of the British Atlantic might have been changed if they had successfully done so). Rather, they attempted to appeal to more established traditions of British society, at the same time failing to keep up with shifting moral and cultural expectations in the eighteenth century. In struggling to prove how anglicized they were, the planters were loathe to take any actions which might dissociate themselves from their putative British counterparts and were anxious to establish connections with Britain to the greatest extent possible. As John Pinney explained in sending his son from Nevis to England, "By no means do I view him, or would I wish to have him viewed, in the light of a West-Indian, though there are many worthy characters, yet, collectively, they are a dissipate unthinking race...I hope therefore my friends will endeavour to inculcate in his tender mind, the principles of an honest, independent Englishman." To another friend, Pinney insisted, "Consider him as one of our own Country-men, no West-Indian!"[15]

This anxiety to demonstrate an unqualified loyalty to Britain had not always been the case. At the turn of the eighteenth century, the British Caribbean often appeared the region most likely to rebel against the Mother

---

[14] T. G. Burnard, "'Prodigious Riches': The Wealth of Jamaica Before the American Revolution," *Economic History Review*, LIV (2001), pp. 506–24; S. D. Smith, *Slavery, Family, and Gentry Capitalism in the British Atlantic: The World of the Lascelles, 1648–1834* (Cambridge, 2006). Cf. S. Max Edelson, *Plantation Enterprise in Colonial South Carolina* (Cambridge, MA, 2006).

[15] John Pinney to George Warry, Nevis, June 10, 1770, Pinney Letterbook 5, University of Bristol Library (hereafter UBL), Special Collections.

Country. Just as 1689 provided New England colonists with the opportunity to flex their muscles against Imperial control as part of a defense of English liberty against Stuart tyranny, the decade after the Glorious Revolution marked a period of contest between the colonies of the West Indies and Mother England. Frustrated by heavy impositions on sugar and the meddling of inexperienced colonial officials in local affairs, the planters complained with increasing stridency that they were being deprived of their rights as English subjects and effectively being "cast out" of England. Barbados planters, in particular, at the peak of their success among the sugar islands, vehemently protested the duties imposed on sugar. Perhaps the most strenuous of the opposition statements could be found in a 1689 pamphlet by Edward Littleton entitled *The Groans of the Plantation.* Though an absentee by the time he wrote his piece, Littleton had once been one of the largest landowners in Barbados and remained an outspoken advocate of planter interests. Littleton began by stressing the colonists' devotion to their Mother England, even when she proved unkind, but concluded by hinting that there was talk of an alternative to English rule:

We of the Plantations cannot hear the mention of being cast off by England without regret. Nevertheless, if it must be so, we shall compose our minds to bear it. And like children truly dutifull, we shall be content to part with our dearest Mother, rather than be a burden to her, But though we must part with our country, yet we would not willingly part with our King: and therefore, if you please, let us be made over to *Scotland.* We are confident that Scotland would be well pleased to supply us with people, to have the sweet trade in exchange. And we should agree well with them: for we know by experience that they are honest men and good planters.

Coming at a time when England was growing more and more concerned over Scotland's imperial ambitions at Darien, such a threat was no laughing matter.[16]

Littleton's menacing words hit a raw nerve, and no doubt helped stir concerns that there could be a future competition for the allegiance of the Caribbean sugar islands. When *The Groans of the Plantations* and its subsequent reprinting raised hackles in London, Barbadians responded to attacks on their loyalty with statements of their important contributions to the

---

[16] Edward Littleton, *The Groans of the Plantations or A True Account of their Grievous and Extreme Sufferings by the Heavy Impositions Upon Sugar...* (London, 1689), pp. 1, 8–9, 15, 17, 20, 23–4, 32.

benefit of all of the crown's subjects. They exalted the military role of Barbados as the citadel of the British Caribbean and emphasized the great economic and social benefit the plantations provided in supplying Britain with sugar, generating trade and money, and putting surplus labor populations to work. Other West Indian colonies also jumped into the debate in the 1690s to challenge London's right to legislate for the islands and emphasize their own position and importance to the Empire.[17]

Well after the flurry over *Groans of the Plantations* subsided, conflicts erupted across the Caribbean from Jamaica to Barbados, as island assemblies and governors quarreled over what should be taxed and who should have the authority to control public monies in the colonies.[18] Tensions between governors and assemblies were common throughout the British colonial world, but only in the Caribbean did hostilities reach such a level that a group of Antiguan planters took it upon themselves to assassinate Governor Daniel Parke in 1710.[19] This was an extreme case, to be sure, but the incident did little to improve the British picture of West Indian politics. The more the planters squabbled with their officials and with one another, the more they began to realize that their image was not one of defenders of British rights and liberties but one of factious troublemakers. Aware of their damaged reputation, they lashed out against their critics, the men "who make it their daily study, to impose so upon the judgments of such as are strangers to their measures and designs... misrepresenting persons and things, both abroad and at home, and industriously raising

[17] *The Interest of the Nation, As it respects all the Sugar-Plantations Abroad*... (London, 1691), pp. 6–7; *A Discourse of the Duties on Merchandize*... (London, 1695), pp. 10, 16; *A True and faithful Account of an Intire and Absolute Victory over the French Fleet in the West Indies, by Two East-India Ships*... (London, 1690); *A State of the Present Condition of the Island of Barbadoes*... (London, [1698?]), p. 3; *Some Considerations Humbly Offered to Both Houses of Parliament, concerning the Sugar Colonies, and chiefly the island of Barbadoes* (London, 1701), pp. 4, 7–8; Thomas Dalby, *An Historical Account of the Rise and Growth of the West-India Collonies*... (London, 1690); *Journals of the Assembly of Jamaica*, July 30, 1691, I, (Jamaica, 1795–1811), p. 140.

[18] "Some Observations & Reasons Offered on Behalf of the Government of Jamaica in Support of the Bill lately passed there called the Duty Bill," BL, Sloane Manuscripts 3986, ff. 5–7; *Journals of the Assembly of Jamaica*, I, pp. 219, 280, 286, 344–5, 352–3; *The Politics and Patriots of Jamaica. A Poem* (London, 1718); John Egerton Bridgewater papers, Huntington Library (hereafter HL), San Marino, California, Manuscripts EL 9730–9731.

[19] Natalie Zacek, "A Death in the Morning: The Murder of Daniel Parke," in Robert A. Olwell and Alan Tully (eds), *Cultures and Identities in Colonial British America* (Baltimore, 2004), pp. 223–43.

factions and divisions which otherwise would never have happen'd among the inhabitants."[20]

Nevertheless, the planters did seem to have recognized that the belligerent stances of the late seventeenth and early eighteenth centuries had done little to endear them to the British public. They began to shift to a new tack, one that would be less abrasive when protesting unpopular duties and policies imposed on them from London. During the 1720s, 30s, and 40s, the standard refrain from the Caribbean centered on the colonists' dire circumstances rather than their demand for equal rights. A pamphlet of 1714 hoping to reduce restrictions on sugar and the slave trade made it a point to *"demonstrate how near the desolation of the Sugar Islands is at hand."*[21] In 1731, 1734, 1735, and 1736, the Jamaica Assembly repeatedly asked the crown to ease the tax burden on sugar, lamenting the "low and languishing circumstances" under which they lived.[22] When Britain considered new duties on sugar in the 1740s, the planters stressed their inability to bear any additional taxes and denied that they lived in luxury and pleasure. For every single wealthy man in the islands, they argued, "hundreds are there obliged to labour hard, and struggle under many Difficulties for a bare Subsistence."[23] Pamphlets in support of the planters also emphasized the many dangers the islanders faced: the danger of the French and Spanish; the threat of slave rebellions; heavy taxes; high prices; hurricanes; and bad weather.[24] The Assembly of Barbados in a petition to George II lamented the dangers they faced from the power of the French in the region and warned of the "sad and distressful condition, to which this and all your Majesty's West India islands must inevitably be reduced," if measures were not taken to secure the islands against the French.[25] Britons who read these addresses and pamphlets from the West Indies and took them at face value would no doubt have thought

[20] *An Account of some of the many grievances of Jamaica, touching the multiplication of offices, in the person of Mr. Richard Rigby*... [London, 1713?], p. 3.

[21] *Some Observations showing the danger of losing the Trade of the Sugar Colonies, humbly offer'd to the consideration of Parliament. By a planter* (London, 1714), p. 4.

[22] A. B. to Charles Wager, Jamaica, September 16, 1733, BL, Additional Manuscripts 19049, f. 7; *Journals of the Assembly of Jamaica*, III, pp. 259, 302, 395.

[23] *Considerations Against Laying any New Duty upon Sugar*...(London, 1744), p. 9.

[24] *Considerations Relating to a New Duty upon Sugar. The Second Edition. To which is now added, A Supplement* (London, 1746), pp. 34–7; *Considerations Against Laying any Additional Duty on Sugar*, pp. 14–16, 19; *Journals of the Assembly of Jamaica*, IV, pp. 155–6.

[25] Address of the Governor, Council, & Assembly of Barbados to George II, enclosed in letter of Henry Grenville, February 20, 1751, Grenville Papers, HL, STG 25(30).

that for most of the first half of the eighteenth century, the West Indies were in a perpetual state of desperation.

It is important to recognize the very real disadvantages under which the West Indies labored and the sense of physical insecurity that helped cement their allegiance to Britain. Destructive hurricanes and weather did ruin many a planter; the French and Spanish were very close by in a period when war was as common as peace; the numbers of slaves were growing dramatically, so much so that the white settlers found themselves drastically outnumbered; and in Jamaica the struggle with the Maroons (substantial communities of runaway slaves long established in remote regions of the island) caused widespread concern until peace was reached in 1739. At the same time, it is also important to consider the cultural insecurity which kept the West Indians anxious to protect their relationship with Britain and their reputation as Britons. Desperate to be accepted as true Britons, they were wary of antagonizing their compatriots across the Atlantic with overt attacks on Imperial policy. It was far safer to call upon their brethren for pity and sympathy in their dire plight.

Unfortunately for the planters, the repeated emphasis on Caribbean weaknesses did little to boost any sense of West Indian confidence or pride, and it was not particularly effective in Britain, where people mocked the wealthy planters' attempts to claim poverty. In 1737, the acting governor of Jamaica proposed a sumptuary law "to discourage excess" and reduce the appearance of luxury, reasoning that "we can hardly expect our misfortunes should affect others, so as to give us relief, if we live as if we did not seem to feel them ourselves."[26] The Assembly not only rejected the proposal but expressed their offense at the implication that they exaggerated their suffering:

It is the opinion of this committee, that the inhabitants of this island are greatly misrepresented in that part of his honour's speech, wherein he recommends a sumptuary law; insinuating thereby, that they live in a state of luxury and great expence, when it is but too visible, that the whole face of the country exhibits the most evident marks of poverty and distress, and the inhabitants never lived in so frugal, not to say mean, a manner as they do at present.[27]

Plagued by their negative image, and yet blind to whatever steps they might take to improve their standing, the West Indians stolidly continued their

---

[26] *Journals of the Assembly of Jamaica*, June 21, 1737, III, p. 411
[27] *Journals of the Assembly of Jamaica*, June 23, 1737, III, p. 412.

campaign to convince the British at home of their financial distress and attendant suffering. It was a non-confrontational strategy but it did little more than add the charge of hypocrisy to the standard aspersions about the planters' alleged addiction to luxury and excess. If anything, by the middle of the eighteenth century, it was more difficult than ever to take pride in the appellation and identification of West Indian.

This is not to say that the West Indian colonists meekly submitted to Imperial rule. Assemblies continued to fight with governors, factions divided island populations, and both royal officials and colonial assemblies guarded their rights and challenged any attempts the other made to overstep their authority. Edward Trelawny, considered one of Jamaica's more successful governors, was so fed up from his long term in office from 1737 to 1752 that he argued the institution of the colonial assembly, "which of all farces is surely the greatest, & most stupid," should be done away with.[28] When a battle between the Jamaican Assembly and Governor William Lyttelton erupted in 1764–66, following the Governor's perceived over-extension of prerogative powers at the expense of the assemblymen's privileges, the Assembly framed the "privilege controversy" in language echoing Parliament's seventeenth-century challenge to the prerogative powers of the Stuart kings. They accused Lyttelton of an "arbitrary exercise of power" and prepared to petition the king to protect them "from such open and manifest violations, destructive of our rights, and subversive of our constitution." An "intense and prolonged" constitutional debate emerged over the origins of the colonists' rights as Britons, and the Assembly went so far as to defy a Privy Council decision and appeal directly to the House of Commons, exposing important constitutional questions for the Empire.[29] Other islands followed suit and called for confirmation of their assembly rights, but these contests over privilege and prerogative in the 1760s never reached the severity of their equivalents on the mainland and to some extent distracted the island assemblies from larger Imperial controversies.[30] Often, the conflicts over authority in the West Indies remained local disputes based on splits between

[28] Trelawny to Henry Pelham, Jamaica, May 1747, National Library of Jamaica (hereafter NLJ), Manuscripts 306.

[29] Jack P. Greene, "The Jamaica Privilege Controversy, 1764–66: An Episode in the Process of Constitutional Definition in the Early Modern British Empire," *Journal of Imperial and Commonwealth History*, XXII (1994), pp. 20, 33, 47–9.

[30] Andrew J. O'Shaughnessy, *An Empire Divided: The American Revolution and the British Caribbean* (Philadelphia, 2000), pp. 115–30; Greene, "Jamaica Privilege Controversy," p. 25.

rival factions and were resolved by a change in governor. This nearly constant infighting gave the islands a reputation as hotbeds of faction and obstinacy, but as one contemporary pamphlet stressed, there was no reason to fear the planters' devotion to Britain fading, for "nothing is more common than to hear the Creols, who can have no notion of Great Britain, or knowledge of persons there, talk of going home."[31]

When "home" invariably meant Britain, the Caribbean colonies found creating a separate identity for themselves extremely difficult. While the wealthy absentees in Britain could serve as powerful political advocates for West Indian issues, their absence at the same time challenged attempts by the resident planters to gain acknowledgement of the value and importance of the islands. If the grandest, wealthiest, and most powerful planters repeatedly flocked to London, how were West Indians ever to overcome the perception that those who could leave the Caribbean did so? Try as they might, the planters seemed unable to gain the recognition and approval they craved. The Seven Years' War and the ensuing Treaty of Paris in 1763 merely confirmed these fears.

As British politicians debated the terms of a peace in the waning years of the war, they opened the way for an intense discussion of the Empire's future and the relative merits of the mainland and the islands. By the end of the war, Britain controlled both New France and all the major French sugar islands save St. Domingue. Peace would not be possible if Britain attempted to keep both regions, and a pamphlet war debating the merits of "Canada versus Guadeloupe" occupied controversialists from 1759 onward. Some British politicians worried that there was an independent spirit on the mainland that might be unleashed by removing the French threat in Canada. The British sugar islands did not appear to raise such concerns, and many acknowledged that Guadeloupe and the other French sugar islands were more immediately valuable than Canada. Nevertheless, the government ultimately concluded that the mainland offered greater potential for British expansion and development and chose to return the captured islands to France.[32]

This decision is often seen as a "triumph of British West Indian interests" in that "British planters were powerful enough to block the acquisition of

---

[31] *The Importance of Jamaica to Great Britain, Consider'd. With some account of that Island, from its discovery in 1492 to this Time* ... (London, c. 1740), p. 7.
[32] Theodore Draper, *A Struggle for Power: The American Revolution* (New York, 1996), pp. 3–25.

territories which would flood England with tropical produce."[33] Initially, to be sure, influential absentee plantation owners (particularly those from Jamaica) did lobby for the acquisition of the French islands for the purpose of destroying their sugar-based agriculture. When this alternative came to seem unlikely, they instead argued against territorial acquisitions in the Caribbean. Yet one must be careful about conflating the actions of the absentees with those of the West Indian planters more generally, for their interests often diverged. With sugar prices trending upwards since the 1730s, planters were less concerned about an enlarged sugar supply than they had been earlier in the century. Many of the smaller planters in Barbados and the Leeward Islands contributed to the conquests of Guadeloupe and Martinique and subsequently advocated their retention, eager to expand into new land and eliminate much of the smuggling of sugar between North America and the French islands that so irked the British West Indians.[34] They were bitterly disappointed when the decision turned in favor of Canada: Britain had turned a deaf ear to resident planters' cries and seemed content to leave the French in their midst, while extending the territories of the mainland colonies so that the North Americans might grow stronger and expand their illicit trade with the French islands.[35] The West Indians had viewed themselves as the most commercially valuable of Britain's colonies, but the Treaty of Paris suggested that the ministry's focus was shifting for the future to the mainland colonies. As contemporaries had feared, the removal of the French from Canada emboldened the mainland colonists. For the colonists of the West Indies, it indicated the low regard with which they were held at home

---

[33] David Brion Davis, *The Problem of Slavery in Western Culture* (Ithaca, NY, 1966), p. 162; Frank Wesley Pitman, *The Development of the British West Indies, 1700–1763* (New Haven, 1917), pp. 334–60.

[34] George Metcalf, *Royal Government and Political Conflict in Jamaica, 1729–1783* (London, 1965), pp. 20–1, 77; J. R. Ward, "The British West Indies in the Age of Abolition," in Marshall (ed.), *OHBE*, II, pp. 418–19; Richard B. Sheridan, *Sugar and Slavery: An Economic History of the British West Indies, 1623–1775* (Baltimore, 1973), p. 453.

[35] "Reflections on the True Interest of Great Britain with respect to the Caribbee Islands: as well as the Old Settlements; as the Neutral Islands and the Conquests. In which the importance of Martinique is particularly considered (1762)", BL, Additional Manuscripts 32938, ff. 356–364; see also John Campbell, *Candid and Impartial Considerations on the Nature of the Sugar Trade; the Comparative Importance of the British and French Islands in the West-Indies*...(London, 1763), p. 73; Martin to Martin, Jr., Antigua, July 20, 1762, BL, Additional Manuscripts 41347, f. 150; George Brydges Rodney, "Description of the Caribee Islands as seen from Martinique Dec. the 3rd, 1762," typescript and copy of manuscript held in the National Library of Jamaica; Pinney to Shaw and Coker, October 15, 1762, Pinney Letterbook 3, UBL.

and struck yet another blow to their already battered self-esteem. When, in the wake of the Seven Years' War, Parliament began to take greater interest in colonial affairs, the mainland colonies and the Caribbean islands, though sharing a common sense of grievance, entered into the controversy from different starting points, acted on the basis of different assumptions, and often pursed incompatible priorities.

For historians working to reintegrate the West Indies into a more complete picture of British imperial policy in America, this divergence raises the complex question of why the islands failed to join the Revolution on the mainland. Simply because the West Indies ultimately did not join in the American Revolution is no reason to view developments in the islands and mainland in separate contexts. One can certainly find examples of West Indians speaking out against Parliament's new measures in much the same language as the mainland colonists, vociferously objecting to what they saw as violations of their British rights and privileges.[36] When Parliament passed the Stamp Act in 1765, the West Indians were at least as upset as the mainland colonies, if not more so. The islands were subject to higher rates under the Act and suffered from a shortage of currency, which added to the burden of paying the new duties. Samuel Martin complained from Antigua that such a foolish policy would be "killing the hen that lays the golden eggs," and lectured his son (a supporter of the Stamp Act in London) on the many ways in which the Stamp Act violated the "rights and privileges of British subjects," as well as the "the very spirit and essence of Magna Charta, & the declaration of Rights, at the Revolution."[37] When his son replied that the Act was a measure born out of "apprehensions of the Americans tendency to independency," Martin dismissed the argument as a poor excuse to trample upon the rights of all British colonial subjects:

… the Parliament, by laying an internal tax upon the British subjects of the Colonies, counteracted the very fundamental principles of the British Government, and in contradiction to the long establishment of legislatures in each colony which no doubt, were first instituted in conformity to those principles, & have been continued ever since their first settlement. Therefore to impose internal taxes upon British subjects of landed property by a Parliament in which

---

[36] Jack P. Greene, *Peripheries and Center: Constitutional Development in the Extended Politics of the British Empire and the United States, 1607–1788* (Athens, GA, 1986), pp. 138–40.

[37] Martin to Martin, Jr., Antigua, July 1, 1765, May 30, 1766, BL, Additional Manuscripts 41347, ff. 203, 226.

they have no representatives, is treating them as slaves to arbitrary power; for tyranny may be as well displayed by <u>many in conjunction</u> as by one man.[38]

Martin's rants would not have seemed out of place in the company of the similar protests against Parliament coming from the mainland colonies.

While Martin protested the new impositions with his pen, others joined the "Americans" in protesting with force. On October 31, the night before the Stamp Act was to take effect, as well as on November 5, riots broke out in St. Kitts and Nevis (the outbreak of this latter riot on the anniversary of the Gunpowder Plot, a day to celebrate England's deliverance from popery and tyranny, was likely no coincidence). The colonists of St. Kitts threatened to hang the stamp "Distributor" and proceeded to burn the stamps at a bonfire where "they gave three huzzas crying out Liberty! No Stamps!"[39]

Customs officials found themselves forced to walk about Jamaica armed with swords and pistols to ensure their safety.[40] The Jamaican Assembly, which had spent the past few years protesting the policies of the Board of Trade, passed a resolution in November 1766 defending their privileges as the true "representative body of the people of this island."[41]

Though the Assembly was promptly prorogued, the settlers had made their point known. One wealthy planter's agent wrote from Kingston of the general uneasiness among the island gentlemen at the new tax, questioning whether the planters together with the colonists of the "Northern Continent," people who "have an independent situation, [are] numerous & not with out daring & enterpryzing genius's will tamely submit to the hard gripe of Ministerial oppression?"[42] Such ominous talk evaporated when Parliament repealed the Stamp Act in 1766, but the controversy left a sour aftertaste. From the response of some of the West Indians to the despised Stamp Act, one could argue that there was very little difference between their outlook and that of their mainland counterparts.

At the same time, however, there were already hints of a rift between the two regions. The Molasses Act of 1733 that outraged mainland colonists had

---

[38] Martin to Martin, Jr., Antigua, July 1, 1765, May 30, 1766, BL, Additional Manuscripts 41347, f. 226.

[39] Pinney to Hinton, Nevis, May 30, 1766, Pinney Letterbook 3, UBL.

[40] Daniel MacLean to the Commissioners of his Majesty's Customs, Jamaica, January 6, 1769, Grenville Correspondence, HL, STG 13(11).

[41] *Journals of the Assembly of Jamaica*, November 19, 1766, VI, p. 4.

[42] Robert Graham to Chaloner Archdeckne, Kingston, September 20, 1765, Archdeckne Correspondence, University Library, Cambridge, Vanneck-Arc/3A/1765/1–18.

been an effort to protect British West Indian planters from their French competitors. For years the Caribbean planters had been angered by the lax enforcement of the Molasses Act and the blatant way North Americans continued to engage in foreign trade, including and especially trade with the French sugar islands. The planters had repeatedly pushed Parliament to crack down upon the mainlanders, and earned the ire of mainland interests when Britain passed the Sugar Act in 1764 in a new attempt to limit French competition.[43] There was also a sense among some West Indians that much of the warfare of the first half of the eighteenth century, supposedly fought to the advantage of the British colonies, in fact primarily benefited the northern colonies while subjecting the sugar islands to danger, difficulty, and inconvenience.[44] Furthermore, as Samuel Martin's letters demonstrate, there was already a common perception in 1765 that the Americans (a term Martin uses for inhabitants of the mainland) had provoked measures like the Stamp Act through their spirit of independence. As Parliamentary impositions continued in the late 1760s, men like Martin wondered at Britain's efforts to stifle the manufacture and trade of the North Americans, but they were even more perplexed that the West Indies were included in the Acts when it was the mainland colonists who should be contributing a greater share to the imperial coffers:

But what astonishes still more is that these parts of America should be included under the same taxation, tho' we pay to the Revenue such monstrous duties upon all our productions, while N America pays little or nothing to that Revenue. Pray explain to me this wonderfull partiality to the disadvantage of the British Sugar colonies, at the very juncture when France is giving all possible encouragements to its Sugar Colonies.... [45]

The presence of British troops also did not have quite the same impact in the West Indies, as the settlers there had grown accustomed to the necessity of these troops in the event of a foreign attack or internal slave revolt.[46]

---

[43] *Journals of the Assembly of Jamaica*, IV, 209–11, V, pp. 320–1; Martin to Martin Jr., Antigua, September 15, 1752, BL, Additional Manuscripts 41346, ff. 36–37; O'Shaughnessy, *An Empire Divided*, 63–9; Richard B. Sheridan, "The Molasses Act and the Market Strategy of the British Sugar Planters," *Journal of Economic History*, XVII (1957), pp. 62–83.

[44] Letters of James Knight, C. Long, and planters and merchants of Jamaica, BL, Additional Manuscripts 22677, f. 42r.

[45] Martin to Martin, Jr., Antigua, September 29, 1767, BL, Additional Manuscripts 41347, f. 286r.

[46] O'Shaughnessy, *An Empire Divided*, pp. 54–7.

Though the West Indians sympathized with the mainlanders over the injustice of the new policy of internal taxation, they also found ways to protest their own inclusion in the Acts, arguing that they really should apply only to North America.

Another stumbling block to solidarity in the western Atlantic was the extremely confrontational approach the mainlanders were taking in their protests against British policy. Only at St. Kitts and Nevis had there been a mob response to the Stamp Act. Barbados, Jamaica, and Antigua had grudgingly complied, while Montserrat ignored the Act.[47] When the Stamp Act prompted riots and violence in the mainland colonies, the Committee of Correspondence in Barbados initially drafted a letter that criticized the "rebellious opposition" of the mainland colonists. They later softened this language, but not before initial drafts of the letter made their way north, infuriating the American colonists. John Dickinson composed a pamphlet lambasting the Barbadian planters for failing to stand by their fellow oppressed countrymen.[48] Dickinson's pamphlet in turn enraged some Barbadians, prompting yet another heated exchange between the Caribbean and mainland.[49] Two years after the Stamp Act fury, George Frere published a history of Barbados, in which he noted the "pernicious" nature and dangerous precedent of the Stamp Act but nevertheless highlighted the island's loyal acquiescence in British authority, proclaiming his goal in writing was "principally to shew, that Barbados hath always preserved a uniform and steady attachment to Great Britain, and therefore is intitled to the affections and indulgence of the mother country."[50] The West Indians agreed the Stamp Act was a loathsome policy and they rejoiced at its repeal, but they also prided themselves on their trusting submission to authority and their faith that Parliament would realize the error of its ways.

---

[47] O'Shaughnessy, *An Empire Divided*, pp. 91–2, 95–6.

[48] John Dickinson, *An Address to the Committee of Correspondence in Barbardos...* (Philadelphia, 1765), in Paul Leicester Ford (ed.), *The Writings of John Dickinson* (Philadelphia, 1895), I, pp. 252–76.

[49] *An Essay Toward the Vindication of the Committee of Correspondence in Barbados...* (Barbados, 1766), pp. 4, 6–7, 14, 17–18, 20; *Candid Observations on Two Pamphlets lately published...* (Barbados, 1766), pp. 3–4, 35–6; [John Gay Alleyne], *A Letter to the North American, on Occasion of his Address to the Committee of Correspondence in Barbados* (Barbados, 1766); O'Shaughnessy, *An Empire Divided*, p. 101.

[50] [George Frere], *A Short History of Barbados, From its First Discovery and Settlement to the Present Time* (London, 1768), pp. iv, viii, 75–6.

In his analysis of the Barbadian response to the Stamp Act, Jack Greene has argued that by "turning the defences of Barbadian behavior during the Stamp Act crisis from an apology for their own timidity to a celebration of their own prudence and realism, these Barbadian settler defenders adroitly used this episode to both sharpen and to reinforce the image of themselves as a people among whom moderation was 'the Prevailing Principle'."[51] While the West Indian settlers no doubt wished to convey this image of moderation and restraint to their fellow Britons, it was a difficult peg on which to hang their hats given their reputation for excess and violence. Moreover, having defended their indecision over the Stamp Act crisis, the West Indians both came to believe in their own propaganda and found themselves obliged to maintain their trumpeted restraint when confronted with the increasing rebelliousness of their fellow American colonists. As the North American mainland rejected Parliamentary authority and edged closer to armed resistance, the West Indians disavowed the dangerous actions of the American colonists and attempted to characterize themselves as true and loyal Britons. Resenting this perceived betrayal of American colonial interests, North American merchants boycotted the islands that complied with the Stamp Act, further damaging the relationship between the two regions. Over the next decade, British colonial policy tightened controls over the mainland but often exempted or reduced the impact upon the West Indies.[52] While the West Indians' pledges of loyalty seemed to have garnered some favor in London, their vacillation did little to endear the islands to mainland America.

Studies of the Caribbean during the American Revolution have tended to conclude that the West Indies were far too vulnerable to foreign invasion and servile insurrection to cast off their connection to Britain, and that the West Indians were predisposed to loyalty due to their much stronger ties to Britain. There can be little doubt that the islanders' limited means of defending themselves, and the potential threats they faced from foreign neighbors and massive slave rebellions, were an overwhelming factor in keeping them within the British Empire.[53] Andrew Jackson O'Shaughnessy,

---

[51] Jack P. Greene, "Liberty, Slavery, and the Transformation of British Identity in the Eighteenth-Century West Indies," *Slavery and Abolition*, XXI (2000), pp. 24–5.

[52] O'Shaughnessy, *An Empire Divided*, pp. 98–9, 104–7.

[53] This has been the traditional conclusion of early work on the eighteenth-century Caribbean. Metcalf, *Royal Government*, 2; Cyril Hamshere, *The British in the Caribbean* (Cambridge, MA, 1972), pp. 111, 136–7, 209; Gordon K. Lewis, *Main Currents in Caribbean Thought: The*

in the most complete study to date of the West Indian position in the American Revolution, argues that "close cultural and social ties with Britain" prevented the West Indies from rebelling. Pointing to high levels of West Indian absenteeism, the tendency of Caribbean settlers to send their children to be educated in England, and the prominence of several West Indians in Parliament and British social circles, O'Shaughnessy contrasts their flight to Britain with the sedentary behavior of the mainland colonists.[54] To be sure, the West Indian planters tried to give the impression that they were the most connected, most anglicized of peripherals, but we should not let their propaganda belie the full story. In retreating to Britain at the first opportunity, the West Indians were not necessarily demonstrating the strength of their transatlantic connections, but rather their concerns that these connections were in jeopardy. The West Indians, in fact, were insecure, culturally and psychologically no less than physically. Resent their colonial status the planters surely did, but the notion of independence from the Empire was a far more horrifying prospect.

The Caribbean colonists ultimately refused to break from the mold they had forged for themselves: weak, loyal, and devoted to their merciful British brethren. Characteristically anything but moderate in action or temperament, the West Indians nevertheless found themselves locked into such a pose by their own rationalizations and justifications for their earlier hesitancies over mainland colonial protests. This awkward stance even led the Jamaican Assembly to undertake a foolhardy attempt in 1774 to mediate between Britain and the mainland colonies, an effort one historian has politely described as "sadly misguided."[55] The assemblymen challenged Parliament's ability to legislate for the colonies but insisted they were acting as neutral mediators and adamantly reiterated in their time-honored fashion that "weak

---

Historical Evolution of Caribbean Society in its Ideological Aspects, 1492–1900, 2nd edn (Lincoln, NE, 2004), pp. 239–40; Robert W. Tucker and David C. Hendrickson, The Fall of the First British Empire: Origins of the War of American Independence (Baltimore, 1982), p. 60. The realities of the danger certainly hit home in Jamaica when plans of a significant slave insurrection were uncovered in 1776, perhaps inspired by the revolutionary rhetoric of the Americans: Richard B. Sheridan, "The Jamaican Slave Insurrection Scare of 1776 and the American Revolution," Journal of Negro History, LXI (1976), pp. 290–308.

[54] O'Shaughnessy, An Empire Divided, pp. xv, 3–33. A similar argument on the inherent structural differences between the mainland and Caribbean colonies is put forward in Kamau (Edward) Brathwaite, The Development of Creole Society in Jamaica, 1770–1820 (Oxford, 1971), p. 67.

[55] Metcalf, Royal Government, p. 189.

and feeble as this colony is, from its very small number of white inhabitants, and its peculiar situation, from the encumbrance of more than two hundred thousand slaves, it cannot be supposed that we now intend, or ever could have intended, resistance to Great-Britain."[56] In the end, their petition only served to irritate British officials, and incur the scorn of the Continental Congress, who sent the Jamaican assemblymen "the warmest gratitude for your pathetic mediation in our behalf with the crown."[57] The Caribbean islands may have started closer to the mainland than not in their hostility to British colonial policy, but the distance between the two quickly grew.

The more the Americans seemed to be determined to push for liberty, the more the West Indians began to see the interests of the two regions diverging. By 1774, Samuel Martin was outraged to read in the papers "the several resolutions of the Boston people to starve the Sugar Colonies out of spite to Great Britain Most inhuman & unchristian resolutions!" Martin grew convinced the "N. Americans have done great injuries to the British Sugar Colonies," and was frustrated that Britain had indulged them for so long that they "set up now for independence."[58] Sympathy for the North American cause faded between 1775 and 1776 as armed conflict escalated. The ensuing shortage of goods and currency in the islands, particularly the lack of cheap foodstuffs to feed the slaves, generated outright and heartfelt hostility toward the pretensions of the Americans.[59] The situation on the sugar plantations was described as "truly alarming from being deprived of that great supply we used to get from North America."[60] Exacerbated by a series of hurricanes and earthquakes in the early 1780s, this "crisis of slave subsistence" led many planters to fear mass slave insurrections might erupt at any moment.[61] The planters' reactions ranged from plaintive to vengeful. Nevis planter John Pinney filled his letters with hopes that the Americans and Britons might yet be reconciled, while Samuel Martin prayed more vehemently that the Americans would be "reduced to submission."[62] Martin's

[56] *Journals of the Assembly of Jamaica*, December 23, 1774, VI, pp. 569–70.

[57] *Journals of Congress*, I, pp. 122–3, quoted in Metcalf, *Royal Government*, p. 189.

[58] Martin to Martin, Jr., Antigua, July 6, 1774, BL, Additional Manuscripts 41348, f. 189.

[59] O'Shaughnessy, *An Empire Divided*, pp. 154–67.

[60] Edward East to Roger Hope Elletson, January 16, 1776, Brydges Correspondence, HL, STB 25.

[61] Richard B. Sheridan, "The Crisis of Slave Subsistence in the British West Indies during and after the American Revolution," *WMQ*, 3rd ser., XXXIII (1976), pp. 615–41.

[62] John Pinney to Mills's & Swanston, Nevis, May 3, 1777, Pinney Letterbook 4, UBL; Martin to Martin, Jr., Antigua, December 19, 1774, BL, Additional Manuscripts 41348, f. 202.

son communed with his father: the Americans were "ignorantly arrogant" and filled with "self flattering imaginations" and "a fantastical conceit of their own importance."[63]

A minority of islanders, often those with the closest ties to the mainland, did express support for the Revolution, and British ministers nervously received reports of West Indians toasting Washington and "Independency," smuggling goods and supplies, and providing information to "the Rebels." Moreover, brewing discontent over wartime shortages in the islands led a group of West Indian MPs to call for the impeachment of Lord George Germain (Secretary of State for America). Together with the continued standoffs between island assemblies and royal governors, this generated some concern in official circles over the strength of West Indian loyalty. Yet no united opposition emerged either in the islands or among the West India interest in London to provide any serious threat, and the West Indians repeatedly voiced their fervent wish "to maintain the integrity of the British Empire."[64] In fact, the American Revolution provided the West Indians with precisely the opportunity they had been looking for to affirm their genuine British identity. William Vassall, a Jamaican landowner who had spent the years before the Revolution living in New England, spent the 1780s attempting to retrieve his confiscated properties there, insisting that "I am a Real British Subject, as I was born in Jamaica."[65] For others, the Revolution made them even more anxious to avoid the taint of the rebellious mainland colonies. By 1778, John Pinney was eager to tie up his concerns in Nevis and return to his "native-land." "My greatest pride," he wrote, "is to be considered as a private Country Gentleman, therefore, am resolved to content myself with little and shall avoid even the name of a West-Indian."[66] In 1784, Bryan Edwards proudly proclaimed that "it is to Great Britain alone that our West India planters consider themselves as belonging," insisting that "even such of them as have resided in the West Indies from their birth look

---

[63] Martin, Jr., to Martin, Westminster, January 27, 1777, BL, Additional Manuscripts 41348, f. 298.

[64] O'Shaughnessy, *An Empire Divided*, pp. 143, 182–5, 213; Andrew J. O'Shaughnessy, "The West Indian Interest and the Crisis of American Independence," in Roderick A. McDonald (ed.), *West Indies Accounts: Essays on the History of the British Caribbean and the Atlantic Economy in Honour of Richard Sheridan* (Kingston, Jamaica, 1996), pp. 138–41.

[65] William Vassall to Simeon Potter, Clapham, March 23, 1784, Vassall Letterbooks, Sheffield Central Library (microfilm, HL).

[66] Pinney to Coker, Nevis, June 1778, Pinney Letterbook 4, UBL.

on the islands as their temporary abode only, and the fond notion of being able to go home (as they emphatically term a visit to England) year after year animates their industry and alleviates their misfortune."[67] Though the Caribbean settlers lacked the cultural confidence and self-assurance of the Americans prior to the Revolution, the conflict provided the West Indians with the opportunity to rethink their true ties and connections. They chose to demonstrate once and for all that their hearts, as they had always claimed, were in Britain.

In the wake of the Revolution, the West Indians enjoyed a brief moment of self-satisfaction. Believing they had finally cemented their British allegiance by joining forces against the ungrateful mainland rebels, the planters might have found the cultural space to embrace an identity that was both British and distinctively West Indian. But the moment passed almost before it appeared. For it was precisely at this point that the anti-slave trade movement, and later the push for abolition, took center stage in British politics. Abolitionism was far from universally popular, but the abolitionists were a vocal group whose tireless efforts to expose the brutality, inhumanity, and injustice of slavery kept the issue prominent in Britain's press, politics, and parlors. With the spotlight turned sharply on the violence and horror of slavery, there was little hope of ever convincing Britons that the sugar islands were civilized "little Englands" dotting the other side of the Atlantic.

In adopting the approach that preserving the slave trade was a life or death issue for white settlers, the planters set themselves up for even greater humiliation when Britain moved toward banning the trade.[68] Jamaican gentleman Nathaniel Phillips wrote to fellow settlers of the disturbing developments he was witnessing:

Sorry am I to say that the dreadful clamour (rais'd in England against the Slave Trade) has already reach'd the ears of the slaves, and <u>they</u> now say that the whites

---

[67] Bryan Edwards, *Thoughts on the Late Proceedings of Government Respecting the Trade of the West India Islands with the United States of North America*, 2nd edn (London, 1784), p. 29, quoted in O'Shaughnessy, *An Empire Divided*, p. 3.

[68] For recent work on the combined impact of the American Revolution and abolition on the British West Indies, see Edward L. Cox, "The British Caribbean in the Age of Revolution," 275–94, and Trevor Burnard, "Freedom, Migration, and the American Revolution," pp. 295–314, both in Eliga H. Gould and Peter S. Onuf (eds), *Empire and Nation: The American Revolution in the Atlantic World*, (Baltimore, 2005); Brown, *Moral Capital*; David Brion Davis, *Inhuman Bondage: The Rise and Fall of Slavery in the New World* (Oxford, 2006); Seymour Drescher, *Abolition: A History of Slavery and Antislavery* (New York, 2009), pp. 205–66.

in Great Britain are their <u>Friends</u> & wish to make them <u>free</u>. Impress'd with these ideas, I fear we are not to expect that these people can be kept long in due subjection. I really tremble for the mischief that is likely to arise from it.[69]

That their supposed brethren in Britain were siding with the slaves against the interest of the planters was a crushing realization. Robert Hibbert of Kingston believed the slaves might soon revolt in 1788 as they had every reason to assume that if they did so "<u>they</u> and not <u>we</u> should receive assistance from England."[70] Even those planters on the older sugar islands who may have been privately reconciled to the end of the slave trade (content with their established slave populations and encouraged that a ban might hurt potential new competitors), could take little pride in how their lifestyle was castigated in an ever-increasing mass of abolitionist literature. The planters' failure to craft a distinctive sense of identity was well underway by the Revolution; anti-slavery propaganda merely cemented their sense of insecurity and unpopularity.

Despite the efforts of the West Indians to develop their tropical paradise into a slightly warmer and more eccentric version of Britain, the challenging environment and the problematic nature of slavery, particularly once it came under attack from the metropole, prevented them from ever wholly succeeding. Historian Richard Dunn noted of the planter class in the English West Indies at the end of the seventeenth century:

They became far richer than their cousins in the North American wilderness. They lived fast, spent recklessly, played desperately, and died young... By the close of the century, when Englishmen in the mainland colonies were turning into Americans, Englishmen in the islands had one consuming ambition—to escape home to England as fast as possible.[71]

Dunn's conclusions also ring true for the planters of the eighteenth century. Absenteeism was both an effect of the crisis of island identity and a further cause of its intensification.

---

[69] Nathaniel Phillips to Hibbert, Fuhr & Hibbert, May 25, 1788, Stowe Brydges Correspondence, HL, STB 27(33).

[70] Robert Hibbert to George Hibbert, May 14, 1788, Stowe Brydges Correspondence, HL, STB 27(33); for more on the interplay between slave rebellion and the abolition movement, see Claudius Fergus, "'Dread of Insurrection'": Abolitionism, Security, and Labor in Britain's West Indian Colonies, 1760–1823," *WMQ*, 3rd ser., LXIV (2009), pp. 757–80.

[71] Richard S. Dunn, *Sugar and Slaves: The Rise of the Planter Class in the English West Indies, 1624–1713* (New York, 1972), pp. xiii–xv.

Absenteeism, it should be noted, was not an entirely negative phenomenon. Having influential friends and connections in London could be a powerful resource for colonial settlers when the interests of absentees and residents coincided. Furthermore, there were certainly plenty of individuals who remained in the islands and worked to make them as comfortable and impressive as possible.[72] Absenteeism may not have been as extensive and detrimental as contemporaries reported, but the ambition of ultimately "returning home" was certainly pervasive.[73] On this front, observers saw a divergence between the islands and the mainland well before the outbreak of the Revolution. For all the improvements Caribbean settlers made to their islands, contemporaries were repeatedly struck by the way the planters regarded their region as a mere stopping place. When one British officer traveled through the West Indies and North America in the mid-1760s, he noted some interesting differences between the two cultures. In Jamaica, he found that the island produced "many of the conveniencies and more of the luxuries of life—but the generality of its inhabitants look upon themselves there as passengers only." In New England, there did not appear to be a pressing desire to return to Britain or send one's children there as in the Caribbean (and, as the officer noted, in South Carolina, a colony heavily populated by West Indian planter immigrants). The officer found Boston society to be well established and strongly rooted but in no way an alien culture. In fact, the officer felt "the men here resemble much the people of Old England, from whence most of them are sprung."[74]

Here the officer presents a view subsequently echoed and expanded in a long tradition of colonial American historiography, which holds that of all Britain's colonies in the New World, those of New England most closely resembled traditional English society. In more recent years, Jack Greene's work in particular has challenged the centrality of New England, arguing that with their egalitarian social structure, communal faith, and tightly knit

[72] John Robertson, *Gone is the Ancient Glory: Spanish Town, Jamaica, 1534–2000* (Kingston, Jamaica, 2005), pp. 68–71, 94–102.

[73] On the debate over the impact of absenteeism, see Douglas Hall, "Absentee-Proprietorship in the British West Indies to About 1850," *Jamaican Historical Review*, IV (1964), pp. 15–35; Trevor Burnard, "Passengers Only: The Extent and Significance of Absenteeism in Eighteenth Century Jamaica," *Atlantic Studies*, I (2004), pp. 184, 189; B.W. Higman, *Plantation Jamaica, 1750–1850: Capital and Control in a Colonial Economy* (Mona, Jamaica, 2005).

[74] Journal of an officer who travelled over a part of the West Indies, and of North America in the course of 1764 & 1765, BL, King's Manuscripts 213, ff. 11v, 26r, 68r.

families, the New England colonies were actually atypical examples of the
colonial experience, while the materialistic, volatile, competitive, more
secular, socially stratified societies of the Chesapeake region represented
a more normative model of British colonial society.[75] It may well be true
that the independent, egalitarian yeomen farmers, artisans, and merchants,
well-attended parish churches, and nuclear families set the northern mainland colonies apart from the realities of the vast estates in Britain and the
gross levels of inequality in British society. Yet they conformed quite well to
the prevailing *perceptions* of Britishness. The northern colonies presented
images of morally upright, frugal societies, with relatively stable family
dynamics, small farms, and a culture where deference and reciprocal relationships worked to the benefit of all. The criticisms heaped upon the
Caribbean colonists for their moral decay and tyrannical rule over their
slaves were not likely to be directed at the New Englanders. Of course, not
every mainland colony looked like Massachusetts or Connecticut, and
colonies where slaves comprised a significant part of the labor force were
vulnerable to the same kinds of caricatures as the West Indies (though not as
easily or as often), just as New Englanders found themselves targeted by
British satires for their proud rusticity. But the diversity of the mainland
colonies meant that their inhabitants could never be as easily characterized
under a single heading and then dismissed out of hand. The West Indians,
despite their actual diversity, were all lumped together in a stereotype of the
planter that they found endlessly frustrating and discouraging.

Secure in their belief that they lived as true Britons should, mainland
colonists had little reason to cling to Britain itself or to return there or send
their families back across the Atlantic to prove they had not degenerated into
something "other." Mainland colonists who did travel to Britain in the
middle decades of the eighteenth century quickly grew disenchanted with
metropolitan society, deciding its inequalities, titles, corruption, and ex-
travagance were a poor match for the frugality, restraint, and peaceful life
of the colonies. They found the British to be "superficial, greedy, and
debauched," while the colonies were "unaffected and pure," and they advised

---

[75] Jack P. Greene, *Pursuits of Happiness: The Social Development of Early Modern British
Colonies and the Formation of American Culture* (Chapel Hill, NC, 1988), pp. xiii, 26–9, 37–9;
Dunn, *Sugar and Slaves*, pp. 337–8. Nicholas Canny makes a similar argument for the excep-
tional case of New England in his "The Anglo-American Colonial Experience," *Historical
Journal*, XXIV (1981), pp. 486–7.

their friends and relations not to bother making the difficult transatlantic journey.[76] Mainland British colonists worried about perceptions of backwardness, but at the same time many embraced their rusticity and took pride in their "hardiness, activity, and courage."[77] For West Indians, the great fear was not of being labeled primitive but of being found degenerate, a group hopelessly corrupted by plantation slavery and the decadence, immorality, and licentiousness that accompanied it. Consequently, the bulk of the Caribbean settlers were unwilling to jeopardize their ties to Great Britain because affirming their Britishness was a fundamental priority. The inhabitants of the mainland American colonies found it painful to abandon their British identity, but abandon it they did.[78] In the West Indies, such a break was all but inconceivable. It was not that the planters were truly more British than the fledgling Americans, but that they were more concerned, first and last, about being accepted as Britons. When push came to shove, laboring under their attenuated sense of cultural identity, the West Indies clung tightly to a Britain they hoped would one day embrace them.

Select Bibliography

SUSAN D. AMUSSEN, *Caribbean Exchanges: Slavery and the Transformation of English Society, 1640–1700* (Chapel Hill, NC, 2007).

BENEDICT ANDERSON, *Imagined Communities*, rev. edn (London, 1991).

BERNARD BAILYN and PHILIP D. MORGAN (eds), *Strangers Within the Realm: Cultural Margins of the First British Empire* (Chapel Hill, NC, 1991).

THOMAS BENJAMIN, *The Atlantic World: Europeans, Africans, Indians, and Their Shared History, 1400–1900* (New York, 2009).

---

[76] Susan Lively also found Southern colonists far more likely to make extended journeys to Britain than New Englanders. Susan Lindsey Lively, "Going Home: Americans in Britain, 1740–1776" (Ph.D. diss., Harvard University, 1996), pp. 10, 54, 139, 265–75.

[77] Richard L. Bushman, "American High Style and Vernacular Cultures," in Jack P. Greene and J. R. Pole (eds), *Colonial British America: Essays in the New History of the Early Modern Era*, (Baltimore, 1984), p. 369; Michal J. Rozbicki, *The Complete Colonial Gentleman: Cultural Legitimacy in Plantation America* (Charlottesville, VA, 1998), pp. 103–11; Kenneth Lockridge, *The Diary, and Life, of William Byrd II of Virginia, 1674–1744* (Chapel Hill, NC, 1987), pp. 25–9, 155–7.

[78] Studies which emphasize the difficulties inherent in casting off things British include Maya Jasanoff, *Liberty's Exiles: American Loyalists in the Revolutionary World* (New York, 2011); Brendan McConville, *The King's Three Faces: The Rise and Fall of Royal America, 1688–1776* (Chapel Hill, NC, 2006); Wilson, *Sense of the People*, pp. 237–84; Gordon S. Wood, *The Radicalism of the American Revolution* (New York, 1991); Gordon S. Wood, *The Americanization of Benjamin Franklin* (New York, 2004), pp. 82–104, 124–51.

T. H. BREEN, "Ideology and Nationalism on the Eve of the American Revolution: Revisions *Once More* in Need of Revising," *Journal of American History*, LXXXIV (1997–98), pp. 13–39.

CHRISTOPHER L. BROWN, *Moral Capital: Foundations of British Abolitionism* (Chapel Hill, NC, 2006).

TREVOR BURNARD, *Mastery, Tyranny, and Desire: Thomas Thistlewood and his Slaves in the Anglo-Jamaican World* (Chapel Hill, NC, 2004).

TREVOR BURNARD, "Passengers Only: The Extent and Significance of Absenteeism in Eighteenth Century Jamaica," *Atlantic Studies*, I (2004), pp. 178–95.

NICHOLAS CANNY and ANTHONY PAGDEN (eds), *Colonial Identity in the Atlantic World, 1500–1800* (Princeton, 1987).

LINDA COLLEY, *Britons: Forging the Nations, 1707–1837* (New Haven, 1992).

DAVID BRION DAVIS, *Inhuman Bondage: The Rise and Fall of Slavery in the New World.* (Oxford, 2006).

SEYMOUR DRESCHER, *Abolition: A History of Slavery and Antislavery* (Cambridge, 2009).

RICHARD S. DUNN, *Sugar and Slaves: The Rise of the Planter Class in the English West Indies, 1624–1713* (New York, 1972).

JOHN D. GARRIGUS and CHRISTOPHER MORRIS (eds), *Assumed Identities: The Meaning of Race in the Atlantic World* (College Station, TX, 2010).

ELIGA H. GOULD and PETER S. ONUF, *Empire and Nation: The American Revolution in the Atlantic World* (Baltimore, 2005).

JACK P. GREENE, "Liberty, Slavery, and the Transformation of British Identity in the Eighteenth-Century West Indies," *Slavery and Abolition*, XXI (2000), pp. 1–31.

JACK P. GREENE, *Peripheries and Center: Constitutional Development in the Extended Polities of the British Empire and the United States, 1607–1788* (Athens, GA, 1986).

JACK P. GREENE, *Pursuits of Happiness: The Social Development of Early Modern British Colonies and the Formation of American Culture* (Chapel Hill, NC, 1988).

JACK P. GREENE and PHILIP D. MORGAN (eds), *Atlantic History: A Critical Appraisal* (Oxford, 2009).

MAYA JASANOFF, *Liberty's Exiles: American Loyalists in the Revolutionary World* (New York, 2011).

ROBERT A. OLWELL and ALAN TULLY (eds), *Cultures and Identities in Colonial British America* (Baltimore, 2004).

ANDREW JACKSON O'SHAUGHNESSY, *An Empire Divided: The American Revolution and the British Caribbean* (Philadelphia, 2000).

RICHARD B. SHERIDAN, "The Formation of Caribbean Plantation Society, 1689–1748" in Peter Marshall (ed.), *The Oxford History of the British Empire*, II (Oxford, 1998), pp. 394–414.

RICHARD B. SHERIDAN, *Sugar and Slavery: An Economic History of the British West Indies 1623–1775* (Baltimore, 1973).

KATHLEEN WILSON, *The Island Race: Englishness, Empire, and Gender in the Eighteenth Century* (London, 2003).

8

American Indians in the British Imperial Imagination, 1707–1815

Troy Bickham

When Ostenaco arrived at the head of a Cherokee delegation in London in 1762, he was following a long tradition of American Indian visits to Britain. Even before the English had established colonies on the North American seaboard, natives of the Americas had walked the streets of London and entertained royalty and commoners alike. But Ostenaco's visit was different. For the most part, his predecessors had been paraded as curiosities.[1] Even the much celebrated, and written about, visit of the "Four Indian Kings"—in fact, four Iroquois headmen—in 1710 had been little more than a publicity move orchestrated by a handful of American colonists and their British collaborators to garner state support for an invasion of New France.[2] Although hardly dupes in the venture, the "Indian kings" were orientalized by their hosts and the British public. Dressed in colorful turbans and capes for an audience with Queen Anne and depicted in popular prints as the Magi, they reflected the limits of turn-of-the-century British cosmology, which only occasionally differentiated between the various peoples of the world. To the vast majority

---

[1] For a comprehensive examination of Indian visits to Britain, see Alden T. Vaughan, *Transatlantic Encounters: American Indians in Britain, 1500–1776* (New York, 2006). For a useful study that looks beyond American independence, see Kate Flint, *The Transatlantic Indian, 1776–1930* (Princeton, 2008). For more on Ostenaco's visit, see John Oliphant, "The Cherokee Embassy to London, 1762," *Journal of Imperial and Commonwealth History*, XXVII (1999), pp. 1–26. The best contemporary account is from the embassy's escort and impromptu interpreter, Henry Timberlake. His journal has been reprinted as *Lieutenant Henry Timberlake's Memoirs, 1756–1765* (ed.), Samuel Cole Williams (Marietta, GA, 1948).

[2] On the Iroquois visit, see especially Eric Hinderaker, "The 'Four Indian Kings' and the Imaginative Construction of the First British Empire," *WMQ*, 3rd ser., LIII (1996), pp. 487–526; Richmond P. Bond, *Queen Anne's American Kings* (Oxford, 1952); and John G. Garratt, *The Four Indian Kings* (Ottawa, 1985).

of educated and uneducated Britons alike, "Indian" was synonymous with non-European. The "Indian" curiosity cabinets collected privately by the elite were a mix of American, African, and Asian artifacts. Portrayals of a single primitive character on the theatrical stage could move from Asiatic to American and back with little notice. Even when a London gang of young ruffians assumed the name "Mohacs" in the 1720s, they mistook their name-sakes as "mohamattan [Muslim]" Asians, adorning themselves with turbans and crescent tattoos. Despite widespread awareness of the gang—Jonathan Swift referred to them as the "meanest" gang in London—no one seems to have noticed its muddling of geographies; or, if they did notice, they did not think it sufficiently important to comment on it.[3]

Responses to Ostenaco's visit five decades later reflected a new Imperial age in Britain and a shift in the British Imperial imagination. Although plenty of gawking accompanied the visit, complete with tavern owners dressing as Indians in hopes of luring customers, the public discussion was far more somber. Printed images of Ostenaco were authentic represen-tations rather than those of generic European or Oriental kings: instead of wearing a turban and cape, he posed in his own clothing, which he supposedly later donated for his model in the celebrated London tourist destination, Mrs. Salmon's Waxwork.[4] In the printed press, detailed discus-sions of Cherokee politics, maps, demography, and military tactics replaced the likes of Joseph Addison's thinly veiled use of the "Indian Kings" in 1711 as a literary device to critique polite society in *The Spectator*.[5] In contrast to previous Indian visits, the public discussion in the press in 1762 was both knowledgeable and concerned with the Imperial implications. As the *Royal Magazine* representatively concluded, "In short, there is sufficient reason to think that this visit of the Indians will be of very great consequence to the British colonies in America," because the visitors would witness the great-ness of Britain and thus expel the "false ideas they have conceived of the English nation, by the unjust and artful representations of the French."[6]

[3] Troy Bickham, *Savages within the Empire: Representations of American Indians in Eight-eenth-Century Britain* (Oxford, 2005), pp. 26–8.

[4] Richard D. Altick, *The Shows of London* (Cambridge, MA, 1978), p. 52; M. Willson Disher, *Pleasures of London* (London, 1950), p. 200; *The London Guide* (London, 1782), p. 116; *A Companion to the Principal Places of Curiosity and Entertainment in and about London and Westminster*, 6th edn (London, 1783), pp. 87–9.

[5] *Spectator*, No. 50, April 27, 1711.

[6] *Royal Magazine*, July 1762, p. 16.

The eventual independence of the United States and the rise of the Empire in Asia has cast a long shadow over the eighteenth century, obscuring the significance contemporaries in Britain placed on American Indians. England established its first successful companies for both American and Asian trade at the start of the seventeenth century but it was the American side of the Empire that had garnered the most national interest in the eighteenth century. While Members of Parliament still laughed patronizingly at names from the Indian subcontinent as late as the 1780s, American Indian nomenclature needed little explanation.[7] As a reader's letter to the *London Chronicle* remarked in 1759, "The American war has so familiarized our ears and tongues to the barbarian names of Indian tribes, towns, or rivers, that we can now attend without laughter to, nay gargle over ourselves the guttural sounds of Ogéchee, Ouagamies, Ticonderago, and Michilimakinac." It continued: "We are well enough informed too of the customs of the American Indians to want no interpreter, when we read of their taking up or burying the hatchet of war; of their tomohawking or scalping their enemies; and of planting the tree or smoking the pipe of peace."[8]

As the British government and public became increasingly Imperialminded during the mid-eighteenth century, American Indians were at the center of the experience, portrayed and discussed in an array of contexts— from the British Museum to tobacco advertising.[9] This chapter focuses on three of the most prominent of those contexts: Imperial governance; the newspaper and periodical press; and the Scottish Enlightenment's discourse on human socio-economic development. While each context is distinct, the

---

[7] On the laughter of Members of Parliament over the names of Asian towns and individuals at the impeachment of Warren Hastings in 1786, see J. R. Osborn, "India, Parliament and the Press under George III: A Study of English Attitudes Towards the East India Company and Empire in the Late Eighteenth and Early Nineteenth Centuries" (D.Phil. thesis, University of Oxford, 2000), pp. 172–3.

[8] *London Chronicle*, October 9, 1759.

[9] Images of American Indians during this period were prolific, and they have received increasing attention from scholars in recent years. For broader examples, see the bibliography at the end of this chapter. For depictions of American Indians in eighteenth-century museums and advertising, see especially Troy Bickham "'A conviction of the reality of things': Material Culture, North American Indians, and Empire in Eighteenth-Century Britain," *Eighteenth-Century Studies*, XXXIX (2005), pp. 29–47; Catherine A. Molineux, "Pleasures of the Smoke: 'Black Virginians' in Georgian London's Tobacco Shops," *WMQ*, 3rd ser., LXIV (2007), pp. 327–76; and Bickham, "Eating the Empire: Intersections of Food, Cookery, and Imperialism in Eighteenth-Century Britain," *Past & Present*, 198 (February, 2008), pp. 71–110.

overlap of assumptions and conclusions regarding Indians is substantial and
ultimately serves to highlight more general conclusions about how American
Indians fitted into the British Imperial imagination. Few Britons during this
period took a great interest in Indian culture for its own sake, as almost all
concurred that Indians were savages whose intercourse offered little inherent
benefit to the civilized British. Missionary societies proved modestly successful
in raising funds to convert and "civilize" Indians, although their success
amongst the Indians was, with such notable exceptions as the Mohawk,
limited.[10] But such efforts as these to improve the plight of Indians were
often mixed with larger, self-interested Imperial aims. This is not to suggest
that individuals who scraped together a few shillings to support a school for
Indians or braved the perils of teaching in it were disingenuous in either their
sympathy or religious zeal. Yet, the membership rolls of missionary societies
that focused on the Americas, such as the Church of England's Society for
Propagation of the Gospel, read like a *Who's Who* of the British Imperial
establishment. Moreover, the sales pitch of these organizations to the general
public often focused heavily on the geopolitical strategic benefits of bringing
Indians into the loyal British Christian community to the detriment of
Catholic New France.[11] Not surprisingly, in the wake of the American Revolution, public interest in missions to Indians virtually disappeared.[12]

By the mid-eighteenth century, most Britons agreed that Indians were an
integral part of the most important part of the British Empire: North
America. In consequence, the British largely discussed and portrayed Indians
in the course of broader deliberations about empire, and when the majority
of the North American colonies left the Empire, interest in Indians rapidly
waned. The Empire had few outspoken critics during the period in which
Indians featured most prominently in the contexts examined here, and so
Indians were discussed in predominately pragmatic terms. Number of warriors, political organization, and martial abilities took center stage as Britons
discussed Indians in terms of their being either obstacles or aids to British
expansion in North America. Only after the American Revolution did the
British become more vocal and astute critics of their own Imperial practices,

---

[10] Jon Butler, *Awash in a Sea of Faith: Christianizing the American People* (Cambridge, MA,
1990), p. 127.

[11] Bickham, *Savages within the Empire*, chap. 6.

[12] P. J. Marshall, *Remaking the British Atlantic: The United States and the British Empire after
American Independence* (Oxford, 2012), p. 301.

targeting African slavery and abuses in the East Indies in particular, and only then did the American natives become widely used symbols of the dark side of Imperial expansion and rule.

****

The Seven Years' War (French and Indian War in North America) was the catalyst for a dramatic British imperial awakening.[13] War with France was the norm by mid-century, but Britain had previously devoted the vast majority of its resources to fighting its European enemies in and around Europe, generally leaving the North American colonists to fend for themselves against their French and Spanish counterparts, who likewise received limited support from their home countries. During the Seven Years' War, the British government shifted strategies and focused on fighting France and its allies overseas rather than in Europe, resulting in unprecedented expenditures of blood and treasure on the Empire.[14] The reasons were primarily economic, although more elaborate justifications rooted in nationalism and a sense of shared Anglo-Protestant culture were also prevalent. The North American colonies included a large free white population that, along with their black slaves and Indian commercial clients, numbered in the millions and together comprised the largest overseas market for British goods.[15] As a result, North America attracted the most government and public interest by far, despite troops and ships being sent across the world.

For most Britons, the war began in 1755 when a force of British regulars embarked for America under the command of Edward Braddock, one of

---

[13] See especially H.V. Bowen, "British Conception of Global Empire, 1756–83," *Journal of Imperial and Commonwealth History*, XXVI (1998), pp. 1–27; Bob Harris, "'American Idols': Empire, War and the Middling Ranks in Mid-Eighteenth-Century Britain," *Past & Present*, 150 (February, 1996), pp. 111–41; P. J. Marshall, "A Nation Defined by Empire, 1755–1776," in Alexander Grant and Keith Stringer (eds), *Uniting the Kingdom? The Making of British History* (London, 1995), pp. 208–22; and Eliga Gould, *The Persistence of Empire: British Political Cultures in the Age of the American* Revolution (London, 2000).

[14] Fred Anderson, *Crucible of War: The Seven Years' War and the Fate of Empire in British North America, 1754–1766* (New York, 2000). The war itself cost an unprecedented 70 percent of government expenditures during the war years, or twice the estimated gross national product for 1760. For a detailed discussion of the economic costs of the Seven Years' War, see especially Nancy F. Koehn, *The Power of Commerce: Economy and Governance in the First British Empire* (Ithaca, NY, 1994), pp. 3–18.

[15] Jacob M. Price, "The Imperial Economy, 1700–1776," in P. J. Marshall (ed.), *OHBE*, II: *The Eighteenth Century* (Oxford, 1998), p. 101.

the king's favorites and a general in one of his household regiments, the
Coldstream Guards. Although British forces had fought in the Americas
before, this was the first time a substantial force of regulars had been sent
to fight in the North American interior. The British assumed Braddock and
his force would quickly defeat the French encroaching on British-claimed
territory along the Ohio River as well as make a show of force to impress the
surrounding locals, both colonist and Indian. The British press followed the
movement of the troops, with newspapers introducing the reading nation to
the American interior by means of travel accounts and colonial letters.
Although Indian visits had attracted public attention and related travel
accounts and captivity narratives had been printed in England for nearly a
century, the British had never before taken so sustained an interest in the
Indians.[16] The moment was an awakening even for the likes of Horace
Walpole, who enjoyed the benefits of one of the largest private libraries in
the country. He prided himself on a robust knowledge of the world yet
announced that "[the war] has thrown me into a new study: I read nothing
but American voyages, and histories of plantations and settlements....
Indeed I was as barbarous as any polite nation in the world, in supposing
that there was nothing worth knowing among these charming savages."[17] He
then proceeded to pick a tribe to follow in the press, and recommended that
his correspondents did the same. Walpole's quaint enthusiasm was erased
when the British regulars under Braddock's command were annihilated by a
French-lead force comprised mostly of allied Indians at the Battle of the
Monongahela in July 1755. Braddock was mortally wounded and over two
thirds of the British regulars in his force were killed or wounded. The
Virginia militia that accompanied Braddock suffered casualties of nearly 80
percent and, of the roughly fifty women following the force, only four
returned with the survivors.[18] This rough introduction to warfare in North
America immediately made the Indians a matter of acute national interest.

Before the Seven Years' War, the British political elite's interest in North
America was patchy at best. North America took up little parliamentary time
and there was no cabinet post dedicated to Britain's Empire and colonies

[16] Linda Colley, *Captives: Britain, Empire, and the World, 1600–1850* (London, 2003), pp. 150–2.
[17] Walpole to Richard Bentley, November 3, 1754, *The Yale Edition of Horace Walpole's Correspondence* (ed.), W.S. Lewis, et al. (London, 1937–83), XXXV, pp. 186–7.
[18] Ian K. Steele, *Warpaths: Invasions of North America* (Oxford, 1995), pp. 188–9; Francis Jennings, *Empire of Fortune: Crowns, Colonies, and Tribes in the Seven Years War in America* (London, 1988), pp. 153–7.

until after the war. Until 1768, the colonies came under the authority of the Secretary of State for the Southern Department, whose responsibilities also included southern England, Wales, Ireland, and the Catholic and Muslim states of Europe. Communication channels were so unclear on the eve of the war that the lieutenant governor of Virginia, Robert Dinwiddie, wrote to no less than seven different departments and individuals to complain about colonial disorganization in the hopes that his concerns would be heard by someone able and willing to take action.[19] A lengthy, expensive war in which Indian allies tipped the balance in favor of the French for several years changed this administrative myopia, and for the first time the British government attempted to exercise a sustained, centralized management over a large body of native peoples.

Most British officials involved with the war in America placed the blame for the early setbacks squarely on the shoulders of the colonists, whose failure to cooperate with each other and history of poor relations with Indians turned what might have been a relatively short engagement into a war that lasted over a decade and ignited further hostilities across the globe. Even when France agreed to British peace terms in 1763, many of France's former Indian allies continued their fight against the British Empire in what became known as Pontiac's War. The British government responded by committing more resources to North America and asserting greater directional control over colonial and Indian affairs. This new "empire of authority" in which the metropole significantly increased tighter, more centralized management of the governments, defenses, and economies of Britain's Empire was felt throughout the globe and established the style of Imperial rule for centuries to come.[20] While its complete failure with the majority of white colonists in North America is still remembered with celebrations of American independence, the system was successful with the vast majority of other peoples around the world over whom Britain claimed dominion, including, for the most part, the American Indians.

The new system of affairs for American Indians was a multi-faceted program designed with a clear goal: to place Indian affairs under the direction

---

[19] He wrote to them all on May 10, 1754, *The Official Records of Robert Dinwiddie, Lieutenant-Governor of the Colony of Virginia, 1751–1758* (ed.), R. A. Brock (Richmond, VA, 1883–84), I, pp. 156–65.
[20] P. J. Marshall, "Empire and Authority in the Later Eighteenth Century," *Journal of Imperial and Commonwealth History*, XV (1987), pp. 105–22. This thesis is elaborated and refined in Marshall's *Making and Unmaking of Empires: Britain, India, and America c. 1750–1783* (Oxford, 2005).

of the crown or, more aptly, the king's ministers and agents, in order to prevent conflicts that would disrupt the all-important colonial economies. By the end of the Seven Years' War, the system was roughly in place. The problem, British officials had determined, was that some of the colonists' bad apples were provoking the Indians by cheating them and that the colonial governments were unable to control the situation. As Lord Shelburne, Secretary of State after the war, remarked in his plan for the "Future Management of Indian Affairs," the whites who traded with the Indians were "the most worthless and abandoned Fellows of the Provinces and such men could not fail of impressing the Indians with bad Sentiments of all White people in general, of whom they took their Traders to be true examples."[21] Through a series of royal proclamations and directives, the colonies lost their powers to negotiate separate commercial and political treaties with Indian nations, while colonial expansion beyond fixed western boundaries was prohibited. Two superintendents, who were outside the colonies' jurisdiction and reported directly to the British establishment, were given staffs and large budgets and charged with placating the Indians. While these superintendents and their staffs, usually in consultation with the commander-in-chief of the British forces in North America, handled day-to-day operations, final directional authority rested firmly in the hands of the king's ministers, who made the major policy and strategic decisions.

The British leadership believed that compensation and placation were more expedient than threats of violence when it came to Indian diplomacy. Most short-term problems were solved by material contributions in the form of "gifts" to key Indian leaders and their supporters.[22] European goods flowed freely into communities of Indians that had come to cherish and depend upon such European products as firearms, steel, and alcohol.[23] At a single Indian congress just after the Seven Years' War, gifts distributed

---

[21] William L. Clements Library, Shelburne Papers, vol. 60: "Shelburne's Observations upon a Plan for the future Management of Indian Affairs," c. 1766.

[22] On the role of gifts in British diplomacy, see Wilbur R. Jacobs, *Diplomacy and Indian Gifts: Anglo-French Rivalry along the Ohio and Northwest Frontiers, 1748–1763* (Stanford, 1950); Timothy Shannon, *Crossroads of Empire: The Albany Congress of 1754* (Ithaca, NY, 2000), pp. 36–48; James H. Merrell, *The Indians' New World: Catawbas and Their Neighbors from European Contact through to the Era of Removal* (Chapel Hill, NC, 1989), p. 149.

[23] On American Indian dependence and use of European goods, see especially Colin G. Calloway, *The American Revolution in Indian Country: Crisis and Diversity in Native American Communities* (Cambridge 1995), pp. 11–13; Richard White, *The Roots of Dependency: Subsistency, Environment, and Social Change among the Choctaws, Pawnees, and Navajos* (Lincoln, NE, 1983).

included 1077 rifles, 2300 shirts, 500 brass pans, 576 hatchets, 79 looking glasses, 36,500 gun flints, 190 saddles, 798 bridles, and an abundance of gunpowder.[24] Strategic gift-giving not only helped mollify aggrieved Indians, but kept in power individuals sympathetic to alliances with Britain. Armed force simply was not a viable alternative after the war. Inadequate funding and heightening tensions with the colonists kept the British army from garrisoning the borderlands to the level early planners had hoped, resulting in a flood of illegal settlers on Indian lands. On multiple occasions, Thomas Gage, the commander of British forces in North America, appealed to Cabinet ministers for a withdrawal from the frontier, expressing concerns that if tensions between illegal settlers and Indians erupted into armed hostilities the British troops would be caught in the crossfire.[25] A combination of this vulnerability and the overall British program of appeasement meant that, far more often than not, British military demonstrations of force after fighting ended in 1765 were used to intimidate white colonists rather than Indians, with detachments of British regulars evicting white squatters and destroying illegal settlements on Indians lands—much to the ire of the increasingly hostile colonial population.[26]

Failure to comply with Britain's program for the American interior carried serious consequences. In 1767, the governor of West Florida, George Johnstone, was recalled for conducting an unauthorized war against the Creek Indians in his territory. Despite Johnstone's claim that he was reacting to violence first committed by the Indians, British ministers were unmoved. Lord Shelburne, as Secretary of State, wrote directly to Johnstone to inform him of his dismissal, detailing the British government's acute dissatisfaction with his failure either to follow the spirit of the policy or to wait for direct orders:

The King disapproves entirely of every Measure which can tend towards rashly rekindling the war between the Indians and His Subjects in North America, which has been so lately extinguished. His Majesty views your late conduct in this Respect, as opposite to the spirit of your Instructions, and extremely disapproved your entering into an Affair of so important and serious a Nature, without

---

[24] The National Archives of the UK [TNA]: PRO CO 5/65, part 2, f. 74: Stuart to Board of Trade, no date.

[25] Bickham, *Savages within the Empire*, pp. 164–5.

[26] For several poignant examples, see Matthew C. Ward, " 'The Indians our Real Friends': The British Army and the Ohio Indians, 1758–1772," in Daniel P. Barr (ed.), *The Boundaries Between Us: Natives and Newcomers along the Frontiers of the Old Northwest Territories, 1750–1850* (Kent, OH, 2006), pp. 66–86.

waiting for answers to your former Letters, by which the Error you have fallen into, would have been prevented.[27]

Ministers then used Johnstone's recall as a warning to other governors. In a letter to the lieutenant governor of Virginia, a colony that had a history of violence with neighboring Indians, Shelburne described the consequences of disregarding Imperial orders:

...the King is extremely displeased to hear of Hostilities being commenced against the Creeks in West Florida. This is a Step diametrically opposite to the System which has been recommended in the strongest terms to the different Governors and the Superintendents of Indian Affairs.... His Majesty's Intentions on this head are so decided, that he Recalled Governor Johnstone; and he will expect that all the Governors Act in concert to conciliate the Affection of the Indians.[28]

In letters to the governors of South Carolina, North Carolina, and East Florida, as well as to Johnstone's temporary successor, Shelburne expressed similar sentiments, first informing them of the recall and then reiterating the king's commitment to peace with the Indians.[29] The royal governors quickly acknowledged that Indian affairs were to be taken seriously and British directions would be followed. The governors of North and South Carolina each responded that they had issued further proclamations calling for illegal settlers to withdraw; the governor of Virginia noted that he too was "requiring and enjoining all Persons who have seated themselves on Lands belonging to the Indians to evacuate." The governor of East Florida was quick to assure Shelburne that his colony was complying with the king's directions and that there had been no violence against the Indians.[30]

By comparison to the policies and programs of the United States, British intentions may appear benevolent, but practical considerations ultimately

---

[27] Shelburne MS, vol. 53: Shelburne to Johnstone, February 19, 1767. For Johnstone's justification of his actions see Shelburne MS, vol. 52: Johnstone to Shelburne, October 4, 1766.

[28] Shelburne MS, vol. 50: Shelburne to Francis Fauquier, February 19, 1767.

[29] Shelburne MS, vol. 53: Shelburne to Lord Charles Greville Montagu, Governor of South Carolina, February 19, 1767; Shelburne MS, vol. 53: Shelburne to William Tryon, Governor of North Carolina, February 19, 1767; Shelburne MS, vol. 53: Shelburne to James Grant, Governor of East Florida, February 19, 1767; Shelburne MS, vol. 53: Shelburne to Browne, Lieutenant Governor of West Florida, February 19, 1767.

[30] Shelburne MS, vol. 52: Tryon to Shelburne, July 18, 1767, Shelburne MS, vol. 52: Montagu to Shelburne, no date, Shelburne MS, vol. 52: Grant to Shelburne August 2, 1767.

motivated the officials in Britain who orchestrated Indian policy. This is not to suggest that individual officials in Britain were callous about the struggles of the Indians. On more than one occasion, individual Cabinet ministers and army officers expressed their contempt for the colonists and pity for the Indians. Yet such passing comments did not affect the overall pragmatism of the British approach to Indian affairs. The British government saw little advantage and great expense in fighting a war of annihilation against the Indians to clear lands that were far away from central British control and still vulnerable to counter-attack. Critics in America called the gifts Britain gave to Indians "tribute" as if it was a shameful business, but officials in Britain saw the situation in terms of a cost–benefit analysis, and tribute was cheaper than war.[31] As Adam Smith reflected at the time in his *Wealth of Nations*, "nothing can be more contemptible than an Indian war in North America."[32] Even so, officials in Britain complained constantly of the expense of the gifts, often chastising the superintendents for spending too much and reminding them the top priority was economy. In the words of Lord Hillsborough, Secretary of State, to one of the superintendents: "The relieving this Kingdom from every Expence that can with safety be avoided, is, in its present state, a consideration of the greatest importance; it is one great object of this plan, and I have it in command from the King in an especial manner to recommend to you the strictest economy in those services."[33] The point was to have peace as cheaply as possible.

Britain's new empire of authority backfired miserably amongst a majority of its North American colonists, who came to resent the British military presence and taxation measures as infringements on their liberties. However, Britain's new approach was generally a success with the American Indians who lived in British-claimed territories. The decade of warfare in the American interior that began with Braddock's defeat was followed by a decade of comparative peace shepherded by British policies. Many Indians came to see the metropolitan British as a people separate from the colonists and developed strong independent economic and political relationships with them. Not surprisingly, the vast majority of Indians who participated

---

[31] Bickham, *Savages within the Empire*, pp. 151–3.

[32] Adam Smith, *An Inquiry into the Nature and Causes of the Wealth of Nations* (London, 1962), II, p. 183.

[33] TNA: PRO CO 5/241, f. 55: Hillsborough to Johnson, October 12, 1768.

in the American Revolution allied themselves to Britain.[34] Yet the overall pragmatic disposition of the British government did not alter: Britain abandoned the vast majority of its Indian allies at the conclusion of the war in 1783, despite the fact the Indians had been largely successful against the American Revolutionary forces throughout the conflict. Shelburne, the one-time secretary of state who had expressed more sympathy for the Indians than perhaps any other Cabinet minister, had risen to the rank of prime minister in 1782 and had assumed primary responsibility for the peace negotiations. Yet even he readily abandoned Britain's Indian allies once he concluded that Britain's best interests lay in maintaining good relations with the new United States. Thus the treaty between Britain and the United States that concluded the American Revolution did not even mention Britain's Indian allies and ceded sovereignty over much of their land to their inveterate enemy, the newly independent United States.

****

During the second half of the eighteenth century American Indians became one of most publicly discussed, recognizable non-European peoples in Britain. Throughout the Seven Years' War, newspapers served as key media through which Britons discussed and disseminated information about Indians, ultimately making North America and its native inhabitants part of the daily diet of news. This sudden increase in attention was linked closely to the rapid rise in public interest in the Empire as a whole from the mid-eighteenth century, as the wider public came to link the overseas Empire with security and prosperity at home. Asia, Africa, and the Americas filled the pages of London and regional newspapers alike, but North America received the most attention by far. The *Whitehall Evening Post* representatively summarized the public view in 1755 when it stated "whatever Nation remains sole Master of North America, must, in Consequence of that Acquisition, give Law in Europe."[35] And, Britons broadly concluded, mastery of North America would depend on good relations with American Indians. Maps, minutes from diplomatic exchanges, and comments on the demography and

---

[34] Calloway, *American Revolution in Indian Country*; Robert S. Allen, *His Majesty's Indian Allies: British Indian Policy in Defence of Canada, 1774–1815* (Toronto, 1992).

[35] *Whitehall Evening Post*, September 4, 1755.

ferocity of Indians packed the press, as the public came to think of Indians in terms remarkably similar to how the British government perceived them.

Sensationalist reporting fueled the growth of British newspapers, which emerged during this period as commercially viable enterprises that profited most when editors paid attention to their readership.[36] As the *Idler* noted when commenting on newsmongering in 1758, nothing sold like the gore of Indian warfare: "Scarce any thing awakens attention like a tale of cruelty... the writer of news never fails, in the intermission of action, to tell how the enemies murdered children and ravished virgins; and if the scene of action be somewhat distant, scalps half the inhabitants of a province."[37] Letters and reports from the ravaged American colonies filled the press with one horrific report after another. Most of the material was not credited, but readers almost never questioned its authenticity or accuracy, appearing readily to accept even the most gruesome tales. The tenor of the press coverage not surprisingly led to a narrow view of Indians as largely two-dimensional, war-focused, masculine, savage characters. As the *Universal Magazine* reflected in 1757, "Almost the sole occupation of the American [Indian] is war, or such an exercise as qualifies him for it. His whole glory consists in this; and no man is at all considered until he has increased the strength of his country with a captive, or adorned his house with the scalp of one of its enemies."[38] Accounts that highlighted Indians' endurance, stealth, bravery, and accuracy with firearms appeared regularly in the press, and few questioned the prevailing assumption that, man-for-man, an Indian was a better warrior than a Briton. In consequence, public pressure to obtain Indian allies against the French and their Indian allies was intense, and men like Sir William Johnson and Robert Rogers, who brokered Indian alliances and employed their military tactics, became heroes in the British press.[39]

One casualty of these prolific but narrow accounts was any public sympathy for Indians who endured atrocities at the hands of British forces. The suffering of Indian civilians rarely invoked the ire of the British editors or readers, who seldom recognized Indians in this period as anything but

[36] Hannah Barker, *Newspapers, Politics, and Public Opinion in Late Eighteenth-Century England* (Oxford, 1998); Troy Bickham, *Making Headlines: The American Revolution as Seen through the British Press* (DeKalb, IL, 2009), chap. 2; Jeremy Black, *The English Press in the Eighteenth Century* (Philadelphia, 1987).

[37] *Edinburgh Magazine*, editor's preface to 1758, p. iv; *Idler* 31, reprinted in the *Edinburgh Magazine*, November, 1758, p. 402.

[38] *Universal Magazine*, May 1757, p. 198.

[39] Bickham, *Savages within the Empire*, pp. 256–8.

combatants. A typical case was the reaction to the desolation of the Abenaki mission village of St. Francois in October 1759. Fully approved by the British high command, the raid conducted by Rogers and 141 of his rangers targeted a village of no immediate strategic significance in order to demonstrate the adaptive capabilities of the British and the vulnerability of even distant villages.[40] Accounts printed in the British press vividly depicted the brutality of the attack, leaving little room to imagine it for anything other than what it was: an explicit act of revenge against a civilian target. The *Derby Mercury* summarized an account from New York in which a French priest "perished in the flames" alongside two hundred Indians—almost all of whom were women, children, and elderly men.[41] Estimates of British losses did not exceed a dozen. Despite the brutality of the attack, there was no outcry in the British press. The public response was that such raids were necessary to quiet the Indians, and justified in the context of an Indian war. As the *Scots Magazine* explained, the Indians were merely reaping what they had sown: "The severe treatment which these Indians met with from Rogers and his party, if upon any occasion such usage can be justified, surely it might be here." Recounting tales that the warriors from this village had been guilty of "inhumanities, bloodshed, and murders" and claiming that Rogers and his men saw "6 or 700 British scalps waving in the wind" as they entered the village, the magazine drew the conclusion that "it seems they have now been punished for their cruelty: and that a just providence never designed that these bloodthirsty Heathen should go down to the grave in peace."[42]

The public depiction of Indians as merciless instruments of destruction reached its apogee during the American Revolution. Throughout the conflict, the British press reinforced the image of Indians as war-obsessed savages. Although not nearly as extensive as in the Seven Years' War, Indian participation on the British side during the American Revolution became one of the most publicly detested aspects of what many in Britain considered to be a civil war.[43] As the *Gentleman's Magazine* warned in September 1775,

---

[40] Steele, *Warpaths*, p. 228.

[41] *Derby Mercury* January 18, 1760. The same account also appears in *Edinburgh Magazine*, January 1760, p. 48.

[42] *Scots Magazine*, March 1760, p. 154.

[43] On the divisiveness and unpopularity of the war in Britain, see especially Bickham, *Making Headlines*; Kathleen Wilson, *The Sense of the People: Politics, Culture and Imperialism in England, 1715–1785* (Cambridge, 1995), chap. 5; John Sainsbury, *Disaffected Patriots: London Supporters of Revolutionary America, 1769–1782* (Montreal, 1987); James E. Bradley, *Popular Politics and the*

"introducing them [Indians] upon the stage of action for the purpose of butchering our fellow-subjects . . . is equally impolitic and anti-christian."[44] Only a tiny minority of even the most ardent rebel-haters publicly viewed Indian involvement as a fit punishment for rebellion. William Markham, Archbishop of York, embraced Indians as viable tools for restoring "the supremacy of law" in America in a sermon, and he was publicly ridiculed for it for the remainder of the war. As one reader remarked in the *Gazetteer*, "The ground on which the prelate ventured to tread . . . is so boggy and rotten that [he] could not prevent bemiring both himself and his subject in the dirt of worldly policy."[45] A satirical print appearing in the *Westminster Magazine* showed Markham landing in America to distribute scalping knives and crucifixes to the Indians, as they butcher a colonist.[46]

Capping the public outcry over Britain's Indian alliances during the American Revolution was what observers declared to be the greatest oration from one of the most celebrated politicians of the age, Edmund Burke. Rising to his feet late on the night of February 6, 1777 in the House of Commons, Burke railed against the government's Indian alliances:

The Indians of America had not titles, sinecure places, lucrative government pensions, or red ribbons, to bestow on those who signalized themselves in the field; their rewards were generally received in human scalps, human flesh, and gratification arising from torturing, mangling, scalping, and sometimes eating their captives of war.

According to Burke, this was no way to regain the affection of disgruntled colonists, and it certainly was no way to treat one's own countrymen.[47] Burke's speech was printed and reprinted in newspapers throughout the country, all describing it as his best ever. The *Public Advertiser* asserted that

---

American Revolution in England (Macon, GA, 1986); Paul Langford, "London and the American Revolution," in John Stevenson (ed.), *London in the Age of Reform* (Oxford, 1977); J.H. Plumb, "British Attitudes to the American Revolution," in his *In the Light of History* (London, 1972); John Money, "Taverns, Coffee houses and Clubs: Local Politics and Popular Articulacy in the Birmingham Area in the Age of the American Revolution," *Historical Journal*, XV (1971), pp. 168–86.

[44] *Gentleman's Magazine*, September 1775, 446. Early British efforts to secure Indian allies first appeared in 1774.

[45] *Gazetteer*, August 20, 1777.

[46] "The Allies," in the *Westminster Magazine*, February 3, 1781.

[47] Because the House was closed to visitors, several versions of the speech circulated. The most widely reprinted first appeared in the February 7, 1778 edition of the *Morning Chronicle*, which was renowned for its parliamentary reporting.

"[i]t is agreed on all Sides, that Mr. Burke's Speech, on moving for an Inquiry about employing Savages . . . was the best and most fancif'l he ever delivered." George Johnstone declared that "he rejoiced there were no strangers [spectators] in the [House of Commons] gallery, as Burke's speech would have excited them to tear the ministers to pieces as they went out of the house."[48]

Such a clear demarcation between colonists and American Indians highlights the hierarchy in which the British public viewed Imperial subjects. Whereas the British had come to see American colonists as fellow nationals during the Seven Years' War, such a perception had limits that stopped well short of including American Indians.[49] While politicians and commentators alike plausibly argued that there was no difference between Boston in Lincolnshire and its sister town in Massachusetts, no one had the audacity to make similar comparisons to Iroquois settlements. Even colonial rebels received more sympathy than allied Indians. As the *Gazetteer* declared in December 1777 in response to news of British-allied Indians attacking colonial settlements: "What a dreadful mode of carrying on war is this, and calculated to gratify the insatiable revenge of those who direct such nefarious measures, but which are prohibited by the laws of every civilized nation throughout the world!—What English and Hessians must not in honour do, is left to be perpetrated by Savages."[50] And the press, which at the end of the war was inundated with complaints about the abandonment of the loyalist colonists, was tellingly silent about Britain's complete desertion of its Indian allies.

With a national audience of millions, the newspapers acted as the primary influence in shaping the public sense of American Indians' character, but this is not to say that more balanced and positive representations of Indians did not exist. A handful of literary representations were far more sympathetic, as were the small number of longer histories of Indians that began to appear during the Seven Years' War. An often-cited example is

---

[48] *Memorial and Correspondence of Charles James Fox*, 4 vols. (ed.), Lord John Russell (London, 1853–7), I, p. 355.

[49] On the formation and disintegration of a widespread British insistence on a shared nationality with American colonists, see especially Gould, *The Persistence of Empire*; and Stephen Conway, "From Fellow-nationals to Foreigners: British Perceptions of the Americans, circa 1739–1783," *WMQ*, 3rd ser., XLIX (2002), pp. 65–100.

[50] *Gazetteer*, December 16, 1777.

James Adair's *History of the American Indians* (1775), which is a 464-page account that offers what is perhaps the most balanced assessment of the history and culture of the Indian peoples that bordered and intermingled with the southern colonies.[51] Yet the notion that his history circulated widely is doubtful at best, even though scholars have utilized Adair's account as representative of wider British attitudes. The text was expensive at fifteen shillings, which was about a week's wages for a junior clerk in London or roughly a year's subscription to a weekly newspaper or leading magazine, and it appeared in only one edition in Britain. The universal hostility to Adair from the review press, upon which individuals, book clubs and circulating libraries relied when selecting new titles for purchase, further hurt circulation of his views.[52] The *Critical Review* declared that every "unprejudiced reader, we are persuaded, will subscribe to our opinion, that it is whimsical, inconsistent, and totally destitute of foundation."[53] In this rare instance its rival, the *Monthly Review*, concurred, declaring that "We wish it were allowable for us to pronounce the execution of it as meritous as the subject is useful and important."[54] Not surprisingly, Adair's history is virtually absent from the surviving holdings lists of the era's private and circulating libraries. Moreover, the handful of identifiable extracts from it that appeared outside review magazines totally contradicted the broad and balanced nature of his account, further revealing the press's selective understanding of American Indians. Carrying headlines such as "An Account of the North American Indians Barbarity to their Captives, and their Manner of devoting them to Death" and "Instances of the Constancy, Fortitude and Presence of Mind of the North American Indians, when suffering from the fiery Tortures," the selected passages are by far the most gruesome paragraphs of this voluminous book.[55]

Such unrelenting depictions of American Indians as merciless warriors left little room for alternative portrayals of them as sentimental, noble, or

---

[51] Gary B. Nash, "The Image of the Indian in the Southern Colonial Mind," *WMQ*, 3rd ser., XXIV (1972), p. 224.

[52] M. Kay Flavell, "The Enlightened Reader and the New Industrial Towns: A Study in the Liverpool Library, 1758–1790," *British Journal for Eighteenth Century Studies*, VIII (1985), pp. 17–20; Antonia Forster, "Review Journals and the Reading Public," in Isabel Rivers (ed.), *Books and Their Readers in Eighteenth-Century England: New Essays* (London, 2001), pp. 171–90.

[53] *Critical Review*, June 1775, pp. 459–60.

[54] *Monthly Review*, March 1776, pp. 261–8.

[55] *London Magazine*, contents headings for April 1775 and May 1775.

romantic savages. Nevertheless, some commentators occasionally developed an Indian character into a noble savage in order to critique British society. One of only a handful of examples is in John Shebbeare's *Lydia; or Filial Piety*, published in London in 1755, in which the forests of North America are favorably compared to London. In the opening pages, the hero, Canassatego, laments the corrupting influence of the Europeans. "He beheld the Indian Chiefs wrapt in European manufactures, as men bearing the badge of slavery," writes Shebbeare.[56] The hero is a purist, never drinking alcohol, wearing only animal skins, and refusing to visit the American cities, detesting the colonists for their broken faith and lies. He also earnestly assumes that the colonists are nothing more than exiles, due to their dishonest nature, and wonders "whether that king and [British] people answered to all the grand accounts which he had heard about them."[57] Not surprisingly, the young Indian travels to Britain, only to experience the severest of disappointments. Shebbeare uses Canassatego's naivety to attack the false politeness, hypocrisy, and dishonesty of politicians. At one point, Canassatego meets the Prime Minister, whom he describes as "faithless."[58] Ultimately, Canassatego determines that his own culture is superior and that man is happier in the wilderness, to which he returns. As poignant as Shebbeare's tale and others like it were, they were but a few drops in an ocean. The appearance of Indians in fiction was rare before the American Revolution. Such works did not sell well, and few of the plays portraying Indians in a favorable light were ever performed.[59] Shebbeare's *Lydia* was exceptional in that it went through two editions. In contrast, Peter Williamson's vivid account of Indians' slaughter of civilians and torture of captives in his *French and Indian Cruelty: Exemplified in the Life and Various Vicissitudes of Fortune, of Peter Williamson*, published around the same time, went through four editions in the first year of publication alone.[60]

---

[56] John Shebbeare, *Lydia; or Filial Piety* (London, 1755), p. 6. The work was reissued in 1769.

[57] Shebbeare, *Lydia*, pp. 7–8.

[58] Shebbeare, *Lydia*, p. 205.

[59] Benjamin Bissell, *The American Indian in English Literature of the Eighteenth Century* (New Haven, 1925), p. 78.

[60] For the most recent discussion of the interesting life of Williamson and the impact of his experiences in North America on his identity and later life, see Timothy J. Shannon, "King of the Indians: the Hard Fate and Curious Career of Peter Williamson," *WMQ*, 3rd ser., LXVI (2009), pp. 3–44.

Rather than portraying Indians as symbols of lost innocence, most Britons instead used Indians as benchmarks for barbarity and depravity. Horace Walpole often played on popular perceptions of Indians to insult those whom he loathed: impolite companions were "Iroquois," and the rabble were "Cherokee." When commenting on London's tumultuous Gordon Riots in 1780, he remarked that "when prisons are levelled to the ground, when the bank is aimed at, and reformation is attempted by conflagrations, the savages of Canada are the only fit allies of Lord George Gordon and his crew."[61] Reporting on a murder at "a little Public House at Kill y cwm" in Wales in 1772, *Jackson's Oxford Journal* drew on the popular image of Indian brutality as a reference point, describing the crime as "one of the most shocking Acts of wanton Cruelty and most savage Barbarity ever heard of. It is of so brutal a Nature that Decency will not suffer the most distant Hint of the horrid Deed. . . . We shudder at the Barbarity of Indians, who roast their Prisoners alive; but the detestable, the hellish Brutality of these Villains is far more horrible."[62] Thus the shaming of Britons came not from the naïve, innocent Indian unmasking the failings of civilized society, but from likening them to Indians, who were depicted as the lowest and cruelest of peoples.

****

Although not as focused on the practical issues of empire building as the British government and general reading public, Britain's intellectual elite offered little that challenged the prevailing stereotypes of American Indians (and much that supported them). Scotland's union with England in 1707 and integration into the British Empire created a new world, transforming the country's political, economic and intellectual culture. Leaders of the Scottish Enlightenment responded during these challenging times by categorizing, sorting, and explaining new information and ideas, which often subverted British cosmologies. With regard to understanding the great diversity of peoples and civilizations the British encountered globally, this process took the form of what Edmund Burke famously referred to as "the Great Map of

---

[61] Walpole to Lord Stratford, June 12, 1780, *Walpole Correspondence*, XXXV, p. 354. For other examples of Walpole and his correspondents using reference to Indians to insult or criticize, see Walpole to Stratford, September 4, 1760, XXXV, p. 306; Walpole to Lady Ossory, August 18, 1792 and January 29, 1793, XXXIV, pp. 152, 177; Walpole to Lady Lennox, November 26, 1790, XXXI, p. 357; Horace Mann to Walpole, October 11, 1748, XXV, p. 109.

[62] *Jackson's Oxford Journal*, March 7, 1772.

Mankind."[63] Using methods that paved the way for the modern social sciences, the Scots philosophers examined European accounts of a host of peoples and civilizations past and present in an attempt to explain how societies develop (and why they do so at varying rates). Predominately devout members of the Presbyterian Church of Scotland, most assumed that the peoples of the world originated in a single, common creation and subsequently shared the same biological history.[64] This made the variations in human societies particularly intriguing and in need of explanation, and in this context American Indians became the living representatives of humanity in its earliest stages of socio-economic development.

Scots philosophers had taken considerable interest in primitive human society since the seventeenth century, but the societies which the likes of Hume and Hutcheson examined were fictitious, generic ones with no fixed geography or time in history. The Seven Years' War experience changed this. Like ordinary Britons, the Scottish intellectual elite was bombarded with printed accounts of Indians, and, just as with regular readers, it piqued the interest of a number of Scots philosophers, including the likes of Adam Smith, Adam Ferguson, John Millar, Lord Kames, and William Robertson. The answers to common fundamental enquiries—how humanity evolved from primitive hunter-gatherers into commercial societies and why societies had progressed, or regressed, at different rates—varied, but Indians quickly became the near universal face of all primitive societies past and present in the Scottish Enlightenment. As William Robertson remarked in his influential *History of America* (1777), "In America, man appears under the rudest form in which we can conceive him to subsist. We behold communities just beginning to unite, and may examine the sentiments and actions of human beings in the infancy of social life."[65] Notably, these studies were not specifically examinations of Indians—although the implications for them were ultimately profound. Instead, Indians, or rather selective descriptions of them by whites, served as illustrative examples of how societies in their infancy behaved. In essence, Scots philosophers treated Indians as living relics. As Adam Ferguson explained in his seminal

---

[63] Thomas W. Copeland (ed.), *The Correspondence of Edmund Burke* (Chicago, 1958–78), III, pp. 350–1.

[64] An exception to this was Lord Kames, who proposed a second creation for American Indians, although he did not suggest Indians were any less human than Europeans.

[65] William Robertson, *The History of America* (London, 1777), I, p. 282.

Essay on the History of Civil Society (1767), "It is in their [American Indians'] present condition, that we are to behold, as in a mirror, the features of our own progenitors, and from thence we are to draw our conclusions with respect to the influence and situations, in which, we have reason to believe, our fathers were placed."[66]

Most of these histories were designed for broad audiences, rather than for a handful of intellectual elites. These were commercial as well as intellectual enterprises. The books were published in multiple editions by the major London publishers of the day, and they garnered substantial profits for authors and publishers alike, with leading authors such as William Robertson said to have earned "no less than 4,500 Sterling" for one of his histories.[67] The books appeared in virtually all of the major subscription libraries, as well as in many of the smaller ones, and the review press consistently praised their merits. The subject of human socio-economic development was a hot topic of the day, as the *Monthly Review* declared in the opening lines of its assessment of Adam Smith's *Moral Sentiments*: "Of all the various enquiries that have exercised the thoughts of speculative men, there are scarce any which afford more genuine or lasting pleasure, to persons of a truly liberal and inquisitive turn, than those which have Man for their object. Indeed, what can be more worthy to be studied, and distinctly known?"[68] Using the native inhabitants of the Americas as illustrative examples was, therefore, at least partly about appealing to potential readers. The Seven Years' War had made Indians household topics, and so employing extended examples that drew on this awareness made the works much more appealing and accessible to potential audiences. That the shift in the awareness of the public, rather than in that of the authors, was key is made evident from the fact that most of the material on Indians came from the pre-Seven Years' War travel narratives of French missionaries, which had circulated in English translations in Britain for decades.[69] The decision to employ these examples seems to have paid off, as the extracts in newspapers and magazines overwhelmingly focused their attention on those portions of the books that dealt with primitive societies

---

[66] Adam Ferguson, *An Essay on the History of Civil Society* (Edinburgh, 1767), p. 122. Ferguson believed that the "Canadian[s] and Iroquois" bore the best resemblance to ancient Northern Europeans.

[67] *Scots Magazine*, April 1772, p. 196.

[68] *Monthly Review*, July 1759, p. 1.

[69] The most heavily used accounts were Lafitau's *Moeurs des Savages Ameriquains, Comparées aux Moeurs des Premiers Temps* (1724) and Pierre Francois Xavier de Charlevoix's *Histoire et Description Général de la Nouvelle France* (1744).

and Indians.[70] In typical fashion, the *Gentleman's Magazine* enthusiastically declared in its review of Robertson's *History of America* that his enquiry into the development of early humanity through his exploration of the Americas was "the most original, and for philosophical and contemplative readers, will be the most interesting part of the work."[71]

The portrait that the Scots philosophers painted of life at the first stage of human socio-economic development was decidedly grim. First published at the height of the Seven Years' War, Adam Smith's *The Theory of Moral Sentiments* was the first major work to make explicit use of Indians as empirical evidence. Smith described first-stage peoples as emotionally limited and inherently egocentric, explaining that "all savages are too much occupied with their own wants and necessities, to give such attention to those of another person."[72] Sympathy, which Smith depicted as the height of emotional evolution, could not be articulated in such societies; in fact, he asserted, it was disdained. Only in more advanced stages were there sufficient opportunities—made possible by a hierarchy of social ranks and leisure time—for moral sentiments to develop. To illustrate his point, he turned to the "savages of North America, [who] we are told, assume upon all occasions the greatest indifference, and would think themselves degraded if they should ever appear in any respect to be overcome, either by love or grief, or resentment."[73] In Ferguson's *Essay on the History of Civil Society* Indians received greater attention but fared no better. Here too Indians were depicted as lacking remorse, pity, or any sense of civic duty. Perpetual warfare, limited ambition, the virtual absence of personal comforts, and physical torture dominated his descriptions of both the early stages of human society and the Indian peoples he used to illustrate it. William Robertson went so far as to represent the Indians as incapable of complex reasoning or understanding abstract ideas, claiming for example that a Cherokee Indian could not comprehend a number above one hundred.[74] This shortcoming, he asserted, ultimately prevented genuine conversions to Christianity.[75] Missionaries'

---

[70] For examples, see *Gentleman's Magazine*, April 1767, p. 177; *Scots Magazine*, March 1767, p. 150; *Monthly Review*, May 1767, p. 345; *London Chronicle*, August 17 and 27, 1771.

[71] *Gentleman's Magazine*, January 1778, p. 26.

[72] Adam Smith, *The Theory of Moral Sentiments*, 2nd edn (London, 1761), p. 313.

[73] Smith, *Moral Sentiments*, p. 312; for another, similar example see p. 319.

[74] Robertson, *History of America*, I, p. 311.

[75] Robertson employed Hume's skeptical theory of knowledge, in which conceptions of time, space, substance, and causation are held to be rooted in custom and education. Nicholas

primary mistake, contended Robertson, who was a prominent figure in the General Assembly of the Church of Scotland, was their belief that the ability to comprehend futurity and the rational explanations of Christianity were natural to all humans.[76]

Not surprisingly, arguments like these fueled the narrow, predominately negative British perception of Indians. There were alternatives, such as that offered by the Mohegan Presbyterian minister Samson Occom, who toured Britain in 1767–8 to raise money for an Indian charity school. Yet Occom's, like the voices of so many Indians and their supporters in Britain, was drowned out in the public discourse of the time, when a single issue of the London Chronicle could reach more Britons than Occom could in over a year of sermons and when Occom's funds could be readily stripped from him to build not an Indian school, but an institution for white colonists, Dartmouth College. Practically-minded British had little time for such counter-intuitive alternatives as Rousseau's French Enlightenment noble savage— a subject of wide ridicule in the British press. As the London Chronicle representatively remarked in a review of Rousseau's Social Contract in 1762, "the meanest Christian must make a better patriot, and a much more social human being, than the model of perfection which John James exhibits in his Natural Man, who runs wild and naked in the woods upon his hands and legs, eats acorns, shuns his species, [except] only when the spirit of copulation moves him, and lives and dies among his brother-brutes." For more on the noble savage, the reviewer advised the reader to "see the Dissertation on the Causes of Inequality of Mankind by this same John James Rousseau, designed by nature to howl in a wilderness, but converted by force and pernicious influence of the social contract, into a citizen of Geneva."[77]

The Scottish Enlightenment version of the harsh primitive life that American Indians illustrated seemed far more realistic. In fact, critics and readers alike praised the Scots for refuting the idea of the idyllic, noble savage. As the Annual Register declared in 1778, the Scots philosophers had definitely disproven any advantage to a primitive existence:

Phillipson, "Providence and Progress," in Stuart J. Brown (ed.), William Robertson and the Expansion of Empire (Cambridge, 1997), pp. 69–70, asserts that Robertson elaborated the Augustinian position that the Word of God was revealed only when the world was ready to receive it by proposing that the revelation was an ongoing process in which societies received parts, or meanings, of the Word as they advanced in their ability to comprehend it.

[76] Robertson, History of America, II, pp. 384–6.
[77] London Chronicle, June 29, 1762.

Poets, philosophers, and politicians, had in vain exerted their genius, wisdom, and talents, to describe or discover the state of simplicity, innocence, and nature, the origin of society, and the source of laws. As they all wandered in the dark, their songs and theories were equally erroneous. That chasm is now filled up. That age, which was supposed to be golden, we now behold; and discover it affords only a state of weakness, imperfection, and wretchedness, equally void of innocence, and incapable of happiness. If we find man without property, and feeding on acorns, we also find him a sullen, suspicious, solitary, and unhappy being; a creature endued with a few good, and cursed with numberless ill qualities; unjust and cruel from nature and habit, treacherous on system, implacable in revenge, and incapable of gratitude, friendship, or natural affection.[78]

To be fair, Smith, Ferguson, Robertson and a solid majority of their colleagues did not deliberately seek to justify racism. In fact, Scottish philosophers critiqued the focus on biological differences that was developing on the European continent. Most praised the qualities of bravery and individualism they believed Indians possessed, but admiring commentary received little attention in the reviews and extracts that appeared in the press. Far more prevalent were the descriptions about how primitive peoples generally, and Indians particularly, would have difficulty advancing to more developed stages of civilization and how such developments were a time-consuming, uncertain process for which there was no roadmap. William Robertson remarked in an often-cited passage, "we may conclude, that the intellectual powers of man in the savage state are destitute of their proper object, and cannot acquire any considerable degree of vigour or enlargement."[79] Such views ultimately bolstered widespread views that the Indians were irredeemable and helped to create a colonial legacy of separation and abuse of native peoples in North America and across the growing British Empire.

****

The formal recognition of the independence of the United States significantly changed the place of American Indians in the British Imperial imagination. For a start, American Indians ceased to be part of the daily diet of news. After the war, Britain's retention of Quebec and what became Upper Canada meant that Indians remained an object of some interest in

---

[78] *Annual Register* for 1777 (London, 1778), p. 214.
[79] Robertson, *History of America*, I, p. 314.

British Imperial policy, but changes in the administration of the colonies and a sharp shift in attention away from North America meant that Indians never again held a major place in the British Imperial imagination. Even as the war wound down and independence had been accepted as inevitable by most Britons, the Indians all but disappeared from the British press. Whereas the plights of American loyalists and African slaves who had fled to British lines received consideration in both the treaty negotiations and the public discussion surrounding them, Britain abandoned its Indian allies with scarce a peep of public protest. To some extent this was a part of the war fatigue that pervaded Britain and the desire of the public to wash its hands of the American debacle and move on, but this desertion and lack of controversy surrounding it also stemmed from the generally dismal view of Indians held by the vast majority of Britons.

After 1783, American Indians rarely featured in geopolitical discussions in Britain. Of course, they remained crucial to British strategic interests in North America, but then what remained of the British Empire there barely figured in either popular discourse or government discussions. When war was imminent with the United States in 1812, the British government refused to reinforce Canada despite desperate pleas and the army's expectation that most of it would be quickly overrun by invading American armies. Only at the end of the War of 1812, and following a herculean publicity effort by the Anglophone colonial elite and their supporters in Britain, did British North America become widely accepted in Britain as an important jewel in the Imperial crown.[80] Moreover, while the war figured substantially in the press at the time, Indians did not. And although Indian allies proved crucial to the defense of the Canadas, and government ministers individually expressed pity for their suffering at the hands of the Americans, Britain once again abandoned its Indian allies at the war's end in exchange for a quick and amicable treaty with its greatest overseas trading partner, the United States.[81]

Only after the virtual disappearance of Indians from British public and political discussions at the end of the America Revolution did the Indian

---

[80] Troy Bickham, *The Weight of Vengeance: The United States, the British Empire, and the War of 1812* (Oxford, 2012).

[81] On American Indians' role in the defense of the Canadas, see especially Carl Benn, *The Iroquois in the War of 1812* (Toronto, 1998); Jon Latimer, *1812: War with America* (Cambridge, MA, 2008), chap. 2–3; and Alan Taylor, *The Civil War of 1812: American Citizens, British Subjects, Irish Rebels, and Indian Allies* (New York, 2010). On Indians' place in the negotiations for the Treaty of Ghent, see Bickham, *Weight of Vengeance*, chap. 8.

emerge in some circles as representing a powerful critique of European imperialism. Against the backdrop of the sensational trial of Warren Hastings, the governor of Bengal, for what were essentially crimes against humanity, Richard Sheridan, one of the prosecutors, staged *Pizarro*—an acute critique of imperialism in which the Spanish actions in the Americas were but a thin vale for the real target: the British in India. In the decades that followed, Southey, Wordsworth, Coleridge, and Shelley were the most celebrated of the host of literary figures of the day who employed romanticized versions of American Indians to critique European imperialism, British society or both.[82] Moreover, in these cases, Indians were not cameo characters or minor influences, but instead central subjects. The representations were of physically and morally strong Indians, strikingly set against a backdrop of the corruption and confusion of European commercial societies. The extent to which these images of Indians replaced earlier, more widespread perceptions is impossible to say. However, unlike earlier attempts such as Shebbeare's *Lydia*, these writers were not dismissed, publicly condemned, or overwhelmed by contradictory depictions in the press. Thus the use of Indians in this way can at the very least be described as having become generally palatable to a broad range of audiences.

This reversal was enabled by a number of factors, not the least of which was the effective removal of real Indians from the front line of British Imperial aspirations. (Britain still had colonies in North America but the public and government paid them scant attention in comparison to other parts of the Empire or to America before independence.) The sensational coverage of the daily carnage in Revolutionary France also more than satisfied the public's morbid curiosity. Accounts of the killings of poor settlers on another continent were no match for tales of royals being executed before crazed mobs just a few hundred miles away. Most important of all, the British became more openly critical of the Empire and imperialism through their experience of the American Revolution and the crisis years preceding it. For two decades American colonists and their sympathizers in Britain had lashed out against the British establishment, resulting in the replacement of the blind, righteous public confidence that followed the Seven Years' War by a far more reflective national mood that came to question the present practices of the Empire, most notably rule in

---

[82] For the most comprehensive study, see Tim Fulford, *Romantic Indians, Native Americans, British Literature, and Transatlantic Culture 1756–1830* (Oxford, 2006).

India and African slavery.[83] Although the rise of a powerful and determinedly expansionist United States meant that it was arguably too late for the British to halt the sufferings and decline of the vast majority of North American Indians, who would ultimately fall under American sovereignty, critics of empire in Britain found in the images of Indians a useful foil to denounce similar treatment of native peoples in other parts of the world.

Select Bibliography

ROBERT F. BERKHOFER, JR., *The White Man's Indian: Images of the American Indian from Columbus to Present* (New York, 1978).

TROY BICKHAM, *Savages within the Empire: Representations of American Indians in Eighteenth-Century Britain* (Oxford, 2005).

STUART J. BROWN (ed.), *William Robertson and the Expansion of Empire* (Cambridge, 1997).

COLIN G. CALLOWAY, *Crown and Calumet: British-Indian Relations, 1783–1815* (Norman, OK, 1987).

LINDA COLLEY, *Captives: Britain, Empire and the World, 1600–1850* (London, 2003).

TIM FULFORD, *Romantic Indians: Native Americans, British Literature, and Transatlantic Culture, 1756–1830* (Oxford 2006).

TIM FULFORD and KEVIN HUTCHINGS (eds), *Native Americans and Anglo-American Culture, 1750–1850: The Indian Atlantic* (Cambridge, 2009).

KATE FLINT, *The Transatlantic Indian, 1776–1930* (Princeton, 2008).

ERIC HINDERAKER, "The 'Four Indian Kings' and the Imaginative Construction of the First British Empire," *WMQ*, 3rd. ser., LIII (1996), pp. 487–526.

P. J. MARSHALL and GLYNDWR WILLIAMS, *The Great Map of Mankind: British Perceptions of New Worlds in the Age of Enlightenment* (London, 1982).

DANIEL K. RICHTER, "Native Peoples of North America and the Eighteenth-Century British Empire," in P. J. Marshall (ed.), *OHBE*, II, *The Eighteenth Century* (Oxford, 1998), pp. 347–71.

RONALD MEEK, *Social Science and the Ignoble Savage* (Cambridge, 1979).

STEPHANIE PRATT, *American Indians in British Art, 1700–1840* (Norman, OK, 2005).

RUSSELL SNAPP, *John Stuart and the Struggle for Empire on the Southern Frontier* (Baton Rouge, LA, 1996).

---

[83] For a more detailed argument, see Bickham, *Making Headlines*, pp. 251–3. The contrast between the language, depth, and extent of public interest in India before and after the American Revolution is most vividly detailed in Osborn, "India, Parliament and the Press under George III." Simon Schama makes a case for the connection between the rise of the British abolitionist movement and the American Revolution in *Rough Crossings: Britain, the Slaves, and the American Revolution* (London, 2005). On the connections between the Revolution and abolition of the slave trade, see also Christopher L. Brown, *Moral Capital: Foundations of British Abolitionism* (Chapel Hill, NC, 2006).

TIMOTHY SHANNON, *Crossroads of Empire: the Albany Congress of 1754* (Ithaca, NY, 2000).

LAURA M. STEVENS, *Poor Indians: British Missionaries, Native Americans and Colonial Sensibility* (Philadelphia, 2004).

ALDEN T. VAUGHAN, *Transatlantic Encounters: American Indians in Britain, 1500–1776* (New York, 2006).

9

The American Revolution (I)

The Paradox of Atlantic Integration*

Nancy L. Rhoden

For most of the two centuries since the event itself, the American Revolution has been a profoundly American tale, intimately bound up in popular imagination and scholarly presentation alike with national mythologies and the imperatives of civic identity. The familiar historical narrative posits a "first American Revolution," more or less complete by 1760, in which long-term cultural maturation and adaptation gradually create a distinctive, non-British society. Then, the second American Revolution, the one that begins in 1775, more or less inevitably rewards cultural divergence with political autonomy.[1] Although this narrative retains much of its traditional power, many recent accounts of the same events emphasize the growing integration of the colonies in the course of the eighteenth century into an Imperial and Atlantic world, suggesting that American separatism, when it comes, is not an unfolding of the inevitable but a revolutionary achievement.[2] These two narratives, one prominently featuring Americanization and the second Imperial and/or Atlantic integration,

* The author thanks Stephen Foster and Ian Steele for their suggestions and encouragement.

[1] For an early nationalist history, see George Bancroft, *A History of the United States, from the Discovery of the Continent*, III, *The American Revolution* (Port Washington, 1967, reprint of 1885 edition).

[2] Cf. Carole Shammas, "Introduction" in Elizabeth Mancke and Carole Shammas (eds), *The Creation of the British Atlantic World*, (Baltimore, 2005), pp. 1–16, esp. 1–5. On Atlantic revolutions and/or Age of Revolutions, see R.R. Palmer, *The Age of the Democratic Revolution: A Political History of Europe and America, 1760–1800* (Princeton, 1959–64), esp. I, pp. 3–24, 232–5; and Jacques Godechot, *France and the Atlantic Revolution of the Eighteenth Century, 1770–1799* (New York, 1965), pp. 1–26; David Armitage and Sanjay Subrahm, "Introduction: The Age of Revolutions, c. 1760–1840—Global Causation, Connection, and Comparison," in David Armitage and Sanjay Subrahm (eds), *The Age of Revolutions in Global Context, c. 1760–1840* (Houndmills, 2010), pp. xii–xxxii.

have encouraged debate about the nature of the transition from colonies to nation and have fed the ongoing controversy over just how much genuinely radical change can be attributed to the American Revolution.[3]

Most historical accounts focusing on the Revolutionary era routinely assume that the rival trends, Americanization and Imperial integration, are mutually incompatible. This dichotomy, however, is potentially misleading at best. There is certainly good evidence that, by the late colonial era, the British colonies were shedding many of the differences produced by their diverse origins. In patterns of social or political convergence[4] as various as the inter-colonial spread of African slavery or the rise of colonial assemblies one may find seeds of Americanization. Yet, Imperial integration largely provided the opportunities for contemporaries both to engage in inter-colonial exchanges and to share in common causes, such as warfare against the French in the name of liberty and Protestantism or the creation of shared concepts and vocabulary for criticizing British colonial policy.

The notorious lack of connection between the historiographies of the colonial and Revolutionary eras can only further the confusion.[5] In the historiography of the late colonial period, integration is a prominent, even ubiquitous theme, having largely displaced previous work that arguably allowed the long shadow of the American Revolution to obscure understanding of the eighteenth-century Empire on its own terms.[6] However, the scholars most interested in integration have rarely pursued their theme past the 1760s, leaving an obvious question unaddressed: if, as recent scholarship strongly suggests, transatlantic communication, political networks, and mercantile dynasties were increasingly integrated and interdependent in the Atlantic world of the middle eighteenth century, then how did a major part of colonial

---

[3] Cf. Alfred F. Young, "How Radical Was the American Revolution?" in Young (ed.), *Liberty Tree: Ordinary People and the American Revolution* (New York, 2006), pp. 215–61; Gordon S. Wood, *The Radicalism of the American Revolution* (New York, 1992), pp. 4–8, 169–89, 232; and related forum, "How Revolutionary Was the Revolution?" in *WMQ*, 3rd ser., LI (1994), pp. 677–716.

[4] Jack P. Greene, *Pursuits of Happiness: The Social Development of Early Modern British Colonies and the Formation of American Culture* (Chapel Hill, NC, 1988), pp. 170–206.

[5] On the colonial–Revolutionary disjunction, see Pauline Maier, et al., "The State of Early American History: A Forum," *Historically Speaking*, VI, No. 4 (March/April 2005), pp. 19–32; Stephen Foster, "British North America in the Seventeenth and Eighteenth Centuries," in Robin W. Winks (ed.), *OHBE*, V, *Historiography*, (Oxford, 1999), pp. 73–92; and Doron Ben-Atar, "The American Revolution," in Winks (ed.), *OHBE*, V, pp. 94–113.

[6] Charles McLean Andrews, *The Colonial Period of American History* (New Haven, 1934–38), esp. I, pp. xi–xiii.

society develop so profound a sense of grievance and so firm a conviction by 1776 that negotiation was futile and that only independence would save them from enslavement and impoverishment? This chapter considers this question in two steps. It begins by defining the concept of integration, exploring the phenomenon along the familiar lines of economic, military, and political developments, as well as weighing its relevance to family relations, religion, and society and culture broadly. Then it addresses directly the seemingly contradictory and paradoxical themes of Americanization amidst Atlantic integration in order to suggest that the coming of the American Revolution might make more sense as a crisis of Imperial or Atlantic integration rather than as an almost inexplicable reversal of the same trends.[7]

****

A legacy of the rise of Atlantic Studies, "integration" refers to the multi-faceted process by which the British overseas provinces became increasingly linked politically, economically, socially, and culturally to Great Britain. The components of integration may be defined as including: commercial patterns of trade and consumption; warfare and territorial expansion; government and administrative policies; and the creation of common social, religious, or cultural values.[8] As employed in this chapter, integration presupposes a whole variety of processes and patterns with different, often conflicting, effects. Forms of integration include anglicization and metropolitanization,[9] but it was possible to have one without the other, as in the case of the British and Dutch financial markets in the eighteenth century, which became highly integrated without the two societies coming to resemble each other any more than they had in earlier centuries. Both integration and anglicization could be the products of increased administrative oversight of trade and politics, as well as structural changes in colonial society, but also on occasion

[7] Cf. P. J. Marshall, "Britain and the World in the Eighteenth Century: II, Britons and Americans," *Transactions of the Royal Historical Society*, 6th ser., IX (1999), pp. 1–16, esp. p. 2; John M. Murrin, "The Great Inversion, or Court versus Country: A Comparison of the Revolution Settlements in England (1688–1721) and America (1776–1816)", in J. G. A. Pocock (ed.), *Three British Revolutions: 1641, 1688, 1776* (Princeton, 1980), pp. 368–453, esp. p. 387.

[8] Richard R. Johnson, "Empire," in Daniel Vickers (ed.), *A Companion to Colonial America* (Malden, MA, 2003), pp. 99–117.

[9] On anglicization, see John M. Murrin, "Anglicizing an American Colony: The Transformation of Provincial Massachusetts" (Ph.D. diss., Yale University, 1966), and for a more recent version T. H. Breen and Timothy Hall, *Colonial America in an Atlantic World: A Story of Creative Interaction* (New York, 2004), pp. 298–323.

were attributable to colonists' deliberate emulation of English culture. Integration could be both hierarchically imposed and voluntarily assumed, and its form in any given case was the result of negotiations between metropole and periphery.[10] Parliamentary legislation, most prominently the Navigation Acts, regulated colonial–British economic interaction and facilitated economic integration, but after 1763, when British administrators attempted a new kind of political integration, they inadvertently contributed to the fracturing of Empire.[11] The spectacular collapse in 1776 of that final attempt at integration has tended to shape our understanding of the entire phenomenon, and has misled us into portraying the late era as a simplistic tug-of-war between centralization and resistance. A closer look at the variety of developments subsumed under the single heading "integration" and its presumed subsets reveals a much more complicated form of interaction.

Over the course of the eighteenth century, as the result of population growth, urban development, social stratification, and a variety of other parallel phenomena throughout the colonies, many American communities, particularly eastern cities, came to share characteristics with their English counterparts. Economic integration—the increasing availability of affordable British goods and of markets for colonial products that provided the credits to buy them—and a parallel process in which emergent colonial elites cast about for visible ratification of their newly won status both fostered a self-conscious cultural convergence. Colonists became eager consumers of British architecture, books, religion, politics, and other markers of civility and polite learning. The importation into the colonies of prestigious commodities, such as Staffordshire china, similarly promoted the privileging of British items that the elite, the middling sort, and even, some of the time, the common people could all potentially share in, even though others lacked the financial means to participate and still others were obliged to purchase less expensive copies of the British original. At times transcending class or local concerns, integration was a polymorphous force that could certainly unify people and regions, but in so doing it also clarified and illuminated potential

---

[10] See Elizabeth Mancke, "Negotiating an Empire: Britain and Its Overseas Peripheries, c. 1550–1780," in Christine Daniels and Michael V. Kennedy (eds), *Negotiated Empires: Centers and Peripheries in the Americas, 1500–1820* (New York, 2002), pp. 235–65, esp. p. 236; Jack P. Greene, "The American Revolution," *AHR*, CV (2000), pp. 93–102, esp. p. 94; Bernard Bailyn and Philip D. Morgan (eds), "Introduction," *Strangers within the Realm: Cultural Margins of the First British Empire* (Chapel Hill, NC, 1991), pp. 9–10.

[11] For pre-1763 attempts at Imperial reorganization see Steven Sarson, *British America, 1500–1800: Creating Colonies, Imagining an Empire* (London, 2005), pp. 191–210.

points of division. Integration was not simply or exclusively pro-British in its effects; it also led to an internal colonial contest over its terms and pace.[12]

Integration can also be conceived of as both *Imperial* and *Atlantic*. One or another version of the concept has been prominent in early American historiography as far back as the work of Charles M. Andrews.[13] It was also employed by later Imperial-minded scholars who argued for English roots of American culture,[14] and has an appeal as well for contemporary Atlanticists, who attempt to comprehend the Atlantic Ocean's basin and its people in their entirety in order to imagine a transnational community forged through common Atlantic experiences.[15] The extent of this proposed transnational and transcultural unity requires further analysis and debate, but there is little question that the reigning Atlanticist framework in early American historiography has turned the concept of "integration" from the somewhat marginalized preoccupation of a relative handful of scholars with Imperial interests to a matter of central concern in our contemporary understanding of the British Atlantic in the colonial period.[16] The conse-

---

[12] Neil McKendrick, John Brewer, and J.H. Plumb, *The Birth of a Consumer Society: The Commercialization of Eighteenth-Century England* (Bloomington, IN, 1982); T.H. Breen, "An Empire of Goods: The Anglicization of Colonial America, 1670–1776," *JBS*, XXV (1986), pp. 467–99; and the same author's *The Marketplace of Revolution: How Consumer Politics Shaped American Independence* (New York, 2004), esp. pp. 53–9, 153–7.

[13] Charles McLean Andrews, *The Colonial Background of the American Revolution: Four Essays in American Colonial History* (New Haven, 1924), pp. 121–2; and Richard R. Johnson, "Charles McLean Andrews and the Invention of American Colonial History," *WMQ*, 3rd ser., XLIII (1986), pp. 519–41, esp. p. 520, 524, 531.

[14] Influential works include Bernard Bailyn, *The Ideological Origins of the American Revolution* (Cambridge, MA, 1967), esp. pp. 1–54; and Pauline Maier, *From Resistance to Revolution: Colonial Radicals and the Development of American Opposition to Britain, 1765–1776* (New York, 1972), pp. 12–16, 27–48. By the mid-1980s prominent works promoting an Atlantic perspective included: Ian K. Steele, *The English Atlantic, 1675–1740: An Exploration of Communication and Community* (New York, 1986); Jack P. Greene, *Peripheries and Center: Constitutional Development in the Extended Polities of the British Empire and the United States, 1607–1788* (Athens, GA, 1986); Bernard Bailyn, *Voyagers to the West: A Passage in the Peopling of America on the Eve of the Revolution* (New York, 1986).

[15] Comparative Atlantic studies include J. H. Elliott, *Empires of the Atlantic World: Britain and Spain in America, 1492–1830* (New Haven, 2006); and P. J. Marshall, *The Making and Unmaking of Empires: Britain, India, and America c. 1750–1783* (Oxford, 2005). For an appraisal, see Trevor Burnard, "The British Atlantic," in Jack P. Greene and Philip D. Morgan (eds), *Atlantic History: A Critical Appraisal* (Oxford, 2009), pp. 111–36.

[16] David Hancock, "The British Atlantic World: Co-ordination, Complexity, and the Emergence of an Atlantic Market Economy, 1651–1815," *Itinerario: European Journal of Overseas History*, 2 (1999), <http://www.let.leidenuniv.nl/history/itin/hancock.htm,1>. Transatlantic studies, however, can also emphasize divergences. See for example J. C. D. Clark's argument that political-religious dissidents, Britain's outcasts, launched the American Revolution in the colonies:

quences for the study of the Revolution and immediate post-Revolutionary period are profound: scholars still interested in emphasizing distinctive American qualities in the late colonial era must confront the concept of integration in some measure,[17] while the various schools of integrationists seem to be reverting to a neo-Andrewsian perspective in which the American Revolution is a discontinuity so profound (of the order of the Irish Potato Famine or World War I) that it is no longer their subject, but rather belongs to other historians whose remit is properly the period 1776 to 1850.

The remainder of this chapter is an attempt to transcend this impasse. It will follow the contemporary predilection for emphasizing the growing integrative ties that bound the periphery to the center and promoted British Imperial unity. The familiar broad categories of economic, military, and political linkages will be discussed in that order. What will become apparent as a result is the double-edged nature of Atlantic integration throughout the colonial period and, as the final quarter of the eighteenth century began, its capacity both to bring on and to retard the final separation.

****

The British Atlantic may be depicted quite convincingly as an increasingly integrated economic unit, the ligaments of which were trade routes, markets, and finance. However disparate the constituent parts, however initially intermittent and incomplete the contacts between colonies and metropole, by the middle of the eighteenth century people, goods, and information were being exchanged across the Atlantic in a progressively more efficient manner.[18] Escalation in the volume of trade and improve-

---

The Language of Liberty 1600–1832: Political Discourse and Social Dynamics in the Anglo-American World (Cambridge, 1994), esp. pp. 318–19.

[17] For a gradual Americanization argument advanced explicitly as a challenge to prevailing "Europeanization," see Jon Butler, *Becoming America: The Revolution Before 1776* (Cambridge, MA, 2000), pp. 4–5, passim, which should be compared with the review by John M. Murrin and David S. Silverman, "The Quest for America: Reflections on Distinctiveness, Pluralism, and Public Life," *Journal of Interdisciplinary History*, XXXIII (2002), pp. 235–46. Earlier treatments of American nationalism in the Revolutionary era include J.M. Bumsted, "'Things in the Womb of Time': Ideas of American Independence, 1633 to 1763," *WMQ*, 3rd ser., XXXI (1974), pp. 533–64; Paul A. Varg, "The Advent of Nationalism, 1758–1776," *American Quarterly*, XVI (1964), pp. 169–81; and Max Savelle, "Nationalism and Other Loyalties in the American Revolution," *AHR*, LXVII (1962), pp. 901–23.

[18] Steele, *The English Atlantic*, pp. 273–6. For a contrary view see S.D. Smith, *Slavery, Family, and Gentry Capitalism in the British Atlantic: The Worlds of the Lascelles, 1648–1834* (Cambridge, 2006), p. 357.

ments in navigation turned the Atlantic Ocean into a highway that linked distant parts of the Empire and facilitated exchange within the Atlantic basin. New-world supplies of fish, timber, furs, tobacco, and sugar enriched London businesses and contributed vitally to the fiscal health of the British state, while colonial exporters, merchants, and agriculturalists became increasingly tied to the British world of finance, credit, and markets. American colonists could participate in an expanding consumer culture by buying a wide variety of British goods. The received wisdom was that all would benefit from participation in a beneficent Empire governed by a wise monarch and Parliament.[19] Only later events would shake that confidence.

British Imperial unity depended also on military prowess. The Empire was preserved, defined, and expanded, in part, by war, and much of the effort to achieve metropolitan–colonial integration was justified in terms of mobilizing support for the four worldwide wars between 1689 and 1765 in which the New World colonies of the rival European powers were part of the high stakes game. Since American colonists needed British military protection against rival European and Native American empires they were inclined, when necessity dictated, to accept the legitimacy of royal government in the colonies, even if they haggled over the exact terms. By the time of the Seven Years' War even British subjects living in colonial backwaters understood that the most distant British victories on land or sea mattered to them too. For Britons and British colonists alike, persistent fears of the Bourbons strengthened their self-identification with their own presumptively unique virtues of liberty and Protestantism.[20] Yet such nationalism, often more Imperial than Atlantic, was never sufficient to maintain mass enthusiasm for very long. In the American theatres of the War of the Austrian Succession and the Seven Years' War military spirit petered out well before the end of the European side of the conflicts.[21] While colonists in

---

[19] P. J. Marshall, "Introduction," in P. J. Marshall (ed.), *OHBE*, II, *The Eighteenth Century* (Oxford, 1998), pp. 1–27.

[20] On British nationalism, see Linda Colley, *Britons: Forging the Nation, 1707–1837* (New Haven, 1992), pp. 11–100, esp. pp. 53–4, 55–6; Kathleen Wilson, *The Sense of the People: Politics, Culture and Imperialism in England, 1715–1785* (Cambridge, 1995), pp. 169–74, 274–8; Dror Wahrman, *The Making of the Modern Self: Identity and Culture in Eighteenth-Century England* (New Haven, 2004), pp. 199–217.

[21] Alan Rogers, *Empire and Liberty: American Resistance to British Authority, 1755–1763* (Berkeley, 1974), pp. 37, 41–50; Fred Anderson, *Crucible of War: The Seven Years' War and the Fate of Empire in British North America, 1754–1766* (New York, 2000), pp. 225–30, 286–8, 317–24, 370–2.

America understood war within a global context, the intensity of their participation depended upon local circumstances, and cooperation could easily be replaced by disillusionment and outright resistance.

Political integration had disparate origins. Shared political institutions and values, including an appreciation for Britain's mixed and balanced constitution, the frequent, if not always entirely harmonious, cooperation between institutions of Imperial governance and the representatives of colonial interests, and the rise of colonial elites interested in participating in British political culture as full members, all point to an increasingly integrated British Atlantic political world in the eighteenth century.[22] British Imperial oversight operated lightly in the first century and a half of colonization: while mercantile matters seemed to receive substantial attention, colonial politics was largely left in the hands of the local elites.[23] Whether this inattention was inadvertent or deliberate, over time the effect was to cultivate a presumption of the legitimacy of this semi-autonomy in colonial governance and of the status of the local elites as its informal stewards, a flattering self-estimation that was further reinforced when ways began to be found to influence Imperial politics.

Scholarship on the role of interest groups in Imperial governance has characterized the early eighteenth century as an age of colonial participation and even collaboration, albeit through unofficial channels.[24] By securing favor at Whitehall, presenting petitions to Parliament, or appealing successfully to a London interest group, the colonial elite became integrated, and domesticated, into British politics. Such activities also brought home to them their dependence, even as it pulled them into the metropolitan orbit. For example, after Virginia's General Assembly passed the Two Penny Act in

---

[22] On colonial self-conceptions, see Jack P. Greene, "Search for Identity: An Interpretation of the Meaning of Selected Patterns of Social Response in Eighteenth-Century America," *Journal of Social History*, III (1970), pp. 189–220. For a contrary view, see Savelle, "Nationalism and Other Loyalties," pp. 903–4.

[23] James A. Henretta, *"Salutary Neglect": Colonial Administration under the Duke of Newcastle* (Princeton, 1972); Ian K. Steele, *Politics of Colonial Policy: The Board of Trade in Colonial Administration, 1696–1720* (Oxford, 1968); Marshall, *The Making and Unmaking of Empires*, pp. 57–85.

[24] On successful American lobbying of Whitehall and Westminster see Alison Gilbert Olson, *Making the Empire Work: London and American Interest Groups, 1690–1790* (Cambridge, MA, 1992), pp. 108–25; Richard R. Johnson, *Adjustment to Empire: The New England Colonies, 1675–1715* (New Brunswick, NJ, 1981), pp. 306–63; and see also the chapter by Dan Hulsebosch in this volume.

1758, the province's gentry strenuously defended it against transatlantic demands for its repeal or its disallowance by the Privy Council. This local controversy set the gentry and the Anglican clergy in Virginia against each other, while it also provided an opportunity for local apologists, most famously Landon Carter and Richard Bland, to articulate and defend their constitutional right of self-determination through the elected lower house of the Virginia legislature.[25] The more intra-colonial politics looked like its British domestic equivalent, the more members of the colonial legislatures might begin to conceive of themselves as British parliaments in miniature with all the power and rights thereunto appertaining, and consequently deeply resent any intervention in their affairs from either Whitehall or Westminster. Somewhat like the Stamp Act and its repeal in 1765–66, the Two Penny Act was resolved by a mix of obfuscation and compromise, leaving neither side satisfied and metropolitan–colonial relations in disarray.[26] Repeal of this law, like the Stamp Act at a later date, may be seen as proof of the old system working effectively,[27] but without a resolution of the competing underlying claims in the controversy, repeal is also evidence of the transatlantic governance machine beginning to tear itself apart through its own internal workings.

The rise of the colonial assemblies[28] is perhaps the central ambiguity of Imperial governance. By aggrandizing power at the expense of royally appointed government, the colonial assemblies mimicked the ascendancy of Parliament in the government of Britain, a process of both imitation and integration, certainly, but one with a built-in potential for conflict. By the

[25] Warren M. Billings, John E. Selby, and Thad W. Tate, *Colonial Virginia: A History* (White Plains, NY, 1986), pp. 257–9.

[26] The Acts passed in 1755 and 1758 would have relieved taxpayers for two years from their legal obligation to pay taxes in tobacco during a period of poor crop yields and consequent high prices. The Privy Council disallowed the 1758 Act (the 1755 version went largely unnoticed), but did not declare it null and void *ab initio*, so that despite its criticisms, the Assembly's action was upheld in practice.

[27] Michael Kammen, *A Rope of Sand: The Colonial Agents, British Politics, and the American Revolution* (Ithaca, NY, 1968), pp. 117–24 presents 1765–66 as the last success of the old system. Cf., however, Mary Sarah Bilder, *The Transatlantic Constitution: Colonial Legal Culture and the Empire* (Cambridge, MA, 2004), pp. 181–5.

[28] On the rise of the assembly as a pan-colonial development, see especially Jack P. Greene, *The Quest for Power: The Lower Houses of Assembly in the Southern Royal Colonies, 1689–1776* (Chapel Hill, NC, 1963), pp. vii–viii, 3–18; and Greene, "The Role of the Lower Houses of Assembly in Eighteenth-Century Politics," *The Journal of Southern History*, XXVII (1961), pp. 451–74.

1720s, the governance of every colony except Connecticut and Rhode Island pitted an appointed governor against an elected lower house of assembly. Although the style of the contest varied from colony to colony, the most effective governors tended to be the ones who had learned how to use patronage and persuasion (and some degree of concessions) to work successfully with the assembly.[29] The locus of political power had shifted in response to the rise of the assembly throughout the colonies, and these common experiences of self-governance later assisted, even emboldened, colonial legislators in their protest against Parliamentary innovations after 1763.

In their re-enactments of Parliament's triumph over the crown, the colonial assemblies, like the legislature of Great Britain, paid tribute to the notion that contemporary English governance was founded on the Revolution of 1689, but in contrast to Britons, colonists were more likely to claim that the Glorious Revolution affirmed the supremacy of the legislative branch in general rather than the sovereignty of Parliament in particular.[30] Additionally, Americans interpreted sovereignty in the British constitution as residing in the King-in-Parliament, effectively embodied in statute. Though no Hanoverian king would have failed to consent to a bill enacted by both houses, whatever its content, Americans made crucial use of this obsolete part of the British constitution in the Declaration of Independence and later, as the veto power of the federal executive and most state governors, wrote it in to their constitutions.

Economic and political institutions may have provided the formal structures of Imperial integration, but supplementing and underwriting them were ties of blood, affinity, and mutual identities of various sorts, as well as the even more incorporeal qualities that fall under the general category "culture." As economic and social units, families organized themselves to take

---

[29] On categories of colonial political analysis, see Jack P. Greene, *Negotiated Authorities: Essays in Colonial Political and Constitutional History* (Charlottesville, VA, 1994), pp. 68–71, 118, 166–83; Greene, "Changing Interpretations of Early American Politics," in Ray Allen Billington (ed.), *The Reinterpretation of Early American History: Essays in Honour of John Edwin Pomfret* (San Marino, CA, 1966), pp. 151–2, 170–7. For an alternative to Greene's typology of factionalism see John M. Murrin, "Political Development," in Jack P. Greene and J.R. Pole (eds), *Colonial British America: Essays in the New History of the Early Modern Era* (Baltimore, 1984), pp. 408–56, and Murrin, "Great Inversion," in Pocock (ed.), *Three British Revolutions*, pp. 383–5. On factionalism, cf. Bernard Bailyn, *The Origins of American Politics* (New York, 1968), pp. 63–6, and Jack P. Greene, "Political Mimesis: A Consideration of the Historical and Cultural Roots of Legislative Behavior in the British Colonies in the Eighteenth Century," *AHR*, LXXV (1969/70), pp. 337–60.

[30] Sarson, *British America*, pp. 214–18.

advantage of Imperial opportunities for trade and for political advancement. Traditionally, overseas merchants relied heavily on close relatives and sometimes on co-religionists, such as fellow Jews, Quakers, or Huguenots, to insure the reliability of long-distance trade. Similarly, diverse London merchants actively sought to coordinate and integrate their business interests geographically and operationally, largely through personal and familial networks.[31] Well-to-do colonial families also used their Imperial connections to advance family members' names to be considered for appointed political positions, from governor to stamp distributor.

Here, too, the impact of colonial maturation was double edged. As the colonial elites expanded faster than the pool of Imperial jobs, competition for places inevitably stiffened and with it the resentments of the "outs" against the "ins." Success at using transatlantic channels to get and keep office angered the local elites when they failed to secure their own choice and it upset the citizenry in general, who identified the far-flung Imperial networks with corruption and venality. One person's integration could produce another's alienation. Consider the case of the Gedney Clarkes, a mercantile connection consisting of two Salem, Massachusetts families, linked by marriage, who developed a formidable web of business activities stretching to Barbados, London, and the Dutch West Indies by the middle of the eighteenth century. They were integrators and entrepreneurs certainly, but from the point of view of Salem's inhabitants, these once leading town families had become agents of a distant power base that combined wealth, office, and corruption in a classic manner. The family's practice of restricting business to its own ranks and a select handful of allies, such as the Lascelles of Barbados, promised to mitigate financial risk, give them an Imperial perspective, and expand their collective influence, but simultaneously it antagonized those shut out from its favors in a manner that was, arguably, destabilizing for the Empire in the long run. To add insult to injury, Gedney Clarke Sr.'s donations in the 1730s and 1740s to the Church of England in Salem and Boston, including bells for North Church in Boston, and the renting of pew number one in St. Peter's,

---

[31] Nuala Zahedieh, "Making Mercantilism Work: London Merchants and Atlantic Trade in the Seventeenth Century," *Transactions of the Royal Historical Society*, 6th ser., IX (1999), pp. 143–58; Zahedieh, *The Capital and the Colonies: London and the Atlantic Economy 1660–1700* (Cambridge, 2010), pp. 106–13; Perry Gauci, *The Politics of Trade: The Overseas Merchant in State and Society, 1660–1720* (Oxford, 2001), pp. 39–43, 71–5; David Hancock, *Citizens of the World: London Merchants and the Integration of the British Atlantic Community, 1735–1785* (Cambridge, 1995), pp. 16–17.

Salem were not likely to endear him to the Congregational citizenry of New England.[32]

Empires depended on war and commerce for their nourishment in a visible way but they also thrived on less tangible forms of sustenance. Despite perennial concerns over the demoralizing effects of exposure to English society, colonials perceived Britain as a vital source of learning, culture, and civility. The southern colonial elite in particular, like their West Indian counterparts, frequently preferred to educate their sons at the English universities or Inns of Court.[33] The purchasing and reading of English and European books reinforced and reflected the middling and elite colonists' emulation of the presumed cultural sophistication of the metropole, but so did the emergence, particularly in colonial cities, of private societies for the exchange of ideas and information, as well as such other foci for intellectual exchanges as taverns, coffeehouses, and the elaborate social ritual centered on the tea table. Educated colonial gentlemen coveted membership of London's Royal Society and also created their own local clubs for the pursuit of natural philosophy, while colonial lawyers and physicians imitated their metropolitan counterparts in their professional organizations.

News, like much else in Atlantic culture, was Janus-faced, creating Imperial loyalties and a consciousness of a distinctive American identity at one and the same time. The mushrooming colonial newspapers largely dedicated themselves to European affairs until the renewal of world-wide warfare and the arrival of a visiting revivalist, George Whitefield, forced this anglicized and anglocentric medium to focus more heavily on American news.[34] Nonetheless, a study of *The Pennsylvania Gazette* recognizes the American focus of much news after 1739 but also finds that the war years

---

[32] S.D. Smith, "Gedney Clarke of Salem and Barbados: Transatlantic Super-Merchant," *New England Quarterly*, LXXVI (2003), pp. 499–549, esp. p. 524. For the suggestion that when markets fell in 1760s and 1770s "gentry capitalism" was "perfectly positioned to destabilize Britain's first colonial empire in the Americas," see pp. 544–5. See also Smith, *Slavery, Family, and Gentry Capitalism*, pp. 91–138.

[33] Lucille Griffith (ed.), "English Education for Virginia Youth: Some Eighteenth-Century Ambler Family Letters," *Virginia Magazine of History and Biography*, LXIX (1961), pp. 7–27; Jack P. Greene (ed.), *The Diary of Colonel Landon Carter of Sabine Hall, 1752–1778* (Charlottesville, VA, 1965), I, pp. 372–3; Julie Flavell, *When London Was Capital of America* (New Haven, 2010), pp. 66–9; Andrew Jackson O'Shaughnessy, *An Empire Divided: The American Revolution and the British Caribbean* (Philadelphia, 2000), p. 22.

[34] Charles E. Clark, *The Public Prints: The Newspaper in Anglo-American Culture, 1665–1740* (New York, 1994), pp. 258–66.

witnessed more detailed, better-informed coverage of British politics than the pre-1739 period and, further, that after the peace in 1763 the newspaper continued to cater to the new taste for such British material even before the onset of the first Imperial crisis.[35] Colonial newspapers became a forum for the discussion of the *local* impact of global events and, in turn, the articulation of colonial interests distinct from those of Britain and ultimately critical of Imperial policy. In addition, London as the center of Imperial trade also inadvertently functioned as a vehicle of inter-colonial integration: news from, say, Georgia was likely to reach Boston via the Imperial capital and was only then reprinted in the local press.[36]

Although many aspects of the concept, "identity", may seem elusive, material culture offers somewhat firmer evidence of various colonists' sense of self. Spurred on by colonial population growth, the share of English domestic exports going to American markets increased from just over 5 percent at the beginning of the 1700s to over 25 percent by the early 1770s.[37] In their purchase of furniture, books, or bone china, or in the construction of their modest versions of the English country home in the Georgian style, provincial elites displayed their wealth and their fine taste. Such deliberate imitation of English models was a measure of Imperial economic integration and colonial cultural allegiance to the metropole. There were of necessity some concessions to local circumstances, such as the use of native wood instead of imported varieties, for reasons of affordability or availability,[38] but such adaptations did not necessarily suggest a rejection of the metropolitan model. When carved wooden pineapples were painted grey and placed above doorways, they appeared at a distance to be chiseled out of marble and so approximated as closely as feasible the English style. One could describe the hybrid result as an instance of either anglicization or Americanization, but the obvious point is that imitation of English fashions was the main goal. While other innovations, such as plainer, simpler

---

[35] Charles Wetherell, "The Measure of Maturity: The Pennsylvania Gazette, 1728–1765," *WMQ*, 3rd ser., XLVI (1989), pp. 279–303.

[36] Clark, *The Public Prints*, pp. 6, 10, 168–71, 252–3; David S. Shields, *Civil Tongues and Polite Letters in British America* (Chapel Hill, NC, 1997), pp. 242, 286.

[37] Jacob M. Price, "Who Cared About the Colonies? The Impact of the Thirteen Colonies on British Society and Politics, circa 1714–1775," in Bernard Bailyn and Philip D. Morgan (eds), *Strangers within the Realm*, pp. 395–436, esp. pp. 417–19; Price, "The Imperial Economy, 1700–1776," in Marshall (ed.), *OHBE*, II, pp. 78–104.

[38] Butler, *Becoming America*, pp. 131–84, esp. pp. 144, 152, 156.

furniture styles,[39] may have foreshadowed an up-and-coming American style just over the horizon, one wonders whether contemporaries saw such adaptations to American circumstances as anything more than necessary compromises when a wholly anglicized style would have been preferable under ideal circumstances.

The development of American religious denominations over the course of the eighteenth century is a study in ambivalence. Despite scholarly attempts to discover in this period the origins of what will become in the nineteenth century a distinctly anti-institutional American evangelicalism, between 1680 and 1760 religious organizations in America actually showed signs of moving back toward European-style establishmentarianism and centralized ecclesiastical governance. At the same moment the expansion of religious societies and the rapid pace of colonial church building resulted in the "sacralization" of the landscape. In many parishes, older buildings were replaced or renovated for the greater glory of God and to conform to gentrified taste.[40] As the skyline of colonial towns and cities filled with bell towers and church steeples, contemporaries might have noted how like London or at least the smaller English cities they had become, even as they argued about which local structure should be highest.

Defining the relationship between the mother churches of Europe and their colonial offspring was a well-developed tangle. A few denominations, of which the Presbyterians were the largest, formally separated themselves from the governance of their British equivalent but still chose to cooperate concerning matters of joint interest, be it the transatlantic revival known as the Great Awakening or the threat posed by the potential appointment of a colonial Anglican bishop. Baptists and Congregationalists had nothing to separate from but communicated with their British co-religionists on the same two heads all the more avidly for lack of a suitable institutionalized alternative.[41] Conversely, Anglicanism in the colonies remained dependent on the metropolitan Church of England until the American Revolution. Anglican colonial clergy were obliged to travel to Britain for ordination, and the Society for the Propagation

---

[39] Butler, *Becoming America*, pp. 158–64.

[40] Jon Butler, *Awash in a Sea of Faith: Christianizing the American People* (Cambridge, MA, 1990), pp. 98–128, esp. pp. 98, 109, 106–16.

[41] Ned C. Landsman, *Scotland and Its First American Colony, 1683–1765* (Princeton, 1985); Marilyn Westerkamp, *Triumph of the Laity: Scots-Irish Piety and the Great Awakening, 1625–1760* (New York, 1988); Carl Bridenbaugh, *Mitre and Sceptre: Transatlantic Faiths, Ideas, Personalities, and Politics, 1689–1775* (New York, 1962).

of the Gospel in Foreign Parts provided personnel and financial support for Anglican missions to Native Americans and to Anglicans in those colonies where the Church of England was not established. Yet even in the case of this most English of churches, the majority of the clergy were American-born by the eve of the American Revolution and the laity were seriously divided on whether to support proposals for a colonial episcopate.[42] And if such matters as the disputes over infant baptism kept colonial Calvinists of different stripes at odds with one another, they still shared an anti-Catholic, anti-French crusading zeal, confident of the wholesale destruction that must descend upon French Catholics when they were finally defeated by a united Protestant Empire.[43]

Members of non-Anglophone religious groups weighed the advantages of colonial cooperation with the Church of England. The Huguenots were largely absorbed, or joined Anglican parishes, intermarried with the English and disappeared as a distinct community.[44] In Pennsylvania, the Lutheran pastor Henry Melchior Muhlenberg, who organized the first Lutheran synod in 1748 in the face of considerable opposition, advocated cooperation with Anglicans to the point of merging the two denominations and favoring plans for English-language charity schools for German children. His son Peter Muhlenberg shared his father's vision and extended it: a licensed Lutheran minister, he took Anglican orders in 1772, a requirement for assuming leadership of a German Lutheran congregation in Dunmore County, Virginia.[45]

[42] Joan R. Gundersen, "The Search for Good Men: Recruiting Ministers in Colonial Virginia," *Historical Magazine of the Protestant Episcopal Church*, XLVIII (1979), pp. 453–64; Nancy L. Rhoden, *Revolutionary Anglicanism: The Colonial Church of England Clergy During the American Revolution* (New York, 1999); Frederick V. Mills, Sr., *Bishops By Ballot: An Eighteenth Century Ecclesiastical Revolution* (New York, 1978); James Bell, *The Imperial Origins of the King's Church in Early America, 1607–1783* (Houndmills, 2004); Peter M. Doll, *Revolution, Religion, and National Identity: Imperial Anglicanism in British North America, 1745–1795* (Madison, NJ, 2000).

[43] Nathan O. Hatch, "The Origins of Civil Millennialism in America: New England Clergymen, War with France, and the Revolution," *WMQ*, 3rd ser., XXXI (1974), pp. 407–30.

[44] Robert M. Kingdon, "Why did the Huguenot Refugees in the American Colonies Become Episcopalian?" *Historical Magazine of the Protestant Episcopal Church*, XLIX (1980), pp. 317–35; Butler, *The Huguenots in America*, pp. 34–7, 77–8, 84–5, 112–20, 134–6, 169–73, 189–93.

[45] Jürgen Heideking, "Muhlenberg, John Peter Gabriel (October 1, 1746–October 1, 1807)," in John A. Garraty and Mark C. Carnes (eds), *American National Biography*, XVI (New York, 1999), pp. 60–1; Wolfgang Splitter, "Muhlenberg, Henry Melchior (1711–1787)," in H.C.G. Matthew and Brian Harrison (eds), *Oxford Dictionary of National Biography*, XXXIX (Oxford, 2004), pp. 654–5; Thomas N. Rightmyer, "The Holy Orders of Peter Muhlenberg," *Historical Magazine of the Protestant Episcopal Church*, XXX (1961), pp. 183–97; Nancy L. Rhoden, "Is God American or English?: The English Clergy as Political Agents of Loyalism and Revolutionary Order," in Hermann

The Lutheran predicament was typical of German speakers generally. Over the century, increasing immigration to the colonies from the Continent created inward looking, exclusionary communities based on ethnicity and religion. To counter this trend, Benjamin Franklin had promoted English schools in Pennsylvania, arguing that the increasing number of German immigrants threatened to "Germanize us instead of our Anglifying them."[46] Patterns of German migration instead point to just the opposite, a vibrant German Atlantic community[47] that was largely shunted aside by the Anglophone majority in the British Atlantic world.

One way or another most of the Protestant denominations in the colonies participated in the evangelical awakening of the mid-eighteenth century. Self-consciously transatlantic and even global in some respects, the first Great Awakening could be classified under any number of rubrics. Nearly simultaneous waves of revivalism in England, Scotland, and British North America, paralleled by the spread of pietism on the Continent, encouraged a radical reconsideration of traditional religious expression that transcended denominational boundaries and led to continued contact between evangelicals from all the affected areas for decades to come.[48] An anti-authoritarian strain enhanced solidarity among those favoring revivalism, but also inadvertently promoted unity among those rationalist denominations critical of revivalism.[49] Transatlantic evangelicals joined together, while moving away from their nominal co-religionists who disapproved of revivalism, thereby creating an evangelical union amidst denominational divisions. In effect,

---

Wellenreuther, Thomas Müller-Bahlke, and A. Gregg Roeber (eds), *The Transatlantic World of Heinrich Melchior in the Eighteenth Century*, Hallesche Forschungen, 35 (Halle, forthcoming).

[46] Benjamin Franklin, *Observations Concerning the Increase of Mankind* (1751), as quoted in Roger Daniels, *Coming to America: A History of Immigration and Ethnicity in American Life*, 2nd edn (New York, 2002), p. 110.

[47] Marianne Wokeck, *Trade in Strangers: The Beginnings of Mass Migration to North America* (University Park, PA, 1999).

[48] Michael J. Crawford, *Seasons of Grace: Colonial New England's Revival Tradition in its British Context* (New York, 1991); Leigh Eric Schmidt, *Holy Fairs: Scottish Communions and American Revivals in the Early Modern Period* (Princeton, 1989); Frank Lambert, *Pedlar in Divinity: George Whitefield and the Transatlantic Revivals, 1737–1770* (Princeton, 1994); Lambert, *Inventing The "Great Awakening"* (Princeton, 1999). Cf. Jon Butler, "Enthusiasm Described and Decried: The Great Awakening as Interpretative Fiction," *Journal of American History*, LXIX (1982), pp. 305–25.

[49] Gerald J. Goodwin, "The Anglican Reaction to the Great Awakening," *Historical Magazine of the Protestant Episcopal Church*, XXXV (1966), pp. 343–71, esp. pp. 352–6; Harry S. Stout, "Religion, Communications and the Ideological Origins of the American Revolution," *WMQ*, 3rd ser., XXXIV (1977), pp. 519–41; Thomas S. Kidd, *The Great Awakening: The Roots of Evangelical Christianity in Colonial America* (New Haven, 2007), pp. xv–xvi, 287, 323–4.

the Awakening intensified the links spanning the Atlantic and created new divisions within the societies located on both sides.

Close analysis of the multi-faceted characteristics of the phenomenon of integration has perhaps increased a sense of the complexity of the subject and induced a wariness of simple dichotomies. But the paradox with which this discussion began has only deepened. If so many deeply held cultural values were shared between Britons and the colonists and if the ties between the two were arguably strengthening, it seems even more remarkable that the American Revolution succeeded in achieving American independence and reversing the trend of Imperial and Atlantic unification. Was it possible that the forces of Imperial integration in the final decades of the Empire actually *contributed* to the revolution that destroyed it?

****

From 1763 onwards, the recurring program of Imperial restructuring demonstrated that the politicians and civil servants in Whitehall and Westminster, as well as the political nation more generally, had come to have a very different idea of what it meant to be both British and colonial from the inhabitants of the colonies themselves. When attempts at reconciling these competing versions failed, the idealism underwriting a sense of being part of a single whole evaporated and pretensions to a common identity were abandoned by all the parties involved. The narrowly political and constitutional claims of the revolutionaries then promptly expanded into a broader denunciation of many British cultural traits and a selective redefinition of other transatlantic characteristics as distinctively American. The crisis of integration had gone full circle by the creation of the American Constitution in 1787: constitutional balance in a federal system, once hailed as the defining and unique genius of the British Empire, was proclaimed to be quintessentially American. Atlantic integration may have provided an improbable point of origin for Americanization, but Americanization offered a solution, a drastic one, to the enduring problems it created.

The political essayist Arthur Young confidently wrote in 1772 that Great Britain, Ireland, and its colonies throughout the world should be viewed "as parts of one whole."[50] His optimistic pronouncements, however, failed to

---

[50] P. J. Marshall, "Introduction," in Marshall (ed.), *OHBE*, II, pp. 7–8, (quotation, p. 8). Cf. Eliga H. Gould, *The Persistence of Empire: British Political Culture in the Age of the American Revolution* (Chapel Hill, NC, 2000), p. 122.

address contemporary concerns over whether the British Empire could effectively absorb the huge territorial gains acquired at the end of the Seven Years' War and incorporate new, potentially disloyal, subjects who were as culturally distinct as Asians, Indians, Native Americans, and French Canadians.[51] Even the Scots, the Irish, and the Scots Irish would not necessarily welcome political and cultural integration centered on London. While other groups, more suspect still, faced discriminatory treatment, presumptively safer British colonials learned how to play the game of Imperial insider. Imagine the exasperation of the Shawnee and Delaware, for example, upon learning that certain well-placed Virginian gentlemen had in the course of a visit to London secured astounding land grants in the Ohio country. Ironically, despite British politicians' concern after 1775 about the potential loyalty of Native Americans and of migrants who had arrived in the colonies only in the previous decade and a half,[52] it was actually the disloyalty of subjects of British descent long resident in America that the Imperial authorities had most to fear.

In yet another irony, British policies concerning newly acquired territories in North America, be it the Royal Proclamation of 1763 that sealed off the trans-Appalachian West to prevent the provocation of Native American inhabitants or the Quebec Act in 1774[53] that secured the religious and legal rights of the French-Catholic population, generally upset residents of already established British colonies, including hitherto pro-Imperial colonial elites. Many British colonists felt these Imperial decisions ran counter to their interests and contrary to their idealized vision of an integrated empire: a single administrative system that would embody and propagate Protestantism, English liberties including the Common Law, and self-government through legislative assemblies. The colonial elites ordinarily acted as intermediaries between Imperial initiatives and local interests. In the decade after the end of the Seven Years' War, these stabilizing functions were seriously

---

[51] Cf. Gordon S. Wood, *Radicalism of the American Revolution*, pp. 213–15, 232, 240–3; P. J. Marshall, "Britain and the World in the Eighteenth Century: I, Reshaping the Empire," *Transactions of the Royal Historical Society*, 6th ser., VIII (1998), pp. 1–18, esp. pp. 2–3; Marshall, *The Making and Unmaking of Empires*, 45–56.

[52] Almost 100,000 British migrants arrived in the thirteen colonies, 1760–1775. See Bailyn, *Voyagers to the West*; James Horn, "The British Diaspora: Emigration from Britain, 1660–1815," in Marshall (ed.), *OHBE*, II, pp. 28–52, esp. p. 32.

[53] For the Quebec Act, see Philip Lawson, *The Imperial Challenge: Quebec and Britain in the Age of the American Revolution* (Montreal, 1989), pp. 126–45.

undermined in two directions at once: they themselves became suspicious of the actions and motives of the crown at just the moment when their hitherto valuable Imperial connections suddenly contaminated them in the eyes of their colonial compatriots, who were visceral anti-Catholics and who relied on westward expansion as the basis for providing for future generations once choice eastern lands were settled and the remaining undeveloped tracts were claimed by leading families and influential speculators.

After 1763, the backwoods offered no escape from Empire. Territorial expansion perpetuated British conflict with European rivals and the settlers' conflict with resident indigenous populations, refueling imperial rivalries and increasing colonial dependence on British military strength. From a would-be settler's point of view the British, by concluding treaties with Native Americans and by trying to keep land-hungry British-American colonists at a distance, had simply become the French reincarnate.[54] Migration to western parts of existing colonies or to the Ohio Valley produced conflict between settlers and Native Americans and between colonists and Britons, as well as among the colonists themselves, as they all competed for control of the West.

Although British authorities were respectful of the rights of both Native American and French Canadian subjects, they were quite willing to impose innovative and unpopular policies in other parts of British North America. Whitehall was looking for both a rejuvenation of existing forms of government, including a financially independent royal executive and strengthened Admiralty courts, and an augmentation of it through the American board of customs commissioners, the standing army, and sources of revenue that were not dependent on the consent of the colonial legislatures.[55] The older forms of negotiation and collaboration were seen by

[54] William J. Eccles, "Iroquois, French, British: Imperial Rivalry in the Ohio Valley," in *Pathways To The Old Northwest: An Observance of the Bicentennial of the Northwest Ordinance* (Indianapolis, 1988), pp. 19–29, esp. p. 28; Colin G. Calloway, *Crown and Calumet: British-Indian Relations, 1783–1815* (Norman, OK, 1987); Matthew C. Ward, "'The Indians our Real Friends': The British Army and the Ohio Indians, 1758–1772," in Daniel P. Barr (ed.), *The Boundaries Between Us: Natives and Newcomers along the Frontiers of the Old Northwest Territory, 1750–1850* (Kent, Ohio, 2006), pp. 66–86; Michael N. McConnell, *Army and Empire: British Soldiers on the American Frontier, 1758–1775* (Lincoln, NE, 2004); Robert S. Allen, *His Majesty's Indian Allies: British Indian Policy in the Defence of Canada, 1774–1815* (Toronto, 1992); Daniel K. Richter, "Native Peoples of North America and the Eighteenth-Century British Empire," in Marshall (ed.), *OHBE*, II, pp. 347–71.

[55] Cf. Greene, "The American Revolution," pp. 96, 99–100; Marshall, *The Making and Unmaking of Empires*, pp. 75–7.

Whitehall as the means for a long series of colonial acts of aggression effecting a progressive *dis*-integration of empire that had reached a point where some British politicians charged the colonists with aiming for independence long before they themselves were willing to contemplate so drastic a step.[56] Concerns that the existing means of Imperial governance would not be sufficient to hold the Empire together became a self-fulfilling prophecy when measures to curb colonial autonomy backfired, uniting the colonists in the common cause of opposition to Imperial centralization. The view of the Revolutionary leadership was that the individual colonies had first been founded voluntarily, then with their consent had been joined into a loosely united larger whole, and were now, in the 1770s, threatened by unprecedented and illegitimate impositions from the metropolitan center that were intended to subvert the happy constitutional balance they had achieved prior to 1763. What had emerged after that date were different visions or styles of Imperial political integration that diverged, at first subtly, and then sharply from one another.[57]

The new attempt at political centralization called attention to the structural problems in the existing colonial–British relationship. When British authorities tried to use parliamentary statutes to recapture powers given up by previous desperate or clumsy colonial governors they met unexpected, fierce resistance.[58] Recurrent bouts of advance and retreat eventually weakened the confidence of each side in the good faith of the other, while the sheer volume of inter- and intra-colonial disputes engendered in the process overloaded the circuits of an administrative organization that had been created in simpler times, some fifty to seventy years earlier. In the effort to increase formal control of the colonies at once Whitehall risked the total loss of their informal empire.

---

[56] For this interpretation see John M. Murrin, "A Roof Without Walls: The Dilemma of American National Identity," in Richard Beeman, Stephen Botein and Edward C. Carter, II (eds), *Beyond Confederation: Origins of the Constitution and American National Identity* (Chapel Hill, NC, 1987), pp. 333–48, esp. p. 339; Greene, "The American Revolution," p. 99; H.T. Dickinson, "Britain's Imperial Sovereignty: The Ideological Case against the American Colonists," in Dickinson (ed.), *Britain and the American Revolution* (London, 1998), pp. 64–96, esp. pp. 66–7.

[57] See J. G. A. Pocock, "1776: The Revolution against Parliament," in *Three British Revolutions*, pp. 265–88, esp. p. 275.

[58] For the clash, cf. Edmund S. Morgan and Helen M. Morgan, *The Stamp Act Crisis: Prologue to Revolution* (New York, 1976, orig. publ. 1953), pp. 52–4, 57–8; Greene, *Peripheries and Center*, pp. 79–104; Dickinson, "Britain's Imperial Sovereignty," pp. 81–94.

Whitehall is often described as working from out-of-date assumptions. It is no less reasonable to argue that it was in a sense too prescient. Perceiving, however imperfectly, the degree to which the colonists had anglicized in their habits of consumption and their ways of thinking and also aware of the extent to which they had been incorporated, sometimes against sustained opposition, into a functioning Imperial system, politicians and bureaucrats alike underestimated the difficulties of raising revenue in the colonies and of further strengthening the central government. The widely-held belief that the colonists' pretensions to poverty were so much camouflage of substantial wealth, as well as the conviction that they had not paid their fair share of the expenses of the last war, further encouraged the attempt to make the Americans do more towards retiring Imperial debts.[59] British policy-makers were not wholly wrong on any of these counts but the changes in the colonies were actually less complete and more ambiguous than they supposed. Colonial elites profited from their alliances with royal government but were not therefore particularly willing to accept an increase in *Parliamentary* power in America and, even if they did acquiesce in the new measures, colonial society was still not so hierarchical, whatever direction it was ultimately moving in, as to give them sufficient leverage to overcome the opposition of the middling and lower orders to new taxes and tighter regulations. Expecting widespread if grudging American compliance, policy-makers gave little serious consideration to securing colonial cooperation in advance, and banking on the popularity of the British army in America in the final, victorious years of the previous war, they paid no attention to the widespread suspicions of a standing army in peacetime.[60] In general, they assumed that their authority would be recognized without serious opposition and that, if any did develop, the means of coercion could somehow be found from existing resources.

[59] Marshall, "Britain and the World in the Eighteenth Century: II, Britons and Americans," pp. 10–11; I.R. Christie, *Crisis of Empire: Great Britain and the American Colonies, 1754–1783* (New York, 1966), p. 45; Dickinson, "Britain's Imperial Sovereignty," p. 69.

[60] John Shy, *Toward Lexington: The Role of the British Army in the Coming of the American Revolution*, (Princeton, 1965), pp. 45–83; and John A. Bullion, "'The Ten Thousand in America': More Light on the Decision on the American Army, 1762–1763," *WMQ*, 3rd ser., XLIII (1986), pp. 646–57. On the degree to which American fear of a standing army derived from a British tradition that had largely disappeared in the metropole itself, see Gould, *Persistence of Empire*, pp. 110–16; Gould, "Fears of War, Fantasies of Peace: British Politics and the Coming of the American Revolution," in Eliga H. Gould and Peter S. Onuf (eds), *Empire and Nation: The American Revolution in the Atlantic World* (Baltimore, 2005), pp. 28–31.

Colonial responses were in a perverse way a tribute to the Britishness of American political life. An initial willingness to play a British-style political game of lobbying and petitioning ended in disillusionment when it failed to produce much of benefit, though the effort did bring the Americans into close contact with the "Country" critics of government corruption and with radical politicians of the stamp of John Wilkes.[61] While in England, Arthur Lee befriended Wilkes and other English radicals, and Wilkes' supporters in America included the Bostonian Samuel Adams and Chief Justice William Allen of Pennsylvania.[62] The Britishness of colonial protests was also evident in the initial reluctance to entertain a comprehensive indictment of an irredeemably wicked system. Instead, American objectives were limited to seeking the repeal of specific laws and placing the blame for them on named individuals, such as Lord Bute, George Grenville, Charles Townshend, and Lord North.[63]

The content of the American protest was in part home grown, but it can also be interpreted as so many localized restatements of English radicalism. There were well-developed strains within British political thought critical of parliamentary claims to omnicompetence, virtual representation, and the heavy, regressive taxation that was held to be the means to fund government placemen and pensioners, as well as to purchase votes through treating and outright bribery.[64] Over and above any challenge to a given measure was the broader fear, derived from English experience and English radical thought, that new British taxes were just the thin end of a wedge that would eventually

[61] Caroline Robbins, *The Eighteenth-Century Commonwealthman: Studies in the Transmission, Development, and Circumstance of English Liberal Thought from the Restoration of Charles II until the War with the Thirteen Colonies* (Cambridge, MA, 1959); J. G. A. Pocock, *The Machiavellian Moment: Florentine Political Thought and the Atlantic Republican Tradition* (Princeton, 1975); Bailyn, *Ideological Origins*; Colin Bonwick, *English Radicals and the American Revolution* (Chapel Hill, NC, 1977).

[62] Norman S. Cohen, "Allen, William (August 5, 1704–September 6, 1780)," in *American National Biography*, I, pp. 344–5; on Wilkes's connection with John Adams and Samuel Adams, see James B. Bell, *A War of Religion: Dissenters, Anglicans, and the American Revolution* (Houndmills, 2008), pp. 90–106.

[63] For various statements of colonists' rights as Englishmen see "The Declaration of the Stamp Act Congress," October 19, 1765, in Jack P. Greene (ed.), *Colonies to Nation, 1763–1789: A Documentary History of the American Revolution* (New York, 1975, orig. publ. 1967), pp. 63–5, esp. p. 64; Daniel Dulany, "Considerations on the Propriety of Imposing Taxes in the British Colonies...," in Greene, *Colonies to Nation*, pp. 51–9, esp. p. 57; The Virginia Resolves, May 30, 1765, in Greene, *Colonies to Nation*, pp. 60–1, esp. p. 60. See also Gould, *Persistence of Empire*, pp. 123–6.

[64] John Brewer "English Radicalism in the Age of George III," in *Three British Revolutions*, pp. 323–67, esp. pp. 337–41.

make the colonies uniformly overtaxed and over-governed.[65] Appropriately, the classic statement of this case came from a former English exciseman who had only been in the colonies a short period when he published the quintes- sentially "American" *Common Sense*. Colonial patriots drew their arguments from the same wellspring of ideas as apologists for British policy, each side basing their claims on principles of British liberty so fundamental as to forbid any significant compromises. This shared commitment to the unalterable led to intransigence and paranoia on both sides. British politicians came to the position that every British law affecting the colonies needed to be defended with the full force of the government's authority, while insurgent colonists came to see every British law extending to the colonies as another part of the same systematic plot.[66] When the power of vice-admiralty courts (which operated without juries) was expanded, many colonists interpreted the change as an attack on their basic judicial rights, rather than merely a heavy-handed method to enforce trade and revenue laws.[67] Meanwhile, British administrators viewed the actions of American colonists, from the support of the South Carolina assembly for John Wilkes to the destruction of tea in Boston, as part of a single continuum of increasing lawlessness that required firm correction, sooner rather than later. The Duke of Newcastle, a survivor of an earlier era, considered the Declaratory Act a pointless distrac- tion that kept Parliament from repealing ill-considered taxes before they wreaked havoc throughout the Empire. His nephew, Lord North later took the more dogmatic position concerning the tea duty that the more a right was challenged, the more it needed to be enforced, regardless of the material stakes involved. Perceptions of growing American anarchy embarrassed and si- lenced those British friends of the colonies who had argued for the fair treatment of Americans as British subjects and legitimated the coercive approach as the only reasonable British course of action by 1774.[68]

---

[65] Brewer, "English Radicalism," pp. 339–40, 356–7, 362. See also Christie, *Crisis of Empire*, pp. vi, 50.

[66] Bailyn, *Ideological Origins*; Gordon S. Wood, "Rhetoric and Reality in the American Revolution," *WMQ*, 3rd ser., XXIII (1966), pp. 3–32. See also Colin Bonwick, *The American Revolution* (Charlottesville, VA, 1991), p. 70, for ministerial attitudes.

[67] On vice-admiralty courts, see Carl Ubbelohde, *The Vice-Admiralty Courts and the Ameri- can Revolution* (Chapel Hill, NC, 1960).

[68] Jacob Price, "Who Cared About the Colonies?" in Bailyn and Morgan (eds), *Strangers within the Realm*, pp. 395–436; James E. Bradley, *Popular Politics and the American Revolution in England: Petitions, the Crown, and Public Opinion* (Macon, GA, 1986).

The mutual extremism of the final period of the Revolution was not typical of what came earlier. For the better part of a decade American protestors had responded to perceived encroachments on representation, local self-government, or trial by jury, not by rejecting ties with Britain, but rather by trying to employ their understanding of empire to legitimize their opposition to British measures. As well as the familiar devices of petitioning and lobbying, colonial protestors for the first time resorted to non-importation agreements on the presumption—a sign of confidence, if not hubris—that the disruption of American markets for British goods would force repeal of obnoxious legislation as the only alternative to the collapse of the British economy.[69] Consumer goods became politically charged: the willingness to purchase tea became a litmus test for loyalism, while homespun was widely touted as a practical alternative to imported British cloth and, eventually, as a symbol of republican simplicity and virtue. The redefinition of British goods as so many tokens of the British corruption threatening a pristine American society was part of this process of renouncing the Imperial–colonial relationship. Gambling, elaborate funerals, and the genteel pastimes of theatre and horseracing, all formerly markers of civility, were also now luxurious, wasteful, and "aristocratic."[70] Although this reformation of manners might seem an American innovation, the same reforming asceticism had been sweeping through Britain as well.[71] Now, however, the rejection of luxury became a patriot strategy to demonize the British enemy, as well as discredit its colonial supporters with the taint of vice. In a taxonomic sleight of hand luxury became British and virtue American. The process was duplicated across the cultural spectrum: hitherto admirable British qualities were transmuted into defining colonial traits, and their opposites attributed to the metropole.

Britain's federal form of Imperial governance was for a time the genius of successive Continental Congresses, and what were seen as *executive* powers,

---

[69] Breen, "Empire of Goods"; Breen, "'Baubles of Britain': The American and Consumer Revolutions of the Eighteenth Century," *Past & Present*, 119 (May, 1988), pp. 73–104 considers whether the path to America ran through anglicization, and whether American revolutionaries, in turn, attempted to control the process. Breen, *The Marketplace of Revolution* advances this discussion, claiming the expanding marketplace challenged Americans to reconsider their relationship with Britain.

[70] Ann Fairfax Withington, *Toward a More Perfect Union: Virtue and the Formation of American Republics* (New York, 1991), pp. 217–44.

[71] G. J. Baker-Benfield, *The Culture of Sensibility: Sex and Society in Eighteenth-Century Britain* (Chicago, 1992), pp. 215–86.

such as defense and foreign affairs, were stripped from the crown and transferred there.[72] In actuality there was an extensive pre-history to the Continental Congresses in which various projected overhauls of Imperial governance were proposed containing some sort of inter-colonial super-legislature with designated responsibilities in such obvious areas as coordinated military policy and Indian diplomacy. The Albany Plan of Union is the best known of these exercises and the Galloway Plan of 1774 was their last appearance in an Imperial context. At the best of times, metropolitan officials suspected that the projected inter-colonial governments might challenge their authority. In the 1770s, an extra-legal Continental Congress was inevitably seen as latently revolutionary even though the moderate majority of its members likely envisioned the First Continental Congress as a step towards a reformed empire. Galloway's proposed Plan of Union received serious consideration largely because of the influence of these moderates, men who were Imperial integrationists, though of a different stripe from their counterparts among British politicians and Imperial officialdom.[73]

Whatever might have been, between 1774 and 1776 British intransigence and the imperatives of war rendered the moderate position untenable. The sense of loyalty to the king, the most persistent of the Imperial ties, diminished significantly in the first year of the war through the King's own actions.[74] Independence then became the only solution left. Or so radicals claimed. Yet even the Declaration when it finally came in 1776 was not intended as a proclamation of a new American culture so distinct from that of Britain as to require an entirely separate polity to give it expression.[75] Instead, the necessity and urgency of independence derived from the remorseless exigencies of war. As Richard Henry Lee claimed, "It is not choice then, but necessity that calls for Independence as the only means by which foreign Alliances can

---

[72] Jerrilyn Greene Marston, *King and Congress: The Transfer of Political Legitimacy, 1774–1776* (Princeton, 1987).

[73] Bonwick, *The American Revolution*, pp. 80–2; Jack N. Rakove, *The Beginnings of National Politics: An Interpretive History of the Continental Congress* (Baltimore, 1982, orig. publ. 1979), pp. 60–1.

[74] Brendan McConville, *The King's Three Faces: The Rise and Fall of Royal America, 1688–1776* (Chapel Hill, NC, 2006); Winthrop D. Jordan, "Familial Politics: Thomas Paine and the Killing of the King 1776," *Journal of American History*, LX (1973), pp. 294–308; Jeremy Black, *George III: America's Last King* (New Haven, 2006), pp. 209–63, esp. pp. 222–5. However, Pauline Maier, *From Resistance to Revolution*, pp. 198–227, argues the implication of George III occurred earlier, in 1770–1772.

[75] Bonwick, *The American Revolution*, pp. 94–5.

be obtained...."[76] Only by declaring themselves a separate nation could revolutionaries acquire necessary foreign military and naval aid and negotiate crucial treaties of cooperation with France and Spain.[77] The same war that ended the integration of the thirteen colonies within the Empire promoted an independent America's Atlantic integration, in part by forging these new political-military alliances, in part because so much of the fate of the American theatre was tied to European developments.

The defeat of the moderates and the flight of many royal officeholders after the fall of royal governments, colony by colony, made it nearly impossible for the British to find any permanent allies among the American upper classes in their attempts to recover their control over the colonies. The men who took up the leadership of the Revolution had for the most part been enthusiastic integrationists earlier in their careers. Allowing for personal considerations in a few well-known instances,[78] their collective about-face, which left the king bereft of friends among the colonial elite, can only be explained by reference to a combination of structural weaknesses in the Empire itself, distinctive local circumstances, and individual idiosyncrasies. Arguably, the royal governors always lacked sufficient patronage to snare aspiring colonial gentlemen in the Imperial web, while the colonial political leadership depended far more than their British equivalents on the good will of a large electorate and therefore could not flout with impunity the widespread hostility to Imperial measures.[79] When negotiating with British administrators, colonial elites did their best to play at being fellow members of an imagined transatlantic Anglophone aristocracy. In reality, they were also local creatures enmeshed in complex family connections, committed to their farms and businesses, and sensitive by inclination as well as necessity to the peculiar concerns of the various localities where they exercised their uncertain power.

---

[76] Lee also contrasted American efforts, including "earnest, early, and repeated petitions for peace, liberty and safety..." with the actions of "our enemies [who] press us with war, threaten us with danger and Slavery." Richard Henry Lee to Landon Carter, June 2, 1776, in David Brion Davis and Steven Mintz (eds), *The Boisterous Sea of Liberty: A Documentary History of America from Discovery Through the Civil War* (New York, 1998), p. 182.

[77] For a different interpretation see Eliga H. Gould and Peter S. Onuf, "Introduction," in *Empire and Nation*, p. 5.

[78] Gordon S. Wood, *The Americanization of Benjamin Franklin* (New York, 2004), pp. 105–13; 145–51.

[79] Bernard Bailyn, *The Origins of American Politics*, pp. 68–85, esp. p. 80.

This is not to say that Britain entirely lacked support on the American mainland. The considerable difficulty the revolutionaries faced, even after war broke out, in persuading large bodies of their fellow colonists to abandon their traditional allegiances, suggests that several generations of membership in the British Empire had left its mark. Constituting an estimated 20 percent of the colonial population,[80] loyalists could be found at every point on the colonial social hierarchy, from royal officeholders to the most ordinary men and women. This lack of clear social definition was precisely what led to the unease about the loyalties of various dissident groups and to high-handed measures to detect covert Tories. Revolutionaries frequently gave the strength of the loyalists as well in excess of the modern estimate of one person in five and were likely to suspect the sincerity of those claiming to be neutral, such as Quakers and other pacifists.

Like many forms of paranoia, the widespread belief that many loyalists were hidden from official view was a gross exaggeration of a partial truth. Groups outside the main circles of colonial power, including African Americans, Native Americans, or aggrieved religious and ethnic minorities, *did* tend towards loyalism in some circumstances.[81] Fleeing a form of slavery more literal than any imagined in a Revolutionary manifesto, African Americans took the chance opened to them by wartime chaos to escape behind British lines or to respond to such British initiatives as Lord Dunmore's promise of freedom for slaves and servants of patriot masters who joined the British army.[82] Native Americans, who are rarely counted in the estimates of loyalists, correctly anticipated that an American victory would unleash wave upon wave of settlers on to their lands. Consequently, most of those taking up arms sided with the British, and some groups, such as the Mohawks, like other loyalists, relocated to Canada following the end of the war.[83] That at least 60,000 loyalist émigrés and 15,000

---

[80] Paul H. Smith, "The American Loyalists: Notes on their Organization and Numerical Strength," *WMQ*, 3rd ser., XXV (1968), pp. 259–77.

[81] William H. Nelson, *The American Tory* (Boston, 1992, orig. publ. 1961), pp. 89–90.

[82] Sylvia R. Frey, *Water from the Rock: Black Resistance in a Revolutionary Age* (Princeton, 1991); Ira Berlin and Ronald Hoffman (eds), *Slavery and Freedom in the Age of the American Revolution* (Charlottesville, VA, 1983); Woody Holton, *Forced Founders: Indians, Debtors, Slaves, and the Making of the American Revolution in Virginia* (Chapel Hill, NC, 1999); and Holton, "'Rebel Against Rebel': Enslaved Virginians and the Coming of the American Revolution," *Virginia Magazine of History and Biography*, CX (1997), pp. 157–92.

[83] Richter, "Native Peoples of North America"; Colin G. Calloway, *The American Revolution in Indian Country: Crisis and Diversity in Native American Communities* (Cambridge, 1995).

slaves, roughly one in forty members of the American population, fled to Britain, the British Caribbean, or Canada is a testament to the continued integrity of the British Atlantic.[84] After the war, the British government compensated civilian loyalists who could prove their material losses and distributed land grants to former loyalist soldiers, thereby encouraging further movement. Such migrations helped to redefine the post-1783 British Empire and recast Britain's relations with Spanish America and the new United States. (It also illustrates the permeability of national boundaries.)[85] The subsequent reintegration of loyalists within American society and the reconnection of loyalist émigrés with their former communities and distant family members may help to explain why American–British relations rebounded so quickly after 1783, as well as the revival of Anglophilia as a prominent feature of American federalism in the 1790s.

Loyalist ideology has been ably explored as a traditional affirmation of the values of law, order, and moderation, and as an act of faith in king and Parliament, the established church, and rule by a landed aristocracy.[86] What still needs emphasis, however, is the way in which loyalism in America was also a rejection of the Revolution brought on by the more zealous revolutionaries themselves, especially the various committees of safety, whose overbearing actions alienated moderate and potential supporters of the American cause. Consider Massachusetts, a colony famous for its revolutionaries and its long history of intransigence that still managed to contribute proportionately more loyalists from its upper political ranks than any other colony.[87] The reason for this apparent anomaly is one of those political and social disconnections of which much has been made, but at the level of provincial, not Imperial politics. In Massachusetts, Revolutionary leadership consisted, as it did in many other colonies, of younger men who had entered politics only in the 1760s on the basis of a strenuous critique of the reflexive support of the old

---

[84] Maya Jasanoff, "The Other Side of Revolution: Loyalists in the British Empire," *WMQ*, 3rd ser., XLV (2008), pp. 205–32, esp. p. 208; Keith Mason, "The American Loyalist Diaspora and the Reconfiguration of the British Atlantic World," in Gould and Onuf (eds), *Empire and Nation*, pp. 239–59.

[85] Mason, "The American Loyalist Diaspora," pp. 242–5, 257; and Maya Jasanoff, *Liberty's Exiles: American Loyalists in the Revolutionary World* (New York, 2011).

[86] Robert M. Calhoon, *Dominion and Liberty: Ideology and the Anglo-American World, 1660–1801* (Arlington Heights, IL, 1994).

[87] William Pencak, *War, Politics, and Revolution in Provincial Massachusetts* (Boston, MA, 1981), pp. 213–29.

elites for the Empire. By the same token, the colony's prominent loyalists included older, more experienced statesmen who had taken an active part in the wars against France and, uniquely among colonial legislators, endorsed the Albany Plan of Union.[88] Their enthusiasm for the Empire was not bought with patronage but sprang from their ambition to play a part in what they saw as a polity of both global and epochal importance. Once they embraced the Empire this closely they could not pull themselves free. Instead, they were increasingly disoriented by the new imperatives of the post-1763 era, alienated from politics by Revolutionary leaders at the provincial level, and increasingly hostile to popular politics generally. The Imperial patriots of 1759 were the Tory traitors to their country of 1776.

The ability of Great Britain to continue the war in America for an extended period meant that the British Empire, directly and indirectly, had an influence on the shaping of the United States, even during the war that ended its control of most of its North American colonies. For those colonists disgruntled by Revolutionary management of the war, such as Benedict Arnold, or for those disillusioned citizens-soldiers who felt they were unfairly bearing the cost of other people's patriotism, the earlier form of governance regained some of its attraction.[89] Wartime experience in the Continental Army, characterized by physical hardship, shortages of food and supplies, and pay arrears, could lead to defection, desertion, or mutiny, as in the case of the Pennsylvania Line.[90] Whatever their original inclinations, therefore, as the war progressed, the Revolutionary leadership, recognizing the need to buy popular support, endorsed increasingly radical measures. The new states took bold initiatives including religious disestablishment, expanded franchises, state bills of rights, promises of larger land warrants, and (in the North) freedom for slaves whose masters allowed

[88] Pencak, *War, Politics and Revolution*, pp. 214, 222.

[89] James Kirby Martin, *Benedict Arnold, Revolutionary Hero: An American Warrior Reconsidered* (New York, 1997); Martin and Mark Edward Lender, *A Respectable Army: The Military Origins of the Republic, 1763–1789*, 2nd edn (Wheeling, IL, 2006, orig. publ. 1982), pp. 160–1. For a study of the impact of recruitment and conscription on lower and middling people in Virginia, see Michael A. McDonnell, *The Politics of War: Race, Class and Conflict in Revolutionary Virginia* (Chapel Hill, NC, 2007); and McDonnell, "'Fit for Common Service?': Class, Race and Recruitment in Revolutionary Virginia," in John Resch and Walter Sargent (eds), *War and Society in the American Revolution: Mobilization and Home Fronts* (DeKalb, IL, 2007), pp. 103–31.

[90] E. Wayne Carp, *To Starve the Army at Pleasure: Continental Army Administration and American Political Culture, 1775–1783* (Chapel Hill, NC, 1984); Martin and Lender, *A Respectable Army*, pp. 162–5.

them to fight in the American armies. Such incentives recognized that the Revolutionary and British armies were each in their different ways contending for the loyalty of the people.[91]

Imperial experience shaped Revolutionary America in yet another way: long wars require participants to learn from the enemy. To wage war against Britain, the revolutionaries needed a more British state. Their newly independent America was a jerry-rigged polity of decidedly limited firepower and resources, sitting atop a society so under-organized that even its means of coercion, such as they were, were in essence voluntary: the local committees of safety charged with dealing with disloyalty, and the state governments that complied with national military requisitions at their own discretion. Not surprisingly, among those calling most loudly for a stronger central government were the military officers, George Washington not least among them. Similarly, to stand up to its British enemy, the Revolutionary army eventually had to become more like it, abandoning the citizen-soldier mystique of the militias in exchange for the professionalism of a regular army. At first, the Americans reverted to British forms of military culture that were already familiar to the more experienced military leaders. In time, the tried and true from the Imperial Wars was replaced by more workable expedients when Baron Friedrich von Steuben, an expert in Prussian training and drilling procedures, implemented a European plan in his training of American regulars. He insisted on junior officers leading the training of their men, in a manner he believed differed notably from British practice.[92]

The experience of waging war and all that entailed encouraged almost continuous tinkering with the various constitutional orders, state and national, and, with more lasting effect, it led as well to considered reflection about the extent to which American circumstances warranted divergence from a British political culture. A nearly total rejection of the British model in 1776 was followed by a lengthy reconsideration, culminating in a new federal Constitution that maintained many British qualities, though these were frequently reinvented as distinctively American. The first state constitutions written in 1776 reflected the radical, democratic tone of the day in

---

[91] John Shy, "The American Revolution: The Military Conflict Considered as a Revolutionary War," in Stephen G. Kurtz and James H. Huston (eds), *Essays on the American Revolution* (Chapel Hill, NC, 1973), pp. 121–56, esp. 126.

[92] Martin and Lender, *A Respectable Army*, pp. 114–15. While not an egalitarian in any sense, Steuben also promoted loyalty within the field units by having junior officers share quarters with their men.

that they curtailed executive functions and expanded legislative powers. In two cases they even abolished the upper house of the legislature entirely. Later state constitutions took a more moderate approach, emulating the Massachusetts constitution of 1780, while the earlier radical state constitutions were rewritten to restore balance between the two houses of the legislature and to provide a significant role for executive authority. At the national level, innovations in American constitutionalism were greater, despite an early reliance on idealized Imperial models. The Articles of Confederation, legitimating an early wartime improvisation, provided for a unicameral legislature in which each sovereign state would have an equal vote and major decisions required unanimous consent. The Confederation was, in effect, the form of Imperial governance leaders of colonial protests might have wished they had in 1763, one based on the presumptions of the equality of all the parts of the whole.[93] Yet by the creation of the new national Constitution of 1787, the principles of federation once again defeated those of confederation. The document ultimately became a unifying symbol for the new nation, but, like the Declaration of Independence, at the time of its creation it was both controversial and divisive.[94]

The Empire was both model and anti-model for the new Federal Union. Even those welcoming the Constitution as a kind of re-Europeanization of America had to reconcile the document with republican principles, including a widespread aversion to interventionist government.[95] American federalism developed in the crossfire as a conscious refinement rather than a rejection of British values. Revolutionaries had discarded monarchy but, by giving substantial powers to the President, the Constitution maintained a strong national executive, though not a hereditary one. The Revolution cast off hereditary privilege generally but initially did little else to prevent continued rule by the traditional elite. Instead, political leaders in America recast themselves, however optimistically, as Thomas Jefferson urged, as members of the "natural aristocracy." Meanwhile, the Constitution largely preserved British concepts of representation and mixed government.[96]

[93] Don Higginbotham, "War and State Formation in Revolutionary America," in Gould and Onuf (eds), *Empire and Nation*, p. 61.

[94] Murrin, "A Roof Without Walls," p. 346.

[95] Max Edling, *A Revolution in Favor of Government: Origins of the U.S. Constitution and the Making of the American State* (Oxford, 2003), pp. 8–10.

[96] Gordon S. Wood, *The Creation of the American Republic, 1776–1787* (Chapel Hill, NC, 1969), pp. 513–16, 561–2.

It reversed the earlier Revolutionary experiment with a unicameral legislature, the Continental Congress, and instead created a bicameral legislature
that tried to balance equal representation with proportional representation.
The three ideal types of British government, monarchy, aristocracy, and
democracy, had clear American counterparts in the new Federal government, and American Federalists also claimed that other devices, such as the
strict American separation of powers between the executive, legislative, and
judicial branches, further extended and improved on the British notion of a
balanced constitution.[97]

After more than two decades of trying to exorcize British traits from
American governance, national, state, or local, the Constitution in many
ways sounded the retreat. This recovery of a British-style balanced polity
with strengthened powers and resources was made palatable for republicans
by the form of its enactment, which was touted as a continuation of Revolutionary methods and a realization of Revolutionary goals. The legitimacy
of the polity created rested on popular sovereignty in its American
embodiment: elected ratifying conventions. This innovation, theoretical
and practical at once, had a "spill over" effect in affirming and enshrining
egalitarianism as the defining American characteristic. Even so, the Constitution's opponents, among them leading revolutionaries like Patrick Henry,
denounced it as a repudiation of the principles of 1776 in favor of a return to
discredited British principles. They were not wholly wrong, but the mode of
ratification was also a sign of the extent to which the period between 1775 and
1789 had altered the ways in which Americans thought about politics. The
exigencies of independence, of having to govern and not merely to oppose,
could only be legitimated in terms of a revolutionary, egalitarian rhetoric.

In the immediate aftermath of the Revolution, the traditional governing
classes, the colonial gentlemen who had once merely wanted a more equal
role for themselves in the Empire, remained very much in charge of the new
republic. The difference was that their political eminence rested mainly on a
fragile coalition with their sometime inferiors, an awkward but workable
sharing of common goals, not on some assured status in the hierarchical,
English-style society that had seemed to be emerging in the colonies when
the Empire was at its short-lived zenith. There had been a successful

---

[97] On continued disagreement between Federalists and Republicans about whether the
delegates to the Constitutional Convention had gotten it right, see Joyce Appleby, *Inheriting
the Revolution: The First Generation of Americans* (Cambridge, MA, 2000).

political revolution in 1776 that put an end formally to the anglicization of America, one way or another. It had not, however, overthrown other long-standing ties to the *quondam* Mother Country.[98] Once the war concluded, migration from Britain quickly resumed its earlier patterns and then exceeded them. Economic links with Britain were restored and the importation of British goods quickly soared and surpassed pre-1775 levels. Business and familial ties that had been stretched during wartime could be restored with reasonable efficiency, and Americans seemed as willing as they had ever been to export their commodities to British markets. The mechanisms of nationhood that produced the new republic and dramatically recast British political aspirations in an American mould no doubt deserve the attention they have received. One may wonder, nonetheless, if other aspects of the process of Atlantic integration, such as the ties of family, religion, trade, and indeed the whole informal web of associations by which people lived their lives, were not more resilient and, ultimately, more important.

The American nation of 1789 was not merely the British mainland colonies of 1763 with a burnished new facade. Disestablishment during the Revolution ended the religious privileges of the Church of England in America and those of the Congregational churches in New England would go the same way in the early republic. Any social practice that hinted at the former British rule or could be interpreted as in some sense "aristocratic" was subject to searching criticism: the Constitution's prohibition of the use of titles in America quite intentionally laid out how America would be different from Britain. All of these measures required a conscious re-evaluation and sometimes a rejection of the consequences of Imperial and Atlantic integration. In the end, Americans of the Revolutionary generation managed, at least in their own view, to re-balance integration and Americanization. They disagreed in the 1780s about whether they had gotten the mix right and they continued to do so in the opening years of the early republic in the course of hotly contested debates about whether America owed support to France, a fellow republic, when it descended into a reign of terror, anti-clericalism, and lawlessness. Debate over the Jay Treaty similarly revealed deep disagreements over what should be the appropriate trading and international relationship with Britain. Just as the Federalists had argued in the 1790s, Americanization need not be a rejection of Britain.

---

[98] See Jay Sexton, "Epilogue" in this volume.

It was clearly, however, going to be a conscious, selective retention of things Imperial in order to reconcile them with the republican and egalitarian values of the American Revolution.

Select Bibliography

I. R. CHRISTIE, *Crisis of Empire: Great Britain and the American Colonies, 1754–1783* (New York, 1966).

H. T. DICKINSON (ed.), *Britain and the American Revolution* (London, 1998).

JULIE FLAVELL and STEPHEN CONWAY (eds), *Britain and America Go to War: The Impact of War and Warfare in Anglo-America, 1754–1815* (Gainesville, FL, 2004).

ELIGA H. GOULD, *The Persistence of Empire: British Political Culture in the Age of the American Revolution* (Chapel Hill, NC, 2000).

ELIGA H. GOULD and PETER S. ONUF (eds), *Empire and Nation: The American Revolution in the Atlantic World* (Baltimore, 2005).

JACK P. GREENE, "The American Revolution," *American Historical Review*, CV (2000), pp. 93–102.

P. J. MARSHALL, "Britain and the World in the Eighteenth Century: I, Reshaping the Empire," *Transactions of the Royal Historical Society*, 6th ser, VIII (1998), pp. 1–18.

P. J. MARSHALL, "Britain and the World in the Eighteenth Century: II, Britons and Americans," *Transactions of the Royal Historical Society*, 6th ser., IX (1999), pp. 1–16.

P. J. MARSHALL, *The Making and Unmaking of Empires: Britain, India, and America c. 1750–1783* (Oxford, 2005).

BRENDAN MCCONVILLE, *The King's Three Faces: The Rise and Fall of Royal America, 1688–1776* (Chapel Hill, NC, 2006).

JOHN M. MURRIN, "The Great Inversion, or Court versus Country: A Comparison of the Revolution Settlements in England (1688–1721) and America (1776–1816)," in J. G. A. Pocock (ed.), *Three British Revolutions: 1641, 1688, 1776* (Princeton, 1980), pp. 368–453.

KEITH PERRY, *British Politics and the American Revolution* (Houndmills, 1990).

J. G. A. POCOCK, "1776: The Revolution Against Parliament," in J. G. A. Pocock (ed.), *Three British Revolutions: 1641, 1688, 1776* (Princeton, 1980), pp. 265–88.

STEVEN SARSON, *British America, 1500–1800: Creating Colonies, Imagining an Empire* (London, 2005).

PETER D. G. THOMAS, *Revolution in America: Britain and the Colonies, 1763–1776* (Cardiff, 1992).

10

The American Revolution (II)

The Origin and Nature of Colonial Grievances

Daniel J. Hulsebosch

Introduction: A Transatlantic Grievance Network

Colonial grievances were as old as the British Empire. As soon as colonists settled in the Americas, they began to complain about the structure and nature of Imperial governance. Every conceivable problem, large or small, was ripe for a grievance. Complaints arose at all levels of government, from town and county to Westminster. Their number rose and fell over time, and the rate varied across the Empire's territories. But everywhere, they were a constant feature of Imperial governance. The stream of grievances was not, however, evidence that "the spirit of the colonies demanded freedom from the beginning."[1] Paradoxically, grievances helped make the Empire work.

Grievances facilitated Imperial development for two reasons. First, the people lodging grievances could rely on a communication network for processing them, a system that helped integrate the many different subjects and places in the Empire.[2] Second, from the colonial perspective, the Imperial grievance system had a safety valve: war. When the Empire was

---

[1] George Bancroft, *History of the United States, From the Discovery of the American Continent*, 15th edn (Boston, 1854) I, p. vii.

[2] On the Imperial communications network, see Alison G. Olson, *Making the Empire Work: London and American Interest Groups, 1690–1790* (Cambridge, MA, 1992); Michael Kammen, *A Rope of Sand: Colonial Agents, British Politics, and the American Revolution* (Ithaca, N.Y., 1968); Ian K. Steele, *The English Atlantic, 1675–1740: An Exploration of Communication and Community* (New York, 1986); C. A. Bayly, *Intelligence Gathering and Social Communication in India, 1780–1870* (Cambridge, 1996); Harold A. Innis, *Empire and Communication*, rev. edn (Toronto, 1972); Richard R. Johnson, "Intra-Imperial Communications, 1689–1775," in Jack P. Greene and J. R. Pole (eds), *A Companion to the American Revolution* (Malden, MA, 2000), pp. 14–18; Richard Ross, "Legal Communications and Imperial Governance: British North America and

at war, metropolitan policy-makers and local governors were more willing
to compromise with provincial interests and accede to claims that had been
or threatened to become the source of grievances. The two together—the
Imperial grievance system and the leverage enjoyed by colonists during
war—generated the sense throughout North America that the Imperial
constitution was a flexible set of institutions responsive to provincial claims
and yet also efficient enough to facilitate common projects, like carrying out
transatlantic commerce and waging war. The Imperial constitution, with the
grievance system at its core, provided for the possibility of change that is
essential to any workable constitution.

Functionally, people in the colonies used grievances to work out their
relationships with the rest of the Empire, the metropolitan government,
other colonies, and local institutions. By the middle of the eighteenth
century, there were well-developed genres of grievance covering the colonies' internal legislative authority, Imperial trade regulation, customs
collection, legal administration, immigration and naturalization, religious
establishments, land distribution, and Indian affairs. These were the main
subjects, but they did not exhaust the imagination of the colonists or the
capacity of the grievance network.

Unlike the rounds of petitioning preceding the Revolution, colonial grievances did not issue from a unitary group of colonists to a single metropolitan
decision-maker. They flowed in many directions to a variety of audiences.
Colonists often lodged grievances against each other, and Imperial officials
serving in the colonies also transmitted their own complaints back home. In
addition, grievances supplied useful information in the metropole and often
influenced policy. By the middle of the 1770s, however, an effective grievance
system that for decades had integrated the North American colonies into the
Empire, after an unusually long and stable period of peace, had become a
vehicle to divide some British subjects from others, whether in the same
town or county or across the Atlantic. The network had begun to operate
selectively, binding particular provincial groups within each colony to each
other and to similar groups in other colonies. Neighbors who had formerly
worked together became unable to cooperate, while colonists in different
provinces found themselves linked in new combinations. Messages to
London became increasingly overwrought. Only then, in the middle of

Spanish America Compared," in Michael Grossberg and Christopher Tomlins (eds), *The
Cambridge History of Law in America* (Cambridge, 2008), I, pp. 104–43.

1776, were the many and sometimes inconsistent colonial grievances com-
piled into a "history of repeated injuries and usurpations, all having in direct
object the establishment of an absolute Tyranny over these States." The
grievance suddenly became an instrument for civil war.

In English Ways: Grievance Languages and Networks

The Imperial grievance circuit—complaint, rebuttal, response, reply—was
deeply rooted in English constitutionalism. English government had for
centuries, long before transatlantic exploration, possessed this capacity to
handle complaints and make reforms. The process permitted change and
also contained dissent. Formally, a grievance was one of the first steps taken
to convey discontent with a governmental institution or policy and was,
typically, expressed through a petition to the crown. There were calibrated
forms for expressing grievances, which ranged from epistles and manuscript
petitions to printed memorials, periodical essays, and pamphlets that by the
mid-eighteenth century were facilitated by cheap print and the Imperial
postal network.[3] The lines between these genres blurred. A petition might be
published, unsigned, and ignored, while more sustained critiques could
remain in manuscript with limited circulation and great influence. Grievances could worsen and become the source of protests and even more
demonstrative forms of resistance.[4]

Sometimes the audience was not the king himself but rather crown
officials. Other times, it was Parliament. The addressee was not always the
source of discontent. Instead, the petitioner might seek some assistance or
relief from one party, while the source of discontent was another. Petitions
also generated support for a position; they therefore created, not just reflected, popular opinion.[5] Consequently, grievances were not in the form of
an individual addressing an abstract "state." Both sides to a dispute might

---

[3] Steele, *English Atlantic*, pp. 113–88.

[4] For one effective petition, see Stephen D. White, *Sir Edward Coke and the "Grievances of the
Commonwealth," 1621–1628* (Chapel Hill, NC, 1979). See also David Zaret, *Origins of Democratic
Culture: Printing, Petitions, and the Public Sphere in Early-Modern England* (Princeton, 2000). For
calibration of grievances, see Pauline Maier, *From Resistance to Revolution: Colonial Radicals and the
Development of American Opposition to Britain, 1765–1776* (New York, 1972); Larry D. Kramer, *The
People Themselves: Popular Constitutionalism and Judicial Review* (New York, 2004); John Phillip
Reid, *Constitutional History of the American Revolution* (Madison, WI, 1986–93).

[5] Edmund S. Morgan, *Inventing the People: The Rise of Popular Sovereignty in England and
America* (New York, 1988), p. 228.

petition the same audience for relief, each asking the king or his servants to provide aid or to discipline an offending third party.

Many of the institutions that defined England as a constitutional monarchy were communications networks that processed complaints and instituted reform based on them. Petitions reported grievances from the countryside to Westminster through an emissary Member of Parliament. Memorials went to the king's Privy Council. The right to petition was itself claimed as a cornerstone liberty in documents like the English Bill of Rights. Common law institutions were central nodes in this network. Justices of the peace brought the king's writ to the far corners of the realm, writs that often responded to individual complaints. As local men familiar with their community, the justices also transmitted discontent up the court system or into Parliament.[6] Juries learned about royal policy and parliamentary statutes in judicial instructions. But the freeholders who sat in the jury box spoke as well as listened and sent recommendations up the chain of command.[7] In form, royal charters—to towns, schools, churches—delegated power and conferred privileges. In practice, the king often used these instruments to seal his approval of, and thereby gain some control over, going concerns. Everywhere, institutions that looked like hierarchies of control were shot through with ambiguity and accommodation.[8] In this circulatory system of authority, a grievance functioned as the flip side of the royal instruction or parliamentary mandate. It reacted to, but also informed, central policy. Notwithstanding the static models of theorists then and constitutional historians now, this flexibility made government seem like a work in progress, breeding both hope and frustration for those within it, and yet usually working.

Usually. Complexity carried costs. The openness of the communication system prevented it from becoming monopolized by one interest, but that accessibility also made it susceptible to intelligence bottlenecks and confusion. Blockages contributed to domestic unrest, as the central policy-makers lost touch with the desires and responses of the governed.[9] As the network

[6] See, e.g., Norma Landau, *The Justices of the Peace, 1679–1760* (Berkeley, CA, 1984).

[7] See Thomas A. Green, *Verdict According to Conscience: Perspectives on the English Criminal Trial Jury, 1200–1800* (Chicago, 1985).

[8] See Jack P. Greene, *Negotiated Authorities: Essays in Colonial Political and Constitutional History* (Charlottesville, VA, 1994).

[9] For the argument that such a communications failure contributed to the English Civil War, see Kevin Sharpe, "Crown, Parliament, and Locality: Government and Communication in Early Stuart England," *English Historical Review*, CI (1986), pp. 321–50.

extended across the expanding Empire, the clarity of connection became even more variable. Many could participate, and there were several different nodes to choose from. Some grievance mechanisms challenged and even interrupted others, so that messages could be re-interpreted along the circuit, generating accidental as well as deliberate miscommunication. To reduce misunderstandings, the colonists latched on to a common stock of complaints that, they hoped, would express their aims in conventional and unthreatening ways. At the core of the lexicon in the mid-eighteenth century was English constitutionalism and Common Law, which most Anglophone audiences recognized and took seriously.

The common stock was deliberately formulaic. The point was to squeeze new claims into traditional forms that would be comprehensible anywhere in the Empire. The grievance forms were never as static as the common-law writs to which they were related, but they were similarly routine on the surface and flexible in practice.[10] These discursive writs were conveyed through works that were among the most readily available literature in the Empire: law books and political pamphlets generated during metropolitan crises. Rudiments and specifics were found in Sir Edward Coke's *Institutes of the Law of England* and other law books, from court manuals to case reports. But it was the outburst of pamphlets during the Restoration and its serial constitutional crises, culminating in the Glorious Revolution and its settlement, that transmitted the leading languages of the English constitution to all corners of the Empire.[11]

In these competing grievances, British Americans argued about the nature of the Empire and expressed themselves increasingly in terms of its "constitution." These competing arguments informed policy in the metropole, but the flexibility of the communications network meant that each group's influence varied over time and never bore a direct relation to the coherence of the group's message, let alone its representativeness. In addition, each grievance was refracted through British politics, which was also variable in its interests, attention to Imperial affairs, and institutional balance of power. As complaints moved through the machinery of British government, some generated new policies that ranged from subtle and modulated to blunt and catastrophic. These policies then provoked new

---

[10] See F. W. Maitland, *The Forms of Action at Common Law* (ed.), A. H. Chaytor and W. J. Whittaker (Cambridge, 1963).

[11] See Bernard Bailyn, *The Ideological Origins of the American Revolution* (Cambridge, MA, 1967).

or renewed colonial grievances. The spiral of complaints was actually a sign of health, as the Imperial constitution operated through this concatenation of complaint, answer, reply or reformulation, and response.

The Epistolary Constitution of Imperial Governance

When British subjects abroad drafted petitions, composed memorials, penned letters, and even cried out in the streets, they could generally depend on an audience.[12] Someone would read or listen. A grievance was an early step in the ladder of political complaint that, if not entertained in an appropriate forum, could fester and lead to resistance. The network was therefore double edged: it facilitated challenges to governance but also controlled their course. Elaborate means were available to make sure that the process of disenchantment never went too far. Behind each grievance, then, lay a political culture that entertained complaints, provided a set of institutions to process them, and thereby fostered hope for reform. The grievance system's connections and content were widespread enough to permit the development of a common Imperial identity and flexible enough to allow constitutional pluralism.[13]

The epistolary pattern of complaint and response, rebuttal and then reply, was built into the Empire's structure.[14] Behind each colonial government lay a founding document that was, in form, letters patent (or a sealed letter) from the crown. Often these royal letters were granted in response to a petition from subjects who presented their case as to why they deserved it, which illustrates the fundamental Imperial pattern of request and response, or sometimes appropriation and confirmation. Imperial expansion was predicated in the first instance on these ongoing negotiations between subjects and the crown and among competing groups of subjects. Then, as the provincial

[12] See: Stephen A. Higginson, "A Short History of the Right to Petition Government for the Redress of Grievances," *Yale Law Journal*, XCVI (1986), pp. 142–66; Gregory A. Mark, "The Vestigial Constitution: The History and Significance of the Right to Petition," *Fordham Law Review*, LXVI (1997–98), pp. 2153–231; Loretta Valtz Mannucci, "The Contribution of the Common People to American Constitutional Debate," in Roberto Martucci (ed.), *Constitution & Révolution aux Etas-Unis d'Amérique et en Europe, 1776–1815* (Macerata, 1995), pp. 51–65.

[13] Daniel J. Hulsebosch, *Constituting Empire: New York and the Transformation of Constitutionalism in the Atlantic World, 1664–1830* (Chapel Hill, NC, 2005), pp. 105–44. Cf. Benedict Anderson, *Imagined Communities: Reflections on the Origins and Spread of Nationalism*, rev. edn (London, 1991). See also Lauren Benton, *Law and Colonial Cultures: Legal Regimes in World History, 1400–1900* (New York, 2002).

[14] Cf. Hulsebosch, *Constituting Empire*, pp. 77–83.

subjects developed their own creolized institutions, culture, and identities, the negotiations became more complex. Within the network, of course, much of the negotiation was oral. Many colonial interests had agents to lobby their cause in Westminster or the king's court.[15] However, even these oral inquiries and responses were usually preceded, followed by, or memorialized in epistolary form.

The original royal grants of power were fairly simple. Some were in the form of corporate charters that granted power and land to a board of directors. Others were royal charters, delegating authority to a crown-appointed governor. Finally, letters patent functioned much like the charters, only they invested land and government in a proprietor.[16] The particulars of these colonial grants varied widely in such matters as the territory and water rights granted, the nature of local authority, and the relationship between the provincial and metropolitan governments but, appearances to the contrary notwithstanding, the royal grant did not really settle the form of colonial government. Instead, it initiated an ongoing correspondence through which Imperial agents, provincial settlers, and metropolitan administrators worked out governance over time.

Despite their diversity, these crown grants shared common guidelines for allocating governmental power between the colony and the metropole. Most contained what became known as a repugnancy clause, which qualified the grant of power by stating that local legislation must not be repugnant, or inconsistent, with English law. By the late seventeenth century, this clause was understood to require the colonial legislatures to submit their statutes to the Privy Council for review, a process in which those aggrieved by the legislation could petition the metropolitan government for redress. The Privy Council could "disallow" statutes that it deemed repugnant to the laws of England. In practice, the vast majority of colonial statutes were accepted. In a related provision, most founding instruments specified that litigants could appeal decisions from the provincial courts to the Privy Council for review, another mechanism for registering a complaint.[17]

---

[15] Olson, *Making the Empire Work*; Kammen, *Rope of Sand*.

[16] See generally Charles McLean Andrews, *The Colonial Period in American History*, 4 vols. (New Haven, 1934–38).

[17] The two requirements were also imposed on colonies, like Connecticut and Rhode Island, whose charters did not contain the reservation clauses, and met occasional resistance. Relatively few litigants took their cases to London, partly because, with a few exceptions, appeals were restricted to cases involving sums that excluded the bulk of colonial litigation, and partly because appeals were expensive and required knowledgeable contacts in London. Nonetheless,

In a limited but profound way, the statutory review and judicial appeal clauses contained the germ of colonial political development. The standards of review for each process, however, were never clear. In addition, these two clauses did not grant English law and liberties to colonial subjects; nor did they require that the colonies hew precisely to English law. Rather, the first clause placed an indefinite limitation on the provincial law-making power, and the second promised some supervision of the local courts.[18] They set loose boundaries on provincial self-government and established blunt tools for metropolitan oversight. They therefore also opened up much space for rights claims, which became the raw material of grievances.

Other official forms of communication were used more regularly to negotiate the shifting boundaries of provincial autonomy. Going west were governors' commissions and instructions, at least for royal colonies. By the middle of the eighteenth century, each commission contained a long list of what the governor had to accomplish and what he had to prohibit "at your peril." Instructions added new tasks to the list. Returning east went reports from the governors, accounts from other officials, and copies of local legislation. These instruments, most of which were in epistolary form, provided the raw material for Imperial policy. Several departments in London shared responsibility for producing this policy. Most important was the Privy Council, which for most of the eighteenth century had a standing committee on colonial affairs. The King-in-Council granted commissions, issued instructions, reviewed colonial legislation, and heard colonial appeals. It received advice from the Board of Trade, created in 1696 to process most colonial information, outline policy, and make recommendations to the Privy Council. The Cabinet officer responsible for North America—first the Secretary of State for the Southern Department, and after 1768 a new American Secretary—usually played a leading role in nominating colonial appointees and formulating Imperial policy. These departments housed the secretaries and clerks who

there was a steady stream of appeals to London from a few colonies. Jamaica, for example, accounted for almost a third of all judicial appeals from the American colonies between 1696 and 1783. See Joseph H. Smith, *Appeals to the Privy Council from the American Plantations* (New York, 1950), pp. 138–51, 77–88, 215–71, 549, 667–71; and Mary Sarah Bilder, *The Transatlantic Constitution: Colonial Legal Culture and the Empire* (Cambridge, MA, 2004), pp. 54–7, 68–9, 77–90.

[18] Hulsebosch, *Constituting Empire*, pp. 43–5.

drafted the commissions, instructions, and reports that were supposed to guide the Empire.[19]

Royal officials serving in the colonies dominated the formal mechanisms of Imperial communication. Customs officers, surveyors general, superintendents of Indian affairs, and the like—Imperial agents who often made the North American colonies their permanent home—wrote letters to the Board of Trade, the secretaries of state and their assistants, and other crown officials in Britain.[20] They also drafted much of the formal correspondence between the governors and the crown. By the mid-eighteenth century, these long-serving Imperial agents supplied much of London's information about the colonies. They also reached outside the formal epistolary structure of government: their own letters to a variety of metropolitan audiences in response to provincial grievances collectively served as a counter-balance to the petitions from the colonies and the informal influence of colonial interest groups.

Of course these official institutions did not exhaust the epistolary network that formed the Imperial constitution. Grievances were an important alternative. In the early years of colonization, inadequate local representation was the most frequent grievance: colonists wanted to participate in policy-making in their own provinces. In New York, for example, the Duke of York opposed the establishment of an elected Assembly for twenty years, but then capitulated in return for a promise that the Assembly would help collect and raise new revenues. At first, he also accepted the Assembly's bold statement of provincial rights in an Act entitled "The Charter of Libertyes and Privileges." The provincial drafters drew on the English constitutional canon and the charters of neighboring colonies, thus mixing corporate and English liberties, local and Imperial identities.[21] It was a typical creole

---

[19] See: Leonard W. Labaree, *Royal Government in America: A Study of the British Colonial System before 1783* (New York, 1958); Ian K. Steele, *The Politics of Colonial Administration* (Oxford, 1968); Ian K. Steele, "Metropolitan Administration of the Colonies, 1696–1775," in Greene and Pole (eds), *A Companion to the American Revolution*, pp. 8–13; Ian K. Steele, "The Anointed, The Appointed, and the Elected: Governance of the British Empire, 1689–1784," in P. J. Marshall (ed.), *OHBE*, II, *The Eighteenth Century* (Oxford, 1998), pp. 105–27.

[20] On the Imperial agents, see Hulsebosch, *Constituting Empire*, pp. 75–83. See also Ned C. Landsman, *From Colonials to Provincials: American Thought and Culture, 1680–1760* (New York, 1997), pp. 170–7; Thomas C. Barrow, *Trade and Empire: The British Customs Service in Colonial America, 1660–1775* (Cambridge, MA, 1967); and Franklin B. Wickwire, *British Subministers and Colonial America, 1763–1783* (Princeton, 1966).

[21] Cf. John P. Reid, *Constitutional History of the American Revolution: The Authority to Legislate* (Madison, WI, 1991), pp. 172–9.

production in which the drafters selected the most advantageous pieces of English tradition and Imperial experience to institutionalize their practical authority.[22] The liberties and privileges that the Assembly presumed to have been granted included the Assembly itself, triennial sessions, the privilege of determining members' qualifications, jury trials, civilian immunity from martial law, and the "due Course of Law," among other old and new rights of Englishmen.[23] Its form—a legislative statute drafted like a charter of incorporation and claiming liberties that comprehended the substance of a host of grievances—was a remarkable hybrid of delegation and grievance, petition and grant.

When the Duke ascended the throne as James II, however, he and his Privy Council disallowed the Act and dissolved the Assembly. After the Glorious Revolution, a new governor called another Assembly, which passed an amended version of the Charter of Libertyes. In this 1691 Act, the Assembly thanked the king for "restoring to them the undoubted rights and privileges of Englishmen," meaning the Assembly and the institutions of local government that were disbanded late in James II's reign. The Assembly also asked the governor to confirm additional "rights, Priviledges, Libertyes and franchises according to the Lawes and statutes of their Majesties Realm of England." This statute was also shipped back to London for review by the Board of Trade, which advised the king's Privy Council in 1697 that the act assumed "too great and unreasonable privileges" and contained "several large and doubtful expressions." The Council disallowed the act. The Board also attached a marked-up extract from a model charter, drafted for Virginia during the reign of Charles II, for the Assembly's consideration. The marked-up extract stressed the colonists' "immediate dependance on the Crown" and on its agent, the governor.[24] The Privy Council had rejected New York's redaction of real and contested common law rights again.

---

[22] See, e.g., Jack P. Greene, *The Quest for Power: The Lower Houses of Assembly in the Southern Royal Colonies, 1689–1776* (Chapel Hill, NC, 1963); Bernard Bailyn, *The Origins of American Politics* (New York, 1968); Andrew J. O'Shaughnessy, *An Empire Divided: The American Revolution and the British Caribbean* (Philadelphia, 2009), pp. 81–134.

[23] Hulsebosch, *Constituting Empire*, pp. 49, 52–3.

[24] Hulsebosch, *Constituting Empire*, pp. 49–54. For the Board of Trade's report, see "Report of the Lords of Trade Against an Act Declaratory of the Rights, &c., of the People of New York, May 11, 1697," in E. B. O'Callaghan (ed.), *Documents Relative to the Colonial History of the State of New-York*, IV (Albany, NY, 1854), pp. 263–5.

As a practical matter, however, disallowance had little effect. The New York Assembly continued to meet throughout the remainder of the colonial period, as the king's instructions said it should, subject to prorogation and dissolution by the governor. Similarly, a week before it declared New Yorkers' rights and privileges, the Assembly created justices of the peace, county courts, and a Supreme Court. All these conflicted with the governor's commission, which gave him the exclusive power to create courts. But these institutions, too, persisted until the Revolution and rested on ambiguous constitutional foundations. In these and similar ways, provincial grievances were funneled into provincial legislation.[25] Rights that might have been claimed in petitions were simply assumed and converted into immemorial custom, rendering it unnecessary to petition for their recognition. To keep the liberties they claimed, the provincials resorted to informal networks and transmitted grievances through transatlantic religious organizations, commercial partners, extended family, and even voyages in person to London.[26]

This pattern of multiple and competing grievances was established in many colonies by the middle of the eighteenth century, before anyone considered revolution. The formal epistolary structure of Imperial government gave shape to the informal petitionary literature that grew up around it. If one was the supportive skeleton of empire, the other provided ligaments that gave it movement and flexibility.

An Empire of War and Liberty: Grievance Cycles

Although grievances were a constant feature of Imperial administration, their frequency was cyclical. War was a primary driver of the cycles. "War is declared in England—Universal joy among the merchants," a New York lawyer recorded in his diary at the outbreak of the Seven Years' War in 1756,

[25] Alison G. Olson estimates that "something like half the eighteenth-century laws in all colonies originated in petitions." Olson, "Eighteenth-Century Colonists and Their Constituents," *Journal of American History*, LXXIX (1992), p. 556.

[26] For the many ways that colonists communicated with policy-makers in England, see, e.g., Stanley N. Katz, *Newcastle's New York: Anglo-American Politics, 1732–1753* (Cambridge, MA, 1968), Alison Olson, *Making the Empire Work*; Bernard Bailyn, *The New England Merchants in the Seventeenth Century* (Cambridge, MA, 1955); Alison Games, *The Web of Empire: English Cosmopolitans in the Age of Expansion, 1560–1660* (New York, 2008).

"Privateering engrosses the Coffee House."[27] But war was an opportunity not only for prizes from foreign powers. Political gains could be had within the Empire, too. In the eighteenth century, the British Empire was at war for more years than it was at peace.[28] These serial wars gave provincial interests bargaining power with their governors—and opportunities to grab power. Peace permitted Imperial reform, which triggered provincial grievances to protect recently won liberties, until these ongoing constitutional conflicts were interrupted by renewed warfare. Then the cycle started over again.

Getting things done during war required all sorts of compromises by the Imperial agents that, over time, became a *modus vivendi* for dealing with a common enemy. Governors closed ranks with assemblies and approved finance bills they would have otherwise vetoed, sometimes violating their instructions in the process. Militias fought alongside regular British military companies. Merchants received royal letters of marque, armed their ships, and shared their prizes with the crown. The Navigation Act's restrictions on colonial commerce were liberalized or simply not enforced. Of course, most colonists would have joined the war efforts for reasons of safety, kinship, shared Protestant religion, commerce, and allegiance to the king.[29] But interest and affection did not prevent the provincials from reaching for as much freedom as they could get. The colonial assemblies, which increasingly controlled appropriations for defense, used their wartime leverage to gain rights they believed due to them as Englishmen and that also served local interests.[30] They had every reason to believe that this cyclical pattern would persist and that they would continue, at intervals, to increase their control over their own provinces. As late as 1773, leading colonists supposed that, upon the outbreak of another war with France, Great Britain would

---

[27] William Smith Jr., "Diary," July 14, 1756, William Smith Jr. papers, New York Public Library.

[28] See Howard E. Peckham, *The Colonial Wars, 1689–1762* (Chicago, 1964). For the interplay of war and liberty more generally, see Fred Anderson and Andrew L. Cayton, *The Dominion of War: Empire and Liberty in North America, 1500–2000* (New York, 2005); Daniel J. Hulsebosch, "An Empire of War and Liberty: Review of Fred Anderson, *Crucible of War*," *H-Law Reviews* (2001), <http://www.h-net.org/reviews/showrev.php?id=5457>.

[29] See David Armitage, *The Ideological Origins of the British Empire* (Cambridge, 2000); Brendan McConville, *The King's Three Faces: The Rise and Fall of Royal America, 1688–1776* (Chapel Hill, NC, 2006). However, commercial interest sometimes overcame such ties: Thomas M. Truxes, *Defying Empire: Trading with the Enemy in Colonial New York* (New Haven, 2008).

[30] On the southern assemblies' control over colonial finance, see Greene, *Quest for Power*, pp. 49–125, 129–68, 223–50.

once again capitulate to colonial grievances and the Empire would unite in the common cause. "Then," believed Philadelphia's Charles Thomson, "will be the time for the American legislatures, with modesty & firmness, to recapitulate their wrongs, explain their grievances and their rights."[31]

Although governors often accommodated provincial interests in the assemblies, some long-serving Imperial agents never accepted these wartime deals as anything except temporary expedients. After the war, they worked to withdraw whatever privileges provincial forces had won and to develop new mechanisms of administration to bypass colonial institutions. The pattern began at least with the English Civil War in the 1640s, when the Cromwellian government gained greater control over the various transatlantic enterprises begun over the previous half century while at the same time closing down English colonial trade with rivals, such as the Dutch.[32] These efforts are best symbolized by the first Parliamentary Navigation Act (1650) and, later, the seizure of Jamaica from Spain. After a few tumultuous years, the Stuart Restoration (1660) initiated a period of royal examination of all manner of local governments, within the realm and in the Americas. Some charters were revoked and rewritten and new, more centralized polities were created. The Stuarts' Imperial reorganization began with attempts to impose a greater degree of control over the newly created colonies like New York and Carolina, and then extended to the revocation or surrender of all of the New England charters. The re-constitution of Empire culminated in the attempt to create new regional colonies, like the Dominion of New England, efforts that ran aground during the Glorious Revolution and King William's War (1689–1697) with France, which followed the overthrow of James II.[33] As these events concluded, the crown re-constituted, in 1696, the Lords Commissioners of Trade and Foreign Plantations, usually called the Board of Trade. In the same year, Parliament re-authorized and extended the Navigation Acts that regulated trade throughout the empire, adding colonial vice-admiralty courts that had jurisdiction over alleged violations.[34] Queen

---

[31] Quoted in Jack N. Rakove, *Beginnings of National Politics: An Interpretive History of the Continental Congress* (New York, 1979), p. 9.

[32] Steven C. A. Pincus, *Protestantism and Patriotism: Ideologies and the Making of English Foreign Policy, 1650–1688* (Cambridge, 1996), pp. 46–50.

[33] Viola F. Barnes, *The Dominion of New England: A Study in British Colonial Policy* (New Haven, 1923).

[34] See Oliver M. Dickerson, *American Colonial Government, 1696–1765: A Study of the British Board of Trade in its Relation to the American Colonies* (Cleveland, OH, 1912), pp. 20–8; Arthur

Anne's War (1702–1713) stymied these efforts at greater centralization but its conclusion ushered in another period of reform that established several leading principles of royal government in America. These efforts petered out in the face of other military threats—recurrent Jacobite threats in Britain for example, and some brutal Native American wars on the colonial Marchland—as well as a domestic environment during the administration of Sir Robert Walpole that was not conducive to any sort of reform, domestic or Imperial. In addition, although the peace with France was long, it was not seen as permanent.

After King George's War (1739–48), a rejuvenated Board of Trade, led by Lord Halifax and including George Grenville and Charles Townshend— each of whom remained central players in British government for decades— conducted an unusually thorough investigation of Imperial governance in the colonies. An example was its study of New York, which culminated in a lengthy memorandum to the Privy Council recommending a host of reforms. Not much was new in the detail of complaints from the Imperial agents or in the record of provincial grievances. The recommendations were mostly familiar too. But rarely had a metropolitan institution delved so deeply into the particular dynamics of one province. The Board told the Privy Council that it had "thrown together, whatever we thought may tend to give your Lord[shi]ps a just idea of the melancholy State of the affairs of this distracted province."[35] Most of the report was made up of extracts from assembly petitions, replies from the royal governor, and letters from Imperial agents to the Board. They all documented "the fatal measures, by which the legal prerogative of the Crown, (which alone can keep this or any Province dependent on the Mother Country) has been reduced, [and] the most essencial powers of Govern[men]t violently wrested out of the hands of the Governor." The Board referred to the assaults on the prerogative as "these grievances" and proposed several remedies "to restore the prerogative to its just and legal boundaries."[36] Recommendations included the grant of permanent salaries for Imperial officers out of quit rents or some other fund

Basye, *The Lord Commissioners of Trade and Plantations, Commonly Known as the Board of Trade, 1748–1782* (New Haven, 1925), p. 1.

[35] "Report of the [Board of Trade] upon the State of New York," in John R. Bradhead (ed.), *Documents Relative to the Colonial History of the State of New-York, Procured in Holland, England and France*, VI (Albany, NY, 1855), p. 635.

[36] Brodhead (ed.), *Documents Relative to the Colonial History of New-York*, VI, p. 636.

independent of the assemblies, and the appointment of superintendents of Indian affairs to displace the provincial Indian commissioners. The latter succeeded: the Privy Council appointed two superintendents in the 1750s. Independent salaries, however, were not established. But both ideas—independent salaries and the appointment of royal rather than provincial officials to handle Imperial affairs—had been proposed before and remained favorites among Imperial reformers for the rest of the colonial period.

The global contest known as the Seven Years' War put an end to—or at least postponed—this stretch of Imperial reform. In the meantime, the common effort led to the expulsion of the French from North America. Most thought it was the high point of the British Empire. The British gloried in their victory, and the colonists rejoiced in being released from the threat of another French war. Soon, however, conflicts re-emerged in the visions of the newly expanded Empire, and this time there was no external threat to stimulate compromise.

The Grievance Cycle Interrupted: Imperial Reform and the Revolution, 1763–1776

When the Seven Years' War came to an end with the first Treaty of Paris in 1763, Britain had been at war for all but six of the last twenty-four years and had enjoyed only one entirely peaceful decade since the accession of William and Mary in 1689. This peace was different. The acquisition of Canada opened up much land for potential development and eliminated long-running border and trade disputes that had been causes of war. Long-standing disagreements in the Caribbean were also resolved. In addition, France was left even wearier and more in debt than Britain.[37] For the first time in the eighteenth century, another round of the fighting with France seemed unlikely.

Historians have long debated the effect of the apparent elimination of the "Gallic Peril" in 1763. Lawrence Henry Gipson famously argued that the colonists, freed from the need for Imperial defense of their western borders, became almost instantly rebellious, so that the Revolution could be viewed as the "aftermath of the Great War for Empire."[38] John M. Murrin shrewdly

---

[37] France also lacked effective fiscal mechanisms for retiring debt. James C. Riley, *The Seven Years' War and the Old Regime in France: The Economic and Financial Toll* (Princeton, 1986).

[38] Fred Anderson, *Crucible of War: The Seven Years' War and the Fate of Empire in British North America, 1754–1760* (New York, 2000); Lawrence H. Gipson, *The American Revolution as an Aftermath of the Great War for Empire, 1754–1763* (Bethlehem, PA, 1950).

argued that the counter-factual behind Gipson's thesis—without the French cession of Canada, there would have been no Revolution—depended on a host of problematic assumptions. Most important, the thesis did not take the colonists' grievances over the next decade seriously.[39] Murrin was largely correct: the "Gallic Peril" had never compelled provincial interests to cooperate fully with Imperial agents. If anything, the French wars had induced the Imperial agents to accede to provincial demands. Now, however, they felt liberated from that constraint. In this sense, the Revolution *was* in part the aftermath of the last French war. But it was so only because the Imperial agents, no longer forced to compromise, followed a long-deferred program of reform that threatened the vision of governance that creolized provincials had come to equate with the Imperial constitution.

Problems arose as soon as British administrators began to reshape the wartime Empire into a peacetime one. The war did not just remove a foreign enemy. It was a catalyst that accelerated the development of internal divisions concerning the future of the Empire. The colonists had long claimed the status of full and equal subjects;[40] now they felt they had earned it. The renewed conviction of equal standing that came with contributing to the conquest of Canada led them to express this expectation in terms of the liberties of Englishmen. Self-governance was the central liberty. Around it circulated a variety of claims to be free of external regulation.

The Imperial agents and many metropolitan officials had a different conception of the peace. To them, it was an opportunity to exercise greater control over the colonies and to force them to shoulder some of the expenses of the war and of maintaining the military in the colonies.[41] An

---

[39] John M. Murrin, "The French and Indian War, the American Revolution, and the Counterfactual Hypothesis: Reflections on Lawrence Henry Gipson and John Shy," *Reviews in American History*, I (1973), pp. 307–18.

[40] Reid, *Constitutional History of the American Revolution: The Authority of Rights* (Madison, WI, 1986), pp. 82–6.

[41] For surveys of the new regulations, see Peter D. G. Thomas, *British Politics and the Stamp Act Crisis: The First Phase of the American Revolution, 1763–67* (Oxford, 1975); Thomas, *The Townshend Duties Crisis: The Second Phase of the American Revolution, 1767–73* (Oxford, 1987); Thomas, *Tea Party to Independence: The Third Phase of the American Revolution, 1773–1776* (Oxford, 1991); Bernhard Knollenberg, *Origin of the American Revolution, 1759–1766* (Indianapolis, 2002); Knollenberg, *Growth of the American Revolution, 1766–1775* (Indianapolis, 2003); Robert Middlekauff, *The Glorious Cause: The American Revolution, 1763–1789* (New York, 1982); Jack P. Greene, "An Uneasy Connection: An Analysis of the Preconditions of the American

even more ambitious goal was to use some of the revenue from new taxes for the Imperial establishment in America to free its members from reliance on the provincial assemblies for their pay and on fees for services. It was an idea whose time, they thought, had finally come.

The new regulations were extensive and bulk large in the historiography of the Revolution. They restricted trade, western settlement, and provincial legal administration. Attempts at tightening metropolitan control in all of these areas were scarcely new but the latest initiatives were brought on in much greater numbers and at a much faster rate, especially under the guidance of George Grenville (Prime Minister, 1763–1765) and Charles Townshend (Chancellor of the Exchequer, 1766–1767), and were far more effective than in the past. In between these bursts of activity were lulls and even retractions. But the even the most famous retraction—the repeal of the hated Stamp Act—gave offense because it was accompanied by the Declaratory Act of 1766 that proclaimed Parliament's unlimited power to regulate the colonies.[42]

Two additional characteristics distinguished the new regulations from older ones. First, many were passed by Parliament and, in provincial eyes, regulated their internal affairs. Previously, most parliamentary legislation, epitomized by the Navigation Acts, regulated external trade. The distinction between internal and external taxes proved tricky to maintain, and this conceptual cloudiness gradually pushed some colonists toward the clearer but more radical principle that all parliamentary regulation was invalid. Second, the measures came with new methods of enforcement. These included attempts to fund salaries for the Imperial agents out of the new revenue, the appointment of outsiders to provincial judicial offices, and the partial displacement of colonial legal systems by Imperial substitutes.[43] The reforms targeted the assemblies and common law institutions that obstructed the enforcement of Imperial policy, especially by judges and juries. These obstructions had long been the source of the Imperial agents'

Revolution," in Stephen Kurtz and James Hutson (eds), *Essays on the American Revolution* (Chapel Hill, NC, 1973), pp. 32–80.

[42] Knollenberg, *Growth of the American Revolution*, pp. 10–16. The British politics behind Parliament's retraction and its peremptory claim are explored in Thomas, *Stamp Act Crisis*, pp. 185–252, and Stephen Conway, "Britain and the Revolutionary Crisis, 1763–1791," in Marshall (ed.), *OHBE*, II, pp. 325–46.

[43] For details in one colony, see Hulsebosch, *Constituting Empire*, pp. 105–44.

grievances, and they had therefore been prominent on the provincials' lists of deserved English liberties. For decades, the provincials had succeeded in developing fairly well-insulated local legal systems, staffed by local men and local juries, with salaries and fees coming from local sources. Now, creole legal establishments were under assault. The mechanisms were so innovative, and the tax rates so low, that it is fair to conclude that it was the specter of enforcement and the principle of regulation they embodied, rather than the actual taxes that triggered the grievances. Indeed, even a "trifling" tax, according to John Dickinson, was "alarming" evidence of a plan "to establish a *precedent* for future use. To console ourselves with the *smallness* of the duties," he warned in 1768, "is to walk deliberately into the snare that is set for us, praising the *neatness* of the workmanship."[44] In provincial eyes, the new measures threatened to work an administrative and constitutional revolution.

A few examples will suffice. In 1764, the American Revenue Act actually cut the duties on a number of foreign imports that, previously, had been highly taxed in an effort to prohibit such trade. Under the new Act, Britain accepted such trade (which had been going on illegally) in exchange for enforcement of the duties. Crucially, the Act was intended to be a revenue measure and did not use taxation to prohibit foreign trade. The statute itself said as much. Parliament proclaimed, right after noting the recent expansion of the Empire, that "it is just and necessary, that a revenue be raised, in your Majesty's said dominions in America for defraying the expences of defending, protecting, and securing the same."[45] The revenue would pay for troops in America.

This Act is commonly known as the Sugar Act, though the duty on molasses was only one of several in it. But French colonial molasses was particularly important to the economies of the New England and Middle Atlantic colonies. In a grievance to Parliament, a group of New York City merchants called sugar and molasses "the very Sinews of our Commerce."[46] They turned it into rum, which became an export commodity and, more

---

[44] [John Dickinson,] Letter VII, *Letters from a Farmer in Pennsylvania, to the Inhabitants of the British Colonies* (Philadelphia, 1768), p. 37.

[45] "An Act for Granting Certain Duties in the British Colonies and Plantations in America," 4 Geo. III, c. 15.

[46] Petition to the House of Commons, Burgesses, April 20, 1764, *Journal of the Votes and Proceedings of the General Assembly of the Colony of New York. Began the 9th Day of April, 1691; and Ended [1765]*, II (New York, 1766), p. 742.

important, a source of credit crucial for the functioning of their economies.[47] The old duty on foreign molasses, established in the Molasses Act of 1733, was six pence per gallon and had been designed to prevent the trade in foreign molasses. That effort failed: smuggling of French molasses continued to be rampant. The new regulation was designed to legitimate the trade and maximize revenue from it.

The Act—and the suggestion in London that it might be followed by a colonial stamp tax—sparked outrage in all the colonies. Most of the colonial assemblies sent petitions to Parliament. Some, like the assemblies in New York and North Carolina, began to articulate the principle that Parliament could only legislate to regulate trade, not to raise revenue, a distinction which seemed to them to capture the new Act's innovation.[48] "We have by improving a Country inhabited only by Savages," the New York Assembly wrote in a petition to the House of Lords, "and far remote from our native Soil, greatly extended the Dominions and Trade of *Great-Britain*; and will undoubtedly, if not checked by a new Model of our Constitution, and an Abridgment of the essential and fundamental Rights of *Englishmen*, continue the Augmentation of Both, till she shall equal the greatest Empire recorded in the Annals of Fame."[49] John Watts, a merchant who looked askance at many colonial grievances and, a decade later, would remain loyal to the Empire, reported to New York's absentee governor in London that "the Colonys are extremely incensed at the Treatment they have received from the Mother Country.... They seem to wish Canada again French; it made them of some Consequence, which Consequence they lost when it was conquered, if their reasoning be just."[50] It could almost be called the Gallic aegis. And it was gone.

Driving colonial resistance were the means of enforcement in the new regulations. The American Act came with a host of new policing devices that reflected a concerted effort to collect revenue in colonial ports. Two sections

[47] Middlekauff, *Glorious Cause*, 67–8; John J. McCusker, "The Rum Trade and the Balance of Payments of the Thirteen Continental Colonies, 1650–1775," *Journal of Economic History*, XXX (1970), pp. 244–7.

[48] Middlekauff, *Glorious Cause*, p. 68.

[49] Petition to the House of Lords, October 18, 1764, *Journal of the Votes and Proceedings of the General Assembly of the Colony of New York*, II (New York, 1766), p. 774.

[50] John Watts to Gen. Robert Monckton, May 16, 1764, *Letterbook of John Watts, Merchant and Councillor of New York, January 1, 1762–December 1765*, New York Historical Society Collections, LXI (New York, 1928), p. 255.

targeted inter-colonial coastal trade. Previously, such trade had been unfettered and therefore offered a way to shuttle smuggled goods around the colonies. Now, shippers had to post custom bonds to guarantee the quantity and quality of their cargo. The point was to prevent the inter-colonial traffic in enumerated goods, long forbidden but just as long enjoyed.[51] The Act therefore brought local shippers into daily contact, for the first time, with Imperial customs officers.

Traditionally, if a prosecuting officer failed to gain a conviction, he could be liable in colonial courts for damages for wrongly detaining the defendant's property.[52] The American Revenue Act, however, changed the common-law rules so that an officer held to have had "probable cause" would only be liable for nominal damages (two pence) if his prosecution failed. If the trial judge refused to certify that the officer had probable cause, the English Customs Board was authorized to indemnify the officer for damages paid in colonial courts. In addition, the Act shifted the burden of proof from the prosecuting official to the owner of the goods and permitted the officer, rather than the defendant, to select the venue for the action. The Act also created a new admiralty court, which by definition operated without a jury, and had jurisdiction over any alleged violations in any colonial waters. The new court was established in Halifax, Nova Scotia, far from obstructive local judges and juries.[53] Suddenly, customs officials could reach deeply into colonial trade with less fear of reprisal, and then send enforcement cases to juryless courts that were hundreds of miles away.

The Stamp Act, passed the next year, made the colonial protests over the Revenue Act seem in vain. What colonists found galling about the stamp tax

---

[51] Thomas, *Stamp Act Crisis*, pp. 44–50; Knollenberg, *Origin of the American Revolution*, pp. 166–7.

[52] Occasionally, Imperial agents were held liable for false prosecutions in colonial courts even when they secured a conviction elsewhere. One example is Erving v. Cradock, in Josiah Quincy Jr., *Reports of Cases Argued and Adjudged in the Superior Court of Judicature of the Province of Massachusetts Bay, Between 1761 and 1772* (Boston, 1865), pp. 553–7.

[53] Knollenberg, *Origin of the American Revolution*, pp. 127–38, 165–70; Thomas, *Stamp Act Crisis*, 96–7; Peter D. G. Thomas, "The Grenville Program, 1763–1765," in Greene and Pole (eds), *A Companion to the American Revolution*, p. 119. See also Carl Ubbelohde, *The Vice-Admiralty Courts and the American Revolution* (Chapel Hill, NC, 1960). In response to colonial complaints about the remoteness of the Halifax court, the Grenville administration put into motion a plan to establish vice-admiralty courts in Boston, Philadelphia, and Charleston. The plan was aborted with the repeal of the Stamp Act. Thomas, *Stamp Act Crisis*, p. 97.

was that it affected many ordinary transactions between individuals. Stamped paper was required not just for official documents like licenses, land deeds, ship clearances, and court filings, but also mortgages, indentures, newspapers, pamphlets, almanacs, calendars, playing cards, and even every "certificate of any degree taken in any university, academy, college, or seminary of learning."[54] Clearly this was an internal tax, the avowed point of which was to raise revenue. The tax was supposed to be self-enforcing because transactions using non-stamped paper would lack legal effect.[55] Once again, however, open violations could be prosecuted in vice-admiralty courts, without juries, at the discretion of the prosecutor. But the tax was never enforceable in most colonies: popular pressure drove many stamp distributors to resign their commissions before it became effective.

The Townshend Revenue Act (1767) was explicitly designed, in response to protests over the Stamp Act and following the advice of colonial agent Benjamin Franklin, to levy "external" taxes (i.e., duties). Charles Townshend, the chancellor of the exchequer who drafted the legislation, thought that the distinction between internal and external taxation was politically useful but conceptually "ridiculous." John Dickinson of Pennsylvania agreed. His twelve "Farmer's Letters" denied Parliament any right to raise revenue, leaving it only the right to regulate trade.[56] The distinction here was purposive rather than spatial, but it was subject to similar criticism: the line between raising revenue and regulating trade was difficult to draw, and some Imperial laws had in fact raised revenue. The real innovation of the duties was, again, their enforcement provisions. The Act authorized colonial courts to issue general writs of assistance (a power previously much contested) in order to search for smuggled goods and discover violations of the customs laws. These gave customs officials the discretion to examine docks and warehouses regularly, instead of only when they had probable cause of a particular violation. The other notable feature was that the money collected was authorized to pay the salaries of Imperial agents—to "defray the charges of the administration of justice, and the support of the civil government"— rather than for the defense and security of the colonies, like the previous measures. For the provincials, the grievance network worked here too. After

---

[54] Act of March 22, 1765, http://avalon.law.yale.edu/18th_century/stamp_act_1765.asp

[55] Thomas, Stamp Act Crisis, p. 91.

[56] Labaree, Royal Government, pp. 295–6, 340–1, 369; Knollenberg, Growth of the American Revolution, p. 40; Thomas, Stamp Act Crisis, pp. 337–63.

protests that included non-importation agreements, which cut at the heart of the Imperial communication network—namely, commerce—most of the Townshend duties were repealed.[57] The glaring exception was the tea duty, which (like the Declaratory Act) was retained to vindicate the principle of parliamentary taxation.[58]

The Currency Act of 1764, which restricted the issuance of paper money in the mid-Atlantic and southern colonies, offers a similar example. If enforced to the letter, the restriction would have severely damaged the economy in several colonies. Even partial enforcement brought recession and deflation. Some of the affected colonies, however, lobbied for and obtained exceptions, which sapped the repeal movement of critical mass.[59] As after the Stamp Act, provincial resistance decreased because the colonies were not able to maintain boycotts for long. Grievances did not die away in the late 1760s. But they became once again local rather general. Looking forward, there was no way even at that late date to predict revolution.

What continued to change was enforcement: specifically, the more effective enforcement of existing regulations. The trend reflected the growing belief in London that the colonies were becoming ungovernable through traditional means. The emboldened resistance had generated a stronger will to carry through administrative plans long hatched but never fully implemented. In one more effort to bolster customs collection, the Treasury established an American Customs Board in Boston in 1768. This body had the power to support local customs collection by, among other means, calling on the Royal Navy.[60] Boston remained a hotbed of local resistance. In June 1768, merchants and sailors rioted when the Navy began to remove a ship suspected of smuggling from its moorings.[61] In response, the Privy

---

[57] T. H. Breen interprets the boycott movement as an attack on commerce itself in *The Marketplace of Revolution: How Consumer Politics Shaped American Independence* (New York, 2004).

[58] Thomas, *Townshend Duties Crisis*, pp. 161–79.

[59] See Joseph A. Ernst, *Money and Politics in America, 1755–1775: A Study in the Currency Act of 1764 and the Political Economy of Revolution* (Chapel Hill, NC, 1973); Jacob M. Price, "The Money Question: Money and Politics in America, 1755–1775: A Study in the Currency Act of 1764 and the Political Economy of Revolution," *Reviews in American History*, II (1974), pp. 364–73.

[60] Knollenberg, *Growth of the American Revolution*, pp. 66–8. The Customs Board was created by statute rather than through the prerogative, in part to challenge colonial interpretations of Parliament's power. Thomas, *Townshend Duties Crisis*, p. 10.

[61] John P. Reid, *In a Rebellious Spirit: The Argument of Facts, the Liberty Riot, and the Coming of the American Revolution* (University Park, PA, 1979), pp. 86–107.

Council resolved that any defendants could be shipped to England and tried for high treason on the basis of a rarely used treason statute passed under Henry VIII. (Unsurprisingly, no defendants were identified.) This idea—investing metropolitan courts with jurisdiction over crimes arising in the colonies and permitting the removal of defendants across the Atlantic—gained popularity in London over the next few years. Similarly, the "Boston Massacre," in which British regulars stationed outside the customs house killed five Bostonians in March 1770, raised the specter of the use of standing armies to police the colonists, yet the well-publicized incident also made that use more fraught and therefore unlikely.[62]

The very weakness of Imperial law enforcement in the colonies propelled metropolitan decision-makers to embrace the idea of transporting sensitive cases back home. In 1772, Parliament passed the Dockyards Act, which permitted the removal and trial in London of defendants accused of burning or destroying naval ships at any Imperial dock. That same year, after the *Gaspée* affair in which a Rhode Island mob attacked and torched a Royal Navy ship that was enforcing customs laws, the North ministry sought to indict the conspirators for trial in England, again under the antiquated Henrician treason statute. The Dockyards Act did not apply because the *Gaspée* had been under sail, not docked. Its application was nonetheless discussed, which led to its notoriety in the colonies. To similar end, Parliament in 1774 passed the Administration of Justice Act, which allowed the transfer of capital trials of anyone acting under the direction of any magistrate for suppressing riot or collecting customs to another colony or England. The Act also provided for the payment of travel expenses for witnesses. The point evidently was to protect enforcers from prosecution in provincial courts in front of local juries. Both Acts addressed the same problem: biased colonial court systems.

This power to extradite defendants was apparently never exercised, but it symbolized the new enforcement regime and its attempt to displace the provincial legal systems. News of the plan to ship colonial defendants to England spread rapidly in 1773 and led directly to the formation of the thirteen committees of correspondence to keep all the colonies apprised of new legislation in Parliament.[63]

---

[62] John Shy, *Toward Lexington: The Role of the British Army in the Coming of the American Revolution* (Princeton, 1965), pp. 303–20.

[63] Knollenberg, *Growth of the American Revolution*, pp. 91–100.

Even the cession of New France, which eliminated the French threat, had generated a set of administrative innovations and concomitant grievances. The King's Proclamation of 1763 declared that colonists could not settle west of the Appalachian Mountains in what the Imperial agents called "Indian country," and follow-up measures threatened to pull cases arising in that territory or with the Indians out of the colonial courts and into new tribunals supervised by the superintendents for Indian affairs. These measures largely failed, but Parliament's Quebec Act in 1774 again seemed, to the American colonies, to hive off territory they claimed as their own and install within it new, autocratic forms of governance.[64]

Expressions of colonial grievances remained periodic, following closely, as in the past, the rhythm of regulation until the outbreak of the Revolution in 1775. But their function was now very different. Instead of holding the Empire together, they were binding the continental colonies in a unified bloc that challenged the Empire in startling new ways. Grievances became repetitive and widespread by design. The committees of correspondence epitomized the situation. They were outgrowths of the Imperial communication network but now were reconfigured to organize and advance common colonial purposes at the expense of the Empire. Colonists read each other's grievances, imitated them, then copied their own lists in successive petitions, adding and subtracting along the way to tailor them for a specific audience. These regular exercises in sharing and individuation created a new sense of unity in America, instilling at last, after a century and a half of European settlement, a sense of a common cause among thirteen disparate colonies.[65]

In 1774, these colonies formed a Continental Congress and, in July 1775, a Second Continental Congress sent one last open letter to King George III, the so-called Olive Branch Petition. Even some of its signers believed that this petition was too little and too late. It lacked particulars and was more of an invitation to continue negotiations toward reconciliation than a traditional list of complaints, though it did still capture the spirit of the grievance process. It also captured the uncertain state of mind of most colonists, those who would revolt as well as those like John Dickinson, the

---

[64] See Peter Marshall, "British North America, 1760–1815," in Marshall (ed.), *OHBE* II, pp. 372–80.

[65] See, e.g., T.H. Breen, *American Insurgents, American Patriots: The Revolution of the People* (New York, 2010), pp. 17–18, 99–128; Edward Countryman, *The American Revolution*, rev. edn (New York, 2003), p. 49.

petition's lead author, who initially remained loyal. At the end of the Seven Years' War, which Congress called "the most glorious and advantagious [*sic*] that ever had been carried on by British arms" and to which the colonies had contributed much support, the colonists believed that "they should be permitted with the rest of the empire, to share in the blessings of peace and the emoluments of victory and conquest." They were instead "alarmed by a new system of Statutes and regulations adopted for the administration of the colonies, that filled their minds with the most painful fears and jealousies; and to their inexpressible astonishment perceived the dangers of a foreign quarrel quickly succeeded by domestic dangers, in their judgment of a more dreadful kind."[66] The peace that had promised Imperial equality brought, instead, an assault on their customary liberties. The ministry refused to entertain the petition. The king instead proceeded with the plan, formulated that summer in response to the fighting in Massachusetts, to declare the colonies to be outside his law—subject, in other words, to martial law.[67] The next year, 1776, Congress mimed the traditional procedures in order to draft twenty-seven grievances that could not in fact be redressed. The audience for this "petition" was not really king or Parliament but the British public and, crucially, potential foreign allies.[68]

In form, the list of indictments in the Declaration of Independence looks like a familiar petition for redress, except that the diction and syntax were accusatory rather than informative or supplicant. The drafters for the Continental Congress represented thirteen states and collected information from all of them while compiling their complaints against the king.[69] They contained claims common to all colonies, like the opposition to new parliamentary taxes and interference with provincial legal administration, as well as several that were peculiar to individual colonies.

The Declaration's grievances were clustered in six categories. The first group targeted Parliament's interference with the colonies' internal legislative autonomy. These covered long-standing objections to the Privy Council's review of legislation. Also included were changes in assembly meeting

---

[66] Petition to the King, July 8, 1775, *Journals of the Continental Congress*, Avalon Project, <http://www.avalon.law.yale.edu/18th_century/contcong_07-08-75.asp>

[67] Thomas, *Tea Party to Independence*, pp. 248, 260–4.

[68] On the latter function, see David Armitage, *The Declaration of Independence: A Global History* (Cambridge, MA, 2007).

[69] Pauline Maier, *American Scripture: The Making of the Declaration of Independence* (New York, 1997).

places to areas less resistant to Imperial governance, and the dissolution of the assemblies. The second group dealt with metropolitan obstacles to colonial development, like the peopling of the colonies, through restrictions on immigration and naturalization, and restrictions on western land grants.[70] The third covered incursions on provincial judicial administration, which included refusing to allow the creation of colonial courts and denying good-behavior tenure to colonial judges. The fourth group covered the growth of the Imperial bureaucracy within the provinces: new customs officials, standing armies in peacetime, and the appointment of military officers, like General Gage, as governors.

The fifth group targeted the parliamentary statutes of the previous decade. Referring to Parliament's new reach as "a jurisdiction foreign to our constitution," the drafters listed several familiar grievances, from taxation without representation and the forced quartering of troops to the establishment of juryless admiralty courts with the power to enforce customs collection and the extension of the jurisdiction of King's Bench to the colonies for specified crimes. In addition, the drafters mentioned statutes aimed at particular colonies: the suspension of assemblies referred to the Suspension Act that threatened to suspend the New York Assembly in 1767, for example, and the revocation of charters, which included the seventeenth-century revocation of the Massachusetts' charter and the restructuring of its council and judiciary through the Massachusetts Regulating Act (1774). The sixth group concerned the belligerent measures of the previous two years. The king had declared the colonies to be out of his peace and had waged war against them, hired mercenaries, impressed his subjects, and incited the Indians to fight against the colonists.

The coda to this long list of complaints follows so closely that it could be taken for a complaint itself, even perhaps the gravamen of the indictment. It is instead an elegy for a vanished form of government. "In every stage of these Oppressions," wrote the drafters, "We have Petitioned for Redress in the most humble terms: Our repeated Petitions have been answered only by repeated injury." The people of Great Britain had been no more solicitous. "We have appealed to their native justice and magnanimity, and we have conjured them by the ties of our common kindred to disavow these

---

[70] See Woody Holton, *Forced Founders: Indians, Debtors, Slaves, and the Making of the Revolution in Virginia* (Chapel Hill, NC, 1999), pp. 3–38.

usurpations, which, would inevitably interrupt our connections and correspondence." These grievances could not be addressed within the framework of the Imperial constitution. The genre to which they now belonged was the international declaration of war.

Conclusion: A Union of War and Liberty

An exclusive focus on the grievances in the Declaration of Independence can create the illusion that most were new or unusual. They were not. At most times in most places across British North America, people complained that Imperial policies or institutions threatened sacred liberties, invaded cherished customs, and imposed innovative restraints on trade. But this litany creates its own illusion. If one looks only at the petitionary literature—the official and unofficial correspondence from Imperial agents and colonists to their supervisors, lobbyists, relatives, and friends in London—it might seem as if the whole history of British American colonization was a tale of repeated and cascading grievances. It was not.

The provincial petitions are misleading for two reasons. First, they contain only half the story, as there were many other grievances, including those from the Imperial agents on the ground in North America without whose efforts there would not have been an Empire. Second, the monologue of colonial grievances does not capture the compromises that made the Empire work. The grievance network was essential to those compromises. It facilitated dialogue among aggrieved subjects throughout the Empire and provided a process that permitted accommodation or, when grievances failed, the possibility of new grievances and the hope of eventual vindication. Process mattered as much as substance. Disappointing outcomes did not prevent people from continuing to resort to a system that had worked for them in the past and had the capacity to do so still.

Ironically, Britain's greatest Imperial victory helped undo the Empire. A stable peace changed the ecology of the Imperial constitution. In the decade after the war, provincial grievances began to fester. The real differences from earlier periods were, first, the sheer number of grievances, arising from all the colonies in concert; second, the simultaneous effort, at every level of Imperial government, to reform colonial administration; and third, the suspension of the familiar cycle of peacetime confrontation and wartime collaboration by which the colonists had gained some of what they wanted and retained hope of gaining still more at a later date. Provincials therefore lost much of their leverage against Imperial reforms just as metropolitan administrators began to re-evaluate the burdens that the colonies should bear for Imperial defense and administration. Without Imperial war, the colonists turned to civil war. The revolutionaries now used the network to unite diverse interests within each colony against the crown, knit thirteen contiguous but very different colonies together, and then petition the other Atlantic empires for recognition and assistance. It was a request to be restored, in a new sense, behind the Gallic aegis.

Select Bibliography

FRED ANDERSON, *Crucible of War: The Seven Years' War and the Fate of Empire in British North America, 1754–1766* (New York, 2000).

DAVID ARMITAGE, *The Ideological Origins of the British Empire* (Cambridge, 2000).

BERNARD BAILYN, *The Ideological Origins of the American Revolution* (Cambridge, MA, 1967).

BERNARD BAILYN, *The Origins of American Politics* (New York, 1968).

MARY SARAH BILDER, *The Transatlantic Constitution: Colonial Legal Culture and the Empire* (Cambridge, MA, 2004).

T. H. BREEN, *American Insurgents, American Patriots: The Revolution of the People* (New York, 2010).

STEPHEN CONWAY, *The British Isles and the War of American Independence* (Oxford, 2000).

JOSEPH A. ERNST, *Money and Politics in America, 1755–1775: A Study in the Currency Act of 1764 and the Political Economy of Revolution* (Chapel Hill, NC, 1973).

LAWRENCE H. GIPSON, *The American Revolution as an Aftermath of the Great War for Empire, 1754–1763* (Bethlehem, PA, 1950).

JACK P. GREENE, *Negotiated Authorities: Essays in Colonial Political and Constitutional History* (Charlottesville, VA, 1994).

JACK P. GREENE, *Peripheries and Center: Constitutional Development in the Extended Polities of the British Empire and the United States, 1607–1788* (Athens, GA, 1986).

ERIC HINDERAKER, *Elusive Empires: Constructing Colonialism in the Ohio Valley, 1673–1800* (New York, 1997).

WOODY HOLTON, *Forced Founders: Indians, Debtors, Slaves, and the Making of the American Revolution in Virginia* (Chapel Hill, NC, 1999).

DANIEL J. HULSEBOSCH, *Constituting Empire: New York and the Transformation of Constitutionalism in the Atlantic World, 1664–1830* (Chapel Hill, NC, 2005).

MICHAEL KAMMEN, *A Rope of Sand: Colonial Agents, British Politics, and the American Revolution* (Ithaca, NY, 1968).

BERNHARD KNOLLENBERG, *Growth of the American Revolution: 1766–1775* (Indianapolis, 2003).

BERNHARD KNOLLENBERG, *Origin of the American Revolution: 1759–1766* (Indianapolis, 2002).

LEONARD W. LABAREE, *Royal Government in America: A Study of the British Colonial System Before 1783* (New York, 1958).

PAULINE MAIER, *From Resistance to Revolution: Colonial Radicals and the Development of American Opposition to Britain, 1765–1776* (New York, 1972).

BRENDAN MCCONVILLE, *The King's Three Faces: The Rise and Fall of Royal America, 1688–1776* (Chapel Hill, NC, 2006).

ALISON G. OLSON, *Making the Empire Work: London and American Interest Groups, 1690–1790* (Cambridge, MA, 1992).

ANDREW J. O'SHAUGHNESSY, *An Empire Divided: The American Revolution and the British Caribbean* (Philadelphia, 2000).

JOHN PHILLIP REID, *Constitutional History of the American Revolution*, 4 vols. (Madison, WI, 1986–93).

JOSEPH HENRY SMITH, *Appeals to the Privy Council from the American Plantations* (New York, 1950).

IAN K. STEELE, *The English Atlantic, 1675–1740: An Exploration of Communication and Community* (New York, 1986).

PETER D. G. THOMAS, *British Politics and the Stamp Act Crisis: The First Phase of the American Revolution, 1763–1767* (Oxford, 1975).

PETER D. G. THOMAS, *The Townshend Duties Crisis: The Second Phase of the American Revolution, 1767–1773* (Oxford, 1987).

PETER D. G. THOMAS, *Tea Party to Independence: The Third Phase of the American Revolution 1773–1776* (Oxford, 1991).

11

Epilogue

The United States in the British Empire[*]

Jay Sexton

"In the year of grace 1776, we published to the world our Declaration of Independence. Six years later, England assented to the separation." So wrote American nationalist Henry Cabot Lodge in the centenary year of the 1783 Treaty of Paris. "These are tolerably familiar facts," Lodge continued, "That we have been striving ever since to make that independence real and complete, and that the work is not yet entirely finished, are not perhaps, equally obvious truisms." Given the persistence of "colonialism in the United States," as Lodge called it, it is fitting that this volume does not end in 1783. Though the Treaty of Paris recognized the political independence of the United States, the new republic remained within the orbit of the British Empire. Its developing economy relied on access to British markets, finished goods, and capital. Its statesmen formulated policy with an increasingly powerful and expanding British Empire in mind. In cultural terms, as well, Americans—still consumers of the Old World's ideas and goods—labored to create a distinctive national culture of their own.[1]

It would take more than the Declaration of Independence or the 1783 treaty for Americans to consider themselves fully free from the British Empire. The multitude of subsequent declarations of independence reveal this fact: the ink on the Treaty of Paris had barely dried when Noah Webster called for linguistic independence; Americans viewed the War of 1812 as a "second war for independence"; Monroe's 1823 message to Congress soon

[*] The author would like to thank the following for their helpful comments on drafts of this chapter: Stephen Foster, Richard Carwardine, A. G. Hopkins, Donald Ratcliffe, Heath Mitton, Gareth Davies, and John Watts.

[1] Henry Cabot Lodge, "Colonialism in the United States," *Atlantic Monthly*, LVII (1883), pp. 612–27.

became a "diplomatic declaration of independence"; Thomas Cole asserted artistic independence in his essay on landscapes in 1836; a year later, Ralph Waldo Emerson proclaimed the nation's intellectual independence; and J. S. Morgan (the father of J. P.) called for financial independence in 1857. But just as it took a protracted war to achieve the political independence that had been declared in 1776, subsequent declarations of independence reflected hopes more than accomplishments.

Long obscured by inward-looking and nationalist historiographies, the place of the young American republic within the British Empire has been the subject of recent scholarship. Indeed, historians increasingly use the term "postcolonial" in reference to the early national period in order to highlight continuities with the colonial era and to call attention to the ongoing importance of the British Empire.[2] "For all its vaunted claims of distinctiveness," historian Sam W. Haynes contends, "the young republic exhibited a set of anxieties not uncommon among nation-states that have emerged from long periods of colonial rule."[3] A. G. Hopkins has gone so far as to suggest that the early American republic be considered an "honorary dominion" of the British Empire.[4]

This recent work has made clear that the American quest to consolidate independence from Britain in the decades after 1783 was a complex and multifaceted process. If most Americans agreed that the struggle against the British Empire continued after 1783, they argued endlessly about how to achieve nationalist objectives. Britain at times threatened to undermine the independence of the United States. But British power was also essential to the young republic's economic and strategic interests. Furthermore, the widespread fear in America that Britain exercised too much control over the nation's destiny at times bound together the diverse states, sections, and peoples of the new republic. This epilogue examines the central, yet variable, role played by Britain in the United States' economy, statecraft, and culture in what can be considered a protracted "postcolonial" period that lasted well into the nineteenth century.

****

[2] Jack P. Greene (and responses), "Colonial History and National History: Reflections on a Continuing Problem," *WMQ*, 3rd ser., LXIV (2007), pp. 235–86.

[3] Sam W. Haynes, *Unfinished Revolution: The Early American Republic in a British World* (Charlottesville, VA, 2010), p. 2.

[4] A. G. Hopkins, "The United States, 1783–1861: Britain's Honorary Dominion?" *Britain and the World*, IV (2011), pp. 232–46.

The political fracture of 1776 only temporarily disrupted the economic connections between Britain and her former American colonies. In the years after the Revolution, British merchants and financiers quickly recovered their position in the American economy, elbowing aside their opportunistic Dutch and French rivals. By 1784, Britain enjoyed a higher value of exports across the Atlantic than in the years preceding the revolutionary crisis and would soon resume its position as the greatest creditor to the young republic. The volume and value of American exports to Britain also rapidly increased in the years following independence. Though European turmoil at times profoundly disrupted this economic relationship, flows of goods and capital between the two nations reached unprecedented levels after 1815. On average in the years 1815–1861, the United States shipped half its exports to Britain, while receiving 40 percent of its imports from its former colonial master. On the other side of this trade, the United States constituted both Britain's leading export market and its largest source of imports. These commercial links were made possible by the expansion of transatlantic shipping lines, as well as a sophisticated system of finance and credit presided over by Anglo-American banking houses such as the London-based Baring Brothers.[5]

This symbiotic commercial connection formed what has been called "a single, integrated Atlantic economy." It bears pointing out, however, that the United States was the subordinate partner in the relationship. Indeed, mid-twentieth-century historian Frank Thistlethwaite went so far as to group the United States with the new Latin American republics as part of Britain's early nineteenth-century "informal trading empire." Such an argument is premised upon the view of the American republic as a developing outpost of the industrializing British economy.[6] The majority of American exports to Britain were raw materials and agricultural goods (especially, as the nineteenth century progressed, cotton), whereas most of Britain's exports to the United States were finished goods. Jeffersonian Republicans boasted that Britain was more reliant on the "necessary" foodstuffs and raw materials they exported than Americans were dependent on "luxury" British imports. Such thinking underlay the ill-fated embargo of 1807–9, which revealed the

---

[5] This economic relationship is succinctly outlined in J. Potter, "Atlantic Economy, 1815–60: The U.S.A. and the Industrial Revolution in Britain," in L. S. Pressnell (ed.), *Studies in the Industrial Revolution* (London, 1970), p. 239.

[6] These Phrases come from Frank Thistlethwaite, *The Anglo-American Connection in the Early Nineteenth Century* (Philadelphia, 1959), pp. 3–5.

perils of commercial isolation: as the American economy suffered from the closure of European markets, Britain capitalized on other markets within her Imperial grasp. The asymmetry in the diplomatic relationship between the two nations reinforced the unequal terms of their economic dealings, particularly in the early years of American independence. Britain's disregard for the neutral rights of American shipping during the Napoleonic Wars obstructed the overseas trade required by the internationalist American economy and helped to trigger the War of 1812. The United States also suffered from Britain's discriminatory trading system within her empire, which restricted access to markets such as the British West Indies that had been integral to the American economy in the colonial era.

Though Britain retained economic influence and power over its former colonies, this did not translate into the kind of effective economic control that it exercised within its Imperial domains. As P. J. Cain and A. G. Hopkins have made clear, the position of the United States within Britain's economic system differed in important ways from those of the British settler colonies in Canada and Australasia.[7] The American republic, of course, enjoyed unchallenged political independence and could pursue policies of economic nationalism. If the aggregate figures of trade and investment from Britain were high in America, Britain's proportional slice of the overall economic pie in the United States was less than what it enjoyed in its settler colonies— economic historians estimate that foreign investment accounted for only 5 percent of the capital stock increase in nineteenth-century America.[8] The development of inland trade within the young republic, as well as its commercial engagement with Europe, Latin America, and Asia, weaned the United States from reliance upon British markets. Despite its diplomatic failure, the Jeffersonian embargo of 1807–9 had the unintended consequence of stimulating American manufacturing, thus demonstrating the potential of the young republic to diversify and develop its economy. Furthermore, one should not overlook the economic importance of the United States to Britain, both as an export market and as a source of raw materials,

---

[7] P. J. Cain and A. G. Hopkins, "The Theory and Practice of British Imperialism," in Raymond E. Dumett (ed.), *Gentlemanly Capitalism and British Imperialism: The New Debate on Empire* (Harlow, 1999), pp. 206–10.

[8] Lance E. Davis and Robert J. Cull, "International Capital Movements, Domestic Capital Markets, and American Economic Growth, 1820–1914," in Stanley Engerman and Robert Gallman (eds), *The Cambridge Economic History of the United States: The Long Nineteenth-century* (Cambridge, 2000), pp. 733–812.

foodstuffs, and, most of all, cotton (though the Confederacy would discover the limits of this reliance during the Civil War). Indeed, bolstered by Britain's liberal tariff reductions, the balance of trade tilted in favor of the United States in the 1840s for the remainder of the nineteenth century.

In the eyes of most early Americans, however, there was little question that their republic remained an economic vassalage of the British Empire. As Henry Clay put it, the United States was in danger of remaining a "sort of independent colonies of England—politically free, commercially slaves."[9] The question of how to break free of Britain's economic orbit became a principal issue in early American politics. From this debate emerged the political coalitions that constituted the first party system of Republicans and Federalists. Led by Thomas Jefferson, Republicans sought to construct a liberal international order cleared of preferential trading systems. This commercial vision, which aimed to entrench republicanism at home and advance the interests of agricultural exporters, challenged the economic structures of the British Empire. When Britain did not acquiesce in American demands for open trade and respect for neutral rights, Jeffersonian Republicans advocated economic retaliation (either in the form of tariffs, which Jefferson advocated as a temporary measure at various points in the 1790s or, as in 1807–9, in the form of an all-out embargo). At the other end of the political spectrum were the Federalists, led by Alexander Hamilton, who viewed Britain as an indispensable economic partner, as well as a model to emulate. The Hamiltonian program called for the consolidation of the nation's finances through the creation of a national bank and the federal assumption of state debts. The Federalists were prepared to make diplomatic compromises with their former colonial master to achieve their objectives, thus further widening the partisan divide at home. Most notable was the 1795 Jay Treaty, which averted war with Britain in the short term by addressing several left-over issues from the Revolutionary period, but outraged Republicans for aligning the United States with its old nemesis and for its failure to protect neutral rights on the high seas.

If Republicans and Federalists disagreed on how to achieve economic independence, they were of one voice in identifying Britain as their greatest economic rival in the long term. For all their differences, both parties were in agreement on the fundamental objective of establishing American eco-

---

[9] Quoted in Kinley Brauer, "The United States and British Imperial Expansion, 1815–1860," *Diplomatic History,* XII (1988), pp. 19–37 (quotation at p. 24).

nomic independence. Historians of the British Empire have stressed the role played by "collaborating elites" in ensconcing Britain's power in her formal and informal empires. Though the Federalists were a pro-British elite, they differed from "collaborating elites" in Britain's empire by rejecting associations with the old country that infringed upon American sovereignty.[10] Economic and political exigencies also at times blurred the lines between the two parties. A recent examination of the funding of the national debt in this period reveals that, despite their heated political rhetoric, Federalists and Republicans endorsed similar policies and institutions of public finance.[11] Though Republicans advocated retaliatory tariffs in the 1790s, they did not implement them when in the ascendancy after 1800, in large part because of the profits derived from the boom in trade with the European belligerents. The Republicans moved to interrupt transatlantic trade only after Britain (as well as France) devised extraordinary measures during a new phase of the crisis in Europe. Jefferson's embargo of 1807–9 is perhaps most significant for its unpopularity and unsuccessful enforcement. Likewise, Hamilton's report calling for a modest tariff increase to promote American manufacturing fell upon deaf ears even in the Federalist Congresses of the 1790s. In the years immediately following the War of 1812, the perceived British threat to the United States led erstwhile political opponents to find common ground. Even Jefferson himself briefly embraced nationalist economic measures, such as a moderate tariff and national bank, in order to counter British power by continuing the development of the American economy.

Over time, the gap between American political coalitions and sections reopened. Whigs and Democrats of the second party system parted on matters of economic policy in ways similar to the Federalists and Jeffersonian Republicans. Whigs argued that an active federal government would promote national economic development and integration, thus thwarting British neo-colonialism. Henry Clay's "American system" of federally supported internal improvements, a national bank, protective tariffs, and export expansion sought to liberate the United States from the so-called "British system." The Democrats' opposition to these measures drew from

---

[10] The importance of "collaborating elites" is examined in Ronald Robinson, "Non-European Foundations of European Imperialism: Sketch for a Theory of Collaboration," in E. R. J. Owen and R. B. Sutcliffe (eds), *Studies in the Theory of Imperialism* (London, 1972), and P. J. Marshall, *The Making and Unmaking of Empires: Britain, India and America, c. 1750–1783* (Oxford, 2005).

[11] Max M. Edling, "'So Immense a Power in the Affairs of War': Alexander Hamilton and the Restoration of Public Credit," *WMQ*, LXIV, 3rd ser. (2007), pp. 287–326.

the Jeffersonian vision of an international commercial system liberated from the corrupting influences of mercantilism and colonial rivalry. The debate over how best to counter British economic ascendancy increasingly focused on the tariff, which after a brief consensus in the post-1815 period, became a political lightning rod. Both protectionists and free traders claimed to advance American independence and counter British neo-colonialism. Advocates of protectionism argued that the tariff would end economic dependence upon British manufacturers. Free-traders responded that the tariff would subvert republican government and transform the Union into a corrupt mercantilist system not unlike the very British Empire that Americans had rebelled against in 1776. The battle over the tariff also took on a sectional dimension, with cotton-exporting Southern Democrats championing free trade and northeastern Whig manufacturers advocating protection from their British competitors. If the question of how best to counter British economic power did not neatly divide along North-South lines—many northwestern farmers, for instance, advocated free trade, while protectionism appealed to Louisiana sugar planters and border state hemp growers—it did play an important role in the development of sectional identities.[12]

The debate over how best to free the United States from Britain's economic orbit thus became entangled in larger questions about the form of the Union at home, as well as the larger international system that Americans hoped would follow from their revolution. But for as much as Americans anticipated a new global order, they continued to operate in an era of British ascendancy. The Federalist policy of assuming state debts and the Whig program of internal improvements increased American dependence on British capital. Likewise, Jeffersonian opposition to barriers to international commerce furthered the nation's reliance on British manufactured goods. The nationalist objectives of the early republic were contingent upon the exploitation of Britain's economic power.

Britain's role in the economic development of the United States was particularly important in the realm of finance. Long-term foreign investment in the United States increased from $18 million in 1789 to $222 million in 1853, to $1.39 billion in 1869, to more than $7 billion in 1914. The overwhelming majority of this foreign investment was of British origin—in 1861, the first

---

[12] Nicholas Onuf and Peter Onuf, *Nations, Markets and War: Modern History and the American Civil War* (Charlottesville, VA, 2006), pp. 219–342; Brian Schoen, *The Fragile Fabric of Union: Cotton, Federal Politics, and the Global Origins of the Civil War* (Baltimore, 2009).

year for which there are reliable figures, 90 percent of the foreign capital in America came from Britain.[13] This westward flow of capital helped fuel the dramatic economic take-off of the United States in the nineteenth century. British investment kept interest rates relatively low in the capital-starved republic, it underwrote important aspects of the "transportation revolution" of canals and railroads, and it financed the debts of municipalities, state governments, and the federal government itself. By the mid-nineteenth century, nearly half of the United States' national debt was held abroad, chiefly in Britain. British capital also played an important role in the American project of nineteenth century nation and empire building. The United States did not "win" the West on its own—or at least not with its own money. To take one example, the London banking house of Baring Brothers, which served as the United States' official agency overseas for much of the nineteenth century, underwrote several of the key transactions that expanded and preserved the nation: the Louisiana Purchase of 1803; the Mexican War loan and indemnity payment of 1848 (which helped finance the conquest and annexation of northern Mexico); and the refinancing of the Civil War debt at a lower rate of interest in the 1870s. Credit from the Barings also helped American merchants penetrate commercial markets in Latin America. Baring Brothers Bank was thus an important actor in the territorial expansion of the United States, the consolidation of the Union during the Civil War era, and the promotion of American exports overseas.

British investment in the United States also triggered political conflict, particularly when it dramatically increased in the mid-nineteenth century. The Whig (and, later, Republican) successors of Alexander Hamilton viewed the importation of capital as essential to economic development and internal improvement. Those opposed, cut from the political cloth of Jefferson and Andrew Jackson, tended to view British investment as the infiltration of an aristocratic elite—the "money power" or "monied aristocracy," in Jacksonian parlance. The fear that British capitalists wielded power over the United States became dogma in the Democratic Party and spanned the entire nineteenth century, from the state papers of Jefferson and Jackson

---

[13] Mira Wilkins, *The History of Foreign Investment in the United States to 1914* (Cambridge, MA, 1989), pp. 50–1, 137, 147; Lance E. Davis and Robert Cull, *International Capital Markets and American Economic Growth, 1820–1914* (Cambridge, 1994), pp. 16–17. The percentage of British capital would slowly decline after the Civil War. 60 percent of the foreign investment in the US in 1914 was of British origin.

to the speeches of William Jennings Bryan in the 1890s. There was more than a kernel of truth to this argument. The foreign indebtedness of the United States at times encouraged unpopular compromises in foreign policy, special legislation, and, later in the century, judicial rulings favorable to corporations and foreign bondholders. The American economy was also particularly vulnerable to fluctuations in the London money markets, as the frequent transatlantic financial panics of the nineteenth century revealed (1819, 1837, 1857, 1873, 1893). "The barometer of the American money market," one congressman remarked in the 1830s, "hangs up at the stock exchange in London."[14]

Such critiques, however, should be viewed in relation to the benefits British capital brought to the developing American economy. The alternative of restricting the importation of capital was hardly desirable for a nation in need of funds for infrastructure development, as many parts of the Union would discover when foreign investment dried up in the aftermath of financial panics in 1819 and 1837. Compared to the economic difficulties faced by the new states in Latin America, who were unable to attract a consistent flow of capital at the affordable rates their northern neighbor enjoyed, foreign investment in the United States does not appear in such a pejorative light. The United States was able to exercise some control over the public debt that was held in Britain. Unlike the obligations of Latin American states that were denominated in pounds sterling, the national debt of the United States was forever transferred to dollars in 1795. The privileged position afforded to the United States on the London money market owed much to the shared culture and networks that grew out of old colonial ties, in this regard more resembling the "cultural economy" of the late-nineteenth-century British world than the British informal empire in Latin America.[15] It is difficult, for example, to view Baring Brothers as an agent of foreign imperialism in the United States: the bank's London partnership included American citizens; it acted on the advice of its American correspondents and investment partners such as Thomas Wren Ward in Boston; and the head of the firm in the early nineteenth century, Alexander Baring, doubled as an MP and diplomat who labored to preserve Anglo-American

[14] Quoted in Ron Chernow, *The House of Morgan* (London, 1990), p. 4.

[15] For a discussion of the "cultural economy" of the late nineteenth-century, see, Gary B. Magee and Andrew S. Thompson, *Empire and Globalisation: Networks of People, Goods and Capital in the British World, c. 1850–1914* (Cambridge, 2010).

peace. Indeed, when transatlantic financiers involved themselves in American politics and diplomacy it was most often to work for the maintenance of Anglo-American peace, not to construct exploitative, quasi-imperial structures.[16]

The United States differed from Latin America in terms of its financial relationship with Britain in another crucial regard: the absence of "gunboat diplomacy." The Royal Navy played a central role in the promotion of Britain's economic interests in Latin America, even if instances of outright gunboat diplomacy were fewer than is often thought.[17] The story was much different in the United States, where the threat of force to collect debts was unthinkable, even in the 1780s when the young republic failed to abide by its treaty obligation to repay lawful debts to British creditors. Rather than rely upon its powerful navy, Britain counted upon American debtors' enlightened self-interest to repay old loans in order to improve their credit rating for raising future capital. This scenario was repeated in the 1840s when several US states defaulted on their debts (three states even repudiated their debts outright, relishing the opportunity, as one Mississippian put it, to "slap John Bull in the face"). Despite these provocations, the British government declined to involve itself in the situation, leaving a group of City investors to use persuasion, rather than force, in a "restoration campaign," which met with some success.[18]

Two nineteenth-century wars played a key role in fostering the national development of the US economy. The embargo period and the War of 1812 ushered in a brief era of economic nationalism that facilitated a growth in manufacturing and the integration and development of the internal market. The Civil War played an even greater role in the development of the American economy. The political ascendancy of Republicans, whose protectionist nationalism drew power from the fear of British free-trade imperialism, inaugurated an era of protective tariffs that nourished domestic manufacturing. Sheltered from British and European competitors in this "golden era of American protectionism," American industrial output would overtake

---

[16] Jay Sexton, *Debtor Diplomacy: Finance and American Foreign Relations in the Civil War Era, 1837–1873* (Oxford, 2005).

[17] See Alan Knight, "Britain and Latin America," in Andrew Porter, *OHBE*, III, *The Nineteenth Century*, p. 124; Barry Gough, "Profit and Power: Informal Empire, the Navy, and Latin America," in Dumett (ed.), *Gentlemanly Capitalism and British Imperialism*, pp. 68–81.

[18] P. J. Cain and A. G. Hopkins, *British Imperialism: Innovation and Expansion, 1688–1914* (London, 1993); Sexton, *Debtor Diplomacy*, pp. 40–5.

that of Britain by the turn of the century.[19] The Republicans also promoted
the internal development of the nation's vast territories by encouraging
westward migration (in the 1862 Homestead Act) and the construction
of the transcontinental railroad. The drying up of British investment during
the war accelerated the development of the national financial infrastructure
that the United States had previously lacked. No longer able to rely on the
City for financial support, the federal government established a national
banking structure, created a national currency, and turned toward an
emerging group of American capitalists for loans. The increased volume
of transactions on Wall Street necessitated the construction of a new
building in 1863, the New York Stock Exchange, which served as a symbol
of the nation's growing financial independence.[20]

The career of J. P. Morgan reflects the transatlantic dimensions of the
economic rise of nineteenth-century America. Morgan began his banking
career in the mid-nineteenth century as an apprentice to his father's
investment bank in London, which underwrote transatlantic trade and
marketed American securities abroad. Morgan returned to the United
States in time to make his initial fortune from the government contracts
he secured during the Civil War. Throughout the late nineteenth century,
he continued to channel British investment to the United States, primarily
to the railroads that he consolidated into his financial empire. By the
turn of the century, however, the dynamics of the Anglo-American financial relationship were changing: the center of gravity began to shift from
the City to Wall Street, where Morgan now concentrated his activities.
In 1900, it was the American house of Morgan that provided funds to the
cash-strapped British government during the Boer War, an act which
portended the reversal of capital flows across the Atlantic in the years
after 1914.

****

The loss of the thirteen colonies did not mark the end of Britain's North
American empire. Maya Jasanoff's recent study of the loyalist diaspora
reveals how the "spirit of 1783" strengthened and reconfigured the British

[19] Alfred E. Eckes, *Opening America's Market: U.S. Foreign Trade Policy Since 1776* (Chapel
Hill, NC, 1990), p. 28.
[20] Richard Bensel, *Yankee Leviathan: The Origins of Central State Authority in America,
1859–1877* (Cambridge, 1990).

Empire, particularly in British North America where some 6,000 refugees resettled and became ardent supporters of the Empire.[21] Upper Canada's first lieutenant governor, John Graves Simcoe, sought to create a stronghold in Canada that would provide the means from which to regain possession of the lost colonies. In the years after the 1783 Treaty of Paris, Simcoe attracted further American migrants to Upper Canada through generous land grants and low taxes. By 1812, some 30,000 "late loyalists" bolstered the population of Upper Canada. British officials also attempted to undermine the American republic from within by maintaining relations with Indian tribes inside the United States and even occupied forts in America's Northwest Territory until the late 1790s. The contested and porous US-Canadian borderland became the site of what Alan Taylor has called a "cold war" between the new American republic and Britain's "counterrevolutionary regime in Canada."[22] As British imperialists aimed to strengthen their position in Canada, as well as expand their interests around the globe, the fledgling United States struggled to maintain its union and independence. The initial experiment in decentralized republicanism, as manifested in the Articles of Confederation, proved unable to respond to the financial, political, and diplomatic challenges that confronted the new republic. Leaders in independent Vermont toyed with re-entering the British Empire, frontiersmen held out the possibility of breaking away from the Union, and even federal officials such as Tennessee senator William Blount and Jefferson's former vice-president Aaron Burr schemed to detach regions of the trans-Appalachian West.

This context of American instability and insecurity in an era of rising British imperial power is crucial to understanding the politics and statecraft of the young republic. It helps to explain a development that is often taken for granted: the formation of the Union itself in the 1780s. The newly independent states, of course, were not pre-ordained to form a single nation. To be sure, they were connected to one another by networks of trade and communication, a republican ideology, and the experience of collectively fighting the British during the Revolution. Yet, as the contentious debates of the 1787 Constitutional Convention demonstrated, the states were deeply divided. Small and large states argued over the form of political representation, Atlantic seaboard states worried about their status in a westwardly

---

[21] Maya Jasanoff, *Liberty's Exiles: The Loss of America and the Remaking of the British Empire* (London, 2011).

[22] Alan Taylor, *The Civil War of 1812: American Citizens, British Subjects, Irish Rebels, and Indian Allies* (New York, 2010), pp. 5, 28.

expanding union and, most ominously, southern slaveholding states and those abolishing the institution in the north looked upon each other with great suspicion. After all, the fragmented states of Latin America that emerged from the collapse of Spanish rule in the early nineteenth century suggest that union among the thirteen former colonies in North America was only one of many political possibilities after independence.

That the American Union endured until 1861 owed much to the interlocking relationship between union and independence.[23] Even before the Revolution, American leaders feared that independence would result in a cluster of un-stable states or regional federations that would invite further European med-dling. In this scenario the American states would have traded their place within the British Empire for the even less desirable position as pawns of the European powers, pitted against one another in conflicts waged to maintain the balance of power in the Old World. Nationalist John Jay feared that "every state would be a little nation, jealous of its neighbors, and anxious to strengthen itself by foreign alliances, against its former friends." The newly independent states could only be secure if bound together in a strong union. "Weakness and divisions at home would invite dangers from abroad," Jay later asserted when making the case for a stronger central government, "nothing would tend more to secure us from them than union, strength, and good government within ourselves." The benefits of union far outweighed the costs, even in the minds of South Carolinians who, though aware of the proliferation of antislavery doctrines in the northern states, concluded that a more powerful central authority could best secure slavery on their vulnerable periphery. Not only would union pre-empt future conflicts between the states and foreign intervention, but it also provided the means for territorial expansion, the exercise of control over Native Americans, and the economic development and integration of the vast resources of the North American continent. "We have seen the necessity of the Union," James Madison wrote in Federalist 14, "as our bulwark against foreign danger, as the conservator of peace among ourselves, as the guardian of our commerce and other common interests."[24]

---

[23] As explored in David C. Hendrickson, *Peace Pact: The Lost World of the American Founding* (Lawrence, KS, 2003) and *Union, Nation, or Empire: The American Debate Over International Relations, 1789–1941* (Lawrence, KS, 2009), and Peter Onuf, "A Declaration of Independence for Diplomatic Historians," *Diplomatic History*, XXII (1998), pp. 71–83.

[24] Jay quotation from Peter Onuf, "The Expanding Union," in David T. Konig (ed.), *Devising Liberty: Preserving and Creating Freedom in the New American Republic* (Stanford, CA, 1995), pp (quotation at p. 60). 50–80; James Madison, "Federalist no. 14" [1787], in Lawrence Goldman (ed.), *The Federalist Papers* (Oxford, 2008), pp. 26, 67.

The US Constitution of 1787 sought to consolidate the achievements of the Revolution by creating a union powerful enough to maintain its independence. It aimed to walk the tight-rope of conferring new powers on the federal government while, at the same time, satisfying individual states by retaining elements of home rule. In time, contrasting interpretations of whether ultimate power resided in the federal government or within the states would contribute to constitutional crisis and civil war. In the 1780s, however, this balancing act was required to achieve both union and independence: strong central authority might better counter British power, but it could prove fatal to the Union from within; too much delegation of power to the states, on the other hand, might leave the United States incapable of maintaining its independence, a lesson learned under the inadequate Articles of Confederation. The interdependent goals of union and independence thus became the twin pillars of early American statecraft; they "were from the beginning... joined at the hip," as David Hendrickson has recently put it.[25]

Though the former colonies could bind in union to secure their independence, the diplomatic fortunes of the new republic still lay largely outside its control. The very weakness and vulnerability of the United States in its early years could at times be a diplomatic asset. With many British statesmen convinced of the Union's eventual demise, they saw little need to pursue costly policies to hasten the inevitable when their resources were required elsewhere, particularly after the all-consuming conflict with France began in 1793. American statesmen seized upon multiple diplomatic opportunities that were presented to them during the European wars of 1793–1815. "Europe's distress," as Samuel Flagg Bemis long ago argued, undoubtedly was "America's advantage"—from the successful prosecution of the Revolution to the Jay and Pinckney Treaties of 1795 (which opened the Mississippi River to American commerce), to the Louisiana Purchase of 1803.[26] Such diplomatic coups notwithstanding, the geopolitical instability of the period also endangered the young republic. Statesmen in Washington particularly feared that peoples in western territories might align themselves with

---

[25] Hendrickson, *Peace Pact*, p. 21; Max Edling, *A Revolution in Favor of Government: Origins of the U.S. Constitution and the Making of the American State* (Oxford, 2003); Frederick W. Marks, *Independence on Trial: Foreign Affairs and the Making of the Constitution* (Baton Rouge, LA, 1973).

[26] Samuel Flagg Bemis, *Pinckney's Treaty: America's Advantage from Europe's Distress, 1783–1800* (Baltimore, 1926).

Britain or France, thus destroying their independent Union.[27] The history of links between Native Americans and British traders was the cause of further alarm. American officials, such as Indiana Territorial Governor William Henry Harrison, were so convinced of the British–Indian nexus that they viewed dispossessing Indians of their lands as a continuation of the American Revolution.[28] In such ways, the anticolonial struggle against Britain seamlessly merged with the project of American imperial expansion.

A great dilemma for early American statesmen concerned how to harness British power to their own ends without becoming a pawn of their former colonial master. Diplomatic exigency during the Louisiana and Spanish–American crises of the early nineteenth century, for example, led even Thomas Jefferson to recognize that American interests could best be advanced through cooperation with the hated British. American leaders also faced a domestic political challenge: the anglophobic political culture that was a product of the Revolution made it difficult to openly align with the British, even when it was in the national interest. Few walked this tightrope better than George Washington, whose foreign policy tilted toward the British. Indeed, historian Bradford Perkins has argued that the 1795 Jay Treaty sowed the seeds of "the first rapprochement" between Britain and the United States.[29] Yet, in his famous 1796 "Farewell Address," Washington glossed over this fact, emphasizing instead the alleged "great rule" of having "as little political connection as possible" with the Old World and the need "to steer clear of permanent alliances." Modeled after the "political testaments" of eighteenth-century European statesmen, Washington's address drew in both style and substance from the diplomatic traditions of Old World powers. Though his "great rule" of diplomatic non-entanglement is often viewed as a manifestation of American exceptionalism, it should be remembered that British statesmen also sought to limit "foreign entanglements" and cherished their island's "splendid isolation" from continental Europe.[30]

---

[27] Leonard J. Sadosky, *Revolutionary Negotiations: Indians, Empires, and Diplomats in the Founding of America* (Charlottesville, VA, 2009); John Craig Hammond, *Slavery, Freedom and Expansion in the Early American West* (Charlottesville, VA, 2007).

[28] Robert M. Owens, *Mr. Jefferson's Hammer: William Henry Harrison and the Origins of American Indian Policy* (Norman, OK, 2007).

[29] Bradford Perkins, *The First Rapprochement: England and the United States, 1795–1805* (Philadelphia, 1955).

[30] Felix Gilbert, *To the Farewell Address: Ideas of Early American Foreign Policy* (Princeton, 1961); Alexander DeConde, "Washington's Farewell, the French Alliance, and the Election of

If the young republic found benefit from the European turmoil of this period, it did come at the cost of conflict with both France (in the "Quasi-War" of 1798–1800) and Britain (in the War of 1812). In contrast to previous diplomatic coups, the United States achieved none of its objectives in the War of 1812 and was fortunate to emerge from the conflict intact. The invasion of Canada was a disaster that ultimately strengthened loyalty to Britain north of the border. Late in the war, the Union threatened to dissolve from within when disaffected New England Federalists convened in Hartford, Connecticut, to consider pursuing a separate peace with Britain.[31] The 1815 Treaty of Ghent that concluded the conflict did nothing to protect American commerce and sailors on the high seas. When viewed in a broader context, however, the War of 1812 successfully consolidated the achievements of the American Revolution.[32] This "second war of independence," as Americans soon remembered it, secured Britain's acceptance of the American republic. It also consolidated the United States' grip on its western territories, not least by breaking British alliances with Native Americans. The conflict that had witnessed British troops burn public buildings in Washington ended on the high note of Andrew Jackson's decisive victory in New Orleans, which helped foster a passionate nationalism that strengthened the Union from within. The partisan conflict during the war was replaced with an interregnum of single party rule. If this "era of good feelings" was not as harmonious as imagined by some at the time, it did briefly witness politicians from across the spectrum embracing legislation that promoted economic development and the integration of internal markets.

In the decades after the War of 1812, the United States strengthened its position in North America, acquiring Florida from Spain and seizing Native American lands east of the Mississippi. British policy enabled American expansion by repudiating old Indian alliances, demilitarizing the Canadian border, and prioritizing peace during territorial disputes in the 1840s. Though Yankee pretensions of national greatness grated, the "official mind" in Britain came to regard the upstart American republic as an important Imperial collaborator. There was little enthusiasm in Britain for

1796," in Burton Ira Kaufman (ed.), *Washington's Farewell Address: The View from the 20th Century* (Chicago, 1969), pp. 116–36.

[31] James M. Banner, *To the Hartford Convention: The Federalists and the Origins of Party Politics in Massachusetts, 1789–1815* (New York, 1970).

[32] Taylor, *The Civil War of 1812*, esp. p. 437.

pursuing costly, unpopular policies that had little chance of containing American expansion. Fighting the Americans, a Victorian once said, would be like breaking your neighbor's windows with gold coins. Content to maintain their hold on Canada and profit from the Atlantic economy, the British outsourced the job of imperial expansion in North America, reaping the economic benefits of an expanding United States without the overhead costs of imperial wars and administration. As Lord Palmerston put it, "commercially, no doubt we should gain by having the whole American continent occupied by an active enterprising race like the Anglo-Saxons instead of sleepy Spaniards."[33]

The context of the post-1815 period thus differed from what preceded it in that the United States operated from a position of greater security and strength. Much of the scholarship on nineteenth-century American foreign policy has made the case for continuity by highlighting the similarities between expansion in the early republican period and the continental imperialism of the 1840s, which saw the United States annex Texas, parts of the Oregon Territory, and northern regions of Mexico, including California. The "Manifest Destiny" ideology of this period certainly can be traced back to the thinking of early statesmen such as Thomas Jefferson, who celebrated the creation of an "empire of liberty." Furthermore, persistent fears of British intervention in the New World continued to fuel expansionist policies, never more so than in the 1845 annexation of Texas which Democrats and pro-slavery Southerners deemed an act of national security on the grounds that it prevented Britain from establishing an antislavery satellite on the nation's southwestern border.[34] Nonetheless, the different contexts within which US statesmen operated should be kept in view. Historian Reginald Stuart has drawn a line between what he labels "the era of defensive expansion" up to 1815 from the later "era of Manifest Destiny."[35] Indeed, the expansionism of the 1840s revealed that the greatest threat to the United States was no longer Britain, nor renegade frontiersmen, but the zealotry with which its own statesmen expanded the nation's

[33] Kenneth Bourne, *Britain and the Balance of Power in North America, 1815–1908* (London, 1967), pp. 182, 411.

[34] Sam Haynes, "Anglophobia and the Annexation of Texas: The Quest for National Security," in Sam Haynes and Christopher Morris (eds), *Manifest Destiny and Empire: American Antebellum Expansionism* (College Station, TX, 1997), pp. 115–45.

[35] Reginald C. Stuart, *United States Expansionism and British North America, 1775–1871* (Chapel Hill, NC, 1988).

territory. The dramatic expansion of the 1840s proved destructive to the internal dynamics of the Union, deepening the North–South sectional divide and setting in motion a chain of events that would lead to civil war in 1861.

In the case of Latin America, Britain was essential to the achievement of US objectives. Monroe's famous 1823 message that declared opposition to European intervention in Latin America should be viewed in relation to British power. Though later Americans would dub it a "doctrine" that constituted the nation's "diplomatic declaration of independence," its achievement relied upon Britain's Royal Navy. A comparison of Monroe's message of 1823 and the British "Polignac Memorandum" of the same year, which also aimed at blocking European intervention in Latin America, demonstrates a surprising similarity in the two nations' diplomatic object-ives.[36] Upon receiving Monroe's message in early 1824, the London *Times* applauded it for articulating "a policy so directly British."[37] Monroe's 1823 message reveals another important point: the two English-speaking powers could be rivals and allies at the same time. Though the United States and Britain sought to prevent the European powers from intervening in Latin America, they competed to gain control of new commercial markets, if not—particularly in the case of the United States—new territory. Indeed, the "Monroe Doctrine" and the "Polignac Memorandum" also can be read as exercises in public diplomacy that sought to curry favor with potential Latin American collaborators in what would become a prolonged struggle for hemispheric mastery.[38]

This ongoing Anglo-American imperial rivalry helps to explain the endurance of Anglophobia in American political culture in the decades after 1815. Fears of Britain also resulted from the ideological prism through which many Americans viewed the world, which presupposed conflict between republics and monarchies. The versatility and political utility of the British threat, both real and imagined, also accounts for its ubiquity in nineteenth-century America. Memories of previous conflicts with Britain (and, for Irish immigrants, first-hand experiences of living under British rule) made anti-British appeals a favorite tactic of American politicians of

---

[36] Bradford Perkins, *Castlereagh and Adams: England and the United States, 1812–1823* (Berkeley, CA, 1964), pp. 324–5.

[37] *The Times*, January 6, 1824.

[38] Jay Sexton, *The Monroe Doctrine: Empire and Nation in Nineteenth-Century America* (New York, 2011).

all persuasions. Jeffersonian Republicans and, later, Jacksonian Democrats, lost no opportunity to tar their Federalist and Whig opponents with the labels of monarchists and "Anglomen." Whigs and Republicans, such as John Quincy Adams and William H. Seward, also recognized the political value of an occasional twist to the lion's tail. Anglophobia played an important role in binding the diverse political coalitions of the early republic. In the case of the Democrats, for example, opposition to Britain helped bring together an eclectic group of bedfellows: Southern slaveholders, Irish immigrants in northern cities, and expansionists from the Midwest. Conjuring up the British threat helped expansionists mobilize domestic support on behalf of controversial policy objectives. The "Monroe Doctrine" of mid-nineteenth-century Democrats like James K. Polk exploited fears of Britain to secure support for aggressive foreign policies, thus transforming the limited 1823 message into a call for pre-emptive expansion.

If American expansionists tended to overstate the foreign threat in the mid-nineteenth century, Britain continued to threaten the United States in a fundamental regard: the future of slavery. Even before formally committing herself to abolition in 1833, Britain directly challenged American slavery by arming and freeing slaves during the Revolution and War of 1812. African Americans were quick to recognize that British power could be directed on behalf of their own goals. "The English are the best friends the coloured people have upon earth," black abolitionist David Walker asserted in 1829.[39] If British policy-makers retained a cautious sense of *realpolitik*—despite the appeal of an anti-slavery Texas, Britain did not stand in the way of its annexation to the Union in 1845—they nonetheless sought to contain and undermine American slavery, primarily through suppression of the international slave-trade, but also by sympathizing with and supporting the activities of abolitionist societies.[40] Britain, of course, was not the only external threat to the slaveholding South. Haiti represented the terrifying specter of successful slave rebellion, while the Northern states pointed to the model of gradual emancipation.[41] Yet the magnitude of the British threat is

---

[39] Van Gosse, "'As a Nation, the English Are Our Friends': The Emergence of African American Politics in the British Atlantic World, 1772–1861," *AHR*, CXIII (2008), pp. 1003–28.

[40] Steven Heath Mitton, "The Free World Confronted: The Problem of Slavery and Progress in American Foreign Relations, 1833–1844" (Ph.D. dis., Louisiana State University, 2005).

[41] Alfred N. Hunt, *Haiti's Influence on Antebellum America: Slumbering Volcano in the Caribbean* (Baton Rouge, LA, 1988); Robin Blackburn, "Haiti, Slavery, and the Age of the Democratic Revolution," *WMQ*, 3rd ser., LXIII (2006), pp. 643–74.

revealed in how Southerners often viewed these dangers through the prism of British power, fearing that their old nemesis was plotting to spread a Haitian-style insurrection to America or that Yankee abolitionists were the pawns of British antislavery organizations. Britain's antislavery position thus contributed to slaveholders' insecurity, fuelling Southern demands for the protection and expansion of slavery that would lead to civil war.[42]

Britain played another role in the break-up of the union: underlying the secession of the Deep South was the certitude that new political and economic arrangements could be constructed upon the transatlantic cotton trade. For all the antislavery activities of British diplomats and activists, it was the textile mills of Lancashire that consumed much of the cotton picked by the slaves of the Deep South, a fact Southerners lost no opportunity to point out. Britain's conciliatory diplomacy in the 1840s, particularly its acquiescence in the US annexation of Texas, served as evidence to many Southern slavers that the British were dependent upon their cotton. This mistaken calculation of the importance of "king cotton" nurtured secessionism in the Deep South, leading many slaveholders to the conclusion that their interests would best be advanced through an independent confederation allied not to the Northern states, but to their largest consumer of cotton, the British.[43]

British power, in sum, both undermined and benefited the expansionist American republic. Though domestic political considerations generally pulled the United States away from Britain, the nation's strategic and economic interests nonetheless could push the new republic, or sections of it, into accord with the former colonial master. Relations between the United States and Britain, particularly after 1815, thus might best be characterized as "collaborative competition." This oxymoron reflects the unusual circumstance of the United States in the nineteenth century: even as it continued the struggle to free itself from the tentacles of the British Empire, it was itself a nascent imperial power—a proponent of "imperial anti-colonialism," in the phrase of William Appleman Williams.[44]

For all their vilification of British colonialism, Americans formulated their own imperialist programs, which mirrored those of their former

---

[42] Edward B. Rugemer, *The Problem of Emancipation: The Caribbean Roots of the American Civil War* (Baton Rouge, LA, 2008).

[43] Schoen, *The Fragile Fabric of Union*.

[44] William Appleman Williams, *The Tragedy of American Diplomacy* (New York, 1972), pp. 18–58.

colonial master. The settlement of North America in the nineteenth century drew from colonial traditions of settler expansion and, as James Belich has recently argued, shared many traits with Britain's concurrent colonization of its "Wests" in the settler colonies of Canada, Australia, and New Zealand.[45] The American model of granting autonomy to white settlers on the periphery, enshrined in the 1787 Northwest Ordinance, helped to inspire similar programs of "home rule" within Britain's white dominions later in the nineteenth century. Further parallels and synergies can be found in the informal, economic empires in Latin America and East Asia, where American statesmen looked to Britain's model for inspiration, as well as taking advantage of British commercial structures.[46] The very British banks, merchants, consuls, and Royal Navy ships that Americans denounced were integral to the expansion of their own economic and diplomatic interests. Similarly, American missionaries closely collaborated with their British counterparts and focused much energy in British domains, particularly India.[47] Early nineteenth-century residents of Beirut referred to American missionaries as "al-Inkiliz" (the English) due to their Protestantism and the fact that they placed themselves under the protection of the British consulate.[48] Though it would gall Americans to admit it, they were often in this sense "hitchhiking imperialists," as one historian recently put it, or the "cock-boat in the wake of the British man-of-war," to use the phrase of John Quincy Adams.[49]

If American statesmen of the eighteenth and early nineteenth centuries found it difficult to acknowledge their debt to Britain, those at the turn of the century were more forthcoming about their convergence of interest with the British Empire. Frank Ninkovich's recent study of liberal American journals of the late nineteenth century found that most emphasized positive features of British imperialism, even its formal colonial rule of India.[50] "Its strength will be our strength," wrote naval strategist Alfred Thayer Mahan of

---

[45] James Belich, *Replenishing the Earth: The Settler Revolution and the Rise of the Anglo-World* (New York, 2009).

[46] Brauer, "The United States and British Imperial Expansion"; Sexton, *Monroe Doctrine*.

[47] Ian Tyrrell, *Reforming the World: The Creation of America's Moral Empire* (Princeton, 2010).

[48] Ussama Makdisi, *Artillery of Heaven: American Missionaries and the Failed Conversion of the Middle East* (Ithaca, NY, 2009), p. 85.

[49] Frank Ninkovich, *The United States and Imperialism* (Oxford, 2001), p. 158.

[50] Frank Ninkovich, *Global Dawn: The Cultural Foundation of American Internationalism, 1865–1890* (Cambridge, MA, 2009), p. 242.

the British Empire. Mahan's writings mined the history of the Royal Navy for lessons for the upstart US navy. It is perhaps no coincidence that the United States seized Havana and Manila from Spain in the War of 1898 just as Britain had done more than a century before in a conflict studied by Mahan. Theodore Roosevelt was just as explicit: "The downfall of the British Empire, I should regard as a calamity to the race, and especially to this country."[51]

****

Of all the forms of British influence in the early republic, cultural forces were among the most pervasive and enduring. Pirated British novels took up much space on American bookshelves and consumers purchased British textiles, Staffordshire ceramics, and goods from further afield such as British India. American theatres put on productions of British plays (one study of Philadelphia in the 1790s found that only 2 percent of the professional plays in the city were written by Americans). Popular songs—even Francis Scott Key's "Star Spangled Banner" that later would become the national anthem—were set to old British tunes. As late as 1883, Henry Cabot Lodge was disgusted to find that his compatriots continued to internalize cultural colonial subordination. Lodge's call to destroy the "lingering remains of the colonial spirit" provides just one of many examples of nineteenth-century Americans imagining a culture liberated from their colonial past. Yet this cultural nationalism rarely resulted in a total repudiation of British forms, which remained inextricably bound to the nascent national culture of the United States.[52]

An early example can be found in Noah Webster's promotion of "American English." A committed patriot during the struggle for independence and a nationalist thereafter, Webster contended that the political autonomy established in 1783 was only the first step toward total independence. His activities in education and lexicography aimed to create an American version of the English language. In the 1780s Webster produced the first of what would be many spellers to spread this "American English" to the nation's youth. "A national language is a brand of national union," Webster proclaimed, "Let us then seize the present moment and establish a national

---

[51] Mahan and Roosevelt quoted in Howard K. Beale, *Theodore Roosevelt and the Rise of America to World Power* (Baltimore, 1956), pp. 96, 134; Paul A. Kramer, "Empires, Exceptions, and Anglo-Saxons: Race and Rule between the British and United States Empires, 1880–1910," *Journal of American History*, LXXXVIII (2002), pp. 1315–53.

[52] Gordon Wood, *Empire of Liberty: A History of the Early Republic, 1789–1815* (New York, 2009), pp. 543–75; Lodge, "Colonialism in the United States."

language, as well as a national government." Webster argued that a national language would separate Americans from Britons, as well as homogenize the linguistic practices of the new republic's regionally and ethnically diverse peoples (roughly one quarter of the inhabitants of the United States in 1790 were not native English speakers). Despite his denunciations of British imperialism, Webster had no qualms about dictating that everyone in the United States should speak his standardized version of "American English."[53]

Webster's political and linguistic views, however, evolved. By the time he completed his magnum opus, *The American Dictionary of the English Language,* in 1828, he had become disillusioned with the republic he helped create. His ardent Federalism and distrust of non-English speaking immigrants led him to reconsider his earlier hostility to Britain. Webster's research took him to the old Cambridge, where ironically he completed *The American Dictionary.* Though the dictionary helped formalize the new spellings of "American English," Webster did not intend to establish a new language. Indeed, he viewed "American" as a purer form of English, uncorrupted since it had been planted in the New World in the seventeenth century. If anything, Webster slighted "Americanisms" in his dictionary, including only around fifty of the new phrases that were so ridiculed in Britain. The nationalism of his early days now broadened into a cosmopolitanism that tended toward an Anglo-American cultural imperialism (subsequent editions of the dictionary later in the century would be entitled *Webster's International Dictionary of the English Language*). "Our language is the *English* and it is desirable that the language of the United States and Great Britain should continue to be the same," he averred in the 1830s before sending none other than Queen Victoria a copy of his dictionary.[54] Indeed, while in Cambridge, Webster sought to arrange a conference of lexicographers to settle points of controversy between American and British versions of the language in order to standardize what he believed would be "the language of one third or two fifths of all the inhabitants of the globe."[55] Though Webster's conference never occurred, *The American Dictionary* became a widely used reference work in Britain, as well as in the United States.

---

[53] Quoted in Richard Rollins, *The Long Journey of Noah Webster* (Philadelphia, 1980), pp. 63–4.

[54] Rollins, *Long Journey of Noah Webster,* p. 127.

[55] Quoted in Harlow Unger, *Noah Webster: The Life and Times of an American Patriot* (New York, 1998), p. 299.

Webster's story casts an illuminating light upon the complex cultural relationship of the United States with Britain after political independence. As in other postcolonial societies, Americans expended great energy discussing how to create their own cultural traditions and literature. Yet the quest for cultural autonomy often required engagement with the very practices, goods, and ideas that American nationalists railed against. Even as they condemned British cultural forms, Americans sought the approbation of their former colonial master and used its standards as the barometer of civility. Recent literary scholarship has made the case for continuity and synergy between British and American literature in the first half of the nineteenth century.[56] Literary critic Leonard Tennenhouse has gone so far as to view early American literature as part of a British diasporic tradition and to suggest that "America's brand of Englishness... is precisely what made it American."[57] The break from the colonial past was not clean, particularly in terms of material culture. "The consumption of fine fabrics, tasty tea, and delicate chinaware emblazoned with family crests, as well as basic textiles and farm tools," Kariann Yokota points out, "was so deeply embedded in American life that it was not going to be given up after independence."[58]

If few Americans repudiated all things British, exactly which British cultural forms and materials to embrace was a matter of great debate. Just as the new republic's economic and diplomatic relationship with Britain proved politically divisive, the nature of the cultural relationship between new America and old England also produced internal conflict. The promotion of elite British culture in the United States lay behind the 1849 Astor Place riots in New York, one of the largest examples of social unrest in the early republic. They were triggered by the appearance of William Charles Macready, a British Shakespearean actor who, along with his elite American sponsors, countered the home-grown, populist productions of Shakespeare with the more restrained style characteristic of respectable London theatre. The Astor Place riots resulted from this intersection of cultural nationalism and internal class conflict. Yet even the radical workingmen opposed to the appearance of a British actor on the American stage—and the highbrow

[56] Ralph Bauer, "The Literature of 'British America,'" *American Literary History*, XXI (2009), pp. 818–35.

[57] Leonard Tennenhouse, *The Importance of Feeling English: American Literature and the British Diaspora, 1750–1850* (Princeton, 2007), p. 12.

[58] Kariann Yokota, "Postcolonialism and Material Culture in the Early United States," *WMQ*, 3rd ser., LXIV (2007), p. 267.

culture and social control that he and the Astor Place Opera House represented—did not object to the performance in New York of a play written by an Englishman. At Astor Place, Americans rioted and killed one another over the question of which production of an English dramatist was most appropriate for their new republic.[59]

In other instances, the pursuit of cultural independence required political action that ran counter to a tradition of limited central authority that was itself a product of the Revolution. The contentious issue of international copyright provides a good illustration of this dilemma. In contrast to Britain, the United States did not grant copyright protection to foreign authors until 1891. When combined with the limited capital at the disposal of American publishers, the absence of copyright flooded the American book market with cheap, pirated editions of British works. Even American schoolchildren were raised on a steady diet of English textbooks.[60] Opponents of copyright deployed the language of republicanism and opportunity, labeling copyright protection a "tax" on knowledge paid by American citizens to foreign publishers and their aristocratic clients. The budding literati in the United States, not surprisingly, viewed the issue in a different light. "Unless we have a copyright law," James Fenimore Cooper lamented, "there will be no such thing as American literature." Cooper might have overstated the effects of the copyright issue but it is worth keeping in mind that while Scott and Dickens received handsome commissions from British publishing houses, Hawthorne and Melville languished in jobs at the customs house. There was no answer to the question of whether international copyright advanced or hindered cultural independence—both those in favor and those opposed can be seen as working toward the goal.[61]

Britain served as a ubiquitous negative reference point in the early American republic. Resentment of the former colonial master, Haynes argues, "provided ideological scaffolding from which a national sense of self could be constructed." Yet Anglophobia was often twinned in the

---

[59] Haynes, *Unfinished Revolution*, pp. 77–105; Lawrence Levine, *Highbrow/Lowbrow: The Emergence of Cultural Hierarchy in America* (Cambridge, MA, 1988).

[60] Ruth M. Elson, *Guardians of Tradition: American Schoolbooks of the Nineteenth Century* (Lincoln, NE, 1964), p. 106.

[61] Aubert J. Clark, *The Movement for International Copyright in Nineteenth Century America* (Washington, 1960), p. 74.

American imagination with its alter ego, Anglophilia.[62] Many Americans, particularly coastal elites, drew from Old World traditions even as they proclaimed their independence. Ralph Waldo Emerson's famous essay "The American Scholar" reveals such a paradox in early American thought and literature. "Our day of dependence, our long apprenticeship to the learning of other lands draws to a close," Emerson proclaimed in 1837. On one level, it is hard not to read this essay, as would Oliver Wendell Holmes later in the century, as an "intellectual Declaration of Independence." Any reading of Emerson's manifesto, however, must take into account how it was influenced by British and European writings, namely the work of Wordsworth, Coleridge, and the German romantics. In this rich irony, British and European thinkers helped inspire Emerson to proclaim intellectual independence from the Old World.[63]

Such contradictory impulses can even be seen in Americans' views of the British monarchy. The vilification of George III and the metaphorical "killing of the king" in 1776 evolved into a larger hostility to monarchy and the broader social and political system it represented. The allegation of monarchist sympathies became a potent political charge in the early republic. Fourth of July celebrations played a central role in early American nationalism and political culture.[64] Yet this did not preclude mimicry of, and in some cases a lingering attraction to, the very British monarchy that Americans had repudiated in 1776. Though the Constitution rejected the hereditary principle, the President resembled a monarch in fulfilling both executive and ceremonial functions. Presidential practices such as the inauguration, the annual message, and the farewell address all drew from the traditions of Old World monarchs. It was because the President's annual message resembled the annual speech of the British monarch that Jefferson ordered a clerk to deliver his address to Congress, thus establishing a custom that lasted into the twentieth century. The influence of the old order in the early United States went beyond political practices. French observer Alexis de Tocqueville noted the irony of chest-thumping republicans who he met in

[62] Haynes, *Unfinished Revolution*, pp. 11, 23, 294; Elisa Tamarkin, *Anglophilia: Deference, Devotion, and Antebellum America* (Chicago, 2008).

[63] Perry Miller, "New England's Transcendentalism: Native or Imported?," in Joel Porte and Saundra Morris (eds), *Emerson's Prose and Poetry: Authoritative Texts, Contexts, Criticism* (New York, 2001), p. 676.

[64] David Waldstreicher, *In the Midst of Perpetual Fetes: The Making of American Nationalism, 1776–1820* (Chapel Hill, NC, 1997).

America who proudly traced their ancestral roots to the English nobility. As the nineteenth century progressed, Americans openly celebrated the coronations and anniversaries of British monarchs. The presence of Queen Victoria was so great across the Atlantic that it gave rise to the curious appellation "Victorian America." "Had Queen Victoria been on the throne, instead of George III," Secretary of State William Evarts declared in 1878, "or if we had postponed our rebellion until Queen Victoria reigned, it would not have been necessary."[65]

American social reform and religious movements became increasingly interlinked with those in Britain in the nineteenth century. The antislavery movement, for example, is best viewed as transatlantic in nature. As British and American antislavery societies shared tactics and funds, prominent abolitionists, such as Britain's George Thompson and America's Frederick Douglass, crossed the Atlantic to promote the cause. The cosmopolitan nature of the antislavery movement, however, did not stop some American opponents of slavery, most notably the Garrisonians whose embrace of women's rights fractured the 1840 World Antislavery Convention in London, from determining their own methods and objectives.[66] As the example of Garrison suggests, it would be a mistake to characterize American reformers as clones of their British counterparts. Reformers adapted ideas and tactics from one side of the Atlantic to comport with the objectives and contexts on the other. "Double cross," or the return traffic of ideas across the Atlantic, also characterized the transatlantic social and reform movements of the time. This was certainly the case with the transatlantic surge in evangelical Christianity, particularly the booming Methodist church. Imported to the New World in the second half of the eighteenth century, American Methodism soon developed and exported back to the old country (with varying degrees of success, it should be added) the emotive and evangelistic characteristics of the Second Great Awakening such as the camp meeting, the "anxious bench," and freewheeling itinerant revivalists.[67]

---

[65] Quoted in Frank Prochaska, *The Eagle and the Crown: Americans and the British Monarchy* (New Haven, 2008), p. 82.

[66] Betty Fladeland, *Men and Brothers: Anglo-American Antislavery Cooperation* (Urbana, IL, 1972); R.J.M. Blackett, *Building an Antislavery Wall: Black Americans in the Atlantic Abolitionist Movement, 1830–1860* (Baton Rouge, LA, 1983).

[67] For the differences, as well as the links, between American and British Methodism, see Richard Carwardine, *Transatlantic Revivalism: Popular Evangelicalism in Britain and America, 1780–1865* (London, 1978), pp. 102–33.

The rising nationalism of nineteenth-century America thus did not lead to isolation from its former colonial master or, indeed, the wider world more generally. If notions of national exceptionalism were sown in this period, it should not be overlooked that many Americans viewed their nation in cosmopolitan terms—"the home of man," to use Emerson's phrase.[68] Yet in practice there were stark limits to this professed American inclusivity. The presence of slavery, the removal of Native Americans, and the discrimination faced by women and many social and ethnic groups all threw into relief the boundaries of the allegedly universal nature of Americanness. Though the United States had a liberal conception of citizenship when compared to the British doctrine of perpetual allegiance, the protections and rights of US citizenship were not extended to all its inhabitants, most obviously slaves and Native Americans. Furthermore, the Naturalization Act of 1790 introduced the first of what would be many racial restrictions (which would not be completely annulled until the mid-twentieth century, it should be added).

For all their anticolonial nationalism, many Americans embraced and replicated the racial hierarchies that buttressed British imperialism. This was particularly evident in US dealings with Native Americans, which was justified by a paternalistic ideology similar to that employed by British imperialists.[69] Profound changes to the nation's demography and ethnic proportions brought about by immigration from Ireland and continental Europe (and, later in the nineteenth century, from southern and eastern Europe, as well as Asia) further fuelled racial identification with Britain. The census of 1850, the first to record the nativity of US residents, found that recent arrivals from Ireland and Germany (numbering 1,545,493) exceeded those from England, Scotland, and Wales (379,093) by more than a factor of four. The implications of these demographic changes cut both ways. Many Irish Catholic immigrants to the United States brought with them an historic antagonism towards Britain, which further fuelled anti-British sentiment in the United States. Yet the increased presence of non-British and Catholic immigrants led many native-born, Protestant Americans to imagine a kinship with the "Anglo-Saxons" of the old country.

---

[68] Ralph Waldo Emerson, "The Young American," in *the Collected Work of Ralph Waldo Emerson*, I (Cambridge, MA, 1971), p. 241.

[69] Rosemarie Zagarri, "The Significance of the 'Global Turn' for the Early American Republic: Globalization in the Age of Nation-Building," *Journal of the Early Republic*, XXXI (2011), pp. 1–37.

As the nineteenth century progressed, many Americans embraced an Anglo-Saxon ideology that placed them, along with their counterparts in England, at the top of a global racial hierarchy.[70] This Anglo-Saxon racial ideology gained traction as the United States became more secure in its diplomatic and economic independence and began to project its power more assertively outside its borders. Indeed, the rise of "Anglo-Saxonism" roughly coincided with the extended "great rapprochement" of the mid- and late-nineteenth century, in which Britain recognized US supremacy in the Western Hemisphere.[71]

****

The historiography that examines the United States in the decades following independence has long been dominated by grand narratives: the expansion of the nation's territory, population, and economy; the emergence of democratic party politics; the interaction of ethnicities, races, and other social groups in a diverse and de-centralized union; and, of course, the rise of a sectionalism that ultimately would lead to civil war. But often slighted in these largely insular narratives is the position of the young republic within an expanding British Empire. That the United States would become the "superpower" of the twentieth century should not blind us to the fact that the British Empire continued to cast a shadow over the American republic deep into the nineteenth century. "If we understand the republic's formation between 1790 and 1860 as fundamentally postcolonial," Van Gosse recently suggested, "it becomes impossible to tell a strictly 'national' story of American politics, any more than one could of Ireland or India."[72]

Despite the severance of formal colonial links in 1776, nineteenth-century America remained embedded in the economic, geopolitical, and cultural structures of the British Empire. The position of the early United States within the British Empire is perhaps deserving of a category of its own, for it differed in important ways from those of the settler colonies or the Latin American republics that were part of Britain's informal empire. This postcolonial relationship was fraught with tension and conflict, yet it ultimately benefited both parties. Independent America remained the chief destination

[70] Reginald Horsman, *Race and Manifest Destiny: The Origins of American Racial Anglo-Saxonism* (Cambridge, MA, 1981).

[71] Bradford Perkins, *The Great Rapprochement: England and the United States, 1895–1914* (London, 1969), pp. 64–88.

[72] Gosse, "'As a Nation, the English Are Our Friends,'" p. 1027.

for British migrants, capital, and trade, thus making it a central component of the nineteenth-century "British world-system."[73] British power, in turn, underwrote the development and expansion of the American nation and empire, even as it loomed as the young republic's greatest threat.

Select Bibliography

JAMES BELICH, *Replenishing the Earth: The Settler Revolution and the Rise of the Anglo-World* (New York, 2009).

KINLEY BRAUER, "The United States and British Imperial Expansion, 1815–1860," *Diplomatic History*, XII (1988), pp. 19–37.

COLIN G. CALLOWAY, *Crown and Calumet: British-Indian Relations, 1783–1815* (Norman, OK, 1987).

RICHARD CARWARDINE, *Transatlantic Revivalism: Popular Evangelicalism in Britain and America, 1780–1865* (London, 1978).

SAM W. HAYNES, *Unfinished Revolution: The Early American Republic in a British World* (Charlottesville, VA, 2010).

DAVID C. HENDRICKSON, *Peace Pact: The Lost World of the American Founding* (Lawrence, KS, 2003).

DAVID C. HENDRICKSON, *Union, Nation, or Empire: The American Debate Over International Relations, 1789–1941* (Lawrence, KS, 2009).

A. G. HOPKINS, "The United States, 1783–1861: Britain's Honorary Dominion?" *Britain and the World*, IV (2011), pp. 232–46.

REGINALD HORSMAN, *Race and Manifest Destiny: The Origins of American Racial Anglo-Saxonism* (Cambridge, MA, 1981).

DANIEL WALKER HOWE, "American Victorianism as Culture," *American Quarterly*, XXVII (1975), pp. 507–32.

MAYA JASANOFF, *Liberty's Exiles: The Loss of America and the Remaking of the British Empire* (London, 2011).

PETER ONUF, *Jefferson's Empire: The Language of American Nationhood* (Charlottesville, VA, 2000).

BRADFORD PERKINS, *The Cambridge History of American Foreign Relations*, I. *The Creation of a Republican Empire, 1776–1865* (Cambridge, 1993).

DONALD RATCLIFFE, "The State of the Union, 1776–1860," in Susan-Mary Grant and Brian Holden Reid (eds), *The American Civil War: Explorations and Reconsiderations* (London, 2000), pp. 3–38.

EDWARD B. RUGEMER, *The Problem of Emancipation: The Caribbean Roots of the American Civil War* (Baton Rouge, LA, 2008).

BRIAN SCHOEN, *The Fragile Fabric of Union: Cotton, Federal Politics, and the Global Origins of the Civil War* (Baltimore, 2009).

---

[73] John Darwin, *The Empire Project: The Rise and Fall of the British World-System, 1830–1970* (Cambridge, 2009).

REGINALD C. STUART, *United States Expansionism and British North America, 1775–1871* (Chapel Hill, NC, 1988).

ELISA TAMARKIN, *Anglophilia: Deference, Devotion, and Antebellum America* (Chicago, 2008).

ALAN TAYLOR, *The Civil War of 1812: American Citizens, British Subjects, Irish Rebels, and Indian Allies* (New York, 2010).

FRANK THISTLETHWAITE, *The Anglo-American Connection in the Early Nineteenth Century* (Philadelphia, 1959).

MIRA WILKINS, *The History of Foreign Investment in the United States to 1914* (Cambridge, MA, 1989).

INDEX